ORDNANCE SURVEY MEMOIRS OF IRELAND

Volume Forty

COUNTIES OF SOUTH ULSTER
1834–8

Published 1998.
The Institute of Irish Studies,
The Queen's University of Belfast,
Belfast.
In association with
The Royal Irish Academy,
Dawson Street,
Dublin.

Reprinted 2013 by Ulster Historical Foundation

Grateful acknowledgement is made to the Economic and Social Research Council and the Department of Education for Northern Ireland for their financial assistance at different stages of this publication programme.

We should like to thank the office of the Taoiseach and the Department of Education in Ireland for contributing towards the costs of this volume.

Copyright 1998.

Series (vols 1–40) © copyright 1990–98.

All rights reserved. No part of this publication may be reproduced, stored in a retrieval system or transmitted, in any form or by any means, electronic, mechanical, photocopying, recording or otherwise, without the prior permission of the publisher.

British Library Cataloguing-in-Publication Data.
A catalogue record for this book is available from the British Library.

ISBN: 978-0-85389-661-6

Printed in Ireland by SPRINT-print Ltd.

Ordnance Survey Memoirs of Ireland
VOLUME FORTY

Counties of South Ulster
1834–8

Cavan, Leitrim, Louth, Monaghan and Sligo

Edited by Angélique Day and Patrick McWilliams

The Institute of Irish Studies
in association with
The Royal Irish Academy

CONTENTS

	Page
Acknowledgements	v
Sligo, Leitrim and Cavan, with parish boundaries	vi
Monaghan and Louth, with parish boundaries	vii
Introduction	viii
Brief history of the Irish Ordnance Survey and Memoirs	viii
Definition of terms used	ix
Note on Memoirs of South Ulster	ix

List of Parishes

County Cavan

Drumgoon	1
Drumloman	12
Drung	19
Enniskeen	26
Killdrumsherdan	31
Laragh	39

County Leitrim

Manorhamilton Union	47

County Louth

Ballymascanlan	55
Carlingford	57
Castletown	61

County Monaghan

Aghabog	62
Aughnamullen	69
Ballybay	78
Clontibret	85
Currin	86
Donagh	98
Donaghmoyne	106
Ematris	112
Errigal Truagh	120
Inniskeen	124
Killanny	130
Kilmore	136
Magheracloone	137
Magheross	143
Monaghan	159
Muckno	162
Tydavnet	169
Tyholland	174

County Sligo

Emlaghfad	176
Killoran and Kilvarnet	183
Kilmactigue	185
Miscellaneous Papers	198

List of selected maps and drawings

Cootehill	5
Manorhamilton Castle	51
Giant's grave in Lisnadara Townland	73
Round tower in Ennis Townland	126
Castle in Ballymote	178

List of OS maps, 1830s

Cootehill	2
Cavan town	25
Manorhamilton	48
Carrickmacross	145
Monaghan town	160
Castleblayney	163

EDITORIAL BOARD

Angélique Day (General Editor)
Patrick S. McWilliams (Executive Editor)
Professor B.M. Walker (Publishing Director)
Professor R.H. Buchanan

ACKNOWLEDGEMENTS

During the course of the projects to transcribe and publish the Memoirs, many have advised and encouraged us in this enormous undertaking. Thanks must first be given to the Royal Irish Academy which has made available to us the original manuscripts. We are also greatly indebted to Librarian Siobhán O'Rafferty and her staff, especially Íde Ní Thuama, for help over a number of years in deciphering indistinct passages of manuscript.

We should like to acknowledge the following individuals for their special contributions. Dr Brian Trainor led the way with his edition of the Antrim Memoir and provided vital help on the steering committee. Dr Ann Hamlin also provided valuable support, especially during the most trying stages of the project. Professor R.H. Buchanan's unfailing encouragement was instrumental in the development of our work.

Without Dr Kieran Devine the initial stages of the transcription and the computerising work would never have been completed successfully: the success of the project owes a great deal to his constant help and advice. Dr Kay Muhr's contribution to the work of the transcription project is appreciated, as is that of former editor Nóirín Dobson. Mr W.C. Kerr's interest and expertise have been invaluable. Professor Anne Crookshank and Dr Edward McParland were most generous with practical help and advice concerning the drawings amongst the Memoir manuscripts. We would like to thank the Director of the Ordnance Survey, Dublin, and the keepers of the fire-proof store, among them Leonard Hines. Finally, all students of the nineteenth-century Ordnance Survey of Ireland owe a great deal to the pioneering work of Professor J.H. Andrews, and his kind help in the first days of the project is gratefully recorded.

The editors would like to thank Mícheál Ó Mainnín from the Dept. of Celtic at Queen's for his help with this volume. They would also like to acknowledge the financial assistance given by Mrs Maggi Root, Baltimore, and Beth Mullinax of the Irish Genealogical Society International, towards the final 3 volumes of the series.

Since the beginning of the OS Memoirs project in the early 1980s, many different bodies and societies have contributed financial and other support at different times: the Community Relations Council, the Dept. of Environment (now the Environment and Heritage Service Northern Ireland), Derry City Council, Donegal County Council Library Service, the Esme Mitchell Trust, Hon. the Irish Society, the Public Record Office of Northern Ireland and the Ulster Local History Trust.

The essential task of inputting the texts from audio tapes was done by Miss Eileen Kingan, Mrs Christine Robertson, Miss Eilis Smyth, Miss Lynn Murray and, most importantly, Miss Maureen Carr.

We are grateful to the Linen Hall Library for lending us their copies of the first edition 6" Ordnance Survey maps: also to Ms Maura Pringle of QUB Cartography Department for the index maps showing the parish boundaries.

Many other individuals too numerous to name have been of assistance to us and, once again, we are pleased to thank them.

Over:
p(vi) Map of parishes of counties Sligo, Leitrim and Cavan;
p(vii) Map of parishes of counties Monaghan and Louth.

The square grids represent the 1830s 6" Ordnance Survey maps. The encircled numbers relate to the map numbers as presented in the bound volumes of maps for each county. Except for Co. Cavan, names of parishes have been numbered in all cases and named in full where possible.

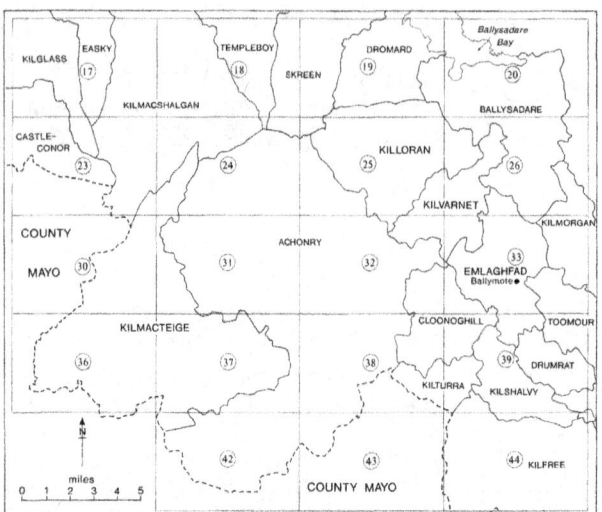
Co. Sligo

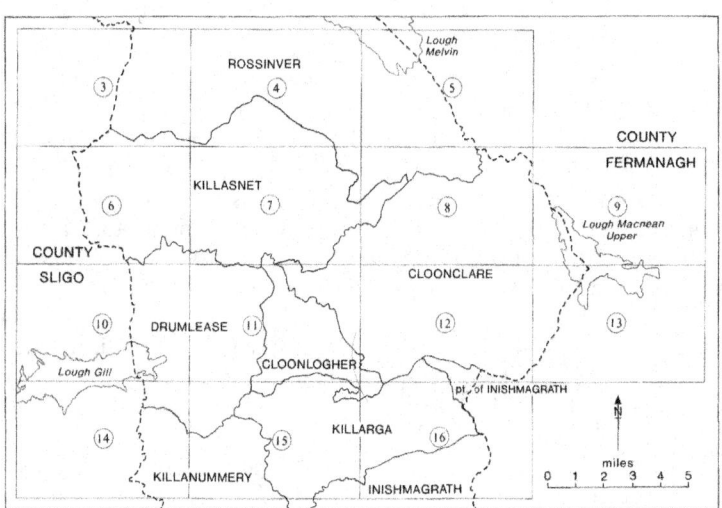
Co. Leitrim

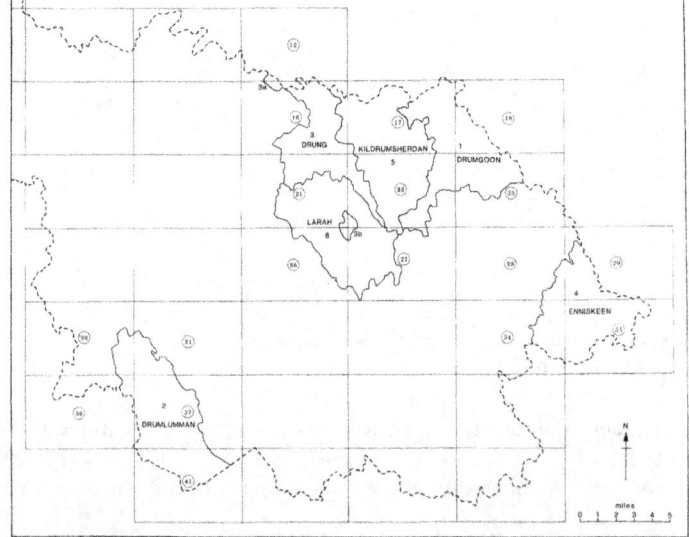
Co. Cavan

Counties of South Ulster

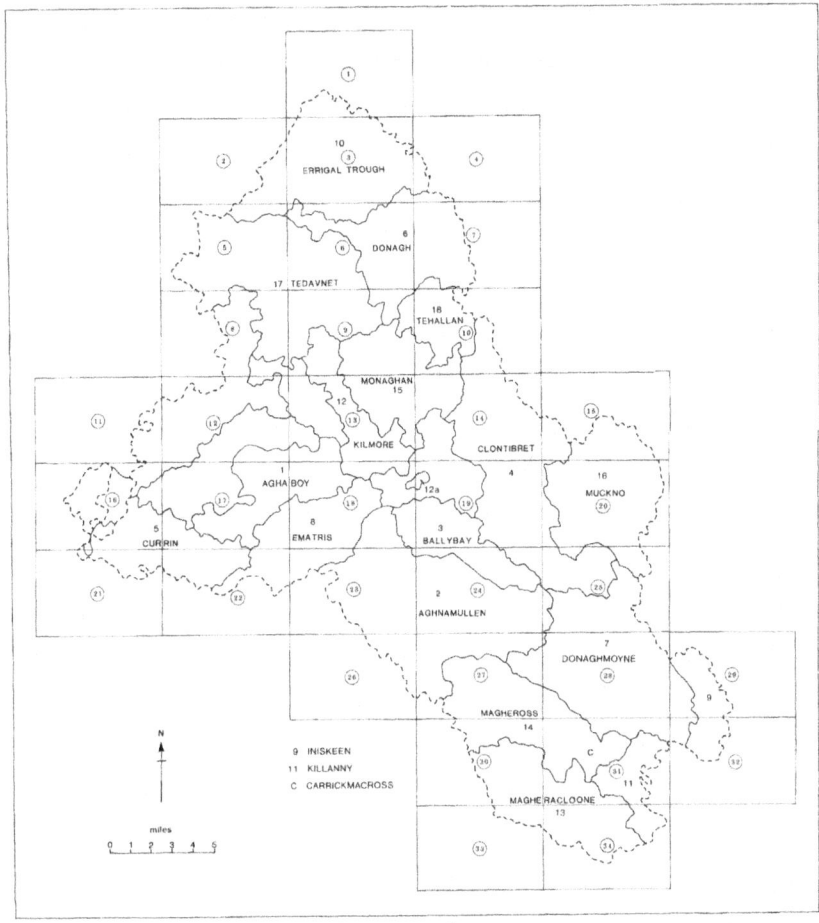

Co. Monaghan

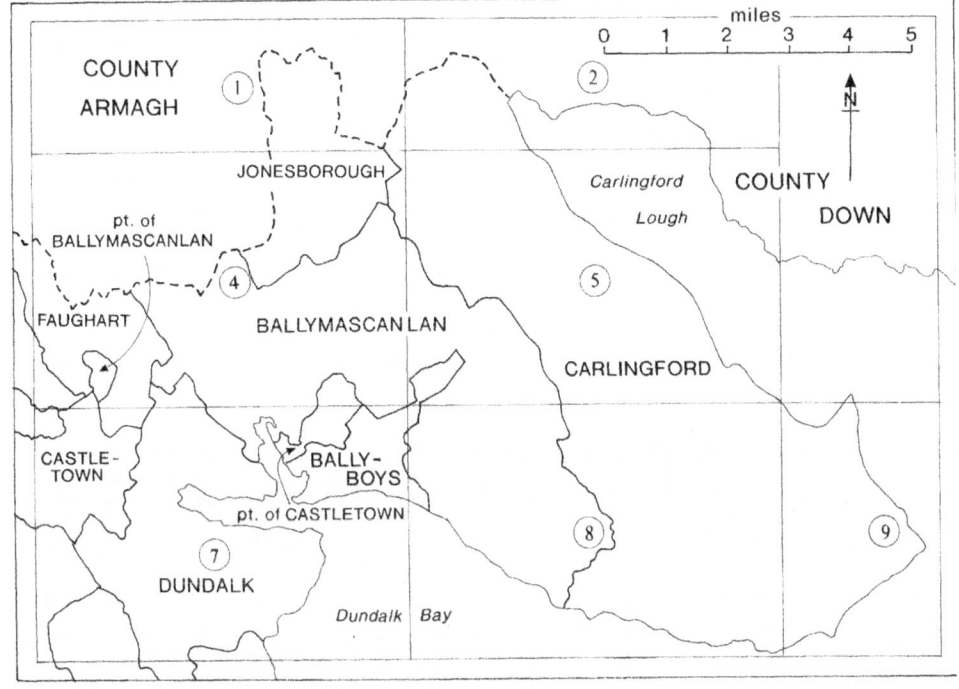

Co. Louth

INTRODUCTION AND GUIDE TO THE PUBLICATION OF THE ORDNANCE SURVEY MEMOIRS

The following text of the Ordnance Survey Memoirs was originally transcribed by a team working in the Institute of Irish Studies at The Queen's University of Belfast, on a computerised index of the material. For this publication programme the text has been further edited: spellings have been modernised in most cases, although where the original spelling was thought to be of any interest it has been retained and is indicated by angle brackets in the text. Variant spellings for townland and lesser place-names have been preserved, although parish and major place-names have been standardised and the original spelling given in angle brackets. Names of prominent people, for instance landlords, have been standardised where possible, but original spellings of names in lists of informants, emigration tables and on tombstones have been retained. We have not altered the Memoir writers' anglicisation of names and words in Irish.

Punctuation has been modernised and is the responsibility of the editors. Editorial additions are indicated by square brackets: a question mark before and after a word indicates a queried reading and tentatively inserted information respectively. Original drawings are referred to in the text, and some have been reproduced. Manuscript page references have been omitted from this series. Because of the huge variation in size of Memoirs for different counties, the following editorial policy has been adopted: where there are numerous duplicating and overlapping accounts, the most complete and finished account, normally the Memoir proper, has been presented, with additional unique information from other accounts like the Fair Sheets entered into a separate section, clearly titled and identified; where the Memoir material is less, nothing has been omitted. To achieve standard volume size, parishes have been associated on the basis of propinquity.

There are considerable differences in the volume of information recorded for different areas: counties Antrim and Londonderry are exceptionally well covered, while the other counties do not have quite the same detail. This series is the first systematic publication of the parish Memoirs, although individual parishes have been published by pioneering local history societies. The entire transcriptions of the Memoirs made in the course of the indexing project can be consulted in the Public Record Office of Northern Ireland and the library at Queen's. The manuscripts of the Ordnance Survey Memoirs are help by the Royal Irish Academy, Dublin, their owners.

Brief history of the Irish Ordnance Survey in the nineteenth century and the writing of the Ordnance Survey Memoirs

In 1824 a House of Commons committee recommended a townland survey of Ireland with maps at the scale of 6", to facilitate a uniform valuation for local taxation. The Duke of Wellington, then prime minister, authorised this, the first Ordnance Survey of Ireland. The survey was directed by Colonel Thomas Colby, who had under his command officers of the Royal Engineers and three companies of sappers and miners. In addition to this, civil assistants were recruited to help with sketching, drawing and engraving of maps, and eventually, in the 1830s, the writing of the Memoirs.

The Memoirs were written descriptions intended to accompany the maps, containing information which could not be fitted on to them. Colonel Colby always considered additional information to be necessary to clarify place-names and other distinctive features of each parish; this was to be written up in reports by the officers. Much information about parishes resulted from research into place-names and was used in the writing of the Memoirs. The term "Memoir" comes from the abbreviation of the word "Aide-Memoire". It was also used in the 18th century to describe topographical descriptions accompanying maps.

In 1833 Colby's assistant, Lieutenant Thomas Larcom, developed the scope of the officers' reports by stipulating the headings or "Heads of Inquiry" under which information was to be reported, and including topics of social as well as economic interest. By this time civil assistants were writing some of the Memoirs under the supervision of the officers, as well as collecting information in the Fair Sheets.

The first "Memoirs" are officers' reports covering Antrim in 1830, and work continued on the Antrim parishes right through the decade, with special activity in 1838 and 1839. Counties Down and Tyrone were written up from 1833 to 1837, with both officers and civil assistants working on Memoirs. In Londonderry and Fermanagh research and writing started in 1834. Armagh was worked on in 1835, 1837 and 1838. Much labour was expended in the Londonderry parishes. The plans to publish the Memoirs commenced with the parish of Templemore, containing the city and liberties of Derry, which came out in 1837 after a great deal of expense and effort.

Between 1839 and 1840 the Memoir scheme collapsed. Sir Robert Peel's government could not countenance the expenditure of money and time on such an exercise; despite a parliamentary commission favouring the continuation of the writing of the Memoirs, the scheme was halted before the southern half of the country was covered. The manuscripts remained unpublished and most were removed to the Royal Irish Academy, Dublin from the Ordnance Survey, Phoenix Park. Other records of the Ordnance Survey, including some material from the Memoir scheme, have been transferred to the National Archives, Bishop Street, Dublin.

The Memoirs are a uniquely detailed source for the history of the northern half of Ireland immediately before the Great Famine. They document the landscape and situation, buildings and antiquities, land-holdings and population, employment and livelihood of the parishes. They act as a nineteenth-century Domesday book and are essential to the understanding of the cultural heritage of our communities. It is planned to produce a volume of evaluative essays to put the material in its full context, with information on other sources and on the writers of the Memoirs.

Definition of descriptive terms

Memoir (sometimes Statistical Memoir): an account of a parish written according to the prescribed form outlined in the instructions known as "Heads of Inquiry", and normally divided into three sections: Natural Features and History; Modern and Ancient Topography; Social and Productive Economy.

Fair Sheets: "information gathered for the Memoirs", an original title describing paragraphs of information following no particular order, often with marginal headings, signed and dated by the civil assistant responsible.

Statistical Remarks/Accounts: both titles are employed by the Engineer officers in their descriptions of the parish with marginal headings, often similar in layout to the Memoir.

Office Copies: these are copies of early drafts, generally officers' accounts and must have been made for office purposes.

Ordnance Survey Memoirs for South Ulster

This volume, the fortieth and final in the series, contains Memoir material for 34 parishes in 5 counties which lie in and along the southern reaches of the province of Ulster. In order to preserve a sense of geographical coherence, the editors have decided to omit from this publication those fragments of Memoir material which do not fall within the general area of southern Ulster and neighbouring counties. Details of these manuscripts are listed below, before the list of drawings.

The editors have used the parish spellings relating to Monaghan contained in P.J. Duffy's *Landscapes of South Ulster, a parish atlas of the diocese of Ulster* (IIS, 1993). For other counties there may be discrepancies between those found on the original Ordnance maps and those found in the Memoir accounts. Where possible, and at times it was a near impossible task, the editors have sought advice in order to try and bring spellings into line with acknowledged use.

The Memoirs in this volume cover a wide range of styles and contain accounts by soldiers mainly from the Royal Engineers. For example, Lieutenant P. Taylor, a very knowledgeable officer interested in geology and natural history, who wrote about Cavan, was a subaltern in the 69th Regiment. Lance-Corporal Trimble, assigned to Sligo, was the only member of the Sappers and Miners to compile a Memoir, though they contributed to the Topographical Department's research into place-names for the maps.

For all the patchiness of the coverage, the five counties being incomplete to some degree, the descriptions contain some fascinating insights into the life in this area in the mid-1830s, the half-way point of the Ordnance Survey in Ireland.

Drawings in the Memoir papers are listed below and are cross-referenced in the text; some are illustrated. The manuscript material is to be found in Boxes 19, 23, 27-8, 49-50 of the Royal Irish Academy's collection of Ordnance Survey Memoirs, and section references are given beside each parish below in their printed order.

Cavan
Drumgoon	Box 19 II 1
Drumloman	Box 19 III 1
Drung	Box 19 IV 1
Enniskeen	Box 19 V 2, 1
Killdrumsherdan	Box 19 VI 1
Laragh	Box 19 VII 1

Leitrim
Manorhamilton Union (Cloonclare, Cloonlogher, Killasnet)	Box 28 II

Louth
Ballymascanlan	Box 23 XII 1
Carlingford	Box 23 XX 1
Castletown	Box 23 IX 1

Monaghan
Aghabog	Box 49 IV II 1
Aughnamullen	Box 49 IV III 1
Ballybay	Box 49 IV IV 1
Clontibret	Box 49 IV V 1
Currin	Box 49 IV VI 1, Box 27 XII 1
Donagh	Box 49 IV VII 1
Donaghmoyne	Box 49 IV VIII 1
Ematris	Box 49 IV IX 1
Errigal Truagh	Box 49 IV XII 1, XI 1
Inniskeen	Box 49 IV X 1
Killanny	Box 49 IV XIII 2, 1
Kilmore	Box 49 IV XIV 1
Magheracloone	Box 49 IV XV 2, 1

Magheross   Box 49 IV XVI 1, IVa 1
Monaghan   Box 49 IV XVII 1
Muckno   Box 49 IV XVIII 1
Tydavnet   Box 49 IV XIX 1
Tyholland   Box 49 IV XX 1

Sligo
Emlaghfad   Box 50 III II 1
Killoran and Kilvarnet   Box 50 III III 1
Kilmactigue   Box 50 III IV 1
Miscellaneous Papers   Box 50 III I 1

Ordnance Survey Memoir papers not published in this series.

Cork: Box 20 I
Galway: Box 28 I
Longford: Box 49 I
Mayo: Box 49 II
Meath: Box 49 III
Queen's County [Laois]: Box 50 I
Roscommon: Box 50 II
Tipperary: Box 50 IV

Drawings

Cavan

Drumgoon [misplaced in Laragh]:
View of Cootehill main street [illustrated].
View of Cootehill showing church and Catholic chapel (by W. Groves).

Drumloman:
Druid's altar in Drumhowna (by A. Beatty).

Laragh:
Two Big Men's Beds, tiny plan (by P. Taylor).

Leitrim

Manorhamilton Union:
Castle of Manorhamilton with dimensions [illustrated].
Castle in Castletown townland, with dimensions.
Old church of Cloonlogher, with dimensions.
Memorial tablet to Catherine Cullen in Cloonclare.
Old church of Cloonclare, with dimensions.
Effigy of Lady Bingham in Cloonclare.
Old church of Manorhamilton.
St Patrick's church in Curraghs townland, Innismagrath parish.
Castle Gore in Newtown townland, parish of Drumlease, with dimensions
(all the above by W. Lancey).

Monaghan

Aghabog: [misplaced in Ematris]
Giant's grave in Carn townland.
Head of giant's grave and trigonometrical station (by W. Groves).

Aughnamullen:
Giant's grave in Lisnadara townland by R. Stotherd [illustrated].

Carrickmacross:
Ground plan of chapel, with dimensions.

Currin:
Hatchet, spearhead, stick or spear (by R. Mayne).

Donagh:
Ground plan of Corracrin chapel in Derryhallagh townland, with dimensions (by J.C. Innes).

Donaghmoyne:
Outline of elk's antler, with dimensions.
Stone circle on Fincarn hill (by R. Boteler).

Ematris:
Dawson's monument.
Crest on Dawson's monument (by W. Groves).

Errigal Truagh:
Ground plan of Errigal church, with dimensions.
Ground plan of Mullylodin Catholic chape (by T.C. McIlroy).

Inniskeen:
Entrance door to round tower.
Round tower in Ennis townland [illustrated].
Ancient inscription in Ennis graveyard.
Cross at a crossroads, with miniature drawing.
Vault or cell near cross.
Circular mound with annotated plan of locality and dimensions.
Section of wall of enclosure near above mound, with dimensions.
Plan of enclosure, with annotations and dimensions.
Outside elevation of arch, with dimensions; elevation of inside arch, with details and annotations (by R. Boteler).

Killanny:
Plan of abbey, sketch of gable wall with annotations and dimensions.
2 drawings of Byrne armorial bearings.
Tombstone of William Tenison in Ballymackney, with coat of arms and inscription (by R. Boteler).

Kilmore:
Ground plan of schoolhouse, with dimensions (by J.R. Ward).

Tydavnet:
Ground plan of Bellanode schoolhouse, with dimensions.

Plan of Catholic chapel at Mullanarockan, with dimensions (by T.C. McIlroy).

Tyholland:
Ground plan of parish church, with dimensions.
Parish school, with dimensions (by J.C. Innes).

Sligo

Emlaghfad:
Ruins of castle in Ballymote [illustrated].
Armorial bearings.
Round tower in Carrownanty townland.
Ruins of castle in Templehouse demesne.
Head over southern door of abbey.
Ruins of Emlaghfad church.
Funerary urn in Templehouse demesne.
Ruins of abbey in Ballymote (all the above by W. Groves).

Kilmactigue:
Plan of original glebe showing castle, ruins of church, and boundary of river (by H. Trimble).

Parish of Drumgoon, County Cavan

Statistical Report by Lieutenant P. Taylor,
[late 1835]

NATURAL STATE

Name and Derivation

The ancient chapel and graveyard of this parish was situated within the circle of a well-defined aboriginal fort on the lofty summit of the townland of Drumgoon. This circumstance is mentioned to assist others more conversant with the Irish language to trace the etymology of the name of the parish, which in this district is wholly unknown.

Locality

Situated in the south eastern extremity of the county of Cavan and in the same position in the barony of Tullygarvey. It is bounded on the north by the parish of Ematris and east of the parish of Aughnamullen, both in the county of Monaghan. On the south it is bounded by the parish of Knockbride and west by the parish of Killdrumsherdan, both in the county of Cavan; and measuring in extreme length and breadth from north to south 8 and east to west 5 English miles; contains 15,463 acres, 14,847 of which are land and 616 acres are water, and paid to the county cess in the year [no further information].

NATURAL FEATURES

Hills

In the subterranean movements and convulsions of the globe, elevating and depressing its crust into the varied forms which can adorn and diversify its surface, the power, glory and providence of God are magnificently conspicuous.

4 hills of beautiful formation characterise the prevailing features of the whole of the parish of Drumgoon: the magna dorsa, elevating their long, carina-shaped forms, are particularly numerous and objects of singular beauty. The cors, rising in the full volume of their capacious and protruberant domes, are next in order and possess equal, if not superior, claims to admiration. The cones are fewer in number but superior in interest to either of the former, from their having been more particularly selected as the site of the atria of the aboriginal nobles of the kingdom. The mullaghs are still fewer but by no means less interesting, in raising their ponderous domes into the shape and form of miniature table mountains.

The most perfect and beautiful specimens of the magnum dorsum formation may be seen in Drumlarkey "the ship hill" and Drumgreen "the sunny hill." Corcloghan "the stony hill" and Corravoghy "the little hill" are equally so of the cor-shaped group. Lisnageeragh "the sheep's fort" and Lisnagoan "the smiths' fort" are perfect resemblances of the cone formation; and in the elevated portion of the townland of Mullaghard may be seen a beautiful representation of the Table Mountain at the Cape of Good Hope.

The drum and cor-shaped hills, so very numerous within the parish, seem to have exhausted the ingenuity of the aboriginal lords of the soil in assigning names to many of their townlands significant of their shape and form, since Barnagrove "the nut top" is a beautiful specimen of a cor-shaped hill of great magnitude and was doubtlessly thus denominated from the hazelwood which then crowned its summit, a remnant of which still covers its base.

Many of the hills appear to owe their appellatives to the particular kind of trees which anciently covered them: Killyrue "the birchwood," Killytee "the housewood," Killyvaughan "the cabanwood" and several others, all elevations of the genuine drum formation.

Hence the natural features of the parish are composed of a most beautiful undulating succession of hills and vales, combining more generally in a construction of long parallel ridges with intervening valleys and groups of dome and cone-shaped hills with inconsiderable variation in their attitude throughout the eastern and western divisions of the parish, developing a considerable depression towards its north and north western boundary.

Mullen, and Mullaghair and Knappagh on the south eastern boundary of the parish elevate their centres 495 feet, 461 feet and 449 feet above the level of the sea. Drumgoon, Dernakish and Toughull on the south western boundary stand 410, 485 and 565 feet above the same level. Mayo and Aughagashland on the north eastern section rise to 602 and 596 feet; and Kelling, Claragh and Lattyloo on the north and north eastern boundary descend to 341, 378 and 376 feet upon the same plane.

Lakes

Barnagrove loch, 315 feet above the level of the

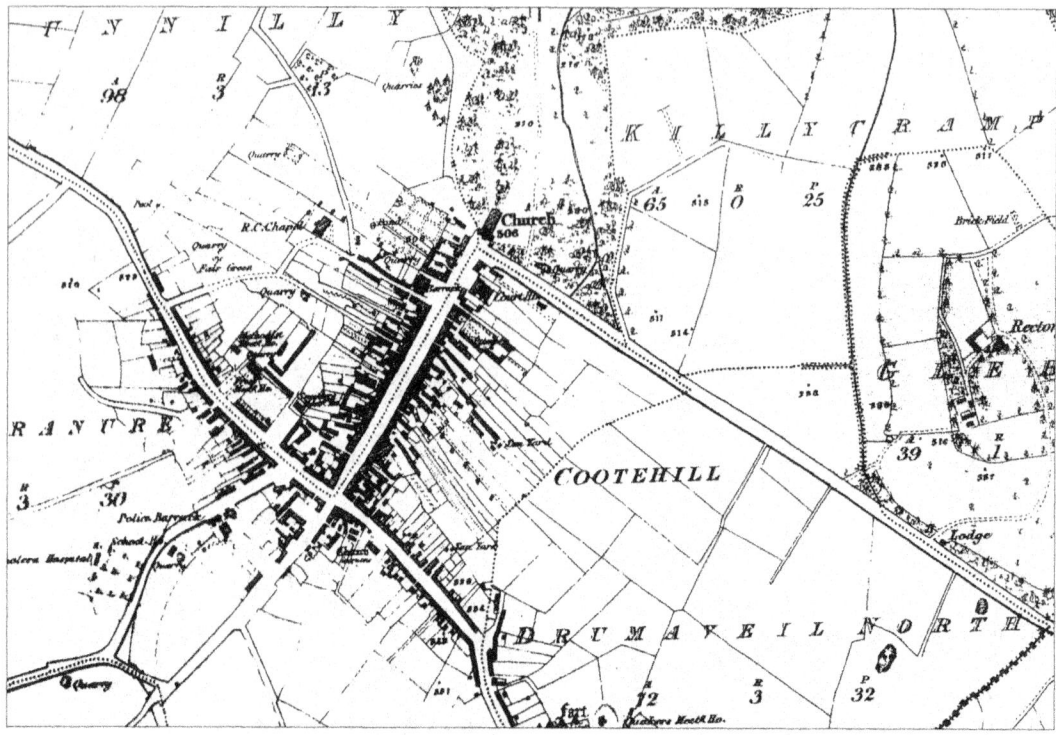

Map of Cootehill from the first 6" OS maps, 1830s

sea, situated in the south eastern boundary of the parish and surrounded by the townlands of Doohatil, Larraweehan and Barnagrove in the parish of Drumgoon and Drumin and Cullys in the parish of Knockbride, is a beautiful expanse of water covering a surface of [blank] acres. A very small streamlet, the general bearing north, connects it with Loch Tucka. It derives its supplies from natural springs and the general drainage of a hilly district.

Loch Tucka, covering an area of 270 acres, is another extensive and beautiful lake on the south eastern boundary of the parish, surrounded by the townlands of Drokabawn, Corcloghan and Mullaghard in the parish of Drumgoon and Oneyfarney and Mullaghbrack in the parish of Knockbride.

The River Annagh, rising from its northern shores, is joined in the townland of Liscloughan by the Knappagh water and, flowing through the parish of Drumgoon, forms a valuable water power to the corn and flour mills of the parish, and was applied during the prosperity of the linen trade to several very extensive bleachfields, the ruins of which are still standing. The waters of the lake stand 302 feet above the level of the sea.

Loch Killyrue occupies the centre of a very beautiful basin surrounded by the gently sloping declivities of the townlands of Killytee, Kilcloghan and Killyrue, and discharges its accumulations of a drain into the River Annagh; its area amounts to [blank] acres. Natural springs and the drainage of the surrounding hills form its supplies.

Annaghard loch near the western boundary of the parish covers 100 acres. Its drains, the general bearing of which flows south westerly, forms a communication with the River Annagh.

Town loch in Bellamont Forest is a beautiful serpentine lake measuring nearly three-quarters of a mile in length by 180 yards of mean breadth and communicates by a drain with Wood loch. Its level is 260 feet above the sea. It derives its waters from natural springs and the drainage of its locality.

Wood loch in the same demesne stands 259 feet above the level of the sea; is half a mile in length and 160 yards in breadth and communicates by a drain at nearly a dead level with Drummore loch.

Coragh loch, another natural embellishment of the demesne pursuing the same north east and south west parallel as Town and Wood lochs, measures 200 yards in breadth by three-quarters of a mile in length and forms a communication with the drain from Wood loch; its level is 269 feet above the sea.

Corsilligo loch, on the north eastern extremity of the parish and common to the parish of Aughnamullen, covers an area of 90 acres and discharges its waters into the river which flows easterly to Dromore loch. Its level is 257 feet and Dromore loch 256 feet above the level of the sea.

Barraghy loch, 410 feet above the level of the sea, situated on the eastern boundary of the parish and is common to the parish of Aughnamullen, barony of Cremorne: it is surrounded by the townlands of Banaghy and Aughnagashland, parish of Drumgoon, and Munniagh and Drumod in the parish of Aughnamullen. It measures in extreme length and breadth 1,160 by 440 yards.

Meaduff loch is also situated on the south eastern boundary of the parish and common to Aughnamullen. It is surrounded by the townlands of Mullaghard and Meaduff in the parish of Drumgoon and Drumcruian in the parish of Aughnamullen, and covers an area of [blank] acres. Its altitude is 371 feet above the level of the sea.

Skerrig loch and Dung loch, Caspinduff loch and numerous others are small and unimportant but diversify the surface of the district in the most beautiful manner. All these lakes derive their supplies from springs in the general drainage of their localities.

Annagh River

The River Annagh, rising from the northern shore of the Loch Tucka, is joined near its source by the Knappagh water, overflowing from Loch [blank] in the county of Monaghan and pursuing its course through the parish, the general bearing of which is north westerly over a rugged grauwacke channel continuing rocky and shallow until it appears [in] the parish of Kill, when its banks deepen and contract and propel the waters onward to Loch Erne.

Bogs

With the single exception of the proximity of Cootehill, turbary is abundant and in many localities. It is densely charged and apparently composed of the comminuted reliquae of oak, fir and sally timber, the stumps of which are numerous and direct, and many of the stems remain indicating great antiquity, branches and leaves of sally in a state of perfect preservation but also in a state of solution from having been so long saturated with water, even thrown out from a stratum 7 feet beneath the surface; and 3 feet deeper a brown and bluish-coloured marl containing abundance of terrestrial shells rest[s] upon the grauwacke rock.

Woods

In the townlands of Boagh and Barnagirve small portions of underwood of oak, birch, beech and alder still testify [to] the former existence of natural woods in those localities, but the most decided specimen of a primaeval forest has been lately developed around the margin of Killyrue loch by the patriotic and public-spirited designs of the Revd A. Duglas, rector of the parish.

The waters of the lake have been reduced by drainage and expose and render available a considerable extent of bogs studded with stumps of oaks, fir and holly and sally. On the northern shore of the lake 70 stumps, mostly fir, many which measure 9 feet in circumference, now rise above the surface, and on its south western margin a more extensive development principally of oak has also been effected.

2 stems, with a portion of the roots attached, of fir in good preservation, have been lately extracted from the reverend gentleman, measuring 40 feet in length by 9 in circumference; and from their laying in the same direction it is probable they were prostrated at the same period and by a powerful south western. One stem of oak, 90 feet long and 13 in circumference, was extracted without exhibiting the appearance of a single branch on its whole length, and converted into valuable household furniture.

Vast numbers of stems of various sizes have been found in the bog, and an offer has been made by a Liverpool timber merchant of 7s a foot for them.

Climate

The great extent of lakes and plantations in the vicinity of Cootehill are supposed to induce rheumatic and febrile afflictions, but the general salubrity of the climate, which is soft and moist, is unquestionable. The following tabular view of the mortality, as furnished by the rector of the parish, establishes the healthiness of the climate most satisfactorily.

Extract from the registry of burials at Cootehill from 1829 to 1835: from 90 to 100 years of age, 1 death; from 80 to 90 years of age, 18 deaths; from 70 to 80 years of age, 16 deaths; from 60 to 70 years of age, 10 deaths; from 50 to 60 years of age, 9 deaths; from 40 to 50 years of age, 7 deaths; from 30 to 40 years of age, 8 deaths; from 20 to 30 years of age, 6 deaths; from 10 to 20 years of age, 8 deaths; from 1 to 10 years of age, 7 deaths.

Natural History

Botany

The sweet, scented vernal grass, smooth and rough-stalked meadow grass, the trefoil and ribwort grass are the most abundant of the spontaneous vegetation. Oak, elm, ash, chestnut, beech and sycamore, plane, poplar and thorn, larch, spruce, silver and scotch firs, hazel, rowan tree and sally comprise the trees of the forest and demesne.

Wildlife

Pike, perch and bream, roach, trout and eel abound in the lakes. Every variety of wildfowl, mallard, widgeon, teal, diver, heron and curlew, gull and crane and cormorant frequent the lakes and marshes. Partridge, snipe and woodcock and plover, hares, rabbits and foxes all exist in the parish but are exceedingly scarce. The bittern, badger, otter and deer are formerly common but are now extinct.

Geology

Associated with the grauwacke rock, which forms the prevailing mass throughout the parish, very extensive developments of siliceous state are frequently obtainable. Quarries of the latter rock were formerly wrought in the townland of Ballynahaigha, supplying the town of Cootehill and surrounding district with coarse roofing slate at 21s a thousand.

Croppings of the rock in any localities indicate the presence of valuable slate, the lamina dipping at an acute angle and frequently approaching to verticality; but although good roofing slate is not at present available within the parish, very large quarries of slate rock, highly valuable as building material, are extensively wrought around.

In a quarry in the townland of Gallenreagh, forming a portion of the glebe of the parish and wrought under the direction of its scientific and benevolent rector, flags of slate rock measuring 5 feet square are easily available, the strata dipping south east 33 degrees. A similar quarry in the townland of Shembless now supplies the town of Cootehill with the same materials, the strata dipping south 15 degrees.

In a quarry in the townland of Dung, near the south side of the road leading to Ballybay, a very interesting specimen of the association of grauwacke with slate rock is particularly observable. One-half of the quarry exposes a section of siliceous rock 12 feet deep and 45 broad, dipping south 72 degrees, of lamina of variable thickness and intersected transversely by parallel lines from 9 to 18 inches apart; the other half of the quarry, losing its lamellated structure, assumes the form of a multitude of arches with their concavities reversed, exceedingly indulated and difficult to work, and the same rock on the right and left of these arches appears in rugged, indescribable confusion.

Iron pyrites in large crystals are frequently observable in the siliceous slated rocks of the district. In the townland of Killytee oblate modules, 3 and 4 inches in circumference, of the sulphate of copper, were found in sinking a drain in grauwacke rock forming a lane on the south margin of Killytee bog.

In the townland of Cloughtucka a vein of galena was discovered many years ago. When preparing the ground for the crops, the specimens being very pure, an examination of the vein was made, a shaft sunk and the work proceeded with but soon after discontinued.

Modern Topography

Town of Cootehill

The town of Cootehill, containing at the last census [blank] inhabitants and situated in the north western extremity of the parish, 52 miles north west of Dublin, was founded in the year [blank]. [Insert note: I could not obtain this information].

The town consists of 2 streets intersecting each other nearly at right angles. Market Street is the principal one and contains the greatest number of shops and constructed buildings: the new church, of Gothic structure, stands conspicuous at its eastern extremity and the old church and churchyard, receding a few yards from the side of Church Street, stands upon the slope of Magheranure, a small elevation of the townland on which Cootehill was originally founded.

In addition to the Established church, it contains 5 other places of public worship, a Presbyterian, Seceding, Methodist, Quaker and Moravian meeting houses and a Roman Catholic chapel, a court house, market house and shambles, and was, during the flourishing condition of the linen trade, one of the most prosperous towns in this division of the kingdom; and from its central position and means of communication ought now to be the depot of the agricultural produce of an extensive surrounding district.

The coach from Dublin arrives every Tuesday, Thursday and Saturday on its way to Clones and returns to Dublin on alternate days. There is also a branch of the Provincial Bank of Ireland open

Cootehill

every Friday (market day), a savings bank and a reading room, which are of great advantage and accommodation.

The town is well supplied with meat, poultry and butter. The cattle for the slaughterhouse are grazed on the gentlemen's estates around the town and the Town Parks rent as high as 3 or 4 pounds an acre. Several new houses have been erected of a superior description within the last 4 years but since that period the improvement in the appearance of the town has been stationary.

Court House

The court house, a handsome modern building, was erected in the years 1831 and 1832. It contains a grand and petty jury room, an office for the clerk of the peace, and reception room, a court and bench with several cells for the safe custody of prisoners. The quarter sessions are held here twice a year, with the assistant barrister of the county presiding.

Market House

The market house, a large, oblong commodious building, was erected in the year 1806, and during the prosperity of the linen trade the upper range was used for the measuring and stamping of linen whilst the lower was, and still is, employed as the general mart of potatoes and corn. The upper portion of the building has been occasionally rented to the government as a barrack for a company of infantry.

Meeting Houses

The Presbyterian meeting house was erected in the year 1728 and accommodates 480 hearers. The Revd James Bones is the officiating clergyman and receives 30 pounds a year from his congregation and the regium donum amounting to 46 pounds 3s 1d.

The Seceding meeting house was erected in the year 1787 and accommodates 220 members. The Revd William Little, the officiating minister, receives the regium donum, 46 pounds 3s 1d, and 36 pounds 10s from his hearers.

Methodist Chapel

The Methodist chapel was erected in the year 1797 and accommodates 300 persons. There is no resident clergyman attached to it. Divine service is performed by 2 ministers who attend on alternate Sundays and these are changed every 2 or 3 years. Their salary amounts only to 16 pounds a year each.

Churches

The old church of Cootehill, a small oblong building, was erected in the year 1639 and continued the parochial and only Protestant Established church within this extensive parish until the year 1819 when the new church, a commodious Gothic building with handsome spire, was built, accommodating 600 persons; the Revd A. Duglas, the officiating resident rector, and the Revd William Tomlinson, curate.

A chapel of ease was erected in the townland of Dernakish in the year 1834, accommodating 260 parishioners; the Revd James Adams, the officiating curate.

Catholic Chapels

There are 3 Roman Catholic chapels conveniently situated within the parish for the benefit of its hearers.

The chapel in the town of Cootehill, erected in the year 1826, is a plain neat building with handsome belfry and cross, accommodating 800 parishioners. The Very Revd Dr Brown, the lord bishop of the diocese, officiates.

Minale chapel, erected in 1821 in the townland of Corcriaghan, accommodates 600 parishioners and Muddabawn chapel, erected in 1824 in the townland of Killytee, accommodates the same number. The Revd Terence O'Reilly and the Revd Pat O'Reilly are the officiating clergymen.

Moravian Church

In the proximity of Cootehill a religious community of United Brethren, more generally known as Moravians, was formed in the year 1752; and a church was erected in 1755, capable of accommodating 400 members. On the 6th July 1765 a congregation was formed and the Revd John Frederick Landen appointed its minister. From that time to the present 11 clergymen have succeeded each other in the ministry. The congregation amounts to 60 and the Revd John Willey, a very learned, pious and godly divine, now presides over the establishment.

The church is a neat oblong building and the Moravian establishment altogether presents a locality strikingly superior in its neatness, cleanliness and order to the wretched cabins <cabans> of its neighbourhood and village.

Gentlemen's Seats

Bellamont Forest, the princely seat of Charles Coote Esquire, surrounded by a cordon of plantation 70 feet broad, the circle of which measures 8 English miles, comprising in demesne, deerpark, ornamental grounds, plantations and lakes [insert note: area wanting], is situated on the northern boundary of the parish, in the immediate proximity of Cootehill.

The beautiful undulating formation of its surface, embracing every variety of drum and cor-shaped hills, the enchanting form and diversity of lakes surrounding and included within its boundary, the vast extent and variety of its plantations, the rapid ascent from the bed of Loch Coragh to the length of Benwith, commanding a northern prospect, altogether combine in forming one of the most splendid and magnificent gentlemen's seats within the province.

The mansion is built of brick, with a handsome portico of Doric order, supported by 4 pillars on an elevation of 14 steps, 30 feet wide. The portico enters into a lofty hall 30 feet square, tastefully ornamented with statuary; and immediately opposite the hall door is the drawing-room of the same dimensions. The walls of this magnificent department are adorned with a full-length portrait of the Earl of Bellamont in the uniform of the Order of the Bath, and a corresponding one of his countess.

This apartment contains also a most beautiful representation of the suicide of the charming Dido, in which the personages are all developed in full length, exhibiting the different passions which that melancholy catastrophe must have created. The painting cost 1,500 guineas.

The dining room contains a beautifully executed portrait of Richard Dawson Esquire, late M.P.; to his memory, a handsome testimonial stands erected in the townland of Carson. The offices, separated from the mansion by highly ornamented and full-grown plantation, are very extensive, divided into square courts and contain a riding house and lofty arched stables; the garden, surrounded by a high brick wall, contains 2 English acres.

The Rectory is a modern quadrangular building presently situated on the elevated portion of the townland of Killycramp, in the immediate vicinity of Cootehill. 24 acres 1 rood 20 perches of land surrounding the rectory were exchanged in the year 1822 for an equivalent portion of glebe in the townlands of Crann and Lisnoore, containing 64 acres, and now form, under the superior agricultural improvements of its highly talented and patriotic incumbent, as finished and perfect a specimen of richly cultivated and exuberantly productive argillaceous soil as is to be found within the kingdom.

Parish of Drumgoon

Bleachfields and Mills

In the townland of Lisnagoan the ruins of extensive premises of a bleachfield are still standing. Its situation, on the banks of the River Annaghlee, and contiguity to an extensive bog render its localities exceedingly favourable for the purpose.

Lower down the river, in the townland of Boagh, are 2 bleachfields with extensive premises. The upper one still carries on business but to a very limited extent, the lower is now converting into a corn mill; its wheel measures 16 feet in diameter and its power is undershot.

Still further down the stream, in the townland of Lisnageera, Mr Murphy has erected an extensive flour and corn mill, the wheel of which measures 18 feet in diameter and 9 feet broad. Its power also is undershot but, as the whole volume of the river is available if necessary, the supply is constant unless in very dry seasons.

There are 2 other corn mills, on a small scale, on the same water, also a flax and clothier's mill, one in the townland of Lurganboy and the other in Lisnaclay; the latter is driven by the Knappagh water.

Communications

The coach road from Dublin to Clones traverses the whole extent of the parish in a north west and south easterly direction. An old road from Cootehill to Shercock runs nearly in the same parallel. A new line of road connecting Cootehill and Bailieborough <Bailyborrow> runs through a large extent of the parish in nearly a north and south direction. A new line of road traverses easterly through the parish to Ballybay and an old line south easterly to Ballytraie. Numerous crossroads intersect these, opening communications to every point and affording every facility for commerce.

The average breadth of the roads is about 40 feet. They are kept in very bad repair and most of them are very injudiciously laid out. The making and repairing of the whole is paid by levies on the parish presented at the half-yearly assizes.

ANCIENT TOPOGRAPHY

Forts

The only remains of antiquity within the parish are the circular forts of the aboriginal lords of the soil which are here particularly numerous, 2 of them having been constructed upon many townlands, over several cromlechs or giant's graves. In the townland of Aughagachland 2 of these graves with attendant fir bregi and a rock of great size in the form of, and representing, a chair are still held in profound and sacred veneration.

In the townland of Quoha, and near the east side of the road connecting Shercock and Cootehill, 2 graves are still distinct, although part of the walls have been greatly disarranged, measuring 40 links long and 3 to 8 broad. John McQuillan, an occupying tenant, was present about 40 years ago when one of these was opened and a human skull, half an inch thick and twice the circumference of a cranium of the present age, together with the femur and several ribs larger than those of a horse, were then exhumed "Credat Judeus Apella;" and several bars of iron, 3 inches square and three-quarters of a yard long, were also found in the grave.

On the western boundary of the same townland another very large cromlech, and much more perfect, measures 40 links long by 10 in its greatest breadth.

Miscellaneous Discoveries

In the townland of Lislea the head and horns of an elk, measuring 12 feet from the top of one branch to that of the other, was found in the bog and now adorns the porch of the Rectory.

In a drain in the townland of Cabragh the branch of one side of the head of an elk was found and was long used as a gate.

In sinking for marl in the bog in the townland of Carpinduff the skeleton of an elk was discovered, but in so soft and pulpy a state as to render its preservation impossible. The skeleton lay in a stratum of blue clay 4 feet beneath the surface, resting upon a bed of marl, in the removal of which the bones were found.

MODERN TOPOGRAPHY

General Appearance and Scenery

The very great uniformity in the general bearing and parallelism of the ridges and valleys, which prevails not only in the parish of Drumgoon but of the parishes in the immediate connection in the barony of Dartry, is a phenomenon in the general appearance and scenery of the district particularly interesting. These beautiful wave-like undulations form the natural reservoirs of the numerous lakes interspersed throughout its surface.

Dromore loch, Wood loch, Town loch and Coragh loch, within the demesne of Bellamont Forest, occupy valleys preserving the same longitudinal direction and developing a very trifling difference in attitude, Dromore loch, standing 256 feet, and Coragh loch, 269 feet above the level of the sea. But from the bed of Coragh to the heights of Benwilt a considerable increase in altitude is immediately involved.

The elevated portions of the townlands of Lisnacerne, Benwilt and Drumcrughil form a chain of heights stretching north west and south east, which naturally separate the northern from the central sections of the parish.

The splendid demesne of Bellamont Forest and the town of Cootehill expand along the northern base of this range, presenting scenery richly diversified with every embellishment; and south of this chain the heights of Mayo and Aughagashland form another range of increasing altitude, in the elevation of which the upheaving power appears to have attained its maximum, since a depression in almost every direction, but more considerably towards the south and west, gradually intervenes.

The central and southern sections of the parish participate in the lower undulating formation, diversified with lakes and cone-shaped hills, crowned with the circular "raths" of its very ancient inhabitants, the River Annagh winding its north westerly course and the cabins of the tenantry thickly studded over its surface.

SOCIAL ECONOMY

Early Improvements

How fast the change which has been effected upon many portions of this country through the agency of agriculture within the last 100 years is fully exemplified in the townland of Carpinduff, the whole surface of which at the above period was covered with heather, within the memory of Charles McArne, who is now above 100 years of age and in full possession of every faculty.

The whole townland was held by Charles Reilly, a descendant of the noble Reillys of Cavan, from Allen Adams, the ancestor of the present proprietor, at 6d ha'penny or, in lieu thereof, a bottle of whisky; and the tenant availing himself of the fluctuation of markets, paid his rent in liquor when the whisky was cheap and in coin when the spirit was dear; and within the last 40 years the land paid only 3s 6d an acre, whereas it now pays from 14s to 23s per acre.

Local Government

Mr Coote of Bellamont Forest, Mr Thomas Coote of Cootehill, Mr Murphy of Newgirve, resident within the parish, Colonel Clements of Ashfield and Mr Boyle of Tullyrin, both in the adjoining parish of Kill, and Mr Clements of Rakenny in the parish of Drum are the presiding magistrates at petty sessions held in the court house every Wednesday, and these gentlemen are firm and decisive in their judgements and highly respected by the people.

One chief constable, 1 constable and 12 sub-constables of police are stationed in the town, and a company of infantry is occasionally quartered in the market house.

56 outrages of an agricultural character, consisting of homicides, rapes, violent assaults and robbery, were perpetrated within this district in the year 1834 and the criminals committed to Cavan gaol for trial at the assizes; and 27 cases of a similar description have occurred within the last half-year ending 30th June 1835, and were either committed or bailed in like manner.

Combination against the payment of tithe exists and prevails throughout the parish. Illicit distillation is carried on when the price of corn is low, but nothing of the kind has been going forward within the last year. Many of the houses in the town of Cootehill are insured but insurance in the country is not resorted to.

Dispensary

Dr Welsh, the resident physician in the town of Cootehill, superintends the dispensary for the town, parish and surrounding district, and pronounces it healthy. Virulent smallpox has appeared in several localities and in some cases the patients had been previously vaccinated.

[Table] fevers, colds, dropsy, bowel complaints and all other accidental diseases: [supported] by subscriptions of the landed proprietors and gentlemen, and by presentments of the grand jury.

Dispensary Report

[Printed] report of the Cootehill dispensary from July 1st 1834 to July 1st 1835.

List of subscribers: Charles Coote Esquire 10 pounds, Colonel Clements 10 pounds 10s, the Lord Bishop of Kilmore 2 pounds 2s, Lady Cremorne 3 pounds 3s, the Lord Plunkett 2 pounds 2s, the Lord Garvagh 2 pounds 10, Colonel Ker 2 pounds 2s, the Right Revd Dr Brown 1 pound 10s, Theophilus E.L. Clements Esquire 5 pounds 5s, John Singleton Esquire 5 pounds 5s, William F. Grevill Esquire 5 pounds, Thomas Burrowes Esquire 4 pounds 4s, Revd A. Duglas 3 pounds 3s, Revd A. Forster 1 pound 1s, Revd J. Harris 1 pound, Revd William Hales 1 pound, Charles Adams Esquire 2 pounds 2s, William Dawson Esquire 1 pound 1s, Thomas Cottnam Esquire 1 pound 1s, Messrs Leslie and Company 2 pounds 2s, Richard Mayne Esquire 1 pound 1s, Richard Montgomery Esquire 1 pound 1s, Michael Murphy Esquire 1 pound 1s, Mr John Boyd Senior 1 pound 1s, Mr John Boyd Junior 1 pound 1s, Mr John Foy 1 pound 1s, Charles Dawson Esquire 1 pound 1s; total 73 pounds 10s.

Abstract of account: balance from last account 38 pounds 10s 11d, account of presentment renewed 30 pounds, by subscriptions 73 pounds 10s, total 142 pounds 11d; cash received 142 pounds 11d, cash expended 138 pounds 13s 11d, balance 3 pounds 7s.

Outgoings: to Dr Welsh, his year's salary, 92 pounds 6s 2d; to Messrs Leslie and Co. for medicine, 31 pounds 19s 5d; paid for spirits and sugar, for syrups and tinctures, 7 pounds 8s 8d; paid for linen and flannel, for bandages, 2 pounds 19s 4d; paid carriage of medicine 1 pound 11s 3d, paid Cowpock Institution 1 pound 1s, paid printing reports 15s, to sundries, stamps, postage and messengers, 13s 1d, [total] 138 pounds 13s 11d.

At a meeting of the committee held February 6th, Thomas Cottnam Esquire, in the chair, the treasurer's accounts were examined and the balance was 3 pounds 7s found to be in his hands; Thomas Cottnam, chairman.

An annual report of the number of diseases treated in the Cootehill dispensary from the 1st July 1834 to the 1st July 1835: remained under treatment to the 1st July 1834, 291; recommended and entered on the dispensary books from the 1st July 1834 to the 1st July 1835, 3,609; visited at their houses 276; children vaccinated 54; remain under treatment 207; [signed] M. Welsh. Johnson, printer, Cavan.

Poor

There is no assistance for the poor within the town or parish. The contributions at the church and benevolence of the people are their only supplies. The collections at the church of Cootehill amount annually to about 25 pounds and the average number of poor upon the church but to 22; and the collection at the chapel of ease in the townland of Dernakish is about 4 pounds per annum and the number of the poor 6.

Religion

The last census of the parish taken in the year 1829 gave the following proportions: Roman Catholics 9,522, Protestants 1,437, Presbyterians 400, Seceders 610, Quakers 42, Moravians 19, Covenanters 9, total 12,039.

The Revd A. Duglas, the Protestant rector of the parish, derives his income from glebe land. Tithe has not been paid for several years but are now paying. The Roman Catholic and Dissenting clergymen are paid by the people.

Habits of the People

Nothing can be more wretched in appearance than the clay and straw-built cabins of the tenantry which prevail throughout the parish, 1-storey high and generally divided into 2 or 3 apartments. Potatoes and buttermilk in its season form the chief article of diet, which undoubtedly conduces to longevity, for many of the peasantry attain a great age. 6 may be stated as the number per family and marriages, although often hastily, are very seldom prematurely formed.

Attendance at markets and fairs are the principal amusements of the people. Patron days or local customs are nowhere observed and no peculiarity of dress distinguishes the district.

Emigration

A few families from the town and parish emigrate during the spring and summer to America, and many others would follow if in possession of the necessary resources. None go from hence to the English harvests.

PRODUCTIVE ECONOMY

Manufacture: Linen

The manufacture of eight, nine and ten hundred linens is still carried on to a very small extent throughout the parish, the profits arising to the operatives not exceeding 2d and 4d a day.

During the prosperity of this trade in the years from 1816 to 1826, the number of webs of 4/4 to 5/4 to 6/4 of from eight to twelve hundred shirting and sheeting sold in the town of Cootehill, and under the impution of an authorised stamper, amounted to about 20,000 annually. The gross value or wholesale price is about 80,000 pounds and the whole of this linen was bleached in the neighbourhood and forwarded to the linen halls of Dublin and Belfast.

Corn

The corn trade is much more extensive now than at any former period. About 15,000 barrels are sold annually in the town of Cootehill, the greater part of which is ground into meal and exported from Dundalk to Liverpool and Glasgow.

Trade and Occupations

Cloth merchants 5, linen merchants 1, wine and spirit merchants 5, grocers 15, drapers 14, smiths 8, nailers 5, coopers 7, cartwrights 2, cabinet-makers 1, leather cutters 6, shoemakers 21, butchers 14, watchmakers 1, lodging houses 40, stationers 0, iron warehouses 7, surgeons 4, apothecaries 1, woollen merchants 5, saddlers 2, public houses 34, coachmakers 2, coppersmiths 1, carpenters 11, gunsmiths 1, innkeepers 1, broguemakers 10, wheelwrights 4, bakers 11, pawnbroker 1, delph shops 3, painters and paperhangers 4, tanneries 2.

Fairs

12 fairs are held annually in the town of Cootehill, one on the second Friday of every month for the sale of horses, cows, sheep, pigs and asses and every other article of agriculture and domestic produce. The cattle are generally of a very inferior description and low priced, horses from 8 to 15 pounds, cows from 4 to 6 pounds, asses from 1 to 2 pounds, sheep from 35s to 55s and pigs according to their weight, the market price 2d to 3d per lb. Beef varies with the season from 3d to 6d per lb., mutton 4d to 6d per lb., lamb from 4s to 5s per quarter and veal from 6d to 7d per lb., butter from 5d to 9d per lb.; poultry are cheap in the season, geese from 10d to 1s each, turkeys the same price, ducks and fowls from 1s to 14d a pair and chickens from 4s to 6s a dozen.

Rural: Proprietors

Mr Coote of Bellamont Forest, Mr Singleton, Mr Ruseton, Mr Girvel, Mr Adams and Lord Garvagh are the principal landed proprietors of this parish, Mr Coote the only resident landlord. Mr Adams resides in the neighbouring parish of Kill, the others and their agents are all non-residents.

The subdivision of farms is carried to a very great extent, varying from 2 to 10 acres on leases of lives and 21 years, but the greater number are tenants at will, at rents varying from 4s to 40s per acre.

Crops and Implements

Potatoes, oats and flax is the chief produce; very little wheat, barley, rag grass or clover are observable. In fact agriculture, throughout a very large extent of this parish, is reduced to the lowest possible state of depression. The soil [is] argillaceous mixed with very minute pebbles of lime and highly productive when blended with a very small quantity of manure. The present crops are luxuriantly abundant.

Lime is very generally burned in small kills [kilns] upon the holdings for manure, and carried from the quarries of Carrickmacross and the parish of Laragh, both at a considerable distance. Burning the soil is much practised and to an injurious extent.

Culture is chiefly by the shovel and loy. The hilly nature of the surface prevents in a great measure the use of the plough. The old Irish car is common but the slide is out of use. The rotation of crops, proportions of seed and produce, marked prices are precisely the same as reported in the parishes of Ematris and Aghabog.

Grazing and Servants

This parish is purely agricultural: no portion of its surface is devoted exclusively to grazing. The cultivation of artificial grasses is very rarely observable.

Very few servants are employed by the peasantry. Female servants receive from 2 to 3 pounds and males from 2 to 3 pounds per annum, exclusive of board and lodgings.

Cattle

The breed of cattle is of the very lowest class. Jobbers purchase up the pigs at the fairs and markets and drive them to Belfast, Newry and Dublin for the English markets.

Fuel

The bogs are wholly used as fuel. No mineral deposits have ever been discerned in them. The turf sold in the town of Cootehill is very dear: from 2s to 4s is charged for a crate. Coal is brought from Newry and Dundalk and sold for 25s per ton.

Planting

With the exception of Bellamont Forest, there is very little plantation within the parish. No nurseries for young trees have been found in it. The forest supplies the builders of the district. Oak is sold at 3s 6d per square foot, ash at 2s 6d, elm at 2s 6d, beech at 2s 6d and fir at 1s 6d per square foot.

SOCIAL ECONOMY

Schools

The great number of schools in active operation within the parish exhibited in the accompanying table testifies strongly the very ardent desire

Parish of Drumgoon

amongst the people to provide education for their children. [Table contains the following headings: name of townland, number of pupils subdivided by religion and sex, how supported, when established].

Town of Cootehill, 4 Protestants, 26 Roman Catholics, 19 males, 11 females, total 30; paid by the scholars.

Town of Cootehill, 3 Protestants, 34 Roman Catholics, 21 males, 15 females, total 36; paid by the scholars.

Town of Cootehill, 26 Protestants, 13 Roman Catholics, 39 males, total 39; paid by the scholars.

Town of Cootehill, 17 Protestants, 3 Roman Catholics, 20 males, total 20; paid by scholars and Hibernian Society.

Town of Cootehill, 35 Protestants, 30 Roman Catholics, 45 males, 20 females, total 65; paid by scholars and Hibernian Society.

Town of Cootehill, 19 Protestants, 16 Roman Catholics, 11 males, 24 females, total 35; paid by the scholars.

Town of Cootehill, 19 Protestants, 16 Roman Catholics, 11 males, 24 females, total 35; paid by the scholars.

Town of Cootehill, 16 Protestants, 8 males, 8 females, total 16; paid by the scholars.

Town of Cootehill, 19 Protestants, 2 Roman Catholics, 21 males, total 21; paid by the scholars.

Town of Cootehill, 12 Protestants, 33 Roman Catholics, 26 males, 19 females, total 45; supported by Mrs Duglas and ladies; infant school.

Town of Cootehill, a large schoolhouse, building, established 1835.

Town of Cootehill, a large schoolhouse, building, in connection with the National Board of Education, established 1835.

Drutainy, 50 Protestants, 15 Roman Catholics, 48 males, 17 females, total 65; paid by the scholars.

Lattully, 12 Protestants, 63 Roman Catholics, 50 males, 25 females, total 75; paid by the scholars.

Rallaghan, 20 Protestants, 40 Roman Catholics, 18 males, 42 females, total 60; paid by the scholars.

Killyclare, 36 Protestants, 9 Roman Catholics, 23 males, 22 females, total 45; paid by the scholars.

Drumgreen, 32 Protestants, 15 Roman Catholics, 20 males, 27 females, total 47; paid by scholars and Hibernian Society.

Killykelly, 7 Protestants, 38 Roman Catholics, 16 males, 29 females, total 45; paid by the scholars.

Tullybrick, 10 Protestants, 32 Roman Catholics, 21 males, 21 females, total 42; paid by the scholars.

Dohatel, 18 males, 12 females, total 30, all Roman Catholics; paid by the scholars.

Lisdoagh, 3 Protestants, 27 Roman Catholics, 22 males, 8 females, total 30; paid by scholars.

Knappagh, 13 Protestants, 52 Roman Catholics, 40 males, 25 females, total 65; paid by the scholars.

Mullaghara, 10 Protestants, 55 Roman Catholics, 49 males, 16 females, total 65; paid by the scholars.

Lisnageeragh, 33 Protestants, 4 Roman Catholics, 18 males, 19 females, total 37; paid by the scholars and the Hibernian Society.

Corcloghan, 35 Roman Catholics, 28 males, 7 females, total 35; paid by the scholars and Hibernian Society.

Remarks on Improvement

The natural resources of the parish of Drumgoon are unbounded. Its soil is argillaceous, formed from the debris of the subjacent slate rocks. Marl is abundant in many localities. The undulatory formation of its surface facilitates drainage. Its water power is vast and means of communication penetrate and ramify in every direction; and, notwithstanding these inestimable advantages in a parish both agricultural and commercial, its surface presents a more wretched and desolate appearance generally than appears in any other parish of the surrounding district, arising entirely from the deplorable system of agriculture and the minute subdivision of the farms which so unhappily prevails. [Signed] P. Taylor, Lieutenant 69th Regiment.

Ecclesiastical Summary

[Table] Name Drumgoon, diocese Kilmore, province Armagh, rectory, no union, patron Revd James Hamilton, incumbent Revd A. Duglas, 213 pounds amount of tithe and belonging to the incumbent.

MODERN TOPOGRAPHY

Drawings

[From Laragh Memoir. Insert note: The sketches are for the Statistical Report of Drumgoon].

View of Cootehill.

View of Cootehill church and Roman Catholic chapel [both] by William Groves.

Parish of Drumloman, County Cavan

Statistical Memoir by Lieutenant Andrew Beatty, November 1835

GEOGRAPHY OR NATURAL STATE

Name

Drumloman <Drumlummon> is derived from 2 Irish words *drum* signifying "a back or ridge" and *lum* signifying "bare or lean." This derivation seems to be supported by the appearance and general character of the parish, the ground being hilly and the soil light and poor.

The ancient mode of spelling the name of this parish was Dromloman. It is so spelt in an old manuscript of the names of proprietors in county Cavan at the time of the Commonwealth, in a "list of Carvaghs" printed in the year 1699 and in the Down Survey. The most modern way of spelling is Drumlummon. It is thus spelt in Beaufort's map of Ireland and modern documents. This mode agrees with its general pronunciation.

Locality

Drumloman is situated in the south westerly part of Cavan, forming, as it were, one of the corners of that county bordering on the counties of Longford and Westmeath. It is in the barony of Clonmahon and is bounded on the north by the parishes of Ballintample and Killashandra <Killysandra>, on the east by Ballintample and Ballymachugh parishes, on the south by Lough Sheelin <Shillan> and the parish of Foyrun in the county of Westmeath, and on the west by Killashandra parish and the county of Longford.

Its extreme length is 9 and a half miles, its mean length nearly 7 miles. Its extreme breadth is about 4 and a quarter miles and the mean breadth about 3 and a half miles. This parish contains 55 townlands, making a total of 16,493 acres 2 roods 23 perches. Of this, 3,262 acres are bog and 195 acres are uncultivated land. Its valuation to the county cess averages about 600 pounds per annum.

NATURAL FEATURES

Hills

None of the hills in the parish deserve particular mention. They are very numerous but unconnected with each other, not forming part of any range. They are generally of the same height, averaging about 350 feet above the level of the sea, a few as high as 400 but not much higher. The general surface of the low-lying ground averages about 220 feet above the level of the sea.

Lakes

The parish is bounded on the south by Lough Sheelin, which is of considerable extent and of good depth. Lough Gowna, another large lake extending into the county Longford, forms part of its western boundary.

Lough Sheelin is elevated 209 feet about the sea at low water mark. This is its mean summer level. It is subject to great floods in winter and, in consequence of this rise, the adjacent lands are annually flooded and remain for some time under water. This flood affects the lands near Finnra which are therefore left in meadow. The deposit left where the water subsides is found to be of service to vegetation, owing perhaps to the quantity of lime held in solution by the water as the bottom of the lake is principally of limestone rocks or gravel.

There are also 6 smaller lakes included in the parish: Lough Islane, adjacent to Drumhourag; Lough Davin, adjacent to Lough Davin; White lough, adjacent to Middletown; Black lough, adjacent to Kilsaran; Killydream lough, adjacent to Killydream; Bracklow lough, adjacent to Bracklow.

Rivers

The River Erne forms part of the western and northern boundary of the parish. Taking its rise in Lough Gowna it runs northward and, being joined by other rivers, gives birth to the fine chain of lakes, Upper and Lower Lough Erne, extending from the borders of Fermanagh and Cavan nearly to the borders of Fermanagh and Donegal, and, narrowing again into a river, falls into the ocean beyond Ballyshannon.

It is 214 feet above the level of the sea, where it takes its rise from the Lough Gowna. The average breadth is about 70 feet; its depth is not greater than 4 feet but it rises very much in winter.

There is another river running through the northern part of the parish, of inconsiderable magnitude and taking its name from the townlands through which it passes. This river affords some good sites for mills; it runs into Lough Gowna.

Springs and Wells

The parish is abundantly supplied with water from wells and springs, especially from the former of which there are a great number.

There is more mineral spar in the townland of Cartronfree. It was formerly tried as a remedy for the sick, but from the fact of its having fallen into disuse it is to be supposed that its medicinal qualities are not of much value.

Bogs

The parish is abundantly supplied with fuel in all parts. In the northern part there is a very extensive tract of bog. Its height above the sea is about 260 feet, about 30 feet above the nearest river.

Timber stills occurs plentifully in some of the bogs, although a good deal is constantly taken away. The trees found are generally oak, fir and deal. The stumps in some cases remain upright, the trunks being separated from them, but the roots always crumble away from the stumps remaining embedded in the soil. The trunks lie indiscriminately and occur both in the interior and edges of the bog. Some remain attached to the stumps, as if torn down by the violence of the tempest; others are detached, bearing the marks of burning and a few of the axe.

NATURAL HISTORY

Zoology

The animals common to the country are found in this parish and do not need individual description.

Lough Sheelin is justly celebrated for the excellent flavour and large size of its trout, and in the summer is frequented by the brothers of the angle from the adjoining counties, particularly during the season of the green drake fly, which occurs about the middle of August. In this lake also, in the winter season, herring are caught rather larger than the sea herring and beautifully speckled.

In all the lakes and river[s] pike, perch, trout, bream and eel are found, and salmon are sometimes taken in the River Erne.

The usual species of birds are found also in the parish.

Geology

Dromloman forms part of the grauwacke formulation of this district which extends from Virginia. The grauwacke rock is very abundant as is also the grauwacke slate. In the south of the parish, townland Carrick, the limestone occurs. This is the extremity of the limestone formation which extends in a southerly direction into the county Meath.

The hill of Carrick is a fine limestone rock. It rises nearly perpendicular above the road to the height of about 100 feet. It is encrival limestone interspersed with nodules and layers of chert, and is carried to a distance of 10 or 12 miles for the purposes of building and burning for manure. The ochreous tough clay is found in the townland of Drumbuckless and is used for making bricks; it would answer very well for potter's clay. The same is found in townlands Drumcor, Legwee and Lower Callenagh. They are found at different depths.

Small islands or patches of hard ground occur in some of the bogs. The bogs vary in depth from 4 to 20 feet and, it is reasonable to suppose, are formed from the successive growth and decay of water plants, grasses and mosses.

Woods

There is no natural wood in this parish but, from the timber found in the bogs, it is natural to suppose that some did formerly exist although, it is probable, not to a very great extent. Grouse Hall was formerly covered with fir

MODERN TOPOGRAPHY OR ARTIFICIAL STATE

Villages

There are 3 small villages in the parish, namely Kilgolah, Kilcogy and Glen.

Kilgolah has fallen completely into decay. The houses are either in ruin or rapidly verging towards that state. There are not 20 houses in the village, all of them in the very poorest description and many of them propped up by pieces of timber to prevent their tumbling down, which gives the village a very desolate appearance. The ruin of an old barrack stands near the centre of the village.

The village of Kilcogy consists of 8 or 10 houses. There is a constabulary [barracks] in which a few police are stationed and a national school.

The village of Glen consists only of a public house and 3 or 4 huts. It is situated on the road from Granard to Ballynagh, in the southern part of the townland of Mullaghorne.

Public Buildings

The places of worship and the schoolhouses are the only public buildings the parish can boast of.

The church of the Established religion is situated in the north east part of the townland of Bracklow, on the left of the road leading from Finnra to Ballynagh. It was built about 50 years ago and is a plain stone building without either a tower or spire. It is of the simplest structure and may defy the church's bitterest enemies to point out any ornament of which they can complain. It will accommodate about 300 persons.

There are 3 Roman Catholic chapels, all of them very neat edifices, built of stone and within the last 10 years. They will accommodate each about 500 or 600 persons.

Gentlemen's Seats

Bracklow, residence of Captain Kerr; Orangefield, residence of Revd Mr Thompson, Protestant curate; the property of Mr O'Reilly; Rockfield, the residence of the Revd Phil O'Reilly P.P. None of these deserve any notice.

The ruins of an old mansion formerly the residence of Squire Pallis, who possesses considerable property in this part of the country, remain in Grouse Hall. The house was burnt down about 30 years ago.

Manufactories and Mills

There are no manufactories in this parish. There are only 3 corn mills in operation, situated in the townlands of Drumbannew, Mullaghorne and Lower Magheraboy. The diameters of the wheels are about 16 feet, the breadth about 2 feet 4 inches.

There is a corn mill in the townland of Legwee, not in use although in a good situation, in consequence of the road leading to it being in such a bad state as to be quite impassable for carts or even horses with any burden.

Communications

The parish is very well cut up with roads. The main road from Granard to Ballynagh runs nearly through the centre, passing from south to north. This road is joined by the main road from Finnra to Ballynagh at the small village of Glen, and about a mile and a half further north the road to Killashandra branches off to the left.

The main road from Ballyjamesduff to Granard runs through the southern part of the parish. It is also well supplied with by-roads.

The main roads are kept in good order at the expense of the county. They are all contracted for and are kept in repair by the rocks and gravel common to this part of the country. These, being of hard materials, seem to answer the purpose very well.

Very little attention seems to be paid to the state of the by-roads. There are no disputes which prevent improvements in bridges or communications.

Ancient Topography

Forts

There are a great number of raths, doons or forts, as they are generally called in this part of the country, scattered through the country. With 2 exceptions they are all of a circular form and have generally a ditch surrounding them.

There are 2 square forts, one of which, situated in the townland of Carrickbawa, differs from the general class of forts. It is built with more regularity and its ditch is of greater depth than usual. It has also an opening in one side, probably constructed to afford facility for ingress and egress. It is the only one which would lead the observer to suppose that the forts were made with any view to purposes of defence.

The supposition that they were intended for purposes of general meeting and assembling together seems more natural. They are generally in situations commanding an extensive view of the surrounding country, which fact would seem to bear out the latter supposition.

None of these forts have been opened. Any attempt to do so would be looked on by the greater mass of the inhabitants of the parish as sacrilege. Only one or two have been laboured, the people, especially the Roman Catholic part of the population, fearing that some calamity would shortly happen to the person rash enough to attempt it, and they relate numerous instances of such calamities having happened.

Druid's Altar

The above [drawing] is a sketch of an old druid's altar situated in the townland of Drumhowna, near the Roman Catholic chapel. The stone on the top is a flat stone about 6 feet long, lying east and west, and supported by 3 upright stones about 4 feet high.

There is another in the townland of Middletown partaking of the same character but the stones are smaller and it does not seem to have been erected with so much care.

From some large stones lying near the altars it might appear that they were formerly encompassed with a circle of stones. Some people think that they were used at the religious rites of the old druids, while others assert that they were used in the wars of Queen Elizabeth as a place where mass was performed. However, the two suppositions are not incompatible: they may have been used for both purposes.

Holy Wells

There are a few holy wells in the parish: one of them in Lower Camagh is distinguished by the name of St Patrick's Well. It has a fine old tree overhanging it, about 15 feet in circumference and, it is said, was formerly used as a station.

Ancient History

This district has very often changed its proprietors. The oldest possessors were the powerful family of the O'Reillys, Cavan being called the O'Reillys' country. A great portion of it was forfeited in the rebellion of 1641. In the time of the commonwealth the O'Reillys did not possess any property in it, but the Lord of Cavan possessed about one-half of this parish along with his other large possession; the remainder of the parish was held by Major William Moore, Lieutenant Burton and other small proprietors not possessing more than single townlands.

Other changes were effected by the forfeitures of 1689. By these, James Dease acquired considerable property, most of which had belonged to the Lord of Cavan. This is now held by his descendant Gerald Dease of Turbotstown. Lord Massereene also acquired considerable property, which has fallen into the possession of Lord Farnham. The family of the Pallises also possess property in this parish but, like too many Irish proprietors, the recollection of it is all that remains to their descendants.

MODERN TOPOGRAPHY

General Appearance and Scenery

The general appearance of the parish is very bleak and uninteresting. No rich planting meets the eye; but ground under tillage or hills topped with sterile rocks and the furze, the emblem of barrenness, are only varied by water and extensive flats of bog. Even the lakes, which are in general such an improvement to the scenery being surrounded by these tracts of bogs, not only lose their natural beauty but seem to add to the dreariness of the prospect; nor have the dry stone fences and the comfortless cabins which man has erected been a great improvement on the wildness of nature. The scenery about Lough Sheelin and Lough Gowna in other parishes is, however, very beautiful.

SOCIAL ECONOMY

Progress of Improvement

Judging from the present state of the parish, and the ample room for improvement which still exists, it would be going far back to look for the time when improvement commenced. In some parts of the parish, however, they are now progressing, particularly on the property of Lord Farnham, who gives much encouragement to his tenants.

No obstructions to improvement, in the shape of legal disputes or uncertainties about rights of land, exist: the boundaries are clearly defined. There are no ancient customs in use to stop its progress; they have been all long discontinued.

Local Government

There are no magistrates resident in the parish. The police force consists only of a sergeant and 3 men stationed in Kilcogy. Manor courts and courts leet have long been abolished. Petty sessions are held in Granard, Ballynagh and in Ballymachugh parish. There are generally 3 magistrates in attendance.

Outrages have greatly decreased of late. There are very seldom very serious cases of assault. Illicit distilling, which was formerly a good deal practised, has been almost entirely put a stop to by the activity and vigilance of the revenue police.

Dispensaries

There is no dispensary situated in the parish, a circumstance much to be regretted for the comfort of the poor, but they derive considerable assistance from one in the neighbouring parish of Ballymachugh.

Schools

Schools have not long enough been established in the parish to enable us to see any improvement resulting from them. Their effect will be more plainly seen in the rising generation. The people are very anxious to have their children instructed and afford them every facility.

There are 3 national schools in the parish and 1 school built and supported by Lord Farnham. In examining the number of scholars in the national schools, the very small number of Protestants which attend is remarkable. This reason of this is because in one case, in Drumhowna, the national school is built close to the Roman Catholic chapel in the chapelyard; in Carrick, although not in the chapelyard, close to the Roman Catholic chapel.

It is much to be regretted that in a national undertaking such as the erection of schoolhouses, the effects of which are intended to confer a benefit on all classes, causes should be allowed to exist which throw a stumbling block in the way of any one denomination of persons. It may be said that this ought to be no obstacle, and to a liberal minded person anxious for knowledge it ought not, but the experience of this and other countries shows what a powerful bias in the home and mind slight circumstances connected with religion effect.

On the other hand, looking at the returns of Lord Farnham's school we find the preponderance of Protestants over Roman Catholics; and when we take into account the number of Roman Catholics in the parish compared with Protestants, about 20 to 1, the preponderance is greater than it seems. It is to be regretted that the difference of religion, and the great stress laid upon that difference, should be thus early implanted in the minds of the young.

Table of Schools

[Table contains the following headings: name of townland, number of pupils subdivided by religion and sex, remarks as to how supported, when established].

Carrick, 1 Protestant, 296 Catholics, 133 males, 164 females, total 297; supported by the National Board; established 1833.

Kilcogy, 7 Protestants, 236 Catholics, 123 males, 120 females, total 243; supported by the National Board; established 1833.

Drumhowna, 3 Protestants, 204 Catholics, 100 males, 107 females, total 207; supported by the National Board; established 1834.

Kilgolagh, 54 Protestants, 19 Catholics, 34 males, 39 females, total 73; supported by Lord Farnham; established 1828.

Poor

There is no provision for the poor, with the exception of the collections made at the different places of worship on the sabbath. They depend for subsistence on the charity of individuals.

Religion

The religion of the people embraces only 2 sects, both Protestants and Roman Catholics. The clergy of the former are supported by tithes and glebe land, those of the latter by the voluntary contributions of their flock and parish dues. The proportion is about 20 Roman Catholics to 1 Protestant; for ministers, see return of Ecclesiastical Commissioners.

Habits of the People

The cottages are generally built of mud, only one-sixth being stone. They are thatched with small glass windows, 1-storey high, with only 2 rooms generally, sometimes 3, and seem to be lamentably devoid of comfort or cleanliness.

The food of the poorer class consists chiefly of potatoes and buttermilk. In winter they are seldom able to get milk and they substitute a drink made of onions boiled in water. Some of them assert that they are in such poverty at times that they are unable to purchase salt. This seems almost incredible.

The only fuel used is turf. The dress of the men is a grey frieze. There is a circumstance connected with this which perhaps is not generally known, but the people of different districts and counties are known by the colour of the frieze they wear, as the clans in Scotland are distinguished by their plaids.

Instances of longevity are not common in the parish: few exceed the age of fourscore. Early marriages prevail, the women being married sometimes at the age of 15. Female cries are still heard but not very often.

Emigration

About 20 or 30 persons emigrate every year to the United States and Canada. A few go annually to England and the counties Dublin and Meath to reap the harvest. They leave their wives and families behind, who generally support themselves during their absence by begging. They rent conacre and sow potatoes for their winter support.

PRODUCTIVE ECONOMY

Weaving

Weaving coarse linens is practised by the men in the summertime, when their farming does not occupy all their time. The women are employed in hand-spinning but of later years this [has] not given any fair remuneration for labour. The produce of the loom is consumed on the spot.

Fairs and Markets

Fairs are held in Kilgolah twice in the year, viz. 17th January and 27th November, for the sale of horses, cows, pigs and sheep; and in Kilcogy four times in the year, 5th February, 25th May,

5th August and 5th November, for the same purposes.

Rural: Proprietors

The principal landed property in this parish belongs to Gerald Dease Esquire of Turbertstown [Turbotstown], county Westmeath. The following is a list of the townland belonging to him, viz. Carrick, Carrickbawn, Cartrasnagh, Callenagh Lower, Carrickakillne, Glasscarrick, Killydoon, Kilsaran, Killydrean, Legwee, Lisnadarragh, Magheraboy Upper, Magheraboy Lower, Toghernaross.

The following is a list of the townlands belonging to Lord Farnham, Farnham, Cavan: Agherboy, Annagh, Carrickabrick, Carnagh Lower, Callenath Middle, Clonloghan, Dundevan, Freeduff, Kilgolah, part of Killikeen. For other proprietors, see Field Name Books.

No gentleman possessing any property in the parish resides in it, nor do any of their agents. The agents are generally paid by a percentage on the rent collected.

Holdings and Rent

The usual size of the holdings averages from 10 to 20 acres. These are generally held by leases of 1 life or 21 years or 3 lives or 31 years. The rent is paid wholly in money. The baneful practice of subletting is too much practised in the parish. The holdings let to the undertenants vary from 3 to 5 acres. The rent paid by them is paid partly by labour. The best land is let from 30s to 2 pounds, land of a middling quality from 20s to 30s and inferior land from 10s to 20s.

There are few respectable yeomen; the great majority are cottiers who farm for subsistence only. There is not much land let in conacre of late years. The size of the fields is generally from 2 to 10 acres. They are, for the most part, badly shaped and the fences are made of loose stones.

Tithes and county cess are the only taxes to which the tenants are liable.

The farm buildings of the better class of farmers, particularly those on Lord Farnham's property, are large and comfortable. Lord Farnham contributed to their erection.

Captain Kerr of Bracklow is the only gentleman who holds any land.

Manures

The soil is generally light. Lime is generally used as manure. It is procured from Carrickrock and carried to all parts of the parish. The kilns are generally the property of the farmers who burn the limestone in their own grounds. Burning the ground does not prevail to any great extent and only for reclaiming bogs and wasteland.

Implements of Husbandry

There are no improved implements of husbandry in use. Spade husbandry is most practised, the plough being only used by the better description of farmers. There are neither threshing nor winnowing machines. The common wheel car is the only conveyance used.

Oxen are very rarely, if ever, used; the plough is drawn by 2 horses.

Crops and Markets

The rotation of crops is generally potatoes, oats and oats, or sometimes potatoes, wheat, oats. The quantity of seed sown is generally 18 stone of wheat per acre, oats 24 stone, potatoes 240 stone. The average produce is of wheat 160 stone, of oats 196 stone, of potatoes about 2,000 stone.

The market towns are Granard, Ballynagh and Ballyheelan. Oats are bought up for exportation to England. They are carried to Drogheda, from whence they are shipped.

Grazing and Wages

There is only 1 farm laid out in grazing. Artificial grasses are little known. Drainage is a little practised, principally on a very small scale on the system of the French drains.

The servants in farmhouses are generally boarded and lodged, and receive from 3 to 4 pounds per year.

Cattle

The breed of cattle is mixed and of an inferior sort but is improving, the short-horned cattle having lately been introduced. The horses are of every breed. The pigs have been improved by a cross of the Dutch breed. Cattle and pigs are brought up by jobbers and taken to Drogheda for exportation to England. Green feeding is not practised in this parish.

Uses made of the Bogs

Some of the bogs are used during the summer months as grazing for young cattle, but in general they are used wholly for fuel. A good deal is carried to Granard, where it is sold at 2s 6d to 3s per cart-load. From the bog adjoining Lough Sheelin it is also carried in boats to supply the parish of Ballymachugh.

The people have free right of turbary. The timber found in the bogs is used for roofing cabins, for which it answers very well when seasoned, particularly the black oak. Some of the fuel is also made into charcoal for smith's forges.

Drainage

No efforts have been made to drain the bogs. There are some which might be drained without much outlay.

Planting

There is hardly any planting in the parish except a few trees around the residence of the better class of farmer. Lord Farnham encourages it very much, giving the tenant the trees gratis and charging them for the ground on which they plant, allowing them to cut down the trees when they are old enough to be serviceable.

Very little timber of the parish is offered for sale. Bog timber and foreign deals, which are purchased, supply the consumption of the district.

SOCIAL AND PRODUCTIVE ECONOMY

Ecclesiastical Summary

Name Drumloman, diocese Ardagh, province Leinster, vicarage; union: united with Granard, Cullinkil, Scrabby and Ballymachugh; patron Fulke Greville Esquire, incumbent Revd Christopher Robinson; extent of glebe 285 acres 14 perches; tithes: vicarial tithes payable to the incumbent 304 pounds 12s 3d ha'penny.

General Remarks

Cultivation has been carried to the highest point of ground in the parish. Northerly and north westerly winds prevail much in the winter season. The soil is light. The manure best suited to it, namely lime, is easily accessible to those in the southern part of the parish but far removed from those in the north.

The land seems to be best adapted for arable purposes. Much of the waste ground might be planted with advantage. There is water power and abundance of fuel to give ample scope to manufacturing industry and the roads and communications are good.

Divisions

Townlands are the only divisions known in the parish. Townlands: see Field Name Book. [Signed] Andrew Beatty, Lieutenant Royal Engineers, 14th November 1835.

Parish of Drung, County Cavan

Statistical Report by Lieutenant P. Taylor

NATURAL STATE

Name

The derivation of the name of this parish is unknown within this district. Tradition refers it to St Patrick observing, when on a mission throughout the country preaching the Gospel, an assemblage of people and, asking the question "what Drung is that?," applied the noun to the name of the parish, which it retains to the present day.

Locality

Situated in the south eastern section of the county of Cavan and in the same position of [sic] the barony of Tullygarvy; it is bounded on the south of parish of Laragh, east by the parish of Killdrumsherdan, west of [by] the parishes of Annagh, Castletarra and Laragh, all in the county of Cavan, and north of [by] the parish of Currin, barony of Dartry, county of Monaghan; and measuring in extreme length and breadth 6 English miles from north to south and 4 from east to west; contains 11,080 acres, 11,019 of which are land, 62 water and paid to the county cess in the year [blank].

NATURAL FEATURES

Hills

The parish of Drung, containing only 11,080 acres and measuring in extreme length 6 English miles, stretches both its extremities in narrow peninsulas along the boundaries of its contiguous parishes and must necessarily participate to a very great degree in the same natural features and formations.

In addition to the cor and magnum dorsum elevations, which stamp its genuine character as undulatory, a variety is here introduced under the denomination of tully which in form are only modifications of the magna dorsa group: Tullywilla "the town hills," Tullyvalla "the cow hills," Tullybuck "the spotted hills" are all assemblages of low tumuli, thickly grouped together and, from their proximity to town and gentlemen's seats, in a state of high cultivation.

The southern peninsula is also termed the mountains, not so much from its altitude compared with its northern or central portions, or its connection with any mountain chain, as from large portions of its surface being still in a state of nature, unproductive and rocky.

Magheratemple and Drumcollick in the northern section stands 415 and 395 feet above the level of the sea; Cornagarren and Leighlin in the central portion 320 and 318 feet; and Cavanreeny and Lappenmore in the southern section 499 and 548 feet above the same level.

Lakes

The lakes of Drung are small and unimportant, contributing more by the diversity of their form to the natural embellishment of the country than in furnishing supplies of water power to the mills of the district.

Cosmutty loch, [blank] feet above the level of the sea and covering an area of 27 acres, occupies a valley bounded on the north and south of the elevated portion of the townlands of Cornagarren and Drumachon. It derives its supplies from springs and the general drainage of the hills in the vicinity, and discharges its excess by a streamlet flowing north west to the River Erne.

Drumherriff loch is located in the centre of a basin-shaped valley enclosed by the elevations of Corrylagh, Nutfield and Drumherriff and, covering a surface of 13 acres, discharges its accumulations of a streamlet flowing north to the River Annagh.

Cornagall loch, containing a small island, lies in a valley of elongation formed of the lengths of Drumshreve <Drumshrene> and Cornagall; its streamlet flows [no further text].

Rivers

The River Annagh, descending through the central division of the parish in a general north westerly course, assumes the name of the Erne and receives a considerable accession to its waters by the junction of the Laragh flowing north easterly through the parish of Drung and, penetrating the parish of Castletarra in the townland of Corraghariff, ultimately flows into Loch Erne.

The Bunno, flowing from the parish of Curran in the county of Monaghan, traverses the parish of Drung in a south westerly course and forms a junction with the River Annagh in the townland of Killmullin.

The Laragh, flowing north easterly through the centre of the parish, forms a junction with the Erne in the townland of Tullywilla.

These rivers are all shallow in summer and fordable throughout their whole length. In winter they swell into powerful streams.

Bogs

In numerous localities within the parish a very great scarcity of bog prevails. In the central division and near Rakenny House a considerable extent happily remains, which its benevolent proprietor very liberally subdivides amongst the surrounding tenantry.

The southern section, locally termed the Mountain, contains it in abundance but in many townlands it is altogether extinct. Wherever it remains, abundant evidence is always present that the debris of oak, fir, sally and pine timber contributed largely to its accumulation.

Woods

The very great scarcity of fuel which has long prevailed within the parish has led to the extermination of every remnant of natural wood upon its surface. That its bogs and the margins of its lakes were originally clothed with timber of the most valuable and unperishable quality is abundantly testified by the stumps and work which are observable around them.

Climate

The sudden vicissitudes from hot weather to cold and from wet to dry are particularly striking. A course of fine weather is almost invariably followed by a storm and rain, of which the west and south westerly winds are the chief conductors.

A considerable difference in the periods of sowing and reaping is well ascertained betwixt the northern and southern extremities of the parish, amounting in some years to a fortnight and 3 weeks; but the climate upon the whole is extremely healthy, the tenants attaining to a very great age.

NATURAL HISTORY

Botany

In the Rakenny demesne oak trees of large dimension and of considerable age predominate in great proportion. Elm, ash, beech and sycamore of great magnitude and Scotch fir have all attained to full maturity. Alder is of uncommon size in this demesne. Larch and spruce are of recent distribution; clover and rag grass are cultivated but in very small quantities.

Zoology

The varieties of plants and animals are precisely the same as reported in the adjoining parishes. The salmonidae family ascend the Annaghlee in the spawning season and would arrive in vast numbers if sandstone instead of the corrugated grauwacke rock formed the gravel of the river. In the sluice of a mill-race in the townland of Knockatoodor a long, tapering, osier basket is fixed into which the salmon occasionally descend and are caught.

Geology

The only kind of rock discernible in this parish is grauwacke, which rises in several townlands in enormous masses and covers extensive portions of its surface. The town of Ballynacargy is built upon it and the northern summit of Cavanrean is one continuous development of the same rock. Vast masses of this unstratified, nonfossiliferous rock rise in the townland of Dercassan in abrupt isolated patches and the elevated portion of Leppanbawn is rendered quite unproductive of its prevalence.

The irregularity of this extensive formation renders it impossible to show the dip and bearing with any determined accuracy, for in any one locality its inclinations point to way [any?] rhomb of the compas[s]; and in consequence of this very great irregularity, it is very little used as building material.

MODERN TOPOGRAPHY

Towns

The village of Rakenny, on the eastern boundary of the parish and on the principal line of road connecting Cootehill with Cavan, contains 14 houses and is neither privileged with market nor fair.

Ballynacargy, on its western boundary and on the same line of road, contains 20 houses. 4 fairs are held here during the year for the sale of horses, cows, asses, pigs and sheep, on the 12th February, May, August and November.

Public Buildings

The vicarage of Drung, an old, lofty, thatched house, its front studded with windows, its rear blank, stands erected upon the elevated position of the townland of Carravaghan, 273 feet above the level of the sea, commanding a very extensive prospect. The house is partially surrounded with orchard, gardens and plantations, a

Parish of Drung

would, if modernized, form a very beautiful locality.

The parochial church in the townland of Drung, a low house covered with shingle, was erected in the year 1635 and accommodates 200 parishioners. The Revd M. Beresford is vicar of the united parishes of Drung and Laragh, and the Revd Fithuston, the officiating curate.

A new church is now erecting in the townland of Ducassan, of neat Gothic structure with accommodation for 450 parishioners and very conveniently situated for a large proportion of the congregation.

In the same proximity a large Roman Catholic chapel, in the townland of Drumownay, was erected in the year 1769, capable of containing 600 parishioners, the Revd Peter Reilly, the officiating divine.

In the townland of Lisleanduff a long clay-built cabin known by the name of the Bunno chapel was erected in the year 1780, the Revd Patrick Fitzsimons, priest. A school is held in the chapel during the week. The chapel accommodates about 500 persons.

Communications

The length of the line of road from Cootehill to Cavan, from when it enters the parish of Drung in the townland of Rakenny to when it makes its exit in the parish of Castletarra, is 4 and three-quarter miles.

The line of road from Cootehill to Stradone, from when it enters the parish of Drung in the townland of Rakenny to when it penetrates the parish of Laragh, is 2 and a half English miles.

Gentlemen's Seats

Rakenny House, the seat of Lucas Clements Esquire, lately erected upon the margin of the River Annagh, is a beautiful modern mansion. The heights around are crowned with valuable timber, an extensive garden is now forming and much improvement in drainage, levelling and planting is in rapid progression.

Mills

4 small corn mills in full activity throughout the winter work up a large portion of the grain of this and the surrounding parishes. One in the townland of Lisbeanduff is propelled by the Bunno river. Its power is breast wheel, diameter 13 feet.

In the townland of Copenagh a corn and flax mill are both wrought by the same water power. The diameter of the wheel is 12 feet and the power undershot.

Another in the townland of Ballynacargy, the diameter of whose wheel measures 12 feet and power undershot.

A fourth in the townland of Carravogy; power is undershot and diameter 12 feet.

The breadth of all these wheels is about 2 feet 6 inches.

Communications

The parish of Drung, stretching along the whole extent of the south western boundary of the parish of Kill, is traversed by the same great lines of communication which penetrate and ramify throughout its surface, the repair and making of which is paid in like manner by the county; and the roads, if possible, are in still worse condition.

ANCIENT TOPOGRAPHY

Forts

The aboriginal forts are particularly numerous throughout the parish and some of them in a state of good preservation. The most perfect, in rampart and fosse, has been protected with much care in the demesne of Lucas Clements Esquire, and in ancient warfare must have presented a formidable position to an invading enemy.

Cromlechs

An ancient cromlech or giant's grave, with a monumental boulder 7 feet high, still immortalizes the Herculean Finny McGool [sic]. The grave is near the side of the road connecting Cootehill with Cavan and in the townland of Cornaleast, and much of it is covered with soil.

MODERN TOPOGRAPHY

General Appearance and Scenery

A close affinity, not only in the natural features and the general appearance but also in many of the peculiarities in the parishes of Drung and Killdrumsherdan, naturally arises from their relative positions. The same naked desolate surface, deprived of all its natural embellishments which indigenous forests or artificial plantations so richly impart, unfortunately characterize its general appearance and scenery.

The elevated and rocky townlands on its south western boundary present a bold outline and its beautiful serpentine river, meandering through its undulatory surface, is peculiarly interesting.

Social Economy

Local Government

Lucas Clements Esquire of Rakenny is the only resident magistrate within the parish, the local government of which is conducted in the court house of Cootehill. Very few outrages of any description have occurred within the past year and the general character and conduct of the people is peaceable and well disposed.

Combination against the payment of tithes is general and successful. Illicit distillation is only carried when the profits arising from the sale of spirits exceed the remunerating price of new grain.

Dispensaries

There is no dispensary within this parish. The eastern division of the tenantry attend the dispensary at Cootehill and the western the dispensary in Stradone in the parish of Laragh. Dr Welsh, superintending the former, pronounces the parish extremely healthy and Dr [blank], the latter, supports the same testimony within his district. The prevailing diseases are catarrh, rheumatisms and fibres [fevers].

Schools

A superior class of teachers, with an increase of salary to render the appointment of importance to candidates, would very greatly improve the present system of education. In many of the schools very young teachers have the charge and instruction of from 50 to 60 scholars, and in very many cases the teachers appear to be incompetent.

6 schools are in full operation throughout the parish, teaching reading, writing and arithmetic, some assisted by the London Hibernian Society and the National Board of Education. [Table contains the following headings: name of townland, number of pupils subdivided by religion and sex, how supported, when established].

Drung, 45 Protestants, 63 Catholics, 48 males, 60 females, total 108 pupils; supported by London Hibernian Society and rector; established 1815.

Cornabeast, 46 Protestants, 24 Catholics, 54 males, 16 females, total 70 pupils; supported by the scholars; established 1825.

Tullewalla, 35 Protestants, 20 Catholics, 30 males, 25 females, total 55 pupils; supported by London Hibernian Society and rector of parish; established 1818.

Lisbeanduff, 40 Catholics, 28 males, 12 females, total 40 pupils; supported by the scholars; established 1815.

Magheratemple, 83 Protestants, 147 Catholics, 137 males, 93 females, total 230 pupils; supported by the Bishop of Kilmore; established 1828.

Greaghcrottagh, 62 Catholics, 35 males, 27 females, total 62 pupils; supported by the scholars; established 1820.

Poor

There is no permanent provision for the poor, lame or blind within the parish. The average number of poor upon the church list amounts to 7 and the annual collection to 5 pounds per annum.

Religion

The last census of the parish exhibited the following proportions taken in the year 1834: Roman Catholics 5,226, Protestants 718, Presbyterians 71, total 6,015.

Habits of the People

In a parish so entirely devoted to agriculture, in which in reality there is neither town nor village, although a few scattered houses on its eastern and western boundaries are dignified with the appellation, the habits of the people must be very primitive.

In industry, unfortunately, they are very defective. Springtime and harvest, turf and hay-making revolve in perpetual succession, giving timely intimation of their approach and departure, and still the labours of the husbandman are continually in arrear. A fair or market, wake or wedding will arrest industry in the most critical season and expose to uncertainty the most pressing demands for subsistence or the liquidation of rent.

The habitations of the tenantry depend very much on the substratum of their soil. If unstratified rock is the prevailing formation, the cabins are built of clay; if stratified, they are formed of stone, a convenience which many other nations avail themselves of.

In food, fuel or dress they conform in every respect to the particulars detailed in the reports which have been furnished of the adjoining parishes.

Emigration

The poverty of the tenantry alone prevents great numbers from emigrating to America. An arden desire pervades the great body of the peasantry to move from their present wretched condition. 3 families holding from 6 to 12 acres sold their interest in their farms and departed last spring for Canada.

PRODUCTIVE ECONOMY

Manufactures: Linen

The manufacture of linen, so actively and profitably pursued 20 years ago throughout this and the surrounding parishes, productive of much comfort to the people, is now almost extinct. A few looms are still in operation, although the remunerating prices of spinning and weaving do not amount to more than 2d a day to an industrious spinner and 4d a day to the weaver.

Cootehill and Cavan are the markets to which they carry the produce of their industry for sale.

Fairs

The village of Ballynacargy is endowed with 4 fairs annually, held on the 12th February, May, August, November, for the sale of horses, cows, asses, sheep and pigs. The price of horses varies from 8 but seldom exceeds 14 pounds; cows from 4 to 6 pounds; sheep from 40s to 50s; asses from 1 to 2 pounds; and pigs according to their estimated weight, the market price ranging from 2d ha'penny to 3d per lb.

Proprietors and Rents

Major Burrows of Stradone in the adjoining parish of Laragh, Lucas Clements Esquire of Rakenny, Maxwell Boyle Esquire of Tullyvin and the bishop of the diocese are the great land proprietors of the parish.

The subdivision of holdings into farms from 2, 4, 6, 8, 10 and 12 acres pervades almost every townland in the parish. The greater proportion of farmers hold their land at will. Some have leases of 1 and 3 lives or 21 and 31 years. The rent per acre is very variable and is fully detailed on the Field Name Books in each townland.

County cess levied by the carvagh is as variable as rent, the carvagh amounting in some townlands to 14 and in others to 40 acres, the rate of carvagh in each being 22s.

Tithe is irregularly paid, some landlords insisting on its liquidation, others declining all interference.

Rural: Agriculture

Soil is argillaceous and highly productive. Wheat is sown in some localities but in very small quantities. Potatoes, oats and a small quantity of flax are the principal produce. The proportions of seed to produce, price etc. are precisely the same as reported in the parish of Kill.

The implements of husbandry are of the most primitive kind. The hilly surface of the country renders the use of the plough frequently impracticable, hence agriculture is almost wholly effected with the loy.

Grazing

Neither the introduction of artificial grasses nor the profitable factors of green-feeding have been adopted in the parish; almost every portion of its soil is devoted to the culture of grain and potatoes.

Cattle

The degeneracy in the breed of cattle throughout this parish and the whole of the surrounding district is reduced to the lowest possible degree. Nothing can be more inferior than the general class of horses and horned cattle exhibited in the fairs.

Pigs are the only animals in which any concern appears to have been taken in their breeding. The low Dutch breed of short-legged, short-eared and small-headed pig are most esteemed and have supplanted in very great degree the long-shanked and hideous-looking animals formerly so common in the country. Jobbers attend at every market and fair, lining up the pigs for the English market.

Uses made of the Bogs

A very great scarcity of bog unhappily prevails in the northern section of the parish and must, within a very limited period, be entirely consumed. None is converted into charcoal for the use of the forges nor have metallic deposits been anywhere observed in it.

Planting

The formation of nurseries or recent plantations are nowhere in progress within the parish. Planting of Bedford sallies and poplars into the bank around the gardens and cottages in the northern section of the parish has very much improved its appearance.

SOCIAL AND PRODUCTIVE ECONOMY

Ecclesiastical Summary

[Table] Name Drung, diocese Kilmore, province

Armagh, vicarage, in union with Laragh, patron bishop of the diocese, incumbent Revd M. Beresford.

General Remarks

The naturally productive argillaceous soil of the parish, its moist and genial climate, its undulating surface, its numerous facilities for communication, the Annaghlee, propelling its powerful streams throughout the centre; these, with many other inexhaustible resources, render the parish of Drung capable of the highest degree of agricultural improvement. [Signed] P. Taylor, Lieutenant 69th Regiment.

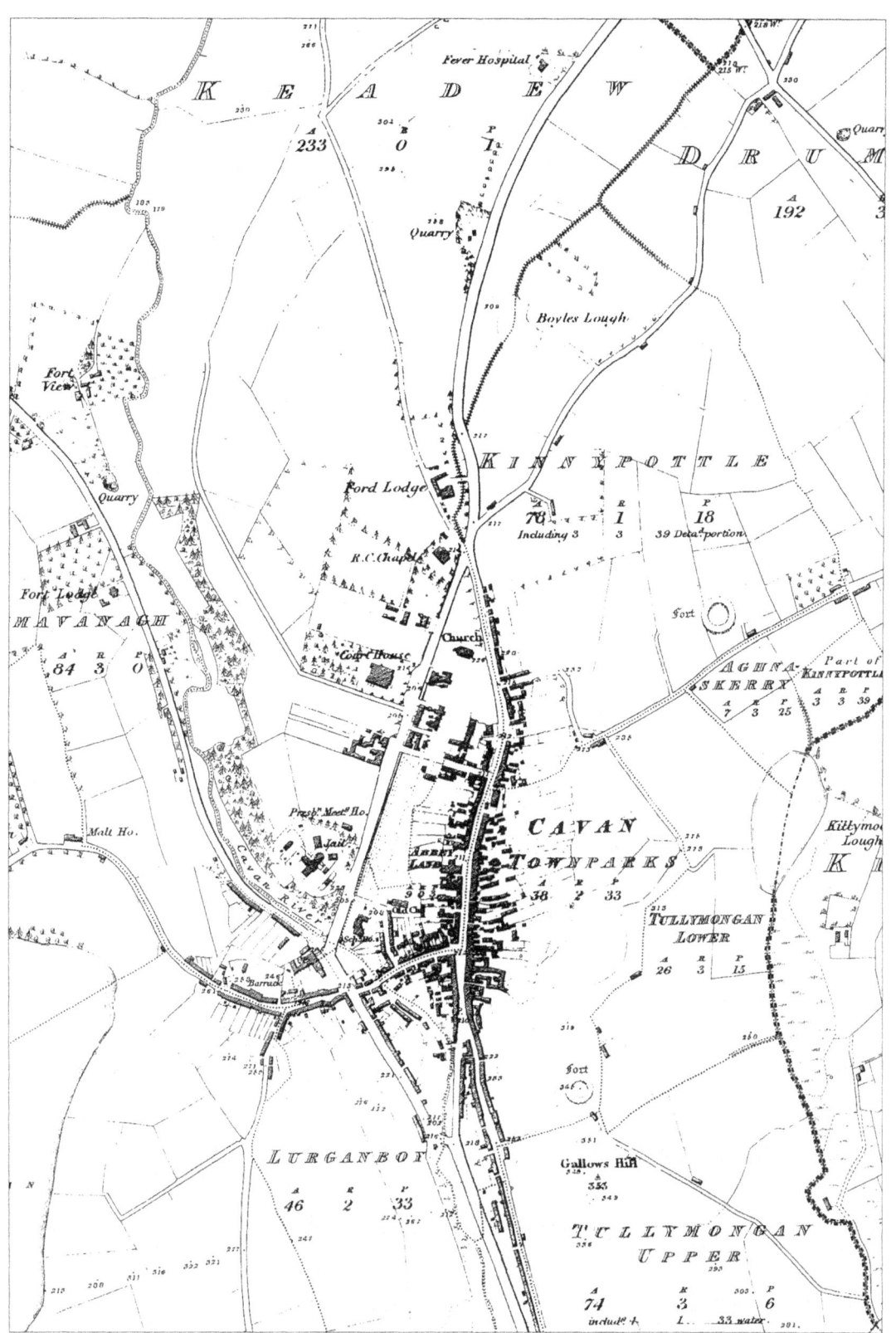

Map of Cavan town from the first 6" OS maps, 1830s

Parish of Enniskeen <Inishkeen>, County Cavan

Letter from Thomas Russell to Education Commissioners, December 1834

SOCIAL ECONOMY

Preamble to Letter

Extract of a letter addressed to one of the Commissioners of Education Enquiry.

Syddan, Ardee, 20th December 1834. Under the head of Public Instruction, the efforts of the Irish Society bear a peculiar and interesting feature. Its labours have been most valuable and effective amongst the adult peasantry in several parts of this kingdom. The schools of this useful society should in some way be brought under the notice of the Commissioners appointed to Enquire into the State of Religious and Other Instruction now Existing in Ireland, but from the very anomalous nature of these schools, the commissioners may perhaps pass from parish to parish without having their attention directed to them.

Allow me therefore, Sir, the liberty, as principal inspector of the society's schools in this district, to submit to you, as one of the commissioners, a brief outline of the object of the Irish Scriptural School Society and the nature and extent of its schools.

I ought to have taken the opportunity of doing this when examined by you as enumerator of Loughnaken parish, where one of these schools (though a very inferior one) is in operation, but such is their peculiarity, the idea of returning one as a school did not occur to me.

Object of Irish Society

The Irish Society has a precisely similar object to that of the Gaelic School Society in the Highlands of Scotland and the Welsh Scriptural School Society in Wales, namely to impart scriptural instruction to the native Irish through the medium of their own language. This society was instituted in Dublin in AD 1818.

There are tens of thousands of the Roman Catholic peasantry in the more retired parts of the country who use and can use no other than the native language, and hundreds of thousands of our countrymen who perhaps speak English tolerably well yet prefer their own tongue in their familiar intercourse amongst themselves and as the most acceptable medium of receiving scriptural instruction. To these 2 classes, amounting to about 1,500,000 individuals, the Irish Society especially directs its attention, to diffuse amongst them the blessing of the light of instruction.

For this purpose schools so called are scattered over various parts of the kingdom formed into districts and placed under the superintendence of pious clergymen, under whom inspectors whose business is periodically to examine into and report the state of each school in their particular circuits or districts to their respective superintendents, by whom their reports are transmitted to the committee.

The Kingscourt district, with which I am connected, comprises portions of the counties of Meath, Louth, Cavan, Monaghan, Derry, Armagh and Tyrone, over which the Revd Robert Winning of Kingscourt, county of Cavan, is general superintendent. This district is subdivided into branches placed under the local superintendence of other clergymen who attend to the schools in their respective localities.

Irish Schools

It may here be necessary, for the sake of perspicuity, to observe that the term "school" is in some respects inappropriate in its application to the elementary department of the society system. The name may, and actually does, convey an erroneous idea to many. It is requisite therefore to define the epithet as understood amongst us, and perhaps the clearest method of doing so is just to give a general description of an Irish school and the mode or system by which instruction is communicated.

An Irish school has but few points of resemblance in common with an English school: there is no regular house for teaching in, no desks, forms, tables; and necessar[il]y no writing, arithmetic, geography taught, no regular hours or stated times or places for giving instruction. To facilitate the reading of the Scripture, being the object and end in view, as to the how and when and where this may be effected, there are no specified regulations laid down.

Teachers

The business is managed in each vicinity by a resident farmer, labourer, English teacher or tradesman of good moral character and competent to read and translate the Scriptures in the native tongue, and willing to instruct his neighbours in the same. Such a person, when engaged for this purpose and supplied at very reduced prices with elementary books and Testaments in the Irish language and character, teaches as many as he can of those who prefer their own language to read the sacred Scriptures in their "own tongue wherein they were born." His places of teaching: sometimes his own house, sometimes the residence of his pupils and not unfrequently under some hedge in the open air.

As generally three-fourths of his pupils are adults, many of whom have families depending on their daily labour for support, it consequently is only on Sundays, holy days and after the usual working hours on other days they can afford time to receive instruction. Hence the master of an Irish school can attend to his usual avocations, whether it be at the plough, the spade, or the shop, and yet be also a useful Irish teacher.

Inspection of Schools

According to one of the economical regulations of the society, "no work, no pay," it gives no fixed salaries to its teachers but remunerates them by gratuities proportioned to their diligence and attention to the improvement of their scholars. This is ascertained in accordance with another provident regulation: "the work must be seen."

To this end an inspector once every 4 months visits each teacher, who on that occasion for the facility of examination collects as many as he can of those he had been instructing. The inspector, after hearing each read, translate, takes down on a sheet or roll prepared for the purpose the name, age, residence and proficiency or improvement of each pupil. These periodical rolls, signed by the inspector and countersigned by the teachers, are deposited with the respective superintendents, who thereby have the opportunity of detecting and correcting any attempt at fraud or imposition.

From these rolls, an abstract is prepared showing at one view the number of pupils throughout a district "produced, examined and passed" in their respective classes at the inspection of each school, distinguishing adults from juniors and males from females. This abstract or return, being signed by the superintendent, is transmitted with his own report or general remarks to the committee, who thereupon award gratuities to the teachers proportioned to the number and improvement of their respective scholars, taking into account also the good conduct, steadiness and local difficulties of each teacher.

On coming to receive these gratuities, each teacher undergoes a strict examination as to his own improvement and advancement in knowledge. This periodical assemblage of the pupils of each teacher for examination thrice every year is what is denominated his Irish school.

From this description, it is very easy to conceive the possibility of an Irish school being in effective operation on the property, or in the immediate vicinity, of a clergyman or gentleman who, if this sentiment in favour of scriptural education be not enamoured and known, may not be aware of the existence of such a school, and if asked on the subject would perhaps assert, and truly too, as far as he knew, that there was no such thing as an Irish school or teacher on his property or in his neighbourhood.

Too many instances of such unfavourable reports have occurred. Therefore the nature and peculiarities of an Irish school cannot be too generally made known to prevent mistake and misconception.

Number of Irish Schools

There have been in the Kingscourt district within the last 12 years 737 such schools, by the instrumentation of which from 35,000 to 40,000 Roman Catholics mostly have been brought more or less in contact with the sacred Scriptures "which are able to make them wise unto salvation." In consequence, however, of deaths, emigrations, removals and the merging of one school into another, more than half the above number of schools are not in operation.

At present there are in this district about 300 schools or teachers under the society, having in attendance or under instruction between 6,000 and 7,000 pupils. On account of various occurrences such as hurry of business, the absence of teachers from home when the inspector calls and sometimes from local difficulties peculiar to Irish schools, several teachers are passed over without inspection of pupils each period, and consequently without being returned to the committee for remuneration for that period. These omissions are always unavoidable, from the peculiar features of these schools and the extent of the district.

Number of Pupils

Last inspection return: by the general return of

inspection for the period ending 17th September 1834, there were 262 schools examined in the Kingscourt district, wherein were produced, examined and passed 5,344 pupils, of whom 165 were 50 years and upwards, 6,186 were adults from 15 to 50 years of age, and 993 juniors; of the total number 3,624 were passed as Testament readers and translators, of whom 106 were reciters who repeat off book and 1,720 were spellers; 900 of the pupils were females.

The number of pupils belonging to a school fluctuates from 8 or 10 up to 60 or 70. Generally not more than two-thirds or three-fourths of those under instruction pass examinations: business of various kinds and timidity prevent many from attending at time of inspection.

Facility of Learning

It is very singular in what a short time an intelligent man may be taught to read the Irish Testament, if he has had a previous knowledge of reading English and can speak Irish. He may be brought to read the Scriptures in the native language and character by even occasional lessons in the course of 3 months or less, and it is no less remarkable than gratifying that wherever the Irish Testament is introduced and makes way, the English Testament is invariably called on to follow and accompany it. Within the 2 last periods were issued to the teachers of this district and paid for by them, 643 English Testaments with references.

Funds and Gratuities

The funds for the support of this institution are derived from private subscriptions and donations, a great proportion of which comes from England and Scotland. Ladies' Auxiliary Societies have proved materially helpful in this department.

The gratuities for remuneration vary from 10s to 60s per period of 4 months. The average, on the whole, of the gratuities for the last period ending 17th September last was only 17s 10d ha'penny per quarter to each teacher.

Libraries and Instruction

Connected with our school system are circulating lending libraries containing selections of useful books for scriptural and general knowledge, and also a loan and widows' fund derived from the voluntary subscriptions of the teachers and of their small gratuities. These helps are looked up to with no small satisfaction, the former as a means of adding to their stock of information, the latter as a resource in cases of distress.

As the London Hibernian Society also affords facility for instruction through the medium of the Irish language, it may be necessary to observe that, as its schools are regular English schools under English masters teaching at certain hours and in certain prepared places, it therefore directs its attention principally to juniors, English education being its prime object; whilst the Irish Society by its desultory schools directs its attention more especially to the adult population, which is beyond the reach of other education societies. (See 14th report Irish Society, 1832).

Utility of Irish Society

From the brief outline here given, it may be perceived that the Irish Society comprises within its system and works all the effective machinery of an adult school society, a Sunday school society, a Scripture reader's society and an English and Irish Bible society.

General examination meeting: at the last general meeting for examination of the schools of this district, held in Ervey meeting house near Kingscourt on the 15th October last and 3 following days, nearly 400 teachers and scholars belonging to this district assembled and were examined by Revd Messrs Robert Daly, Radcliffe, Blackburn, Roper, Whitstone, Winning and others, not only in reading and translating but in the knowledge of the great, leading, essential and fundamental doctrines of Christianity, with proofs from the Bible in support of their views of each doctrine. The result was most satisfactory and encouraging.

Effects of Irish Schools

The effects produced by these schools are most gratifying and cheering to all those who have the religious and moral improvement of the people and the real welfare of the country at heart. Very many through this instrumentality have become acquainted with the sacred word of God as a rule and standard for doctrine and practice; Christian views and Christian conduct and Christian feeling are consequently taking root and spreading wherever our schools are established.

Prejudice and bigotry have to a great degree been cast down and the mists of ignorance are being dissipated before the light of divine truth. Want of funds is the principal hindrance of scattering these beneficent schools in every valley

Parish of Enniskeen

and on every mountain where the native language is still used and venerated.

Conclusion to Report

In conclusion, it may be perceived from the preceding account that, as the inspector has an accurate knowledge of every teacher and of the proficiency of each pupil in his circuit, so, by means of the periodical rolls of the several schools, his superintendent becomes acquainted with the number and state of the schools and number and improvement of the scholars within his district.

The committee, in like manner, by means of the abstracts or returns furnished by the several superintendents, have, at regular intervals, a correct account of a number of districts, number of schools, number and classification of scholars under its care in every part of the country. This summary, showing at one view the state of the society's schools throughout the kingdom, together with extracts from the reports of superintendents, are published periodically, the last number of which I had the pleasure of laying before you.

For further information on the subject of Irish Schools generally, the society's regulations, committee etc., I beg leave to refer to the annual report for the year 1834, which I took the liberty of handing you, and also to any of the gentlemen officially connected with the society.

For further particulars relative to this district, explanatory and confirmatory, I would respectfully refer to the Honourable and Revd Archdeacon Packenham, Ardbraccan; the Revd Richard Radcliffe, Screen Glebe; Robert Bourke Esquire, Hayes near Navan; Revd Anthony Blackburn, Clongill Glebe; Revd Thomas H.C. Finney, Dunleer Glebe, superintendent of the south branch; John McClintock Esquire, Drumcar, Castlebellingham; Richard Benson Esquire, Fathom Park near Newry, superintendent of the Newry branch; Revd Dean Roper, Annamullen Glebe, Ballybay, superintendent of the Clones branch; or to the Revd Robert Winning, Kingscourt, general superintendent of the district.

Entreating you will pardon the liberty I have taken and excuse the prolixity of this statement, I have the honour to be, Sir, your obedient servant, Thomas Russell, senior inspector, Kingscourt district. To [blank], one of the Commissioners for Enquiry into the State of Education in Ireland.

School Inspection Returns, 1836

Report on Schools

Abstract of the inspection returns of the schools in the Kingscourt district, for the period ending 17th day of January 1836. [Table contains the following headings: name of branch, local superintendent, number of schools, number of pupils produced, examined and passed for January 1836, number under instruction last return].

1. Cavan Walk, superintendent Revd Robert Winning, 78 schools; pupils: 422 spellers, 612 readers, 424 translators, 25 reciters, 160 juniors, 1,323 adults; 72 aged above 50 years, 109 females, total 1,483; 2,082 under instruction at last return.

2. Meath Walk, superintendent Revd Richard Radcliffe, 35 schools; pupils: 322 spellers, 445 readers, 293 translators, 17 reciters, 101 juniors, 976 adults; 56 aged above 50 years, 76 females, total 1,077; 1,289 under instruction at last return.

3. Monaghan Walk, superintendent Revd William Roper, 82 schools; pupils: 395 spellers, 498 readers, 432 translators, 47 reciters, 197 juniors, 1,175 adults; 95 aged above 50 years, 125 females, total 1,372; 2,556 under instruction at last return.

4. Louth Branch, superintendent Revd Thomas H.C. Finney, 28 schools; pupils: 139 spellers, 225 readers, 103 translators, 15 reciters, 83 juniors, 399 adults; 10 aged above 50 years, 57 females, total 482; 976 under instruction at last return.

5. Newry Branch, superintendent Richard Benson Esquire; this branch has been detached from Kingscourt and made the basis of a new district.

6. Clones Branch, superintendent Revd Thomas Taylor, 26 schools; pupils: 151 spellers, 139 readers, 136 translators, 75 juniors, 351 adults; 13 aged above 50 years, 43 females, total 426; 678 under instruction at last return.

7. Killashandra Branch, superintendent Revd Francis Saunderson; this branch, in consequence of unfavourable circumstances, has been given up.

8. Castlepollard Branch, superintendent Revd Adolphos Drought, 10 schools; pupils: 75 spellers, 99 readers, 86 translators, 1 reciter, 27 juniors, 234 adults; 23 aged above 50 years, 19 females, total 261; 462 under instruction at last return.

9. Athboy Branch, superintendent Revd Robert Noble, 12 schools; pupils: 61 spellers, 92 readers, 66 translators, 219 adults; 8 aged above

50 years, total 219; 451 under instruction at last return.

10. Tyrone Branch, superintendent Revd Robert Allen, 22 schools; pupils: 260 spellers, 365 readers, 183 translators, 34 reciters, 285 juniors, 557 adults; 16 aged above 50 years, 198 females, total 842; 1,206 under instruction at last return.

11. Draperstown Branch, superintendents Revd Messrs Brown and Hewitt, 27 schools; pupils: 230 spellers, 344 readers, 219 translators, 56 reciters, 217 juniors, 632 adults; 52 above 50 years, 209 females, total 849; 1,333 under instruction at last return.

12. Dungiven Branch, superintendent Revd Henry Kid, 17 schools; pupils: 122 spellers, 189 readers, 141 translators, 69 reciters, 141 juniors, 380 adults; 12 aged above 50 years, 127 females, total 521; 1,176 under instruction at last return.

[Totals]: 337 schools, 2,177 spellers, 3,008 readers, 2,083 translators, 264 reciters, 1,286 juniors, 6,246 adults; 357 aged above 50 years, 973 females, total number of pupils 7,532, 12,229 under instruction at last return.

(Signed) Robert Winning, general superintendent; (signed) Thomas Russell, senior inspector, Kingscourt, February 1836.

Parish of Killdrumsherdan, County Cavan

Statistical Report by Lieutenant P. Taylor,
[late 1835]

NATURAL STATE

Name and Derivation

The etymology of the name of this parish is doubtful, neither does any ruin of its ancient chapel remain, pointing to its probable derivation.

Locality

Situated near the south eastern [insert query: north eastern?] boundary of the county of Cavan and in the same position as the barony of Tullygarvey. It is bounded on the north by the county of Monaghan, south by the parish of Knockbride, east by the parish of Drumgoon and west by the parish of Drung, all in the county of Cavan, and measuring in extreme length and breadth from north to south 8, and from east to west 5 English miles.

Contains 16,619 statute acres 3 roods 21 perches, of which 16,494 acres 3 roods 14 perches are land, 125 acres 15 perches are water; and produced in local taxation to the county cess alone in the year [blank] the sum of [blank].

NATURAL FEATURES

Hills

The southern division of the parish presents a similar beautiful undulatory formation of hill and dale which so particularly characterises the natural features of the surrounding district. The same parallelism of ridges, stretching in a north west and south easterly direction, which has been shown as distinctive features in the more eastern parishes, is here greatly interrupted. Very few valleys of any extent are formed.

One continuous development of mullagh, cor and drum-shaped tumuli rise confusedly in every direction, varying in altitude very inconsiderably over its northern and central portions. Cortubber, Corwillis, Copenagh, Cornaghgarrew, Cornabeagher and Drumhose stand respectively 379, 425, 375, 323, 372 and 372 feet above the level of the sea.

The southern section, locally termed "the mountains," is marked by bolder features. Its elevations and depressions obtain a greater magnitude and the rugged grauwacke rock, emerging in considerable masses from the uncultivated heathy surface, impart a wild and mountainous character, although the difference in altitude betwixt the most elevated and depressed levels does not exceed 534 feet. Drumleage, Drumhart and Drumnagress in the central portion, standing 463, 438 and 416 feet above the level of the sea; and Ratressin, Drumnatraid and Tievenass, the most elevated trigonometrical stations, rise 804, 826, 827 feet above the same plane.

Lakes

The natural formations of the parish into cone and dome-shaped hills thickly grouped together, which universally prevail throughout its area, preclude in a great degree the accumulation of its waters into lakes, which are not only fewer in number but much smaller than in the parish of Drumgoon and in the other parishes in immediate connection.

Its principal lakes are: Barragh loch on the north eastern boundary of the parish; occupies a valley terminating in a cul-de-sac which forms the natural division betwixt the counties of Cavan and Monaghan, and, covering a surface of 20 acres, stands 274 feet above the level of the sea, its streamlet flowing south easterly to the River Bono.

White loch is a beautiful sheet of water enclosed on its south and west by the elevations of Tonnaghlawn and Corlerryquinil, whose summits are adorned with pine, whilst the road from Cootehill to Redhill runs along its northern shore with Ashfield church and spire on the left turning through the surrounding plantation. White loch covers an area of 19 acres and stands 302 feet above the level of the sea.

Drumsheel loch is another small but beautiful lake containing a small artificial island studded with trees. Its area measures 13 acres, its level is 213 feet above the sea. Its streamlet flows south easterly to near the confluence of the Rivers Annagh and Drummore.

Black loch is contained in a basin-shaped valley formed of the elevations of Drumhart, Coravoghy, Cullin and Rakane. Natural springs and the general drainage of the hills form its supply; its superabundance is charged by a small streamlet flowing easterly to the River Annagha; area 12 acres.

White loch, containing a small island clothed with wood, is located in a valley of elongation formed of the elevated ridges of Rakane on the north and Tongin on the south. Its streamlet flows easterly to the Annaghlee.

The whole of these lakes derive their supplies from natural springs and the general drainage of these localities; area of White loch 13 acres.

Rivers

But in the absence of extensive lakes which so much enrich and adorn a country, 2 beautiful rivers bend their particularly tortuous courses through its fertile and productive soil.

The Annagh, rising in Loch Tucka on the southern confines of the parish of Drumgoon, penetrates the parish of Killdrumsherdan in the townland of Degnavanty and, traversing its southern central division bearing severally north west, enters the parish of Drung in the townland of Rakenny, supplying in its course an abundant water supply to corn and flour mills erected within its locality.

The altitude of the river where it enters the parish is 225 feet and its level near its exit is 196 feet above the sea, showing a depression of 29 feet only in 8 English miles.

The Drummore river, rising from the lake of the same name which separates the counties of Cavan and Monaghan, traverses its northern central portion and, flowing through the manor of Ashfield in a beautiful situation, and having the same general north westerly bearing, forms a junction with the Annagh in the townland of Tullyvin. Its waters are also applied in driving corn and flax mills near its boundaries.

Bogs

One of the greatest miseries of human life, the deprivation of fuel, oppresses the peasantry of Kill. Turbary is quite exhausted over a very large extent of the parish. The tenantry located in its central and northern sections are obliged to carry their turf 5 and 6 miles without any hope of ever ameliorating their unfortunate condition.

The same natural causes which prevented the formation of lakes would appear to have operated in like manner in limiting the accumulation of bog. For whenever the elevation of the surface into extended ridges with intervening valleys is formed, bog is either abundant or the traces of it having been so are manifest. Every remaining portion, as well as the marshy margins of the lakes, testify that forests of great size, consisting of oak, fir, sally and yew trees, were anciently within and around.

Woods

The faintest trace of natural woods nowhere exists within the parish. Every vestige has been removed and, with the exception of the plantation around gentlemen's seats, together with Bedford and Lombardy poplars recently planted around the cottages and cabins of the tenantry, the surface of the parish presents a very naked and cheerless landscape.

Climate

In the southern section of the parish, termed the mountains, the crops are considerably later in arriving at maturity than in the north and central portions. In the latter the oats are frequently carried to market for sale before a decided colouring of the crops is manifest in the former, and in wet and unfavourable seasons much of the harvest is lost. Nor does the lateness in ripening arise from a late period in sowing: for fields sown in March are attended with total loss of seed.

Aspect has decided influence in this respect: the southern face of a drum-shaped hill will appear covered with grain closely approaching to maturity, whilst its northern declivity is perfectly green.

NATURAL HISTORY

Botany

Moss is the most abundant of all natural grasses and would cover in a very few years, with amazing thickness, the whole surface of demesnes and would exclude every other variety if the soil was not occasionally broken up. The superabundance of rain, which falls throughout the year, is doubtlessly the proximate cause of this exhuberant vegetation.

3 varieties of pine, Scotch, larch and spruce, with elm, ash, beech and oak, are most predominant in the plantations. Sycamore, chestnut, walnut and holly adorn the demesnes. Rag-grass and clover may occasionally be observed but turnips, vetches or mangle wurzel have little place here. Spontaneous vegetation is the chief dependence of this impoverished tenantry.

Zoology

Salmon ascend the rivers in the spawning season but not in great numbers. Pike, perch, roach and bream, trout and eel are most abundant in the rivers and lakes. Every variety of wildfowl peculiar to the country which has been enumerated in former reports frequent the lakes and marshes in their seasons. Game, viz. partridge and hares and pheasants, are very scarce.

Geology

A siliceous slate-rock associated in the grauwacke is very prevalent throughout the parish, the general arrangement of which is nearly horizontal, although the dip in many localities amounts to 20 and 30 degrees. When the black-blue slate-rock is fine-grained and pure, metaliferous veins traverse it as bright as silver; and iron pyrites abound in the crevices of every stratum.

In the townland of Cornanurny, and amongst a vast development of grauwacke rock, a vein of galena was discovered and wrought for several years by the Royal Irish Mining Company and much valuable ore extracted. In [blank] the works were discontinued.

In the townlands of Lappenbawn and Lappendoo, and in numerous other extensive localities, the rugged grauwacke rock rises to the surface in immense masses unstamped by the faintest trace of organic life, and it is also remarkable that not a single fossil of either animal or vegetable has been discovered in this extensive grauwacke district, although rewards have been offered for every discovery of the kind.

A fine conglomerate is occasionally observable, composed of rounded pebbles of grauwacke and slate-rock with quartz; and the grauwacke itself may frequently be observed to change its component particles from a coarse assemblage approaching to conglomerate to a fine texture apparently running into slate, but the line of transition has not been observed.

A trap-dyke of modular formation, in immediate connection with slate-rock, presents itself in a quarry near the side of the road connecting Cootehill with Cavan and in the townland of Cabragh. The nodules, generally spherical in form, vary from the size of an egg to 3 and 4 feet in circumference and form the perpendicular wall or face in regular piles. The trap nodules exhibit a concretionary form, and coatings in a state of decomposition can be successively separated.

MODERN TOPOGRAPHY

Towns

On the eastern boundary of the parish, and in the townland of Corbeagh, the village of Clementstown, consisting of 41 stone and clay-built cabins, was erected, commenced building at 50 years ago, on the estate of Colonel Clements of Ashfield. Its close proximity to Cootehill rendered the endowment of fairs and markets unnecessary. It stands upon the road connecting Cootehill with Drum and is altogether a very wretched village.

Tullyvin, situated near the western boundary of the parish, is also a very small village consisting of 20 stone and mud-built cabins. One fair is held here during the year for the sale of horses or cows, pigs and a few sheep, on the 4th day of May. A small detachment of police is stationed in the village, which stands on the main road connecting Cootehill with Cavan.

Public Buildings

The parochial church, erected in the townland of Drumhart in the year 1792, is a small oblong building with elliptical windows capable of accommodating 120 parishioners. The Revd Archdeacon Irwin, an absentee, is rector and the Revd Edward Hales, the resident and officiating curate.

In the townland of Tamnaghlawn, and within the manor of Ashfield, a perpetual curacy was formed and a church erected in the year 1797, of which the Revd John Harris is curate. The church, rectangular in structure with handsome spire, is capable of accommodating 400 parishioners.

There are 2 Roman Catholic chapels within the parish, 1 in the townland of Drumhart erected by the Revd Felix McCabe, the Roman Catholic clergyman, in the year 1826, in close proximity with the parochial church; accommodates 750 members.

Corrick chapel, built in the year 1769 in the townland of Drummurry, accommodates 300 parishioners; the Revd Thomas Reilly, the officiating curate.

Gentlemen's Seats

Ashfield Lodge, the seat of Colonel Clements, is sequesteredly situated in the townland of Drumlogan and on the banks of the River Drummore. The southern face of Tannaghbawn rises by a gradual slope from the margin of the river and is beautifully subdivided into fields. Its elevated portion is crowned with plantation, and the spire of the church, rising from its foliage, form its front and northern prospect.

The magnum dorsum of Drumlogan, covered with valuable timber approaching to full maturity, surrounds its eastern and southern face. The ornamental grounds and plantations and the circular "atria" of the very ancient inhabitants adorned with wood, together with the coping of the hills and shading of the avenues, with varieties of pine, render Ashfield a locality of general admiration.

Tullyvin House, the seat of Maxwell Boyle Esquire, is very delightfully situated on an elevation in the townland of the same name, commanding a view of the principal road connecting Cootehill with Cavan. The house, quadrangular in form, is of modern erection with an unhappy irregularity of structure in the southern face. The surrounding plantations are recent and limited.

The offices and gardens are commodious and extensive, and Tullyvin House, almost surrounded with old circular forts which are here particularly numerous and clothed with plantations, presents as beautiful a locality as appears within the surrounding district.

The Vicarage occupies the lofty summit of the townland of Cordoagh and commands from its elevated position a most extensive view of the surrounding country; partially surrounded with young plantation, it forms a pleasing object in a district so very deprived of its natural embellishments.

Annaghlee House, unequalled in the beauty of its site, on the summit of the townland of Annaghlee, with the River Annagh preserving its silent course around its west and northern boundary, forms a very pleasing and delightful landscape. The grounds are regularly subdivided into square and oblong fields surrounded with fences of quickset and trees. The old and recent plantations encircling the house and offices renders the residence exceedingly comfortable in appearance which, unhappily, is suffered to fall into a state of general dilapidation.

Fort William, the residence of the Revd A. Foster, curate of Currin, an active and zealous clergyman, pleasantly situated on the southern slope of the townland of Arigle, within 1 mile of Cootehill and in close proximity to the principal line of road connecting Cootehill with Tullyvin.

Ashfield Glebe, the residence of the Revd John Harris, is delightfully situated on the south western face of the townland of Carrickalinny, near the side of the road leading from the village of Clementstown to Redhills.

Retreat, the residence of Charles Adams Esquire, is situated in a very sequestered locality surrounded with plantation on the north side of the road leading from Rakenny to Tullyvin.

MEMOIR WRITING

Note on Plan

My Dear Stotherd

Have the goodness to take the fair plan and examine how and when the streamlet from Cornagall loch flows; and enter it in this report. Enter also the altitude of Cornealty loch. County cess also wanting. Also enter Dr Halpin's opinion of the healthiness of the tenantry of the parish and all will be right. Yours ever, P. Taylor, 3rd December 1835 [to] Lieutenant Stotherd, Royal Engineers.

MODERN TOPOGRAPHY

Corn and Flour Mills

A large flour and corn mill, the property of Mr Boyle of Tullyvin, erected in the townland of Drumnaquean and driven by a race from the River Annagh, works up a very considerable portion of the grain of the parish and surrounding district, both for home and foreign consumption. The diameter of the wheel measures 16 feet, breadth 10 feet 2 inches and power is breast wheel.

The townland of Drumsillagh contains a small corn mill whose power is overshot and diameter of wheel 12 feet, breadth 2 feet 6 inches.

A small corn mill in the townland of Terryin works up the grain of the southern section of the parish, the diameter of whose wheel measures 12 feet, breadth 2 feet 6 inches and power overshot.

A fourth corn mill in the townland of Leaghan, of small dimensions, is wrought by a streamlet from Lochnacairn, the wheel of which is 11 feet in diameter and power overshot.

A small corn mill in the townland of Corbeagh is wrought by a race from the River Drummore, whose power is undershot and wheel 12 feet in diameter; and lower down the river, in the townland of Killcreeny, a small corn mill and a flax mill with a breast-wheel power are wrought by a wheel 13 feet in diameter, breadth 2 feet 6 inches.

Roads

The parish is traversed by roads in every leading direction. One line through its southern section connecting the town of Cootehill with Bailieborough <Baillyburrow>, sends off a branch westerly to Stradone; a second principal line opens a communication with Cootehill and Cavan through the towns of Tullyvin, Rakenny and Ballyhaze, fending off a diverging branch south westerly to Stradone. A third and main line

Parish of Killdrumsherdan

of road runs through its eastern section, connecting Cootehill with Belturbet, passing through the village of Clementstown and Redhills.

Numerous lines bisecting these ramify through every section of the parish, affording every facility of communication.

Clement's bridge and Corrick bridge, well recognised localities throughout the district, are old erections with several arches and parapet walls 6 feet high.

The making and repairing of the roads and bridges is paid by the parish, by levies of unequal proportion upon the land; and very unfortunately few, if any, are in good condition.

ANCIENT TOPOGRAPHY

Cromlechs

In the townland of Drumhart an ancient cromlech or giant's grave still records the custom of an antediluvian era. A large portion of the grave is covered by the labours of the husbandman and many of the stones have been fractured and removed. 2 very large boulders mark its extremities, the superior one standing 7 feet high.

Another testimonial of this celebrated chieftain (Finny McCool [sic]) is still extant and in greater preservation in the townland of Drumnawhillian. This Cyclopean sepulchre measures 40 feet in length by 12 in its greatest breadth and converging to 4 at the inferior extremity.

Stone Circles

The circular "atria" of the very ancient inhabitants of the kingdom are particularly numerous in this parish, and in several localities they are so disposed as to form lines of telegraphic communication. The summit of the most elevated cor-shaped hills was generally chosen for their erection, but in many other places they are formed in low and sheltered situations.

MODERN TOPOGRAPHY

General Appearance and Scenery

The general appearance of the scenery of the parish, like many others of the surrounding district, is bleak and dreary. Very few trees appear upon its surface. The cabins of the tenantry are wretched in the extreme and, were it not for the plantations surrounding gentlemen's seats and the dwellings of a few superior class of farmers, the observant eye would sweep the circle marked with very faint traces of civilization; and still the natural surface of the parish, beautifully formed into hill and vale with rivers winding through and around their bases, is capable of the highest possible artificial embellishment.

SOCIAL ECONOMY

Local Government

The tenantry of the parish of Kill attend the petty sessions of Cootehill every Wednesday for the redress of grievances. Colonel Clements of Ashfield and Maxwell Boyle Esquire of Tullyvin, both resident within the parish, supported by the magistrates of Drumgoon, comprise the bench.

The character of the parish is quiet and orderly. A detachment of police, consisting of 1 constable and 4 subconstables, are stationed in Tullyvin. Illicit distillation is carried on when the price of corn is much reduced but not otherwise.

Dispensary

The tenantry have the benefit of attending the dispensary in Cootehill, there being no dispensary or resident surgeon within the parish. Dr Welsh, the superintending surgeon, pronounces the parish exceedingly healthy.

[Table] Average number of patients unknown, supported by subscriptions from the landed proprietors and gentlemen and by presentment from the grand jury; complaints: rheumatisms, catarrhus, febres and all other inflammatory and accidental afflictions.

Table of Schools

[Table contains the following headings: name of townland, number of pupils subdivided by religion and sex, remarks as to how supported, when established].

Corberryquill, 70 Protestants, 44 Catholics, 66 males, 48 females, total 114; supported by Colonel Clements 5 pounds, Society for Discountenancing Vice 8 pounds, established 1800.

Doharrick, 120 Protestants, 25 Catholics, 92 males, 53 females, total 145; supported by the scholars' fees, established 1821.

Cortubber, 23 Protestants, 17 Catholics, 20 males, 20 females, total 40; supported by the scholars' fees, established 1828.

Corbeagh, 44 Protestants, 62 Catholics, 65 males, 41 females, total 106; paid by the scholars and London Hibernian Society, established 1826.

Corfad, 40 Catholics, 30 males, 10 females,

total 40; supported by the scholars' fees, established 1830.

Dequavanty, 100 Catholics, 60 males, 40 females, total 100; supported by the scholars' fees, established 1832.

Drumhart, 111 Protestants, 1 Catholic, 64 males, 48 females, total 112; supported by scholars and National Board of Education, established 1830.

Ratressin, 3 Protestants, 43 Catholics, 30 males, 16 females, total 46; supported by the scholars' fees, established 1828.

Arigle, 20 Catholics, 12 males, 8 females, total 20; supported by Mrs Foster.

Lumgelton, 20 Protestants, 100 Catholics, 50 males, 70 females, total 120; supported by the scholars' fees, established 1835.

Aughatotin, 16 Protestants, 46 Catholics, 40 males, 22 females, total 62; National Board of Education 8 pounds, established 1825.

Corravogy, 20 Protestants, 70 Catholics, 48 males, 42 females, total 90; London Hibernian Society 5 pounds and scholars' fees, established 1803.

Leaghan, 11 Protestants, 13 Catholics, 13 males, 11 females, total 24; supported by scholars' fees, established 1833.

Tievnass, 2 Protestants, 20 Catholics, 10 males, 12 females, total 22; supported by the scholars' fees, established 1834.

Drumhart, 50 Protestants, 67 Catholics, 70 males, 47 females, total 117; supported by rector 5 pounds and London Hibernian Society 8 pounds, established 1826.

Much improvement in the morals of the rising generation has resulted from the establishment of schools, and still greater advancement in so desirable an object may be anticipated from the very liberal measures of the legislation.

The number of schools in active operation throughout the parish amounts to 15. The introduction of the useful art of sewing into the schools, which is altogether neglected, and combined with reading and writing, would be highly desirable.

Poor

The average number of poor receiving relief at the parish church of Killdrumsherdan amounts to 19 and the annual amount of collections 6 pounds 10s. The number of poor on the church list of Ashfield averages 30 and the collections upon the sabbath day amount to 26 pounds per annum. These sums, together with the voluntary contributions of the charitable, are the only resources of the poor, asylums for their reception never having been erected within the district.

Religion

The last census of the parish, taken in the year 1832, gave the following proportions: Roman Catholics 7,564, Protestants 1,835, Presbyterians 769, Dissenters 2, [total] 10,170.

Habits of the People

In several localities where slate rocks abound, the cottages are built of stone, with glass windows, divided into 2 and 3 apartments; but when the grauwacke rocks prevail, which are exceedingly irregular in cleavage, the cabins are formed of mud and seldom exceed the ground floor.

Potatoes and buttermilk constitute the chief, and almost only, diet of the people. Very coarse friezes and corduroys with home-spun woollens and fancy cottons form their attire. One striking peculiarity in the dress of the males is their never wearing a neckcloth; and the females, in the hottest days of summer, wear their cloaks and feel undressed without them.

Attendance at fairs, wakes, weddings and markets are their favourite amusements, where mirth, jollity and dancing abound. Many legendary and extravagant tales are rehearsed of their favoured Fin McCool, and many houses have taken fire and families perished for sacrilegiously mutilating the stones forming his grave.

Emigration

A few families dispose of the interest in their leases and emigrate annually to the Canadas, and vast numbers would follow their example if furnished with the means of paying their passage. None return, nor does any depart from hence during the harvest season.

PRODUCTIVE ECONOMY

Manufactures

In connection with agriculture the spinning and weaving of coarse linens is carried on but to a very limited extent throughout the parish, compared with the quantity annually brought to market in former years. Eight, nine and ten hundred linen is the finest quality now manufactured and the market price from 8d to 1s per yard.

Dealers in yarn and linen from the towns of Newry, Armagh and Belfast attend the markets and fairs of Cootehill and purchase up the produce of the district.

Parish of Killdrumsherdan

Fairs

In the village of Tullyvin there is one fair held on the 4th day of May annually for the sale of horses, cows, asses, pigs and very few sheep, which is numerously attended. The cattle are all of the commonest breed and prices proportionate, varying in no respect whatever from those enumerated in the fairs of Cootehill.

Rural: Crops

Very little wheat is sown throughout the parish, owing to the very great scarcity of manure. Potatoes, oats and flax are the great general produce. 2 crops of potatoes are frequently raised from the same field, the first crop being manured, and a succession of 2 or 3 years' crops of oats follows without manure until the productive powers of the soil are exhausted. A small quantity of flax is sown after the potato crop.

Farms and Rents

The size of the farms varies from 4 to 12 acres; very few exceed 12. By far the greater proportion average 6 and 8 acres. Tenancy <tinnse> at will is most generally adopted; leases of 1 and 3 lives or 21 and 31 years are also common.

It is impossible to name the average rent per acre with accuracy: it varies so much in every townland.

Manures

Limestone is carried from the quarries Carrickmacross and Laragh, purchased at 10d per ton and burned in kilns <kills> upon many of the holdings, but in very small quantities. Marl is abundant but very seldom used as manure.

The practice of green feeding has never been adopted.

Seed and Produce

The proportion of seed and produce, with the prices of each, appear in the annexed table.

Potatoes: seed 180 stone per acre, produce 2,160 stones, market price from 1d ha'penny to 3d ha'penny per stone.

Oats: seed 24 stones per acre, produce 240 stones, market price from 6d to 12d per stone; oats, second year: seed 28 stones per acre, produce 224 stones.

Wheat: seed 16 stones per acre, produce 160 stones, market price from 15s to 18s per barrel.

Barley: seed 10 to 12 stones per acre, produce 190 stones.

Flax: seed 12 to 13 pecks per acre, produce 36 stones of lint, market price from 10s to 11s 4d per stone.

Butter is accumulated throughout the season and packed in firkins for the English market, and considerable quantities are transported annually from this parish and the surrounding district.

Proprietors

The great landed proprietors of the parish are Colonel Clements of Ashfield, Major Burrows of Stradone, Maxwell Boyle Esquire of Tullyvin, Charles Coote Esquire of Bellamont Forest, Charles Adams Esquire of Retreat and the bishop of the diocese. The manor of Ashfield comprises 18 townlands in the northern section of the parish.

Colonel Clements and Mr Boyle farm extensively within their demesnes, in which are introduced every improvement of modern agriculture, the beneficial influence of which extends unfortunately but very limitedly amongst their tenantry.

Soil

The soil of the parish is argillaceous, heavy, cold and generally of a brown yellow colour. In the more elevated and rocky townlands in the southern section of the parish it is light and stony but very productive when manured and capable of high agricultural improvement.

Grazing

No portion of the parish is applied exclusively to grazing. Its subdivision into minute holdings precludes this possibility and the cultivation of rag-grass and clover is very rarely observable. Ribwort is the most predominant in the meadows, many of which luxuriate in rushes.

Wages

The general rate of wages to menservants, including board and lodgings, is from 4 to 6 pounds a year and female servants receive from 2 to 4 pounds. Day labourers are paid at the rate of 10d a day in summer and 8d in winter, not including board and lodgings.

Cattle

In Ashfield demesne, and upon the grounds of Mr Boyle of Tullyvin and Retreat and a few other localities, a very superior breed of Ayrshire and Durham cattle are reared; but with these exceptions the general breed of cattle throughout the parish are of the very lowest description. Turnips for stall-feeding in winter are cultivated within these demesnes but nowhere else throughout the parish.

Uses made of the Bogs

The stems of oak and fir trees extracted from the bogs are applied in supporting the thatched roofs of the cottages and cabins of the tenantry, and are excessively sought after and valued for this purpose. The bogs throughout the parish are greatly exhausted and wholly converted into turf. None is prepared as charcoal for the forges. Mineral deposits have not been discovered in any of the bogs of this parish.

Planting

The planting of poplars around the cabins and cottages of the tenantry and also on the hedgerows, which has been in progress for the last few years in many localities in the northern section of this parish, has very quickly improved its appearance. A general adoption of this practice would in a short time impart a very different character to its present naked and desolate features.

SOCIAL AND PRODUCTIVE ECONOMY

Ecclesiastical Summary

[Table] Name Killdrumsherdan, diocese Kilmore, province Armagh, vicarage, union none, patron bishop of the diocese, incumbent Revd Archdeacon Irwin.

General Remarks

The same destructive influence which cramps the energies and paralyses the physical powers of the occupying tenantry, the subletting and subdivision of the soil into small holdings, is equally operative in all its ruinous consequences on the prosperity of the parish of Kill as it is in every other parish of the surrounding district; and until this baneful practice is thoroughly extirpated and new measures of legislation introduced into the agricultural interests of the country, the inexhaustible natural advantages of its soil and climate must continue to languish and ultimately lead to the destruction of the most valuable institutions of the kingdom. [Signed] P. Taylor, Lieutenant 69th Regiment.

Parish of Laragh, County Cavan

Statistical Report by Lieutenant P. Taylor,
[late] 1835

NATURAL STATE

Name and Derivation

The name of this parish is very probably derived from the circumstance of Laragh "the half-parish" having been united to Drung "the tribe," was then formed into and still remains an impropriate vicarage in the baronies of Tullygarvey and Upper Loughtee.

Locality

Situated in nearly the centre of the county of Cavan and in the northern division of the barony of Tullygarvey, its north western section extends also into the barony of Upper Loughtee; and measuring in extreme length and breadth 7 by 8 English miles.

NATURAL FEATURES

Hills

A range of heights locally termed the Mountains, but wholly unconnected with any mountain chain, extends in an east and westerly direction throughout the southern section of the parishes of Kill and Drung, and attains, in the townland of Artany, to the height of 717 feet above the level of the sea. From Artany on the eastern boundary of the parish of Laragh to its southern extremity, through the townlands of Drumcalpin, Carrickcallen and Carrickacrommen, the difference in altitude of these elevations amounts only to 28 feet, their relative heights being 716, 719 and 745 feet.

From Artany through Derrygooney, Cordeggan, Kilcrone and Stradone westerly, the angle of depression is increased, the trigonometrical height of these stations being 476, 420, 413 and 364 feet above the same plane. But from the same position, north and north westerly through the elevation in the townland of Tullyco, a rapid depression amounting to 382 feet immediately supervenes.

An uniformity of level prevailing from thence throughout the western section of the parish, Killygarbit, Lisclone, Corfaghone and Drumlane standing respectively 410, 390, 433 and 424 feet above the same level.

Lakes

6 lakes, diversified in form and of considerable magnitude, beautify the surface of the parish.

Lough-a-cannon, covering an area of 38 acres and elevated 498 feet above the level of the sea, occupies a depression in a beautiful vale bounded on the east by a drum-shaped hill in the townland of Carrickcallan and on the west by a similar elevation in the townland of Tullynashon. Its supplies are derived from springs and the general drainage of a heathy district. Its accumulated waters flow south to the River Laragh, propelling a small corn mill in the townland of Knockataggart.

Lough-a-stirral is another beautiful expanse, located in a considerable depression terminating in a cul-de-sac formed by the elevated ridges of the townlands of Carrickacrommen and Greaghgibney, and measuring half an inch in length by a quarter in breadth, is traversed by the River Laragh, and its altitude is 606 feet above the sea.

Lough-na-lair, on the parish boundary in the townland of Carrickacrommen, is another beautiful lake closed in a valley surrounded by hills almost wholly covered with heather; it discharges its superabundance by a streamlet flowing north westerly to Lough-a-cannon.

Loch-a-curragh is another beautiful sheet of water upon the parish boundary enclosed in a valley of considerable elongation, discharging its waters by a rivulet into Loch-a-stirral.

Cliffernagh lough lies in a flat in the townland of the same name, receiving its supplies from the bogs and marshes of its locality. Its streamlet furnishes water power to a corn mill in the same townland, on its course to Laragh. Its area amounts to 14 acres, its altitude 530 feet.

Killnenagh lough is another magnificent lake deposited in a valley of considerable extent in the western portion of Stradone demesne, bounded on the east by a drum-shaped elevation in the townland of Raheelagh and on the west by the magnum dorsum of Drumkillagh. Its rivulet, flowing easterly, forms a confluence with the River Laragh in the townland of Clonderrigan. It covers an area of 59 acres and stands 294 feet above the level of the sea.

Countenan lough, in the northern section of the

parish, occupies a valley formed by the declivities of the townlands of Broaghderrig, Drumcrow and Countenan, its waters forming a tributary to the River Stradone; its area amounts to 11 acres.

Corfewhone loch occupies a valley formed by the elevations of Raskill, Lisatoo, Corfewhone and Countenan, and discharges its waters of a streamlet flowing north to the parish of Drung; its area measures 13 acres.

Corfand loch, Drumcalpin lochs, Killymeehan loch and several others are small and unimportant but add much to the natural embellishment of the country.

Rivers

The River Laragh, penetrating the parish in the townland of Carrickacrommen and traversing Loch-a-stirral, pursues in a general north westerly course a distance of 6 and a half English miles, forming the natural boundaries of the several townlands through which it flows; and pouring its volume through the deep and rugged ravine of Knockatoodor, changes its direction to a south westerly course for a mile and three-quarters, over nearly a dead level, until met by the base of the beautiful elevation of Drumlonagh, veering its course again on a northerly channel, in which it continues to its exit in the parish of Drung.

The extreme length of the river from its entrance to its exit, including its 3 grand convolutions but rejecting its innumerable contortions, is 11 English miles. In winter it swells to considerable magnitude, inundating the flats and vales in its passage but in summer it diminishes to a very small stream.

The Stradone river, rising in Loch Killnenagh in the eastern section of Stradone demesne, flows in a general course north easterly and forms a confluence with the Laragh in the townland of [blank].

Bogs

In the southern division of the parish bog is in abundance and, were it possible to transfer its superaccumulation to the northern section, its value would vastly increase the rent of land.

In a bog in the townland of Monycass Glebe, a section of which is 12 feet deep, large stems of oak trees are embedded horizontally at the base, with 8 feet of black condensed bog above them, the 4 superficial feet appearing a slightly compressed mass, the greater proportion of which is leaves and branches of fir and sally, a phenomenon of rather difficult solution.

Woods

The bogs and marshes contain the only remnants of natural woods and forests within the parish. From every other portion of its surface they have been removed.

Climate

The climate is exceedingly variable but very seldom severely cold. The winter is generally mild, frost is rarely of any continuance, a vast quantity of rain falls throughout the year but not more so than in the surrounding parishes.

The crops in the southern mountainy townlands are considerably later at arriving at maturity than in the northern section of the parish, amounting frequently to a fortnight and 3 weeks, and the equinoctial gales too often compel the husbandman to cut down his oats to ripen in the stook.

NATURAL HISTORY

Botany

Scotch firs, spruce and larch greatly predominate in the surrounding heights of Stradone demesne. Oak, ash, elm and sycamore of great magnitude adorn the lawn, silver firs and hollies and alder shade the avenue and margins of the lake, and the orchards and gardens abound in fruit trees of apples, peach and cherry of every variety.

Geology

Grauwacke, the prevailing rock of the district, forms the substratum of almost every portion of the parish of Laragh, rising in the townlands of Artany, Altbeag, Muniens and Cormeen, and in many other localities, in immense masses covering extensive areas and rendering the soil unproductive and of little value.

This homogeneous mass, having no determined lines of either stratification or cleavage, and alike devoid of the remains of all organic exuviae, would in many quarries and excavations induce a supposition that it owes its origin as much to igneous as aquaeous interference. That it has undergone disruptive action in the earlier convolutions of the globe is testified by the manner in which it frequently presents its upheaved and broken fragments.

In the townland of Muniens, where its development is fully exhibited, numerous apparently disrupted elevations and, in the immediately vicinity of a corn mill, slate-rock dipping westerly 60 degrees is associated with it; and from the croppings on the surface around the locality the presence of valuable slate is highly presumable.

But amongst the vast fields of grauwacke rocks, carboniferous limestone develops itself in several townlands in the northern section of the parish and is quarried in summer and sold upon the spot for 10d per ton. In the townland of Laragh, in the immediate vicinity of the new church and on both sides of the river, a dark blue limestone, containing organic remains of the nompholus, the cirrus, bellerophon and various other fossils and interstratified with shale, forms an interesting feature of the district.

In the bed of the river at the same place a highly indurated sandstone, strongly effervescing on the application of acids, is raised in flags for building material and both these formations are surrounded and almost covered with grauwacke rock.

Lower down the river, in the townland of [blank], the same limestone formation in nearly horizontal strata, laying deeply under immense accumulations of clay and gravel which forms superficial alluvium of the parish (and is composed of the comminuted and fractured particles of the grauwacke mass), and beneath the level of the stream, can only be wrought in summer by pouring out the water from the excavations; and in several other townlands where it also is found, its position is precisely the same and inaccessible in winter.

A particularly interesting phenomenon is the presence of highly crystallized limestone containing stems of encrini and of a white yellowish colour, laying also in horizontal strata and beneath deep banks of the same detrital accumulations; is wrought in the adjacent townland of Drumlonnagh; and the same crystalline formation of one presents itself on the western bank of the river in the townland of Countenan.

In every direction around these limestone deposits the form is black and earthy and faintly crystallized, the latter white and highly so. The grauwacke rock forms in its comminuted state the rich, argillaceous, alluvial soil and frequently rises to the surface en masse, and is universally wrought in quarries for the making and repairing of roads and occasionally as building material for the surrounding district.

Zoology

Trout of great size and delicate flavour abound in the lakes and rivers of this parish, affording delightful sport and recreation to the scientific and experienced angler. Salmon ascend the river to spawn but in very few numbers, the rugged channel of its stream affording few gravel banks whereon to deposit their spawn. Eel, pike, perch and roach are also in abundance.

Partridge, hares and rabbits abound in Stradone's demesne and [are] strictly preserved. Woodcock, plover, snipe and rail arrive in great numbers and Loch Killnenagh swarms throughout the season with wild duck, widgeon, coot and teal. Every other variety of birds peculiar to rural districts excel here in vast abundance.

MODERN TOPOGRAPHY

Towns

The town of Stradone near the western boundary of the parish, and on the direct line of road connecting Cavan with Bailieborough and Cootehill with Ballyjamesduff, contains 67 dwelling houses, a dispensary and a small detachment of police. 5 grocery shops, 5 spirit retailers and 10 lodging houses denote the occupations of the inhabitants.

No trade or commerce is carried on within the town, the appearance of which, in its present state, indicates rather a stationary condition than any advance in improvement. It is privileged with a weekly market every Monday and 7 fairs during the year, on the 7th February, 28th March, 10th May, 24th June, 16th August, 10th October, 10th November.

It is situated in the diocese of Kilmore, in the province of Ulster, county of Cavan and parish of Laragh, and is [blank] miles from Dublin.

Public Buildings

The new parochial church, erected in the townland of Laragh in the year 1831, is a neat oblong building capable of accommodating about 250 parishioners. The Revd M. Beresford is vicar and the Revd Erskine the officiating curate.

A Roman Catholic chapel in the same vicinity was erected in the year 1770 and accommodates about 500 parishioners; the Revd Hugh Brady, parish priest; and in the townland of Cliffernagh a Roman Catholic chapel was erected in the year 1821, accommodating from 500 to 600 parishioners; the Revd P. Lamb, the parish priest.

Gentlemen's Seats

Stradone House, the seat of Major Burrows, deputy-lieutenant of the county, is a modern handsome building situated in the basin-shaped valley in the townland of Drumlonnagh, extensively surrounded with rich and varied plantation. The mansion is quadrangular in form with extensive offices. The orchards and gardens are large, commanding a southern aspect. The lawn is limited but tastefully adorned with noble ash and sycamores.

Loch Killnenagh, occupying a valley in the eastern section of the demesne, gives rise to the River Stradone which flows elliptically around the northern face of the mansion, thus combining the beauties of nature with the embellishments of art in rendering Stradone House one of the most secluded but delightful residences within the county.

The Parsonage, the residence of the Revd Erskine, recently erected upon an elevation in the townland of Countenan, in the immediate vicinity of Stradone demesne, is pleasantly situated near the north side of the road leading from Stradone to Cavan.

Altbeagh Cottage, recently erected by R. Sanderson Esquire in the vicinity of romantic alpine scenery in the central portion of the parish and surrounded with young plantation, fully developed even in its present state; how capable wild and inhospitable rupes are, of artificial embellishment.

The Beehive, an unfinished residence erected upon the estate of Charles Coote Esquire in the townland of Carrickacrommenn, is pleasantly situated on the new line of road connecting Tullyvin with Bailieborough.

Corn Mills

In the immediate vicinity of Stradone a corn mill 4 feet 2 inches broad and 12 feet diameter with a breast wheel power is driven by a race from the River Stradone and in active employment in winter, grinding the corn of the district.

In the townland of Knockatooder a corn mill 12 feet in diameter and 2 feet 4 inches broad with an overshot power is propelled by a race from the River Laragh. This mill is employed working up the eastern produce of the parish.

The townland of Cormeen contains a corn mill impelled by a race from the Laragh, whose power is breast wheel, diameter of wheel 12 feet and breadth 2 feet 2 inches.

A corn mill 14 feet in diameter and 2 feet 6 inches broad in the townland of Knockataggart is driven by a streamlet flowing from Loch-a-cannon.

In the same locality a tuck mill 12 feet diameter and 2 feet 6 inches broad with an overshot power is driven by the same rivulet.

Communications

Taking the town of Stradone as a centre, 4 principal lines of communication radiate throughout the parish: one north to Cavan, sending off a branch north west to Cootehill; a second south to Virginia; a third south east to Bailieborough; and a fourth south south east to Virginia. The average breadth of these roads is 25 feet.

The mail coach road traversing a small portion of the western section of the parish measures 45 feet and is kept in excellent repair. The new lines of roads have been judiciously laid out but are kept in very bad repair. The making and repairing is paid by rates presented for at the half-yearly assizes and levied upon the parish.

ANCIENT TOPOGRAPHY

Giant's Graves

In the townland of Canfield 2 giant's graves, although much covered with briars and thorns, still pursue very distinctly the outline of their Cyclopean promotion. The most interesting of these antediluvian mausoleums displays the figure of a lozenge, the largest diameter of which measures 50 links, the shorter 25. Very large and massive rocks cover the vault, which is raised a foot above the surface.

The other cromlech is of a common oblong form, measuring 40 links in length by 12 in its greatest breadth, but neither of these interesting antiquities are preserved with care.

In the townland of Knockatoodor, Two Big Men's Beds (local phraseology), placed [at] right angles in the form of the letter "T" [drawing], attract particular attention. The side walls of the graves, composed of large rocks, are in perfect order and several fir bregi stand at each extremity. These graves measure 50 links long by 12 in greatest breadth and 4 at the inferior extremity.

Forts

The circular forts of the aborigines of the country are particularly numerous within the parish, the remains of one at least being found upon almost every townland, and in some 2 are in immediate connection. That these castellae were, in very remote times, the only residences of the inhabitants may be presumed from the absence of every other trace of humble habitation upon its surface.

Modern Topography

General Appearance and Scenery

The imposing altitude of Artany is rendered more particularly attractive by the vast development of rock and dark heathy complexion it presents when viewed from the numerous hills and vales clothed in verdure which rise so beautifully throughout every section of the parish.

The central portion, comprising the townlands of Cormeen, Muniens and Altbeagh, assume a remarkably wild and romantic appearance. Vast masses of grauwacke rock rise in numerous pinnacles 50 and 60 feet high, some at acute angles, others in perpendicular escarpments, the general inclination of which is easterly, the River Laragh winding through and around their bases.

The recent plantations of Altbeagh Cottage and the widely surrounding woods of Stradone demesne, together with the lovely and diversified form of the lakes embosomed within its vales, impart a rich and beautiful appearance within and around these localities, the power of which is vastly increased when contrasted with the naked and cheerless landscape which the greater portion of the surface of the parish exhibits.

Amongst the numerous elevations of townlands denominated cor, drum, knock and kill are the original proprietors of the soil. The 2 former greatly predominate and clearly indicate that valleys of elongation pervade its surface, the magna dorsa forming their late boundaries. But in the townlands of Carrickcallen and Carrickacrommen the handsome rock and squallaceous [squalleron] rock in the southern section of the parish, the size of which are unusually large, every variety of formation may be observed within their boundaries and which characterize not only the section but every other portion, one continuous series of waving undulation.

Social Economy

Local Government

Although the character of this parish and surrounding district is turbulent and disorderly, very few outrages have been committed within the part year. Resistance to the payment of the tithe exists and has prevailed successfully, and illicit distillation is extensively practised whenever the price of spirit is more remunerative than the sale of raw grain.

Major Burrows is the only resident magistrate; the tenants attend the petty sessions in Cootehill and Cavan.

Dispensaries

Unspeakable benefit has resulted to the peasantry by the establishment of dispensaries. The average number of patients attending the dispensary in Stradone, 2 days every week, amounts to 120. Malignant diseases and typhus fevers are of rare occurrence and the general health of the tenantry are well provided for. Dr Halpin, in charge of the dispensary, pronounces the parish particularly healthy.

[Table] Dispensary: catarrhs, febris, rheumatisms, pthysis, accidental diseases; supported by subscriptions from the landed proprietors and gentlemen, and presentments by the grand jury.

Schools

Great anxiety and desire on the part of the people exists for an increase of schools. 9 are in full and active operation within the parish, teaching reading, writing and arithmetic, and which has manifestly led to great improvement in the intelligence and moral habits of the rising generation.

Table of Schools

[Table contains the following headings: name of townland where situated, number of pupils subdivided by religion and sex, how supported, when established].

Drumlonnagh, 15 Protestants, 45 Roman Catholics, 40 males, 20 females, total 60; supported by Major Burrows of Stradone, established 1825.

Ardada, 105 Roman Catholics, 60 males, 45 females, total 105; paid by the scholars' fees, established 1830.

Aghagolrick, 40 Roman Catholics, 28 males, 12 females, total 40; paid by the scholars, established 1828.

Carrickacrommen, 70 Roman Catholics, 30 males, 40 females, total 70; paid by the scholars, established 1831.

Cliffernagh, 7 Roman Catholics, 5 males, 2 females, total 7; supported by the scholars, established 1828.

Drummole, 50 Protestants, 108 Roman Catholics, 100 males, 68 females, total 118 [sic]; supported by Major Nisbet and Revd Marcus Beresford, established 1832.

Cliffernagh, 80 Roman Catholics, 50 males, 30 females, total 80; paid by the scholars, established 1823.

Municass Glebe, 3 Protestants, 3 Roman Catholics, 3 males, 3 females, total 6; paid by the scholars, established 1835.

Moynetta, 1 Protestant, 69 Roman Catholics, 40 males, 30 females, total 70; paid by the scholars.

Poor

The universally acknowledged hospitality and benevolent disposition of the people are the only sources of supply for the indigent poor. The annual amount of collection on Sunday at the church of Laragh averages 20 pounds and the numbers receiving relief 27.

Religion

The census of the parish taken in the year [blank] gave the under-mentioned proportions: [blank]. [Insert note: The census could not be obtained, the enumerator having returned no memoranda of it].

Habits of the People

Would that habits of industry and the desire of accumulation, which so generally prevails in the sister kingdoms, could be imparted effectually into the minds and disposition of this wretched and deplorable peasantry, whose only aim and desire is to secure the means of the lowest possible rate of subsistence.

How the general class of tenantry holding from 6 to 8 acres can possibly pay their rent appears inexplicable. The month of December is fast approaching and a very small portion of the potato crop only is secured; and so fatal is their inactivity that much of it will be in the ground in December and January. The lamentable consequences resulting from which is starvation in the dwelling and rent in arrears.

The greater proportion of the cabins are built of mud, the substrata being extremely difficult to form into building material. The dwellings are generally 1-storey high, consisting of 2 and 3 apartments with very small glass windows. The families are large, amounting in general to 6 members. Markets and fairs are chief resorts, and much valuable time is sacrificed in these perpetual meetings. No singularity in manners or dress distinguishes the peasantry in the parish from those in the more eastern district.

Emigration

One-half of the members of 5 families emigrated during the year to the Canadas, and the want of the means of transport alone prevents the great body of people from removing simultaneously to the same colony.

PRODUCTIVE ECONOMY

Manufactures: Linen

The manufacture of coarse linen has almost ceased within the parish; the noise of the spinning wheel may frequently be heard but the flying shuttle seldom resounds. This profitable branch of trade, formerly so valuable to the occupying tenant as to render him independent of the rent of his land, has almost unfortunately perished and nothing but the outline of an impoverished soil, which he has not the power of manuring, remains, whereon to protract his wretched existence.

Fairs

7 fairs are held in the year in the town of Stradone, for the sale of horses, cows, asses, sheep and pigs, the breeds of which are of very low description and the value of the cattle of the same amount as reported in the parish of Kill and Drumgoon. Nothing can surpass the inferiority of the breed of horses and horned cattles throughout the whole of this district.

Husbandry

The principal labour is manual throughout this parish and the whole of the district. The plough is seldom observable upon the holdings, farming and threshing machines are almost unknown. Culture is chiefly with the loy and shovel. The flail and centre of the road answer every convenience of the threshing machine and barn, and in favourable weather the stackyard speedily diminishes by these means. The old Irish cart is very common in the mountain townlands but the slide has not been observed.

Manures

A rich argillaceous alluvium forms the arable soil of the parish and only requires efficient culture and manuring to render it highly productive. Limestone is burnt and used very generally as manure, but in very sparing quantities. Quarries of the rock are wrought in a few localities in summer in the northern section of the parish and sold at 10d per ton.

Farms

The holdings vary in size from 4 to 12 acres. Very few in the parish exceed 20 and the rent varies from 6s to 40s per acre on leases of 1 and 3 lives but more generally as tenants at will.

County cess is also exceedingly variable and is averaged at about 2s per acre per annum, and churchland is chargeable with tithe averaging 1s per acre.

The holdings are subdivided into innumerable small enclosures and, considering their multitude, many of them are well fenced.

Potatoes, oats and flax are the only product; wheat or barley is seldom sown, even in the demesnes.

Marl is abundant in many of the drains and the bogs but seldom used as manure. Burning of the soil is practised and to an injurious extent.

Proprietors

The great landed proprietors of the parish are Major Nesbit of [?] Crosdong, Major Burrows of Stradone, the bishop of the diocese, Alexander Sanderson of Castle Sanderson and Robert Sanderson Esquire of Drumkeen. Major Burrows and Robert Sanderson Esquire are the only resident landlords, but neither farm extensively upon their estates.

The system of green feeding has nowhere been introduced, and whilst one-half of the soil of the parish lies unproductive, the other half is undergoing a succession of crops with little or no manure, a system alike injurious to the landed proprietor as it is impoverishing to the tenantry of the soil.

Seed and Produce

A considerable quantity of the grain of the parish is conveyed to the large corn mills of the district and sold, and much of it is taken to the surrounding markets for sale for exportation to England. The proportions of seed and produce of the several crops, together with the market prices, vary in no respect from those exhibited in the tables on this head as furnished in the more poorer eastern parishes.

Grazing and Irrigation

Grazing farms are nowhere formed within this parish, neither has the introduction of rag-grass or clover been anywhere extensively tried: in Stradone demesne even they are scarcely observable. On spontaneous vegetation alone the tenantry place their sole dependence.

Simple irrigation by the direction and dispersion of the streamlets over a field is occasionally practised but a regular system of drainage for the improving of the soil or the reclaiming of wasteland is nowhere adopted.

Wages

The rates of wages to male and female servants, very few of whom are employed, are precisely the same in this as has been reported in the parishes of Kill and Drumgoon.

Cattle

A superior breed of horned cattle is observable in Stradone demesne but no attention whatever is paid to the breeding of horses or cows in any other portion of the parish, the degeneracy of which is reduced to the lowest degree. A superior breed of pigs, termed the Dutch breed, has been very generally introduced and a cross betwixt the pure Dutch and native pig is considered a valuable improvement. Poultry of every description, geese, turkeys and fowls are small but delicate in flavour.

Jobbers attend the fairs of Stradone, purchasing up the pigs for the English market. Green feeding is not at all practised within this parish.

Uses made of the Bogs

The bogs are wholly converted to turf as fuel and consumed within the parish. It is also converted into charcoal for the use of the forges. No mineral depositions have ever been discoverable in the bogs. Stems of oak and fir trees of great magnitude are frequently extracted and converted into roofing timber by the tenantry, and highly valued for this purpose.

Drainage

Simple drainage, of the sinking of drains, has been carried to the utmost possible extent in the northern sections of the parish for recovery of bog; and, in summer when the water drains off, much valuable turf is saved in the southern section when bog is in abundance and at a higher elevation. Very little exertion is necessary in draining the winter accumulation of water and very little made for that purpose. A belief prevails amongst the people that if the bog is not increased by immersion in water, it is improved and protected by it.

Planting

In the vicinity of Altbeagh Cottage a considerable extent of young plantation of Scotch fir, larch and spruce are now rising and will ultimately enrich and highly improve this locality, but in no other portion of the parish has improvement of recent plantation been attempted, neither has nurseries of young trees been anywhere found.

SOCIAL AND PRODUCTIVE ECONOMY

Ecclesiastical Summary

[Table] Name Laragh, diocese Kilmore, province Armagh, vicarage, in union with Drung, patron bishop of the diocese, incumbent Revd M. Beresford.

General Remarks

A considerable extent of the surface of the southern division of the parish has not been reclaimed. In the townlands of Cavankallan and Carrickacrommen large portions of the hills and extensive tracts of bogs are still covered with heather. One-half of its cultivated surface is fallow, having surrendered its scanty autumnal crop, and the other bears the impressions of the husbandman but yields neither a suffering of grass or provender for the cattle.

A lonely tree is not observable upon its surface and were it not diversified with a few improved localities, the bisections of roads and ramifying lines of communications, the monotony of same in traversing an agitated ocean could scarcely leave fainter impressions upon the mind than the cone, dome and drum-shaped billows which rise in beautiful succession around this district.

The northern section of the parish is an age at least in advance: cultivation has crowned its very summit; the fields are more regularly divided and very well fenced; quickset hedgerows are frequently and plantings occasionally observable; and the general appearance of increased industry is stamped upon its soil.

But even here, the same destructive influence of subdividing the soil into holdings so minute as to the general average about 8 acres, counteracts and paralyses every effort that can be made to develop the innumerable resources of its soil and climate, and raise it to a scale of agricultural prosperity inferior to none in any country on the surface of the globe. [Signed] P. Taylor, Lieutenant 69th Regiment.

Parishes of Cloonclare, Cloonlogher and Killasnet, County Leitrim

Memoir for Manorhamilton Union by Lieutenant W. Lancey, April 1837

NATURAL STATE

Situation and Locality

Statistical Memoir of the Union of Manorhamilton, comprising the parishes of Killasnet, Cloonclare and Cloonlogher, situated in the baronies of Dromahair and Rosclogher in the county of Leitrim. [Insert footnote: Part of Cloonclare in the barony of Rosclogher was surveyed by Lieutenant Vicars and is not included in this Memoir].

This large district lies near the northern extremity of the county. It is surrounded by Cavan on the east, the county Sligo and parish of Drumlease on the west; on the north is the large parish of Rosinver and on the south Killargy and Killanumery.

Contains [blank] acres; of these, 21,728 acres are cultivated; all the rest, with the exception of [blank] acres of water, is in bog, waste or rocky sheep-walks. The county cess amounts to 617 pounds in Killasnet, 313 pounds in Cloonclare and 232 pounds in Cloonlogher.

Cloonlogher takes its name from Carrickleitrim which stands near its northern end and is said to be the rock from whence the Earls of Leitrim derived their titles.

NATURAL FEATURES

Hills

The surface of this tract of country is much broken by high rocky hills and deep valleys separating the district into distinct and isolated glens. Glencar and Glenade in Killasnet, Glenbuoy, Glenkeel and Glenfarn in Cloonclare and the glen in Cloonlogher are the principal low grounds, each limited by its broken and rough hills. At the junction of these glens, in a central position, stands the town of Manorhamilton.

The ground about Glenade is bold, precipitous and striking, rising on the east and west of the lough to 1,573 and 1,134 feet, and falls in considerable perpendicular steps to the lake which is only 216 feet above the sea. To the north of Glencar the limestone hills vary from 1,273 to 211 feet but on the southern side of this narrow valley they attain the elevation of 1,472 and 1,497 feet. The lough contains [blank] acres and is 97 feet above the low water mark.

Large subsidencies have taken place in this valley, which renders the landscape peculiarly striking. Glenbuoy and Glenfarn are more accessible and there is a considerable stretch of low fertile land in the valley of Cloonlogher skirted by high and barren hills of [blank] feet elevation.

Lakes

The lakes are not numerous. The following [blank] table exhibits their names and contents.

Rivers

The largest stream is the Bonet <Bownet>, flowing from Glenade to the sea by Lough Gill and Sligo. This is a small stream, not attaining more than 70 feet in breadth in its average widest part in Cloonlogher. It is subject to floods from the sudden pouring down of many mountain rills and overflows the adjacent land for 6 feet in depth, and does considerable damage to the hay crops if the season should unfortunately be late. The floods in former times remained on the land for 6 days but now not more than 24 hours as the lands are drained. The Bonet is fordable nearly in all its extent and flows over limestone gravel and ledges of rock.

West of Manorhamilton the Owenmore river falls into it from the east, when it becomes a slower and deeper stream, and the fords not so frequent south of Carrickleitrim.

The principal stream emptying itself into Lough McNain, 173 feet above the sea on the mearing of the county Cavan, is a small brook which accompanies the mail road from Manorhamilton to Enniskillen for some miles and is fordable in almost every place.

The stream flowing into Glencar lough is also insignificant but these rivulets assume a very different appearance after heavy rains, when they are rapid and turbulent.

Bogs

The mountains have considerable tracts of bogs on their summits. Their slopes are frequently fine sheep-walks whilst few bogs are now met with in the lowlands. Fir and oaks are dug up in the low grounds but not very extensively. They are supposed to have been blown down by the westerly winds. Some gold coins and crocks of tallow were found at Coanestack.

The bogs are let at 4 pounds an acre to those not entitled to turf by their leases and fuel is sold from 20s to 25s for 120 barrels when cut, or 8s to 10s per 100 uncut, each barrel containing 24 stones. This is considered cheap. The inhabitants of the town have now to go from 1 to 2 miles for their turf.

Woods

The country was formerly extensively wooded. There are yet traces of extensive woodlands in the district, especially at Glencar and the hills in Cloonlogher and those mearing with it and Cloonclare at the gorge of the valley.

At Lough McNain, on Mr Tottenham's estate of Glenfarn, upwards of 20 Irish acres have been added, and considerable oak copses, perhaps 17 acres, are to the west of Manorhamilton on the Sligo road, and a small park at Screeny in the immediate vicinity of the town. The oak copses appear to be valuable and there is more timber in this country than usual.

Climate

The clouds from the Atlantic, passing over the flat coasts, settle on the highlands of the district and envelop the deep glens in mist and rain for a longer period than in the open country, rendering the climate very damp and moist. The hay harvest is begun usually on the 12th of July, oats about the middle of August and the higher ground from 14 to 30 days later.

NATURAL HISTORY

Zoology

The fish are salmon, trout, pike, perch, eels in the Bonet river. There are a few martins, badgers, foxes and hares but they are scarcely one-tenth of what they were 30 years ago. Eagles at Glenade, goose and sparrow-hawks in the cliffs are not uncommon.

Geology

The country is for the most part mountain limestone, the primitive rocks gneiss and talc slate, rising occasionally on the summits of the higher hills. The mountain limestone is frequently

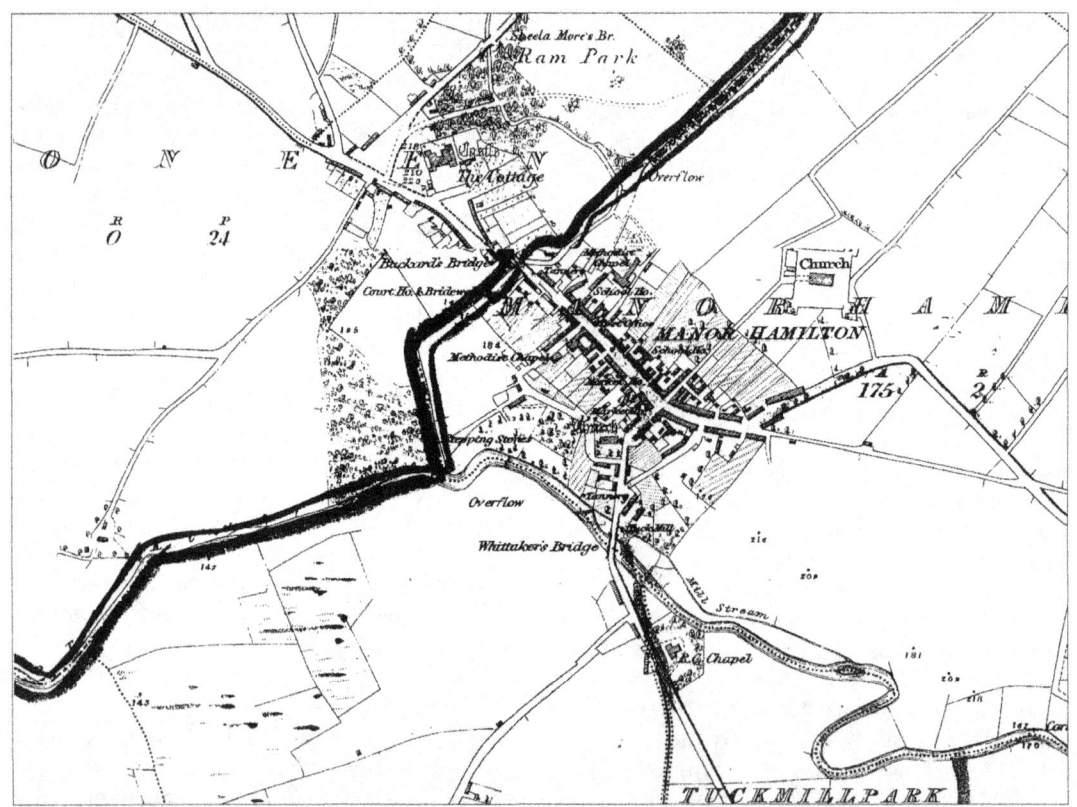

Map of Manorhamilton from the first 6" OS maps, 1830s

filled with shells, zeophytes and other organic remains.

The gold mine in Bulbuoy in Cloonlogher has obtained its name from the glittering iron pyrites found in it.

Modern Topography

Towns: Manorhamilton

Manorhamilton is the only village of importance. It is 3 furlongs in length and was rebuilt by Sir Frederick Hamilton, who erected the castle about 250 years ago, and now belongs to Lord Leitrim. A new market house was erected in 1834-5 and is said to have cost not less than 800 pounds. It is of stone, the lower part a shed for potatoes, the upper part used as offices with a market enclosure in the rear.

The court house was built about 1819 and cost 2,400 pounds. There are 3 prisoners' rooms, 1 for the court, 2 for the petty jury and 1 for the grand jury.

Public Buildings

2 Methodist chapels: the old one with a half-gallery was built in 1801 and cost 300 pounds, and a new one in 1826. It also cost 300 pounds and each can hold almost 300 persons.

The Roman Catholic chapel stands a short distance from the main street. It has galleries and can hold 600 persons, was built in 1828, cost 600 pounds and is a good slated building.

The parish church stands in an old fortified barrack square with bastions on a hill just north of the village. It was built about 100 years ago, had a new stone spire in 1781 and is in excellent repair, has a half-gallery and can accommodate 600 persons in pews.

The ruins of the old church still exist in the town. Its roof was taken off when the new church was built.

There is a post office, tannery, hotel, tuck mill and bridge. This last was erected in 1824 at an expense of 300 pounds.

Social and Productive Economy

Local Government

Detachments of 7 constabulary and 10 revenue police are stationed in Manorhamilton.

The crimes committed are usually distillation, waylaying, beating, stealing and picking pockets. An immense quantity of spirits is consumed but illicit whiskey is not extensively used, owing to the vigilance of the police.

Markets and Fairs

The market day is on Thursday and 12 fairs are held annually, on the 8th May, 1st July, 21st August, 7th October (these are called old fairs); the 8 new fairs are held on the 12th of the other months.

The tolls on cattle are levied only at the old fairs: 6d a milk cow, 4d for dry cattle, 1d for sheep, 2d for pigs, 5d for horses, 1d a sack for potatoes, 2d for meal. These fines are paid to Lord Leitrim and amount sometimes to 20 pounds a fair day.

The market is not well supplied with meat. 2 or 3 persons stall-feed 20 cattle. Butter is produced in large quantities and sells from 6d to 10d a lb. and cows from 3 pounds to 5 pounds apiece.

Rents

The Town Parks let as high as 50s an acre and generally the lands in this district vary from 37s 6d the best to 32s middling and 26s and 18s rough pasture, the Irish acre. The mountain sheep-walks vary from 3s 6d to 7s an acre. The lowlands about Manorhamilton are very fine and produce abundant crops, and the low grounds generally are very productive.

Dispensary

The dispensary surgeon in the town receives 150 pounds per annum, one-half by subscription, the other by the grand jury.

Poor and Schools

Mr Cullin of Glenade in 1824 left 12 pounds a year for 12 widows.

McMaster's charity amounts to 20 pounds a year, for which the rector and the Cullins family are trustees. It affords education to 40 Protestant scholars. This has been in existence for 28 years. The master provides the school apartments and 1 scholar is sent from each house, who is supposed to communicate his or her instruction to the family.

The London Hibernian Society have a school in the village and a sewing school for girls. There is a private one for the Roman Catholics consisting of 30 scholars. These are the chief means of education in Manorhamilton. This last school is supported by the payment of the scholars, about 20 pounds a year each.

Trades and Occupations

The trades are shoemakers (30), tailors (24), nailers (12), grocers (16), smiths (5) and publicans

(20). The town is not increasing in population and wealth as the landlord does not give encouraging building leases.

Conveyances

The conveyances are the Sligo and Enniskillen Mail and Shareholder Cars daily. 3 houses let post-cars and a chaise can be had at the Leitrim Arms Hotel. Mailbags are made up at the post office for Dublin, Enniskillen, Florencecourt, the Blacklion and Sligo.

MODERN TOPOGRAPHY

Gentlemen's Seats

Colonel Cullin's house was built 150 years since. It is a whitewashed building of 2-storeys covered with country slates and stands in a small park in Screeny in which are some good old trees.

Mr Tottenham's, Glenfarn House, lies near the bank of Lough McNain and is in bad repair although built but 16 years ago. The offices are now being repaired. There is an extensive garden and a small pack of hounds on the premises, but the whole estate is very much embarrassed.

Hollymount was improved 2 years ago. The old house belonged to Mr Algeo 100 years since. It is a large pile of building of the plainest description standing in a small park.

Larkfield in Clonlogher is the residence of the descendants of the O'Donnell of Tyrconnell. The last Earl of O'Donnell died here. The grandfather of the present proprietor was Sir Neil O'Donnell and his mother is connected with O'Connor Don. The dwelling house is of the plainest description but the expense of its erection embarrassed the estate.

Glenade House in Killasnet lies on the high road from Manorhamilton to Ballyshannon, on the bank of the lough. It is a small square and stone building of 1-storey, the kitchen sunk on 3 sides (for defence) and a colonnade towards the lough. The offices are unfinished. There is a little young plantation but the whole is bleak and exposed. It was erected 3 years ago and cost 3,000 pounds [insert query].

In Deerpark stands a small house called Rockwood. There is nothing remarkable about it.

Bleach Green and Mills

There is a small establishment in Glenbuide and by the lease must be kept up. There are about 50 acres of fine land. About 10 men are employed on the average and country work is all that is done by its machinery.

There are mills in Milltown, Lower Breccagh and in Stradrian.

Communications

The leading roads from Ballyshannon to the Blacklion, from Sligo to Enniskillen pass through Manorhamilton. They run in glens and are hard and good. The country roads are also good but there are not so many of them as usual and, the limestone being at hand, they are in good repair.

Few cars or carts are used by the country people. Horses and asses are usually employed in carrying burdens. The bridges are of the common construction and kept in order by the county.

ANCIENT TOPOGRAPHY

Castle

The old castle in Manorhamilton has been a large massive pile of building but is now a complete ruin. It was erected by Sir Frederick Hamilton, an officer in the army, in 1641, who obtained a manor from King Charles.

[Drawing of castle with dimensions, height 64 feet].

History of Manor of Hamilton

In the Down Survey the manor of Hamilton is estimated at 2,500 acres. The castle was burnt down by the Irish 7 years after it was built, on account of the treacherous conduct of Sir F. Hamilton in taking vengeance for the death of his son, who had been killed in Roscommon on a foraging party. He invited the Irish chieftains to dine with him, having prepared his servants at a certain signal to dispatch them. The old Irish piper played the tune of *Make your visits short and far between*, but the hint had no effect and they were destroyed. The neighbouring chiefs attacked and burnt down the castle and Sir F. Hamilton left the country.

Tradition concerning Castle

A curious story is told of one McGlaughlin letting the site of the castle to Sir F. H[amilton] for a term of years, at the end of which he was to pay for the improvements; but the massive pile of building erected put it out of the power of McGlaughlin to keep to his bargain and the general outwitted him and kept the castle.

Mr Wilson, agent to Mr Cullin, resided in a part

Manorhamilton Castle

of the castle so lately as 25 years ago. Colonel Cullin has it now for 30s a year forever.

Charles Henry Tottenham Esquire is a descendant of this Hamilton. He left no son but 3 daughters, to the 2 elder of whom he gave the manors of Manorhamilton and Carrickmoiety, and the third daughter was married to a Bingham in Mayo. Lady Bingham is buried in Cloonclare.

A few of the descendants of those who came with Sir F. Hamilton still remain in the country.

Castle in Castletown

The old castle in Castletown in Killasnet at present belonging to Mr Parke was formerly the residence of O'Rourke, Prince of Breffney, who carried off the wife of Dermot MacMurrough in the time of Henry II, which event led to the conquest of Ireland. The roof fell in almost 80 years ago and a high gable crowned with ivy is all that now remains.

[Drawing of castle, 70 feet high by 24 feet across].

Churches of Cloonlogher and Cloonclare

The church of Cloonlogher is a simple rectory. [Drawing of church, height of gables 25 feet, width 25 feet, distance between gables 55 feet].

The old church of Cloonclare: [drawing of tombstone with motto and inscription: "Here lyeth the body of the Honourable Catherine Cullin alias Bermingham, relict of Captain John Cullin. She departed this life 15[blank] Our Lord 1773 aged [blank] years;" 3 feet 10 inches wide, 3 feet 6 inches high].

Old Church of Manorhamilton

[Drawing of Lady Bingham's effigy, 1 foot wide, 2 feet long.

Drawing of old church of Manorhamilton, with bell-tower and tombstone, length 68 feet, height 36 feet].

St Patrick's Church

Curraghs or St Patrick's church, situated on the western side of Lough Allen and in the parish of Inishmacgrath, townland of Curraghs. The time of erection is not known in the country but is supposed to have been built by St Patrick. [Drawing of church, 60 feet long, 30 feet wide, 40 feet high at gable].

Castle Gore

South view of Castle Gore situated in the townland of Newtown, parish of Drumlease. This castle is said to have been erected by the family of the Gores in or about 2 centuries ago. [View of castle elevation with range of back buildings, showing 2 sets of chimney stacks, ancient door and dimensions].

Churches and Graveyard

The old church of Killasnet stands in the townland [blank].

The old church of Manorhamilton is situated in the town and is a complete ruin.

There is an old graveyard in Kilmakernel and one in the fort of Carrickrevagh, and a standing stone near it.

Fortifications

2 ancient fortified barrack enclosures (squares with bastions) are met with, one in which stands Manorhamilton church, the other at the village of Lurganyboy on the Sligo road. They consist of walls with a banquette and were erected at the same period with the old castle.

Forts

Danish forts are found in the following townlands. Killasnet: Kilroosk, Falachartha (2), Largy, Gurteenagunnel, Carrickeery (2), Fenagh (2), Tomrod, Bar of Shancurragh, Castletown, Mulkawn (3), Townatemple, Drimahan, Shracreaghan (2), Ballyglass, Knocknaclapagh, Townamachugh, Shranee (2), Largadoon.

Cloonclare: Gortnaliblut, Minnymore (2), Cornastack, Carrickleitrim (2), Ross, Rathneerey (4), Tullysecarny (2), Screeney (6), Screeney Little (2), Curraghoore, Moneenashinagh, Annagh, Carrickreevagh (2), Aughlerim, Brioselunagh, Kilmakernel.

Cloonlogher: Lisgorman (5), Cloonlogher (3), Cloonagurn (2), Boggan (5), Larkfield (4), Gortgargon (1).

MODERN TOPOGRAPHY

General Appearance and Scenery

This country, being high and running in ridges and glens, is very inaccessible except leading roads which follow the directions of the glens. The mountain limestone hills are very bold in Glencar and Glenade, and are strikingly picturesque in the vicinity of the loughs. The rest of the country is very hilly, opening with a broad valley in which is placed Manorhamilton, a mean insignificant village. The country in its neighbourhood is rich and fertile, and relieved with woods and oak copses.

The lowest lands are cultivated with corn and potatoes on a very limited scale as grasslands are principally sought after. This gives the country a more wild appearance than it really possesses, but the idleness of the people and the risk of additional taxes keep the lands in pasture.

SOCIAL ECONOMY

Improvements

The facilities for cattle and the leading roads through this district have caused it to be well inhabited, and it would become a much more flourishing country were advantageous leases given to the inhabitants of Manorhamilton, who would build good houses and increase its respectability and wealth.

Local Government

Mr Armstrong and Mr Cullin of Glenade are the 2 resident magistrates. The country is quiet, requiring 7 police and [blank] revenue. Quarter sessions are held by Mr Finley, the barrister, and petty sessions every 14 days in the town of Manorhamilton. The causes are of the usual common description; illicit distillation is on the decrease.

Dispensaries: there is 1 in the town. The medical man receives 150 pounds.

Religion

The Roman Catholic population is estimated at 4,754 in Killasnet, Protestants 989; Roman Catholics 2,029 in (see Lieutenant Lancey's report) Cloonclare, Protestants 387. Of these, 5,050 are males and 4,110 females, making a total of 8,160 (not including Cloonlogher).

The Protestant living is a union of the 3 parishes of Killasnet, Cloonclare and Cloonlogher, and the rector is paid 700 pounds a year composition for tithes with 2 glebes.

The rector, Mr Abraham Hamilton, does not reside. He employs 3 curates and visits the parish once a quarter. The Roman Catholic priests are paid in the usual manner.

There are chapels in Glenfarn, 90 feet by 55 feet, erected in 1832, holds 2,000 persons and cost 1,000 pounds, Cartronatemple, Mullies,

Drummonds, Meneenageer and West Bars; and 2 Methodist chapels in Manorhamilton.

Habits of the People

Their habits are bad, being very much addicted to whiskey and party fights. Their houses are of limestone but very little of it is expended in whitewashing the cabins either inside or out.

The cow, horse or ass lives in the same room with the family, and dirt and filth are the common characteristics of their dwellings. In this state of things, some drag out existence for 100 or more years.

They do not marry very early.

The old system of Beal Tinne is kept up on St John's Eve.

Emigration

A great number of Protestants embark for America annually at Sligo. A few of the poorer sort go to England or Scotland for harvest.

Remarkable events: none.

PRODUCTIVE ECONOMY

Manufacturing and Commercial

Spinning and weaving are common for country uses but there are not one-twentieth of the looms now at work that there were formerly. If a woman has to buy her flax, she cannot earn 2d a day by her wheel. The weights and measures are the standard ones.

Proprietors and Holdings

The chief proprietors are Mr Fox, Mr Tottenham, Messrs Cullins, Mr Wynne.

The usual size of holdings varies from 9 to 14 acres arable and the rents from 15s to 35s an acre. The average of the mountain is 2s 6d. About 100 persons have farms above 20 acres in Cloonclare. The bleach green farm is 50 acres, Hollymount 150, Colonel Cullin's upwards of 40 and Mr Rutledge's 50 acres near Glenfarn chapel.

The leases on Mr Fox's estate, which is the largest, are for 21 years but the general leases are for 3 lives or 61 years, usually held from the landlord, the practice of middlemen being scarcely known here. Service days in spring and harvest are bound in the leases.

The fields are badly laid out, of every size and shape. The buildings are erected by the farmer who is subject to the usual taxes, tithe and county cess. No farms are held by the landowners as examples to the tenantry.

Manures

Lime is sold at 8d to 10d a barrel and the whole subsoil of the lower lands lies on limestone rock. Each person usually burns what he requires.

Tillage

The tillage is carried on not by ploughs but by digging with a long narrow spade called a loy. Little, however, is required: a small patch of corn from 2 to 20 gallons of flax and enough potatoes for the year is the extent of the broken-up ground.

Conveyance of Goods

Carts are uncommon: the extra produce is conveyed to Sligo market by contract, 12d a sack for potatoes or oats, and a limited number of persons make their living by this traffic.

Rotation of Crops

Rotation in crops is consequently not required or at least not practised. Lea, 2 crops of potatoes, 2 or 3 crops of oats (sometimes 7 in succession) followed by potatoes is a common method on good ground. Little wheat has been tried; rye is sown in mossy ground. Conacres prevail a good deal, from 5 to 8 pounds an acre if manured. The land is not burnt except in reclaiming.

The value of the produce in good ground is 8 pounds an acre for oats, 12 to 20 pounds for potatoes. The seed for the former is about 24 stones, for the latter 20.

Grazing

There is a good deal of grazing in this district. The limestone hills afford sweet pasture for sheep, but cattle are the principal stock. Green feeding is but very partially, if at all, used and the breed of cattle are of the usual mixed nature, Devonshire and Irish. The meadows are coarse but good.

Wages and Livestock

Wages of servants are about 5 pounds for men and 2 pounds for women per annum. [Insert footnote: In 1831 there were in Killasnet 134 males and 143 female servants and in (see Lieutenant Lancey's report) Cloonclare 55 males and 45 females].

There are a great number of pigs. Horses are worth 5 to 10 pounds.

Uses made of Bogs

They are grazed and burnt; see under the article Bogs.

Planting

Mr Tottenham of Glenfarn House has planted upwards of 20 Irish acres on the banks of Lough McNain. A few acres have been laid down by Mr Cullin of Glenade and Mr Wynne improves his estate by plantations. There is not sufficient wood in the country for its consumption, but Sligo and Ballyshannon afford opportunities for purchasing any that may be required.

Fishing

The River Bonet is preserved by Mr Martin of Sligo, who possesses the right of fishing it and Lough Gill. He pays about 12 or 13 waterkeepers at the rate of 3 pounds a year, who preserve the fish.

Cultivation and Rents

The soil of this district is generally very fertile, especially about Manorhamilton where a farm of 24 acres whose rent is 9 pounds 16s 5d clears to the proprietor 50 pounds per annum. The tenants usually depend on their cattle and butter to pay one-half year's rent and their corn the other. The egg trade is in a flourishing condition.

Some of the highest points cultivated are in the townlands of Glenbuidhe, 573 feet, Lacoon, 802 feet, West Bars, 988 feet, Mure, 680 feet, Boggan in Cloonlogher, 853 feet, Gortnagorn, 774 feet, Carrickdown, 767 feet and Brackrymore, 1,075 feet.

Soil and Improvements

Prevailing soil is heavy clay which, with good tillage, is made into excellent land; some parts are loamy. Abundance of lime can be procured in almost every townland. Plantations thrive extremely well and it is to be much regretted that more timber is not grown, as there are numbers of favoured spots at present comparatively thrown away which might be turned to immense profit, if planted.

Should Lough Gill be connected with Lough Allen, and opportunity afforded for conveying the surplus produce by water to Sligo, the whole face of this country would change its appearance and a well-cultivated district supply the place of one now considered to be backward and wild.

Geology

The country people entertained a notion that gold and silver mines are in the district, which arises from the pyrites so often found. The best manure for rough land is the blue clay and limestones, and dug up from the subsoil. [Signed] William Lancey, Lieutenant Royal Engineers, 21st April 1837.

Parish of Ballymascanlan, County Louth

Townland Statistics by Civil Assistant
A. McLachlan

PRODUCTIVE ECONOMY

Table of Townlands

[Table contains the following headings: name of townland, pronunciation, proprietor and agent, size of farms, leases, rent per acre, county cess per acre].

Edentober, pronunciation Edenthobber; proprietor Mr Fortiscue, agent Mr Wright; farms 3 to 5 acres, leases 1 life, rent 1 pound 10s.

Carrickcarnon, pronunciation Carri-harnon; proprietor Mr Fortiscue, agent Mr Wright; farms 5 to 10 acres, leases 1 life, rent 1 pound 10s.

Ravensdale Park or Rock Aughavarn, pronunciation Revensdale; proprietor Mr Fortiscue, agent Mr Wright Dundalk, no farms.

Dromard, pronunciation Drom-ad; proprietor Mr Fortiscue, agent Mr Wright; farms 8 to 20 acres, no leases, rent 1 pound 10s, county cess 6 pounds 12s.

Feed, pronunciation Fe-ed; proprietor Mr Fortiscue, agent Mr Wright; farms 7 acres, no leases, rent 1 pound 10s, county cess 6 pounds 12s.

Clarret Rock, pronunciation Carret Rock; proprietor Thomas McGrath Esquire; farms 2 to 5 acres, leases 21 years, rent 25s 10d to 21s, county cess 8d [sic] 120 acres 3s 10d; remarks: Lord Claremont the principal proprietor of nearly all these townlands.

Monascribe, pronunciation Monyscrib; proprietors Mr Hale and Mr Batty, agent Mr Coulter; farms 5 to 10 acres, leases at will, rent 36s to 50s.

Plaster, pronunciation Pleaster; proprietor Wolf McNeil Esquire, agent Mr Tippin of Lisnally; leases: but a few for 1 life, the rest at will, county cess 11d.

Upper Faughart, pronunciation Upper Foughort; proprietor Wolf McNeil, agent Mr Tippin; farms 5 to 32 acres, leases 30 years, two of 1 life, rent 47s to 52s, county cess 15d ha'penny.

Lower Faughart, pronunciation Lower Foughort; proprietor James Moore, farms 3 to 10 acres, leases at will, rent 30s to 45s, county cess 10d 3 farthings.

White Mill, pronunciation Belnamonnan; proprietor James Moore, agent Christopher Moore; farms 4 to 20 acres, leases at will, rent 18s to 60s, county cess 16d.

Annies, pronunciation Annies; proprietors Robert Murphy, Castle A., and Jacob M. Murphy, Tower; leases at will, county cess 24d.

Navan, pronounced Navan; proprietor Alexander McNeil, no divisions; leases of lives, county cess 8d.

Aughboys, pronounced Aghluie, proprietor William Skelton Esquire; rent 50s to 63s.

Ballymascanlan, pronounced Ballymascanon; proprietors John McNeil and Wolf McNeil Esquire, agent James Tippin of Lisnally.

Culfore, pronounced Culfure; proprietor James Moore; farms 1 to 3 acres, leases at will, rent 55s to 65s, county cess 10d.

Proleek, pronounced Praleek; proprietor Mr Fortiscue, agent Mr Wright, Dundalk; farms 3 and a half to 8 acres, leases at will, rent 30s to 48s, county cess 10d 3 farthings.

Proleek Acres, pronounced Proleek Acres; proprietor Mr Fortiscue; leases at will, rent 2 pounds, county cess 11d ha'penny.

Broughatten, pronounced Broughatten; proprietor Mr Brush, agents [Mr] John Black Esquire and Thomas Magrath; farms 6 to [blank] acres, leases at will, rent 37s, county cess 11d ha'penny the half-year.

Drumnasylla, pronunciation Drumnasulla; proprietor Mr Fortiscue; farms 6 to 12 acres, leases at will, rent 25s to 30s, county cess 11d ha'penny the half-year.

Drumnacarne, pronounced Drimnacarne; proprietors Wolf McNeil Esquire and James Moore, agent Christopher Moore of Strand Field; farms 3 to 10 acres, leases at will, rent 12s to 34s, county cess 11d ha'penny the half-year.

Aughnaskeagh, pronounced Annaskeagh; proprietors Wolf McNeil Esquire and James Moore, agent Christopher Moore of Strand Field; farms 4 to 10 acres, leases at will, rent 23s, county cess 9d farthing; value to the county cess for the south borough for Dundalk, 740 pounds.

Moneycrockroe, proprietor [Mr] Fortiscue, agent [blank] Wright; farms about 30 acres, [insert note for remaining townlands: only 2 or 3 leases in the whole place, the rest of the occupiers of land are tenants at will]; rent per acre 16 pounds 12s for the holding of 30 acres; county cess 1s 2d.

Spellickanee, proprietor [Mr] Fortiscue; farms about 18 acres, rent 10s to 15s, county cess 1s 2d.

Aughameen, proprietor [Mr] Fortiscue, agent

[blank] Wright; farms about 18 acres, rent 9s 6d to 16s, county cess 4d ha'penny to the pound.

Jenkinstown, proprietor [Mr] Fortiscue, agent [blank] Wright; farms about 15 acres; rent: upper part about 10s, lower part about 35s; county cess 1s 8d ha'penny; upper part pays one-third of the cess per acre levied on the lower of this townland.

Mullaghhatten, proprietor [Mr] Fortiscue; sublet in farms about 12 acres; rent 60 pounds for this townland, sublet 10s to 15s; county cess 4d ha'penny in the pound.

Ballygooly, proprietor [Mr] Fortiscue, farms about 15 acres, rent 9s to 17s 6d, county cess 1s 2d.

Rockmarshall, proprietor [Mr] Fortiscue; farms about 12 acres, rent 30s average, county cess 2s ha'penny; upper part one-third of cess.

Killen, proprietor [Mr] Fortiscue; farms about 10 to 15 acres, rent 30s, county cess 3s 3d.

Analoughan, proprietor [Mr] Fortiscue; farms about 10 to 15 acres, rent 30s, county cess 2s 6d; Mr Moore of Rockmarshall House has a large farm in this townland.

Rampark, proprietor [Mr] Fortiscue; farms about 10 acres, rent 35s, county cess 3s 3d.

Piedmount, proprietor [Mr] Fortiscue; farms about 10 acres, rent 35s, county cess 3s 4d.

Loughanmore, proprietor [Mr] Fortiscue; farms about 12 acres, rent 35s, county cess 3s 4d ha'penny.

Parish of Carlingford, County Louth

Field Note Book [? by G. Conroy]

NATURAL STATE

Name of Parish

Carlingford, *Cathair-linn* "the city or the town on the bay," *Cath-air-linn* "naval engagement." The former is the probable name. The latter takes its name from the engagement of the Irish and Danes in the reign of *Ceallachan MacBuadhachain*, King of Cashel.

PRODUCTIVE ECONOMY

Table of Townlands

[Table contains the following headings: name of townland, size of farms, rent per acre, county cess per acre, name of proprietor].

Greenore: farms 5 to 15 acres, county cess 13d, proprietor Marquis of Anglesea.

Millgrange: farms 5 to 20 acres, rent 2 pounds 9s, county cess 15d to 22d, proprietor Marquis of Anglesea.

Much Grange, farms 2 and a half to 17 acres, rent 40s to 50s, county cess 15d, proprietor Marquis of Anglesea.

Ballitrasna: farms 5 to 24 acres, rent 3 pounds per acre, county cess 14d ha'penny, proprietor [blank] Brabazon Esquire.

Ballenamonymurphy: farms 6 to 24 acres, rent 3 pounds, county cess 14d ha'penny, proprietor [blank] Brabazon Esquire.

Ballagan: farms 4 and a half to 18 acres, rent 2 pounds 13s 4d, county cess 16d farthing, proprietor Marquis of Anglesea.

Whitestown: farms 10 to 30 acres, rent 1 pound 6s, county cess 14d, proprietor [blank] Brabazon Esquire.

Wilvill: farms 5 to 250 acres, rent 1 pound 6s, county cess 15d farthing, proprietor Mr John Gernon.

Templetown: farms 3 to 50 acres, rent 1 pound 10s, county cess 12d ha'penny.

Bellug, no divisions, county cess 12d, proprietor Mr Parks.

Ballenamonybradshaw: farms 3 to 30 acres, rent 2 pounds, county cess 12d, proprietor Mr Parks.

Artholomore, 10 remain only, rent 2 pounds 5s 6d, county cess 14d, proprietor Mr Parks.

Petes: farms 12 to 24 acres.

Old Grange, no divisions, rent 2 pounds 6s, county cess 2 pounds 9s 7d, proprietor Peter Gernon.

Mucklow, 2 divisions, rent 15s, county cess 14d ha'penny.

Monksland, rent 2 pounds 2s, proprietor Richard Vernon Esquire.

Mulabane: farms 7 to 24 acres, rent 2 pounds, county cess 15d ha'penny.]

Notes on Townlands

[Table contains the following headings: name of townland, proprietor, agent, size of farms, length of leases, rent per acre, quality of land, county cess levied at summer assizes 1835].

Ardaghy, proprietor Marquis of Anglesea, agent Colonel Armstrong; farms 1 to 10 acres, leases none, rent 10s to 40s, quality of land bad, county cess 7 pounds 3s.

Artholobeg, proprietor [blank] Hollyoak, non-resident, agent Mr Wright, Dundalk; farms from 6 to 12 acres, leases 1 life, rent 40s, quality of land good; "little hill on high ground," county cess 1 pound 11s 9d.

Artholomore, proprietor Captain Stannus, non-resident, agent Captain Twigg, non-resident; farms: 1 holding, leases forever, rent 8s, quality of land good; "large hill on high ground."

Ballagan, 263 acres, proprietor Marquis of Anglesea, agent Colonel Armstrong; farms 4 to 10 acres, leases none, rent 2 pounds, quality of land middling, county cess 17 pounds 14s 3d ha'penny.

Ballinamoneybradshaw, proprietor [blank] Holyoak, agent Mr Wright, Dundalk; farms 4 to 30 acres, rent 2 pounds, quality of land good, county cess 2 pounds 19s 6d ha'penny.

Ballinamoneymurphy, proprietor H. Brabazon Esquire, agent Mr Wright, Dundalk; farms 10 to 30 acres, leases 3 lives or 31 years, rent 2 to 3 pounds, quality of land good, county cess 4 pounds 10d farthing.

Ballinamarry, proprietor Captain Stannus, non-resident, agent Captain Twigg, non-resident; farms 5 to 20 acres, leases 1 life or 21 years, rent 1 pound 12s, quality of land good.

Ballyonan, proprietor Marquis of Anglesea, agent Colonel Armstrong; farms 1 to 6 acres, leases none, rent 40s, quality of land bad; crops: oats and potatoes; seed to potatoes 32 bushels, crop 180 bushels; seed to oats 3 cwt, crop from 8 to 12 cwt; county cess 7 pounds 3s.

Ballenleskin, proprietor Marquis of Anglesea, agent Colonel Armstrong; farms 1 to 8 acres, leases none, rent 10 to 40s, quality of land bad, county cess 7 pounds 3s.

Ballavarty [insert note: not Ballavarly], proprietor Marquis of Anglesea, agent Colonel Armstrong; farms 10 to 12 acres, leases: 1 lease, rent 1 pound 12s 6d, quality of land good, county cess 7 pounds 1s 5d farthing.

Ballatrasna, proprietor H. Brabazon Esquire, non-resident, agent Mr Wright, Dundalk; farms 3, in content 30 acres; leases none, rent 3 pounds and 3 pounds 5s, quality of land good, county cess 2 pounds 9s 10d.

Baran, proprietor Marquis of Anglesea, agent Colonel Armstrong; farms 1 to 10 acres, leases none, rent 25s to 40s, county cess 7 pounds 3s.

Bena, proprietor Marquis of Anglesea, agent Colonel Armstrong; leases none, farms 8 to 10 acres, rent 1 pound 10s, quality of land middling, county cess 4 pounds 10d farthing.

Bellug, proprietor [blank] Hollyoak, non-resident, agent Mr Wright, Dundalk; farms: 1 holding, 88 acres, leases 3 lives or 31 years, rent 1 pound, quality of land good, county cess 3 pounds 19s 4d.

Castlecarra, proprietors Mr Coulter and Squire Tippin, head proprietor, agent none; farms: 1 holding 105 acres and from 5 to 6 acres, leases none, rent 3 pounds, quality of land good, county cess 14 pounds 2s 10d 3 farthings.

Castletowncooly, proprietors Mr Giles (toties quoties) and Squire Tippin, agent none; farms 4 to 70 acres, leases in perpetuity, rent 7s 6d to 8s, quality of land good, county cess 20 pounds 4s 1d ha'penny.

Carrowkit, proprietor Marquis of Anglesea, agent Colonel Armstrong; farms 4 to 10 acres, leases none, rent 10s to 40s, quality of land bad, county cess 5 pounds 10s 2d.

Carnamucklagh, proprietor Marquis of Anglesea, agent Colonel Armstrong; farms 4 to 10 acres, leases none, rent 10s to 40s, quality of land bad, county cess 7 pounds 3s.

Commons Middle, plots of ground 1 to 3 acres, no county cess.

Commons North, county cess 5 pounds 11s 8d.

Commons South, county cess 4 pounds 10s 10d.

In North and South Commons rent 20s to Widow Goodricke.

Drummullough, proprietor Marquis of Anglesea, agent Colonel Armstrong; farms 1 to 10 acres, leases none, rent 10s to 40s, quality of land bad, county cess 7 pounds 3s.

Earls Quarter, proprietor Squire Tippin, agent Graham Johnston Esquire, non-resident; farms 4 to 5 acres, rent 1 pound, quality of land good, county cess 2 pounds 6d.

Galtrim's Land, proprietor [blank] Hollyoak, non-resident, agent Mr Wright, Dundalk; farms 5 to 20 acres, leases 3 lives, rent 2 pounds, quality of land good, county cess 3 pounds 11s 5d.

Greenore, proprietor Marquis of Anglesea, agent Colonel Armstrong; farms 20 to 100 acres, leases none, rent: held by the lump, quality of land middling.

Glenmore, proprietor Marquis of Anglesea, agent Colonel Armstrong; farms 8 to 15 acres, leases none, rent 15s to 1 pound, quality of land bad, county cess 26 pounds 18s 11d.

Insh Grange, proprietor Marquis of Anglesea, agent Colonel Armstrong; farms 4 to 10 acres, leases none, rent 2 pounds, [quality of land] good, mountain excepted, county cess 10 pounds 11s 6d.

Knocknagoran, proprietor Marquis of Anglesea, agent Colonel Armstrong; farms 2 to 10 acres, leases none, rent 10s to 40s, quality of land middling, county cess 7 pounds 3s.

Lislea, proprietor Marquis of Anglesea, agent Colonel Armstrong; size of farms 1 to 10 acres, leases none, rent 10s to 30s, quality of land bad, county cess 7 pounds 3s.

Liberty of Carlingford, proprietors Lord Claremont 22 acres, Mr Moore 17 acres, North Commons 48 acres, Catherine's Grove 37 acres, Mountain Parks 40 acres, Crossalaney 36 acres, Bellmount 58 acres, Limenenagh 60 acres, Orr and Partners 40 acres, quality of land good, rent 2 to 3 pounds, county cess 64 pounds 13s 7d farthing.

Lower Rath, proprietor [blank] Hollyoak, non-resident, agent Mr Wright, Dundalk; farms 3 to 20 acres, leases 3 lives or 31 years, rent 1 pound 5s to 2 pounds, quality of land good, county cess 4 pounds 19s 2d.

Lugbrisken, proprietor [blank] Hollyoak, non-resident, agent Mr Wright, Dundalk; farms: 2 holdings, leases 1 life or 21 years, rent 2 pounds, quality of land good, county cess 1 pound 4s 9d.

Maddock Land, proprietor Marquis of Anglesea, agent Colonel Armstrong, Portarlington; farms: 1 holding, 1 lease, rent 1 pound 5s, quality of land good, county cess 4 pounds 10d ha'penny.

Maddock's Garden, proprietor Squire Tippin, agent Graham Johnson Esquire; farms 2 to 25 acres, rent 1 pound 5s, quality of land good.

Mill Grange, proprietor Marquis of Anglesea,

Parish of Carlingford

agent Colonel Armstrong; farms 5 to 6 acres, leases none, rent 2 pounds 15s, quality of land good, county cess with Muck Grange.

Monks Land, proprietors Richard De Verdon, Turner and Holyoak, agent none, Mr Wright; farms 8 to 10 acres, leases: 5 perpetuity, rest at will, rent 1 pound 14s 1d ha'penny, quality of land good, county cess 10 pounds 15s 6d ha'penny.

Mountbagnel, proprietor Marquis of Anglesea, agent Colonel Armstrong; farms: 2 holdings, leases 3 lives or 31 years, rent 1 pound and 1 pound 5s, quality of land good, county cess 14 pounds 2s 10d 3 farthings.

Muck Grange, proprietor Marquis of Anglesea, agent Colonel Armstrong; farms 10 to 15 acres, leases none, rent 2 pounds, quality of land good, county cess 28 pounds 5s 9d ha'penny.

Mullabane, proprietor Marquis of Anglesea, agent Colonel Armstrong; farms 4 to 10 acres, leases none, rent 40s, quality of land good, county cess 16 pounds 14s 8d ha'penny.

Muckton, proprietor [blank] Hollyoak, agent Mr Wright, Dundalk; size of farms: 2 holdings, leases 3 lives or 31 years, rent 40s, quality of land middling, county cess 2 pounds 19s 6d.

Mullatee, proprietor Marquis of Anglesea, agent Colonel Armstrong; farms 2 to 10 acres, leases none, rent 40s, quality of land good, county cess included in the Liberties.

Mullhalteen, proprietor [blank] Hollyoak, non-resident, agent Mr Wright, Dundalk; farms 2 to 10 acres, quality of land bad, county cess 4 pounds 14s 3d ha'penny.

Old Grange, proprietor [blank] Hollyoak, non-resident, agent Mr Wright, Dundalk; farms: 1 holding, leases 1 life, rent 2 pounds, quality of land good, county cess 2 pounds 9s 7d.

Petes, proprietor [blank] Hollyoak M.P., agent Mr Wright, Dundalk; farms: 3 holdings, leases 3 lives or 31 years, rent 1 pound 5s, quality of land good, county cess 1 pound 13s 9d.

Rathcor, proprietor Sir F. Hollyoak M.P., agent Mr Wright, Dundalk; farms 4 to 10 acres, leases 1 life, rent 1 pound 16s 11d, quality of land good, county cess 20 pounds 4s 1d ha'penny.

Screen, proprietor Captain Stannus, non-resident, agent Captain Twigg, non-resident; farms: 3 holdings, leases 1 life, quality of land good.

Top Rath, proprietor Sir F. Hollyoak, non-resident, agent Mr Wright, Dundalk; farms 2 to 10 acres, leases 3 lives, county cess 1 pound 4s 9d ha'penny.

Tullaugh, proprietor Marquis of Anglesea, agent Colonel Armstrong; farms 1 to 10 acres, leases none, rent 10s to 40s, quality of land bad, county cess 5 pounds 3s 1d.

Templetown, proprietor F. Hollyoak, agent Mr Wright, Dundalk; farms 7 to 10 acres, leases 3 lives, rent 2 pounds 10s, quality of land good, county cess 12 pounds 17s 10d ha'penny.

Whitestown, proprietor H. Brabazon Esquire, agent Mr Wright, Dundalk; farms 6 to 12 acres, leases 3 lives or 31 years, rent 1 pound 6s, quality of land good, county cess 14 pounds 2s 10d 3 farthings.

Wilvill, proprietor H. Brabazon Esquire, agent none, farms: 1 holding, leases 3 lives or 31 years, rent 26s, quality of land good, county cess 17 pounds 14s 3d ha'penny.

Table of Mills

[Table contains the following headings: name of townland, occupier, diameter and breadth of wheel, type of mill, nature of wheel].

Rathcor, Mr Marks, diameter 13 feet by 2 feet, corn mill, overshot wheel.

Town of Carlingford, Mr McKivitt, diameter 13 feet 10 inches by 2 feet broad, corn mill, overshot wheel.

Ballintiskin, Bernard Rice, diameter 13 feet by 2 feet, corn mill, breast wheel.

Mill Grange, not occupied, 2 mills not in use.

SOCIAL ECONOMY

Dispensary Table

Carlingford, medical practitioner Robert S. Strong M.D., Carlingford dispensary. Very many cases of rheumatism in winter, of a bad description; fever prevalent all seasons but not of a malignant nature.

Table of Schools

[Table contains the following headings: where situated, number of pupils by sex, when established, how supported, remarks].

Rathcor, 25 males, 15 females, total 40; established 1830, payment from the children 2s 6d, 3s 6d and 4s; Arthur McDonald, teacher.

Whitestown, 18 males, 12 females, total 30; established 1825, payment from the children 3s, 4s and 5s; H. O'Rourke, teacher.

Ballagan, 39 males, 17 females, total 56; established 1827, payment from children 3s 3d, 5s 5d; O. Hagan, teacher.

Carlingford, 14 males, 6 females, total 20; established 1828, payment from the children 5s and 6s 6d; James Nugent, teacher.

Carlingford, number not given (forwarded); [blank] Kallowly, [teacher].

Cornamucka, 20 males, 10 females, total 30; established 1832, supported by scholars; Patrick Levans, [teacher].

Drummulligan, 20 males, 10 females, total 40; established 1826, 5 pounds per annum from Marquis of Anglesea and 2d to 3d per week from scholars; John Magery, [teacher].

Knocknagoran, 30 males, 10 females, total 40; established 1796, 3 pounds from Marquis of Anglesea and 2d to 3d per week from the scholars; J. Hollyrood, [teacher].

Carlingford, 12 males, 22 females, total 34; established 1833, paid by the children 3s, 3s 6d and 4s 6d; Maria Savage, [teacher].

Places of Public Worship

[Table contains the following headings: persuasion, average number of attendants (several figures written roughly, so apparent totals only given below), name of clergyman, remarks, where situated].

Protestant: number of attendants: 116; Revd Mr Waring, curate, Mr Forde, rector; town of Carlingford.

Methodist Wesleyan: number of attendants: 43; [service] performed by missionaries once a fortnight; town of Carlingford.

Presbyterian: number of attendants 21; Revd Mr Lunn, town of Carlingford.

Roman Catholic: Grange, number of attendants 350, Revd P. Kearney, parish priest, and Revd Finnagan, church curate; Mullabury or Glenmore, number of attendants 180, Revd P. Kearney, parish priest, and Revd Finnagan, church curate; Carlingford town, number of attendants 350, Revd Holland, parish priest, and Revd McIrath, church curate; Knocknagoran, Omeath, number of attendants 450, Revd Holland, parish priest, and Revd McIrath, church curate.

Parish of Castletown, County Louth

Statistics for Ballyboysbeg and
Ballyboysmore Townlands by
Civil Assistant J. Gilmore

PRODUCTIVE ECONOMY

Table of Townlands

[Table contains the following headings: name of townland, pronunciation, proprietor and agent, size of farms, leases, rent per acre, value to the county cess per acre].

Part of Bellurgan, parish of Castletown, pronunciation Ballurgan; proprietor Francis Tipping Esquire, agent [blank] Pratt Esquire, county Monaghan; farms 4 to 20 acres, tenants at will, rent 52s 6d to 30s, county cess 24 pounds 15s 8d; this part of Bellurgan, parish Castletown, is subject to tithes (at present received by the Revd [blank] Thackery of Dundalk); the other part is tithe free.

Part of Bellurgan, parish of Castletown, pronunciation Ballurgan; proprietor Francis Tipping Esquire, agent [blank] Pratt Esquire, county Monaghan; farms 4 to 20 acres, tenants at will, rent 52s 6d to 20s, county cess 24 pounds 15s 8d; the value to the county cess is taken from Treasury warrants of 1826, which document shows the area of Ballyboysbeg and Ballyboysmore to be 432 Irish acres.

Parish of Aghabog <Aughabog>, County Monaghan

Statistical Report by Lieutenant P. Taylor, June 1835

NATURAL STATE

Name and Derivation

The etymology of the name of this parish appears with every probability to be derived from the words augha "a field" and bohog "a tent," in which divine service was performed in times of merciless persecution and to within the recent period, when a chapel was erected in 1812 and the practice of tent-preaching fell into disuse.

Locality

Situated in nearly the centre of the barony of Dartry in the county of Monaghan, it is bounded on the north by the parish of Killevan, on the south by the parish of Ematris, on the west by the parishes of Currin and Killevan, and on the east by the parish of Kilmore in the barony of Monaghan; and measuring in extreme length and breadth 7 by 4 and one half English miles; contains 11,281 acres of land, 621 of bog and 262 of water, making a grand total of 11,544 acres; and paid in local taxation to the county cess alone in the year 1834 the sum of 572 pounds 1s 5d 3 farthings.

NATURAL FEATURES

Hills

A similar undulatory formation of the surface into hill and vale prevails throughout the whole extent of the parish of Aghabog as was described as forming the western features of the parishes of Currin and Ematris. The very great number of drums indicate clearly that elevated ridges are amongst its peculiar features. Glen and glynch apply to valleys and lis points to forts, and cors to a formation nearly as numerous as the dorsa, but by no means admitting of such exact definition.

The loftiest range within the parish extends through the townlands of Curmoy, Gerran, Carn, Drumhillagh and Calliagh on its northern boundary, standing respectively 614, 622, 677, 696 and 706 feet above the level of the sea; and a parallel range on its southern boundary through Mullaghmore, Corduff, Coranny and Liswiney stands 432, 411, 412 and 448 [feet], and the intermediate points of Feagh, Drumett and Deescort townlands stands respectively 481, 457 and 476 feet above the same level.

Lakes

There are 6 lakes within the parish, all of which are small but highly useful, from their locality, in supplying a constant water power to the mills of the district. Annygoas loch, in the north western extremity of the parish, covers a surface of 39 acres and affords a constant water power to a clothing mill in the townland of Turnary and to a corn mill in the townland of Drummullin.

Drumett loch, measuring in area 28 acres, is also small but supplies a sufficiency of water power to a corn mill in the townland of Aughnacue.

Aughalough is also a very small lake, driving a corn mill in the same townland.

Lismagonaway lake, covering 13 acres, supplies a water power to a corn mill in the parish of Ematris.

Feigh loch, measuring 25 acres, drives a corn mill in the town of Newbliss.

Spring wells abound in every direction, but chalybeates nowhere appear.

Bogs

Happily for the tenantry of Aghabog, turbary is abundant in many localities; and judging from the appearance of many of its sections, presenting a mass of comminuted trunks, stems and branches of trees, and other vegetable substances, a conviction arises that the bog was formed by the accumulation of the debris of trees falling in succession through periods of indefinite duration.

Fir is evidently predominant in the compound, and the appearance of distinct strata, separated by matter more condensed in substance but less combustible, is frequently observable. Several of the sections measure 10 feet deep without arriving at the soil, but when the substratum does appear, it is either a clay of a light colour or the prevailing argillaceous rock of the district.

Woods

The whole surface of the parish is so exceedingly bare and destitute of trees, unless in some very small localities and around the houses and enclosures of holdings of long standing, that no trace whatever of the existence of natural woods, with the exception of the bogs and margins of the lakes, is now to be found; but Killygraghy and Killyleg are both townlands from which it is said thick underwood of thorn and hazel was only removed within the last 40 years.

Climate

The east and north east winds prevailed through a great part of the spring, but the south west wind is much more prevalent throughout the year. The climate is moist and variable, and a very great quantity of rain falls, but is followed by no malaria or epidemic diseases. The medical gentlemen in charge of the parish pronounce the climate salubrious in the highest degree.

NATURAL HISTORY

Botany

The rough and smooth-stalked meadow grass, the meadow foxtail and crested dogstail and ribwort grass are the early spontaneous grasses which most abound. The saintfoin, trifolium and white clover are somewhat later. The recent plantations in the townland of Drumbrain, around the Rectory, and Mr Quin's seat in Rossnalough West comprise several varieties of fir, oak, ash, elms and sycamores.

Zoology

In a parish so purely predial and densely populated, the fields innumerable and imperfectly closed, affording facilities for the destruction of game, the extermination of partridges and hares is almost complete.

Besides the more common species of birds, the merlin and micecatcher are frequently observable, the landrail and quail in the spring, the swallow and swift in the summer. The raven, hooded crow and jackdaw are all very rare, but rooks are innumerable. Herons, waterrails, coots and curlews frequent the lakes and marshes. The woodcock, plover, common and jacksnipe arrive in winter and the starling and lapwing swarm in autumn. The avas, widgeon, teal, black, white and redneck divers approach the lakes and marshes in the evening to feed, and take their early flights to safer pastures by day. The white, blackhead and common gull are observable in the fields and lakes throughout the year.

The otter and badger have become entirely extinct. Pike is abundant and some of great size, weighing from 5 to 5 and 20 lbs. Roach and perch are small. Trout are scarce, weighing from 1 to 5 lbs. Bream are numerous, weight 2 and 3 lbs; and eels are abundant, weighing from 3 to 5 lbs, shad <shade> from 2 to 3 lbs.

MODERN TOPOGRAPHY

Public Buildings

There is neither town nor village, doctor nor lawyer within the boundary of the parish.

The parochial church, a plain rectangular building without a spire, was erected in 1750, upon the summit of [a] gently rising hill in the townland of Gorn, central in position but still very remote from many of its parishioners. It accommodates 400 out of 1,400 parishioners.

The glebe, consisting of 52 acres and the parsonage house, is beautifully situated on the lofty summit of the townland of Aughnacue. The Revd Richard Hood, Dean of Kilmacdoe, is rector, a non-resident, and the Revd Hamilton Hare, curate.

A Presbyterian meeting house was erected in the townland of Aughadrumkeen in the year 1804, containing accommodation for 320 persons; the Revd Richard Ross, the officiating clergyman.

A Roman Catholic chapel was erected in the year 1812 in the townland of Latnamard, accommodating 800 members; the Revd William Harris, rector, and the Revd Hugh McPhillips, parish priest. Previous to this period divine service was performed in the open air.

Gentlemen's Seats

A large quadrangular house with extensive offices recently erected on the summit of the townland Rossnalough West, and purchased by Mr John Quin of Newry, commands a most extensive prospect. The plantations are all recent but promise to add much to the beauty and improvement of the surrounding locality.

In the townland of Drumbrain the Revd Richard Ross has recently erected a very neat small house with young plantations, garden and orchard; and in the immediate vicinity Mr [blank] Phillips' house, Drumbrain. Plantations and grounds are in a very superior state of cultivation.

NATURAL HISTORY

Geology

The geological and mineral character of the rocks which comprise the basis of the very beautiful undulatory formation of the parish of Aghabog differ in no respect whatever from the same formations which everywhere form the substratum in the contiguous parishes of Ematris and Currin. The transition graywacke rock, of a greenish tint, universally pervades the whole parish, the debris of which forming a light productive argillaceous soil.

In a very few localities only does an apparent change in its mineralogical character take place. In the townland of Carn the rock assumes the same reddish colours that are described in the locality of Carnroe in the parish of Currin, but the developments are by no means so extensive.

In 2 exposed sections in the townland of Calliogh, the highest point of elevation within the parish, 706 feet above the level of the sea, the rock rises within an inch of the surface, covered with a thick green sward, and presents 2 sections 20 feet high of a very dark colour, exceedingly brittle and so much fractured and comminuted as to indicate the presence of volcanic agency as the cause of the phenomenon: number 59 and 60 of the geological specimens. The lines of fracture are nearly horizontal and not more than one or two inches apart, and the transverse or perpendicular lines of separation about the same distance, forming the fragments into square and cubical figures, and give to the whole section an appearance of the rock having been at one time stratified.

That its locality was the seat of subterranean, if not volcanic, disturbance is testified by the comminuted state of the whole rock as far as the sections expose it, as well as from the scorched appearance it exhibits. In the townland of Garran <Gerran> several large blocks of trap, locally termed whinstone, are observable, particularly in connection with the cromlechs or giant's graves, but they do not appear in mass in any portion of the parish.

Modern Topography

Communications

The nearest post town is Newbliss for the western division of the parish, and Rockcorry <Rock Curry> for the eastern. The coach road from Dublin to Clones runs north by east through its western section, sending off a branch south west of the village of Drum. The road from Rockcorry through Smithborough <Smythburrow> crosses its western section, sending off 2 branches which communicate with Newbliss. Numerous other crossroads intersect these, some new and others old, opening communications with every market town within the barony.

The new lines of road are tolerably level and in good order. The medium breadth measures about 25 feet and the expense of making and repairing the roads and bridges is paid by the county.

Ancient Topography

Forts

The circular castella of the very ancient aristocracy of the country, so particularly conspicuous throughout the southern parishes of the barony, are equally so here. Lislea, Lisnamusky, Lislamfield and Lismagonaway are forts which have been carefully preserved and attract particular attention; but in addition to these there is scarcely a drum or cor, mullagh or kill within the parish which does not contain one or more of these reliques of antiquity.

Giant's Graves

In the townland of Carn the trigonometrical pile stands within a circle of massive rocks, some of great size, forming the sepulchre of the illustrious Carn Gool. Attached to the circle are 2 alae, representing his arms pendant. His body and lower extremities are marked by 2 rows converging towards the pedes, which are 3 feet broad, 4 across the chest, and the circle 26, the whole length 27 feet. This grave, from its elevated position, is the favourite resort of the people on holiday afternoons.

A somewhat similar monument of antiquity stands conspicuous in the townland of Calliagh, close to the trigonometrical station, measuring 25 feet in length, with pseudo viri guarding in monumental silence the tomb of this illustrious chief.

In the townland of Latnamard 2 enormous boulders forming a portion of a giant's grave still represent the monument of the bard.

In the townland of Garran 2 of these cromlechs still preserve their primitive size and form, with fir breige in close attendance. These graves are only 15 feet long, placed with the lower extremities approaching each other but, unlike Calliagh and Carn, occupying the loftiest position in the parish, they were here very humbly deposited in a bog.

The townland of Garran appears to have been singularly honoured with the presence of this illustrious family. Several localities are pointed to where their Herculean forms repose.

Modern Topography

General Appearance and Scenery

The prevailing feature throughout the whole extent of the parish is characterised by a similar undulating formation of its surface into hill and vale as distinguishes the whole of the surrounding district. In the southern division the undulation is more irregular, on a much lower scale, but very beautiful, the angle of elevation and depression seldom exceeding 5 degrees.

From the centre of the parish the altitude increases towards its northern boundary, presenting a graduated range of parallel heights with intervening valleys, rising in succession and forming the loftiest chain in this division of the country; from the summit of which a prospect embracing the greater portion of the counties of Monaghan, Armagh, Tyrone, Fermanagh, Leitrim and Cavan suddenly unfolds itself, embracing in the foreground the towns of Newbliss, Newtownbutler, Clones, Monaghan and Ballybay, all embosomed in plantations of great extent and beauty.

Social Economy

Local Government

The western division of the parish attends the petty sessions at Clones on every alternate Friday; Colonel Madden, Mr Foster, Mr Smith, the Revd John Wright forming the bench, 3 of whom are generally in attendance. The eastern division attend at Rockcorry on alternate Wednesdays; T.C. Stewart Corry, Richard Mayne and John McEnally Esquires generally presiding.

The character of the parish is stated by these gentlemen to be peaceable and well conducted; opposition to the payment of tithes prevails; and that illicit distillation to a small extent is carried on [in] the autumn and winter.

Dispensaries

There is no dispensary within the parish. The tenantry have the privilege of attending one in Rockcorry and another in Newbliss, and derive very great benefit from these institutions. No epidemic diseases infest the people. Cynanche tonsillaris, catarrhus, asthma and pertussis are the most prevalent complaints. Dr Atkinson of Newbliss and Dr Shannon of Rockcorry both pronounce the parish healthy.

Newbliss dispensary [table contains the following headings: name of complaint, number of patients, number cured, remarks as to how supported].

Cynanche tonsillaris, catarrhus, asthma, pertussis, rubiola, febris, diseases of the skin: average number of patients on the books 170, very few deaths; 88 pounds 15s subscribed by the landed proprietor, ladies and gentlemen of the district, plus 88 pounds 15s paid by the county; medical attendant's salary 60 pounds.

Table of Schools

[Table contains the following headings: name of townland, number of pupils subdivided by religion and sex, remarks as to how supported, when erected].

Feigh (parochial school), Protestants 28, Roman Catholics 4, males 20, females 12, total 32; London Hibernian Society 8 pounds and scholars, established 1815.

Doohatt: Protestants 22, Roman Catholics 5, males 18, females 9, total 27; London Hibernian Society 8 pounds, Mr Pounden 5 pounds, established 1823.

Aughnacue: Protestants 23, Roman Catholics 2, males 21, females 4, total 25; London Hibernian Society 8 pounds and scholars, erected 1826.

Aghabog: Protestants 7, Roman Catholics 24, males 20, females 11, total 31; private school, erected 1825.

Correvan: Protestants 38, Roman Catholics 5, males 23, females 20, total 43; private school, erected 1816.

Drumgarly: Protestants 14, Roman Catholics 28, males 29, females 13, total 42; National Board of Education 10 pounds, erected 1830.

Latnamard: Roman Catholics 28, males 21, females 7, total 28; National Board of Education 10 pounds, erected 1831.

Lismagonaway: Protestants 8, Roman Catholics 18, males 18, females 8, total 26; National Board of Education 10 pounds, erected 1832.

The parish is well supplied with schools, the total number amounting to 8. The usual branches of education are reading, writing, arithmetic and book-keeping. Several of the schools are in part supported by the London Hibernian Society and National Board of Education, and by the quarterly salary of the pupils: reading 1s per quarter, reading and writing 2s per quarter, and the whole course of education 3s per quarter.

Vast improvement has been effected on the morals and habits of the rising generation through the instrumentality of these schools. A superior class of teachers with an increase of salary would still advance this desirable object much.

Poor

The poor are assisted by church collections on the sabbath day and a donation of 10 pounds by Mr Woodwright, granted as an annual legacy. The average number upon the poor list amounts to 20 and the collections to about 14 pounds a year.

Religion

The grand total of the last census taken in the year 1831 was as follows: Roman Catholics 4,121, High Church 1,567, Seceders 1,400, Presbyterians 353, Moravians 1, total 7,442. The tithes were compounded in 1832 for 350 pounds a year, but much opposition has since been made to their payment. The Dissenting clergyman, the Revd Richard Ross, receives the regium donum, 50 pounds a year, and 40 pounds from his congregation. The Roman Catholic clergymen are paid by the people.

Habits of the People

The habitations of the peasantry are formed of a combination of clay and straw. These materials well mixed together, and made into walls 2 feet thick, roughcast and well thatched, last a great length of time. The whole building when completed costs about 10 pounds, when of a superior description, but the expense of building the general class of cabins <cabans> does not amount to more than 3 pounds, and these very seldom stand above 15 or 20 years.

In correspondence with the general state of the very humble domiciles of the poor, for there is no middle class, the whole population, whether cottier or farmer, being literally "the poor," the interior accommodations, furniture, utensils are all of very rude and primitive construction.

6 may be named as the usual number of a family, and the longevity of the senior members is in many instances remarkable, but as no registries were kept till within a recent period, numbers of these cases appear questionable. Grey frieze cloth at 3s per yard and corduroy at 2s per yard constitute the male attire, and house-spun woollens and coarse linens, with fancy cottons, the female.

The Irish language is much more common in the north eastern division of the parish than English, and in all their domestic intercourse the latter is never heard. Many legends of these giants, fir bregi, and supernatural personages amuse the old and interest the younger members of the community, and the extent of their credulity in these traditions is astonishing. Very few, however, could with any propriety be recorded.

The attendance at fairs is their favourite amusement which, together with religious and civil holidays, consume a vast portion of their time. McMahons, McPhillips, McFarrell, Carters, Boylens and Clarkins are very common names.

Emigration

Several families from this parish emigrated last year to the Canadas and several others followed this spring. The want of resources alone prevents vast numbers from following their examples. None depart from thence to the English harvest.

PRODUCTIVE ECONOMY

Manufactures

In a parish so purely agricultural as Aghabog, the attention of the people has not been so much directed to the manufacturing of coarse linen as in the parishes immediately around. A very small trade, however, is carried on, the sale of which is effected on the market and fair days of Newbliss, Rockcorry and Monaghan.

Fairs and Markets

The nearest fair and market for the western division of the parish is held in Newbliss on the first Wednesday of every month, the market every Saturday; and in Rockcorry and Monaghan for the eastern division, the fair of the former on the last Wednesday of every month and market every Wednesday, and the fair of the latter on the first Monday of every month and the market every Monday. The breeds of cattle, pigs and other marketable commodities, together with their prices, vary in no respect from the details given under the same head in the parishes of Ematris and Currin.

Rural Economy

A rich argillaceous alluvial soil, the decomposition of the incumbent rocks which pervade not only every portion of the parish but a district of vast extent around, render this and adjoining parishes peculiarly adapted for agriculture. The natural division of its surface into hill and vale is another advantage of considerable importance in facilitating drainage, which upon a less undulating surface and the same soil would be found impracticable.

Parish of Aghabog

The great land proprietors are the Honourable R. Westenra, Lord Cremorne, Mr Quin, Dr Kerr and Mr T. Coote, none of whom, nor their agents, have seats within the parish, with the exception of Mr Quin.

Farms and Rents

The average size of the farms is given as 8 acres. When they do exceed 10 they are generally subdivided betwixt the occupying tenant and some near relative, but a very great number are as low as 3 and 4 acres. The majority of the farms are held directly from the landlords, and many of these as tenants at will and on leases of 3 lives or 31 years, at a rent averaging from 20s to 30s per acre Irish measure.

There is very little variety in the quality of the soil, the substratum rising occasionally to the surface, as in the townland of Carn, rendering it light and stony, but the difference of rent in these localities is very trifling if any.

Produce and Husbandry

Potatoes, oats and flax are the chief produce. Wheat and barley after the potato crop is occasionally, but very seldom, observable. Turnips, clover or mangel-wurzel <mangle worcil> are nowhere cultivated. The proportions of seed and produce of potatoes and the different kinds of grain, and their prices, are precisely the same as reported in the parish of Currin, and nearly the whole produce in like manner is exported to England.

County cess and tithe form the local taxation, the former averaging about 1s 2d per acre. To the payment of the latter, much opposition has been made for several years. The potato crop is the only one manured, and more so by the burning of the soil than by any other process.

The implements of husbandry are of rude construction. The wooden plough and a large bunch of thorns for harrows are in general use. Much of the grain is carried to market on the old Irish car and the slide is also still retained.

Proportions of seed to produce. [Table contains the following headings: name of crop, quantity of seed and produce per acre, market price].

Potatoes: 60 stone per acre, produce 1,250 stone per acre, 1d ha'penny to 3d ha'penny per stone.

Oats: 16 stones per acre, produce 180 stones per acre, 6d to 11d ha'penny per stone.

Wheat: 16 stones per acre, produce 240 stones per acre, 19s to 21s per barrel.

Barley: 16 stones per acre, produce 240 stones, 10d to 1s per barrel.

Flax: 12 pecks per acre, 2 pounds 8s per acre, produce 36 stones of lint, 12s per stone.

Hay varies from 1s to 3s 6d a cart throughout the year.

Grazing

There are no grazing farms within the parish. The whole of its soil is devoted to agriculture. There are very few servants within the parish. Female servants receive from 2 to 4 pounds a year, exclusive of board and lodging, male servants from 4 to 6 pounds. Day labourers receive 10d in summer and 8d per day in winter.

Cattle

A very inferior class of cattle is employed throughout the parish, horses and cows of a small and very degenerate breed. The low, short-eared and small-headed Dutch breed of pigs is much esteemed. Jobbers in pork frequent every fair, purchasing for the English market. The common kinds of poultry are reared and brought to market. Young turkeys and geese sell for 10d each, fowls and ducks from 14d to 16d a pair, and chickens from 3s to 4s a dozen.

Uses made of the Bogs

The bogs are wholly used as fuel and charcoal for the forges. The superabundance of turf in some localities affords a very salutary supply to many townlands in the adjoining parish of Ematris. Much is prepared and sold in Newbliss at moderate prices, from 18d to 2s for a cart-load. No mineral deposits have ever been discovered. The embedded firs, when highly charged with turpentine, are split into bog-wood, serving the valuable purposes of candle and coal.

Planting

There are no mature plantations within the parish. The very small localities of Rossnalough West, the glebe and on the townland of Drumbrain are the only appearances and those of recent formation.

SOCIAL AND PRODUCTIVE ECONOMY

Ecclesiastical Summary

[Table] Name Aghabog, diocese Clogher, province Ulster, a rectory, no union; patron the bishop of the diocese, incumbent Revd Richard

Hood; extent of glebe 52 acres, tithes compounded for 350 pounds a year.

General Remarks

Nearly the whole surface of the parish presents a southern aspect, securing it effectively from the injurious influences of the nipping northerly winds. The climate is mild and highly salubrious. Abundance of water power is easily available.

Fuel is plenty in many, and accessible in every, section and its naturally productive argillaceous soil presents to the enterprising and intelligent agriculturist a parish in possession of resources, the full development of which could not fail to be productive of unbounded wealth and vast natural prosperity.

But, doomed to the same blasting influences which everywhere exhausts and impoverishes its soil, and hangs suspended as a curse over the moral and intellectual faculties of the country, the larger portion of its area produces food for neither man nor beast, and the lesser half is scarcely sufficient to protract the existence of its wretched inhabitants. [Signed] P. Taylor, Lieutenant 69th Regiment, 20th June 1835.

Parish of Aughnamullen, County Monaghan

Statistical Report by Lieutenant John Chaytor, December 1835

NATURAL STATE

Name

The name of this parish is derived from a ford across a small stream next to which formerly stood a mill. The ford is at present pointed out by the inhabitants, but a small bridge supersedes the necessity of fording. The original was *Ath-na-muillean*, literally "ford of the mills," but it has been corrupted to Aughnamullen, which is the orthography commonly used by the inhabitants.

In *Carlisle's Topographical dictionary*, the *Irish ecclesiastical register*, 1824, Beaufort's map, and in Sir C. Coote's *Statistical survey* it is written Aghnamullen, and in McCrea's barony map, Aghnemullen. It is usually pronounced Annamullen.

Locality

It is situated in the south west part of the barony of Cremorne, county of Monaghan, bounded on the north by the parishes of Tullycorbet and Ballybay, on the east by Ballybay, Clontibret and Donaghmoyne, south by Donaghmoyne, Magheross, Killan and Knockbride, and on the west by Drumgoon and Ematris. It extends east and west 11 and three-quarter miles and greatest breadth is 6 and a quarter miles, and contains [blank] acres, of which [blank] are cultivated, [insert note: to be supplied from the register], 2,172 acres are uncultivated and 1,704 are waste; the average valuation to the county cess 1,500 pounds per annum.

NATURAL FEATURES

Hills

The principal hill, situated nearly in the centre of the parish, is called Bonanimma. The summit is covered with heather and is 886 feet above the level of the sea. In connection with this there is a range of hills extending westwards 6 miles to the parish boundary, the heights of which are as follows: Carrigatee, 884 feet, Fossey, 779 feet, Brackley, 754 feet, Tullynahuinna, 741 feet, Lurgangreen, 730 feet and Carysduff 78 feet.

Westward from Bonnanima are numerous detached hills, nearly of the same height and form, and towards the north are similar hills decreasing in height as they approach the town of Ballybay. In the southern part of the parish the country is undulating.

Lakes

In the interior of the parish there are the following lakes: Lough Eagish, situated in the eastern part, is an irregular sheet of water 1 and a quarter miles long and 292 and a half acres in area. It contains some very small islands and is 532 feet above the level of the sea, and discharges its water by a river at the southern extremity.

Lough Earan, on the boundary of the townlands of Latten, Lisdrumalane, Drumcurrian and Mahon, is 3,600 feet long and 1,450 feet broad, covering 144 and a half acres. It served formerly as a reservoir for Lisnagalliagh bleaching mills. Its altitude above the sea is [insert note: to be supplied from plan].

Creeve lakes, 2 in number, are connected by a small stream 200 feet in length. The smallest, which is the most western, is 1,400 feet long and averages 600 feet in width. It is 620 feet above the level of the sea. The other is 2,700 feet long and 1,000 feet in width, and empties itself at the north west extremity by a stream which has a sluice, so that the water is accumulated in winter and may be let off in summer to supply the Creeve bleaching mills.

Mullinary lough, situated on the boundary of the townlands Anny, Mullinary Glebe and Derryrusk, is 2,200 feet long and averages 1,450 feet in width. It contains 1 island and is 258 feet above the level of the sea.

Corkeeran lough, situated a quarter of a mile west of Mullinary lough, with which it is connected by a small stream, is 34 acres in area and 257 feet above the sea. This is the same height as the Ballybay river.

Lough Morien, which is said to give name to the barony, is situated on the boundary of Lettercrum, Lurgahamla, Aughamakirlin and Drumillard. It is nearly circular and 1,300 feet in diameter. It serves for a reservoir for the mills of Mr Jackson of Royduff.

Corsilligo lough in western part of the parish is 24 and a half acres in area and empties itself eastwards.

Lough Bawn, situated in the southern part of the parish, is 100 acres in extent, consisting of 3 arms, and is quite narrow in the centre. The shores are ornamented with the plantations of Lough Bawn demesne, and the lough contains 2 small islands which are also planted. The altitude is 350 feet above the sea.

In connection with this lough, and situated west of it, are the following: Black lough, area 63 and a quarter, Derrygooney lake, area 78 and three-quarters, and Lacken lough 42 and a quarter acres; and towards the east Lough Bawn is connected with Loughnakilloo Bawn and Ballynean lough, which latter are on the boundary of the parish.

Besides these loughs described, in the interior of the parish there are 24, of very little importance, and on the boundary of the parish with Donaghmoyne there are 2, with Magheross parish there are 3, with Drumgoon 4 and with Ematris 2.

Rivers

The Ballybay river (see Ballybay Memoir) enters the parish at the northern part and runs nearly south west. Three-quarters of a mile from this point it forms a considerable but irregular lake, 1 and a half miles long and varying in breadth from 300 to 1,200 feet. The river leaves the south west extremity of this lake, and three-quarters of a mile from it again opens, forming a small lake which is 700 feet average wide and a quarter of a mile long. The river continues running south west from this lake a quarter of a mile, when it turns nearly north and divides the counties of Cavan and Monaghan.

The parish is well supplied with water, both from springs and rivulets.

Bogs

Lisduff bog, situated in the eastern part of the parish, is 180 acres in extent. In the townlands of Mahon, Minniagh and Mountain Lodge Demesne there are considerable portions of bog. The largest is 120 acres, having a small lake near its centre called Lough Clegg. On the boundary of Carrickatee and Ullienagh is a bog of 75 acres, and on the mearing of Carrickatee and Carrickareilty one of 70 acres. Also on the boundary of this latter townland in the Kilkit there is a bog of 40 acres.

Besides the above, there are numerous patches scattered throughout the parish, affording [a] convenient and ample supply of fuel to the inhabitants. Timber occurs in nearly all these bogs, generally of oak, sally and fir. They are found lying indiscriminately, some whole and others with the roots broken off. The subsoil is either a hard red sand, called by the inhabitants "till," a white gritty clay or a deep blue clay. Some of the bogs are 15 feet deep.

Woods

The plantations of the parish, which are all ornamental, are of the fir and forest tribes, and apparently are thriving.

NATURAL HISTORY

Zoology

The lakes abound in fish of the following kinds, viz. trout, pike, perch, roach, bream and eel. Hares, rabbits and weasels are very general; foxes and badgers are occasionally met with. Partridge and snipe are abundant, as also wild ducks, and the lapwing is a constant visitor to the bogs.

MODERN TOPOGRAPHY

Towns: Ballytrain

The only collection of houses in the parish resembling a town is Ballytrain. Ballytrain is said to have derived its name from Ballagh-train, which is translated by the inhabitants "way to the house of the man of strength," train signifying "pith" or "cause of strength." [Insert note: Tradition has it that a man of extraordinary strength formerly lived in this neighbourhood].

McCrea, in his county map, spells it Ballytrean, but Ballytrain is the orthography commonly used by the inhabitants. It is situated in the southern part of the parish, on the old road between Ballybay and Carrickmacross, and the Cootehill and Dundalk road passes near its northern extremity.

It is a miserable village, with only 1 house of 2-storeys. The remainder are cottages of the poorest description. A small house is now in progress, intended to serve as a chapel and school, raised by subscription of the inhabitants.

8 fairs are held annually in Ballytrain, viz. on the 1st February, 17th March, 1st May, 11th June, 1st August, 29th September, 1st November and 23rd December. The principal business transacted is in the sale and purchase of yarns, black cattle, horses, pigs and sheep. No tolls have been exacted at these fairs for the last 20 years.

Parish of Aughnamullen

Public Buildings

The public buildings of the parish are 2 churches, 2 Presbyterian meeting houses and 4 chapels.

The parish church in the townland of Mullmore is a plain stone building with a tower but no spire. It contains accommodation for 350 persons. The date of its erection is not known, but a monument built in the south wall of the church is dated 1689.

Church in Crossduff, a chapel of ease for the parish, is a neat building with a tower; was erected in 1829, cost about 800 pounds, and contains accommodation for 200 persons.

Creeve meeting house, a plain building with slated roof, was erected by subscription 30 years ago, and contains accommodation for 450 persons.

Corlea meeting house is a small building capable of accommodating only 200 persons.

Roman Catholic chapel in Lisdrumclave, commonly called Latten chapel (because the old chapel formerly stood in the adjacent townland Latten), is a capacious building with galleries. It was built in 1822 and cost about 800 pounds.

Drumcoonien chapel is a large stone building erected in 1833. It is not yet completed and cost up to the present date 640 pounds; it is calculated to hold 800 persons.

Annaghhaghey chapel contains accommodation for 600 persons and Royduff chapel is capable of accommodating the same number. They are both plain buildings with slated roofs.

Gentlemen's Seats

Lough Bawn, in the southern part of the parish, the residence of W.B. Tenison Esquire, is a neat building of 2-storeys and a basement. It was built 20 years ago by the present proprietor, who laid out and planted the whole of the demesne which is extensive and in a flourishing condition. The house is situated on a gentle eminence commanding a view of Lough Bawn, the shores of which are interspersed with plantations and pasture-land in excellent order.

Mountain Lodge, the residence of Colonel Kerr, is situated in the south west part of the parish near the Cootehill and Dundalk roads. [Insert note: The situation is by no means pleasing and it is nearly surrounded by bogs. The house is an old-fashioned low building of 2-storeys with offices attached. The plantations are, for the most part, young trees laid down by the present proprietor].

Bushford House, in the townland of Closhaghbeg, the residence of J. Thompson Esquire, is an old-fashioned building of 2-storeys situated near the Ballybay river.

Aughnamullen House, in the townland of Aughnamullen, is the residence of Thomas Bunker Esquire. It is a neat house of modern architecture.

In addition to the above are the following: the Glebe House in the townland of Mullinary; Carnareagh House, the residence of James Cunningham Esquire; Cremorne Green, the residence of John Jackson Esquire; Creeve House in the townland of the same name, occupied by [blank] Cunningham Esquire. These last 3 houses, which are adjacent to each other, are well surrounded by plantations and bleaching greens, and bear the appearance of an extensive demesne.

Drumfolmas is a neat house of 2-storeys built by Mr John Cunningham, the proprietor of an extensive corn mill situated near it.

In Shantonagh there is a neat house at present occupied by the Revd Mr Mayne, one of the curates of the parish.

In the townland of Tooay there is a good house, the residence of Mrs Forbes.

Farmhill, the residence of R. Robinson Esquire, is situated in the townland of Royduff.

In Laragh is the residence of Mrs Davidson, a modern house of 2-storeys with plantations and bleaching greens around it.

Lisnalony Cottage, the residence of Mr W. Brunker, and Tattybrack Cottage, of the Revd Mr Brennan, are situated near each other on a hill above the Cootehill and Ballybay roads.

In Royduff townland there is a neat cottage the residence of Mr Jackson, the proprietor of the corn mill adjacent.

Fair View, the residence of the Revd Mr Maxwell, in the townland of Corraskea, is a neat cottage with offices attached.

In the townland of Corfad there is a neat house of 2-storeys built in 1828 by the present occupant, Mr James McCullagh.

Bleaching Greens

The bleaching green of the Messrs Cunningham in the townland of Creeve, and of Mr Davidson of Laragh are the only ones remaining of the many which formerly existed in this parish.

Creeve green is now very considerably reduced. It was originally established by Mr Jackson about 80 years ago. There are still standing a number of good mills of every description requisite for bleaching, which are all supplied by the Creeve lakes. The greater part of these buildings are 3-storeys high, the upper storeys being used as storerooms and drying lofts, and the lower storeys for the machinery such as wash mills and beetling mills.

There are 8 mills in the townland of Creeve employed for this bleach green, besides the occasional employment of 2 others, 1 in the townland of Drumfoldra and another in Cumry, both used as beetling mills, overshot wheels, diameter 16 feet, 4 feet broad. The extent of ground used at present as bleaching green is 50 acres.

Laragh bleaching green, the property of Mr Davidson, is situated in the south east part of the parish and contains wash and beetling mills supplied by a stream from Lough Eagish. The diameter of the mill wheels are each [blank], breadth [blank], breast wheels.

A small beetling mill which is occasionally used for this bleaching green is situated in the townland of Corncarrow. It is attached to a small spinning factory and is wrought by a wheel 24 feet in diameter.

Besides these, there was formerly a bleaching green of 57 acres extent called Cremorne green situated in the townlands Edenforan and Corwilliam, though it has not been used for some time. The mill and machinery are still standing and one of the mills at present used as a scutching mill.

In the townland of Lisnagalliagh there was formerly a considerable bleaching green; the buildings and machinery are now in a dilapidated state. The water was led from Lough Erean by a race 1 mile in length.

Another bleaching green was situated in the townland of Aughnamullen, but it is some time since it was used. No part of the mills now exist.

Mr Robinson's bleaching green in Royduff has been discontinued for 10 years. The mills are at present fitting up for corn mills.

Mr Forbes' bleaching green and mills in Tooay has also been discontinued for some time past.

Mills

Corn mill in Drumfoldra townland, the property of John Cunningham Esquire, is 4-storeys high and fitted up with machinery of the very best description. It has a breast wheel 22 feet in diameter and 4 and a half broad, and has 2 pairs of cleaning fans and 2 kilns attached to the mill.

Mr Cunningham is at present fitting up a new flour mill within a short distance of the corn mill. The wheel is 17 feet in diameter and 4 and a half feet in breadth, and worked by the stream which flows from Creeve lough. The building, which is complete, is 5-storeys high.

A flax and corn mill in the townland of Cordevlish, called the Peat Hole mill in consequence of being supplied from a lake in a bog, [insert marginal note: which supply is but scanty]. The wheel, which works both the flax and corn mill, is a breast wheel 14 feet in diameter and 4 and a half feet broad. The building is small and has a thatched roof.

Corfad flax and corn mill, the property of Mr McCullagh, is a low range of stone building, slated roof. The corn mill wheel is 12 feet diameter and 4 feet broad; that of the flax mill is 12 feet in diameter and 2 and a half broad, both breast wheels.

Derryrusk flax mill has a breast wheel 12 feet in diameter and 2 and half feet broad.

Aughnamullen corn mill, a breast wheel 12 and a half feet in diameter and 2 and a half feet broad.

Annaghveyarig corn mill is a good building with slated roof, but the machinery is not yet fitted up.

Edenbrone tuck mill: the building is a mere cabin in a ruinous state and the machinery also in bad order. The wheel is overshot, 13 feet in diameter and 2 feet broad. It has not been worked for the last 2 years.

Corn mill in Grigorna: the building is a good cottage with thatched roof; it has a breast wheel 12 feet in diameter and 2 and a half feet broad.

Lisnalong corn mill has a breast wheel 11 feet diameter and 2 and a half feet broad.

Tieveleney corn mill: the building, a cottage, is in a bad order. It has a breast wheel 10 feet diameter and 2 and a third feet broad.

Cooas corn mill has an overshot wheel, diameter of which is 18 feet and breadth 2 and a half feet.

Derrygooney mills, formerly mills for a bleaching green, are now used as corn mills. They are well supplied with water by a stream from Lough Eagish.

The Rea corn mill in the townland of Royduff is a building of 3-storeys, [insert marginal note: the property of Mr Jackson]. The wheel, a breast wheel, is 18 feet in diameter and 5 feet broad, and has a good supply of water from Lough Morien.

There is also another mill in the same townland, the property of Mr Robinson. This was formerly a bleaching mill but is now fitting up as a corn mill; diameter of wheel 12 feet, breadth 4 and a half.

A mill in Tullyglish, part of Mr Forbes' old bleaching mill, and the beetling mill are yet standing but in a ruinous state. The wash mill is occasionally used by Mr Forbes at present.

Mr Oliver's corn and flax mill in Laragh townland is supplied by the stream from Lough Eagish. It is a long range of 2-storeys high with slated roof.

Manufactories

Mr Davidson of Laragh has a manufactory for the spinning of linen yarn and weaving. The buildings are separate and situated near the southern extremity of Lough Eagish, in the townland of Corweana. The machinery of the spinning factory is worked by a water wheel, which also works a beetling engine for the bleaching green. The house occupied by weavers is small and of 2-storeys. All the looms are worked by the hand.

Communications

The main roads from Ballybay to Clones, Cootehill, Carrickmacross and Shercock pass through the parish, measuring in all 26 and a half miles. They have within the last few years undergone considerable improvements and are now, for the most part, in good order. Cross and by-roads are numerous and in tolerable order.

The only bridges of any importance are Ballycoghill and Ballynascarvy, on by-roads leading to Rockcorry and both over the Ballybay river. The former is of 3 and the latter of 4 arches. They are old and narrow, but the date of erection is not known.

There is a bridge of 6 small arches over the junction of 2 loughs a short distance west of Ballytrain, and another small bridge, called the Vicar's bridge, in the townland of Derrygooney, over the stream running from Lough Eagish. The Ballybay river, during the summer seasons, is fordable in many places.

ANCIENT TOPOGRAPHY

Priory

In the townland of Littuifaskey are the ruins of what is said to have been a priory of the Franciscan order. The side walls, which are 50 feet long, now stand 12 feet high and the gables are 20 feet high and 20 feet wide. There are 3 windows: one, situated in the eastern gable, is 7 feet by 3 feet; another, in the western gable, 2 and a half feet by 1 foot; and a third, in the south east corner, which is roughly arched, is 6 and a half feet high and 1 and a half feet wide. The doorway appears to have been about the centre of the south side wall, but at present it is altogether destroyed.

A small graveyard surrounds these ruins and is still used by the inhabitants as a burial place. There are no stones of any antiquity to be found in it.

Graveyards

In the townland of Anny may yet be traced part of the fences of an old graveyard which is now under cultivation. The oldest inhabitants in the vicinity do not remember to have seen a body interred in it, but the person who farms it states that he found numerous graves and headstones. One of these stones was removed to Bushford, the residence of Mr Thompson, and is at present at the door of his kitchen. It is a rough flag 3 feet by 1 foot 10 inches, with a sunken cross cut upon it.

Tradition states that another graveyard was situated in the townland of Aughnaskew, on the farm at present held by John Dancey, but no trace at present exists of it.

In the townland of Drumconnen there is a trace of a graveyard.

Giant's grave in Lisnadara

Pagan Antiquities

In the townland of Lisnadonogh (southern part of the parish) is situated a giant's grave. This is formed by 2 rows of stones placed upon their ends in the ground 4 feet apart and projecting from the surface of the ground 4 and a half feet.

Plan of the giant's grave, townland Lisnadara [main dimensions 9 feet wide, 24 feet long]; sketch from the west end at A; sketch from the north side at B, with dimensions] by R. Stotherd, Lieutenant Royal Engineers, in 1835.

The parish contains 93 old circular forts, generally termed Danish forts.

MODERN TOPOGRAPHY

General Appearance

The general appearance of this parish is that of a poor and badly cultivated country, but in the vicinity of Creeve and the residences of the Misters Forbes, Maine and Davidson the bleaching greens, with the plantations and numerous mills, form a pleasing contrast; and in the southern part of the parish the chain of lakes, demesne and plantations surrounding Mr Tenison's residence diversify the scenery.

SOCIAL ECONOMY

Local Government

The only magistrates in the parish are Colonel Kerr and Mr Tenison; and the police force in Ballytrain, which consists of a constable and 4 subconstables, is under the direction of the chief constable in Castleblayney. No petty sessions are held in the parish: all cases are referred either to Ballybay, Carrickmacross or Castleblayney.

No dispensary in the parish.

Schools

The various schools now established throughout the country have certainly tended to improvements in the morals of the people. The inhabitants appear anxious for the instruction of their children.

Poor

There is no regular provision for the poor of the parish, who obtain a liberal support by travelling from house to house. It is customary among the better class of inhabitants to appoint one day in the week on which the paupers in the neighbourhood assemble and receive a gratuity. The usual collection is made in the 2 churches during divine service.

Religion

There are 3 denominations, viz. the Established Church, Presbyterian and Roman Catholic, in the following proportions, 1 to 2 and 6.

Habits of the People

Same as Ballybay parish. An instance of longevity at present exists in this parish in the person of George Harper of Mullynagon, who has attained the age of 105 years, and was able a short time ago to walk from his house to Rockcorry, a distance of 2 miles. His memory appears good but his sight and hearing imperfect. As he is the life of a valuable lease where he resides, great attention is paid to his health and comfort.

PRODUCTIVE ECONOMY

Manufacturing

The commercial produce of this parish is for the most part in the hands of the bleachers and corn merchants, who prepare much for the English market. The various small corn mills prepare meal for human consumption or for the markets in the vicinity, and charge in kind usually one-fortieth of the quantity ground, but in some cases as high as one-twenty-eighth.

The flax mills commonly dress the flax for the hackler at the rate of from 9d to 1s per stone, one-half of which is given to the person who works at the scutching handles and the other half goes to the proprietor of the mill who pays all assistants, except 1 at the rollers who is in all cases found by the owner of the flax.

The manufactory of Mr Davidson of Laragh for linen cloth has in it 30 frames for spinning worked by a water wheel and attended by girls. He has about 600 looms which employ as many men. Spinning yarn is the constant occupation of the greater part of the females, but weaving is only resorted to by the men at such seasons as agriculture cannot be followed. A weaver can on an average weave a piece 52 yards in length in 15 days, for which he gets 6s and board and lodgings.

Mr Forbes of Tooay weaves a small quantity of union cloth. The cotton is obtained either from England or Belfast, and the linen for the most part in the county of Cavan. In weaving a piece of 70 yards seven-eighths wide, the weaver gets 5s 6d, and for a piece three-quarters wide, 4s 6d. The

Parish of Aughnamullen

warp is cotton and weft linen. For bleaching such a piece of linen the cost is 1d farthing per yard.

Merchants who prepare meal for the English markets purchase corn in the adjacent markets. At Mr Cunningham's mill, Drumfoldra, 3 men are constantly employed. One receives a salary of 40 pounds per annum and his assistants 1s per diem each. There are also 2 kiln men employed who receive 1s per diem. The mill would grind 120 barrels [insert marginal note: 14 stones each] of oats per diem, but is seldom employed to this extent. 5,000 bags of meal, each 2 cwt, were exported to England last year.

Fairs and Markets

No fairs or markets are held in the parish except those already mentioned with Ballytrain.

Rural Economy

The parish of Aughnamullen belongs to numerous proprietors (see Table of Townlands). Colonel Kerr of Mountain Lodge resides and Mr Tenison is an occasional resident. All the other proprietors and their agents are non-residents.

The farms in the parish are 1,283 under 10 acres, 701 above 10 acres, 125 above 20 acres, 28 above 50 acres and 6 above 100 acres. Of these, by far the greater part are held without leases. The leases granted are within 21 years or a life. The average rent of the best land is 1 pound 15s per acre, for middling 1 pound 5s to 1 pound 7s, and the worst from 15s to 1 pound, always paid in money.

The manures generally used are farmyard manure and lime. The latter is obtained from Carrickmacross and Clones, distant 8 miles from the centre of the parish.

Uses made of the Bogs

The bogs are used wholly as fuel and afford sufficient for the inhabitants and supply the neighbouring towns also. Turf is never made into charcoal for the use of the smithies, coal being readily obtained from Dundalk or Newry.

Planting

The only plantations in the parish are in the demesnes and vicinity of [blank]; appear in a thriving state. Oak and elms are scarce. There is no nursery in the parish for the growth of young trees.

General Remarks

The soil of this parish, though for the most part poor, is capable of great improvement. The great impediment is the difficulty of procuring manures; lime, which is most required, is distant. The roads are good and convenient, but the smallness of the farms, and consequent poverty of the farmers, do not allow them the means of transporting it. Cultivation is carried to the highest point of the parish. [Signed] John Chaytor, Lieutenant Royal Engineers, 17th December 1835.

DIVISIONS

Table of Townlands

[Table contains the following headings: name of townland, proprietor, agent].

Anny, R. Thomson, agent none.

Annaghaghey, C.A. Leslie Esquire.

Annaghveyarig, H. Grattan Esquire, agent none.

Aughakista, [blank] Montgomery Esquire, [agent] R. Scott, Newtownbutler.

Aughamakerlin, [blank] Rothwell, [blank] Tilly, Dublin.

Aughnamullen, [blank] Johnson Esquire, R. Thomson, Bashford [Bushford].

Aughnaskew, [blank] Lucas Esquire, J. Rose, Monaghan.

Baroghy, [blank] Hogshaw, agent none.

Beagh, [blank] Rothwell, [blank] Tilly.

Binmore, D.A. Hamilton, agent none.

Bowelk, J. Brien Esquire, R. Philips, Cootehill.

Brackley, [blank] Montgomery, R. Scott, Newtownbutler.

Cargaduff, D.A. Hamilton, agent none.

Cargabane, representatives of the late Sir H. Crofton.

Carnaveagh and Carrickatee, [blank] Montgomery, R. Scott, Newtownbutler.

Carrickaveilty, Sir H. Crofton.

Chantinee, [blank] Rothwell, [blank] Tilly, Dublin.

Clonawilliam, W. Brunkard, Esquire.

Closhaghbeg and Closhaghmore, Sir F. Foster, A. Fleming, Monaghan.

Cooas, D.A. Hamilton, agent none.

Cooltrim, E. Lucas Esquire.

Cooltrimeagish, W. Hamilton, agent none.

Cordevlish, Colonel Verner, [blank] Crossley, Ballygawley.

Corfad, James McCullough, agent none.

Corgreagh and Corkelshina, W.B. Tenison, no agent.

Corkeerin, [blank] Johnson, R. Thompson, Bushford.

Corlea, E. Lucas Esquire.

Corlatt, Dr Lantaigne, Dublin.

Cormean, J. Thomson Tennent.

Cornecarkaw, [blank] McIntire, Belfast, [blank] Davidson, Laragh.

Corrakarra, W.B. Tenison Esquire, agent none.

Corragaldra, W. Hamilton Esquire, Castleblaney, agent none.

Corryhagan, Colonel Verner, [blank] Crossley, Newtownbutler.

Corsilliga, [blank] Plunket, near Monaghan.

Corlaghard, J. Nixon Esquire, Glasslough.

Cortinel with Killaliss, [blank], A. Swansea.

Cortubbert, W.B. Tenison, agent none.

Corvacken, W.B. Tenison and [blank] Adams, Shercock, agent none.

Corvillen, J. Jackson Esquire and Lord Cremorne.

Creeve, part Mrs Cole.

Crossduff, representatives of W. Tyler Esquire, G. Barkley, Monaghan.

Crosskeys, Colonel Verner, [blank] Crossley, Newtownbutler.

Cumrey, J. Lewis Esquire, Belfast, J. Irwan, Ballydian.

Derry, Dr D. Leslie, J. Marran, Ballybay.

Derrygoony, W.B. Tenison and [blank] Adams, Shercock.

Derrynisk, Mrs Oliver, resident.

Dooragh, [blank] Rothwell, [blank] Tilly, Dublin.

Drumcannea, J. Maine Esquire, [blank] McIntosh, Cootehill.

Drumconien, W.B. Tenison, agent none.

Drumfoldra, Lord Cremorne.

Drumfreehan, N. Grattan Esquire, agent none.

Drumgarr, E. Lucas Esquire.

Drumhilla, H. Grattan Esquire, agent none.

Drumillard, [blank] Rothwell.

Drumload, F. Ellis Esquire, H. Ellis Esquire, Dublin.

Drumskelt, Dr Kerr.

Drumacanny, [blank] Plunkett, Newbliss.

Drummad, J. Maine Esquire.

Edenbane, [blank] Johnson and [blank] Hamilton.

Edenfaran, Lord Cremorne.

Farlagh and Carrownagapple, W.B. Tenison, agent none.

Farmill, H. McMath, agent none.

Garrybane, representatives of Sir H. Crofton.

Garrydoo, W. Hamilton Esquire.

Gartlana, Dean Plunkett.

Gregarna, [blank] Montgomery.

Keenabawn and Keenaduff, [blank] Johnson.

Kilkit, [blank] McMath.

Killaliss and Cortivel, [blank], A. Swansea.

Lacken, E. Lucas Esquire.

Laragh, [blank] McIntire, [blank] Davidson, resident.

Latten, J. Maine Esquire.

Lattenfaskey, [blank] Jones, W. Hamilton Esquire.

Latticrum, representatives of Sir W. Tyler, G. Barkley, Monaghan.

Lay, Colonel Verner, [blank] Crossley, Ballygawley.

Leggan, D. Hamilton Esquire.

Lisdrumclave, W. Hamilton Esquire.

Lisduff, [blank] Montgomery, R. Scott, Newtownbutler.

Lisgillan, Colonel Verner, [blank] Crossley, Ballygawley.

Lisgorran, Dr Kerr.

Lisnadarragh, W.B. Tenison.

Lisnagalliagh, Colonel Kerr.

Lisnalong, W. Brunker.

Lisinisky, W.B. Tenison.

Lurgahaurla, representatives of Sir W. Tyler, G. Barkley, Monaghan.

Lurgangreen, [blank] Jones, D. Hamilton.

Maghon and Minneagh, J. Maine Esquire, [blank] McIntosh, Cootehill.

Moninton, Colonel Verner, [blank] Crossley, Ballygawley.

Mount Carmel and Mountain Lodge Demesne, Colonel Kerr.

Millbeg and Mullmore, Dr Leslie, J. Marron, Ballybay.

Mullenary, Cortinel, [blank].

Mullenary Glebe, Revd Roper.

Mullinagare, Colonel Verner.

Mullinanalt, R. Murdock, Dublin, R. Murdock.

Raw, Dean Plunkett.

Raybane and Rayduff, [blank] Rothwell, [blank] Tilly.

Rooe, [blank] Montgomery, R. Scott, Newtownbutler.

Shankill and Shantonagh, W.B. Tenison, agent none.

Shragh, [blank] Hogshaw.

Tattybrack, Colonel Verner, [blank] Crossley, Ballygawley.

Tamlaght, [blank] Johnson, R. Thomson.

Tivaleeney, [blank] McMath, agent none.

Tooay, [blank] Rothwell, [blank] Tilly.

Tossey, [blank] Montgomery, R. Scott.

Parish of Aughnamullen

Tullinaneagish, [blank] Hogshaw.
Tullyglish, [blank] Rothwell, [blank] Tilly.
Tullynahinnera, J. Hamilton, Clones.
Tullynamatrow.
Tullyrean, [blank] Rothwell, [blank] Tilly.
Ullienagh, [blank] Mongtomery, R. Scott.
Ullmuck, Dean Plunkett.

SOCIAL ECONOMY

Table of Schools

[Table contains the following headings: name of townland, number of pupils subdivided by religion and sex, when established, how supported].

Crosskeys, 40 Protestants, 7 Roman Catholics, 24 males, 23 females, total 47; when established: unknown; private erection, pupils pay 3s 6d per quarter.

Cordevlish, 18 Protestants, 1 Roman Catholic, 14 males, 5 females, total 19; established January 1835; no agreement as to charge.

Cumrey, 13 Protestants, 28 Catholics, 14 males, 27 females, total 41; established about 1824; pupils pay 1s 6d to 3s 3d per quarter.

Aughnamullen, 66 Protestants, 26 Catholics, 65 males, 27 females, total 92; established 1826; Society for Discountenancing Vice allow 7 pounds per annum, rector 2 pounds; pupils pay about 5 pounds and master is parish clerk with a salary of about 10 pounds, free house and 1 acre of ground.

Tiveleney, 4 Protestants, 42 Catholics, 32 males, 14 females, total 46; established 1828; pupils pay 1s 1d to 3s 3d per quarter.

Derragooney, 19 Protestants, 45 Roman Catholics, 39 males, 25 females, total 64; when established: unknown; pupils pay 1s 6d to 2s 6d per quarter.

Creeve, 39 Protestants, 21 Roman Catholics, 10 males, 50 females, total 60; when established: unknown; pupils pay 1s 1d per quarter.

Carnaveagh, 14 Protestants, 11 Roman Catholics, total 25; when established: unknown; pupils pay 1s 1d per quarter; I. Savage, teacher.

Closaghmore, 15 Protestants, 21 Catholics, 19 males, 17 females, total 36; when established: unknown; pupils pay 1s 1d to 3s per quarter.

Carrickaveilly, 4 Protestants, 26 Catholics, 18 males, 12 females, total 30; pupils pay 1s 1d to 2s 2d per quarter.

Raw national, 80 Protestants, 40 Roman Catholics, 75 males, 45 females, total 120; society allows 8 pounds per annum, pupils pay 1s 1d per quarter.

Corrahara, closed.

Crossduff church school, not opened yet.
Ballytrain, not completed.
Leggan, D.A. Hamilton allows a salary and pupils pay by the quarter.
Aghamakerlin, Corlea, Ullienagh, no returns.

Ecclesiastical Summary

Aughnamullen, diocese Clogher, province Armagh, rectory and vicarage, union none; patron, Bishop of Clogher, incumbent [crossed out: Very Revd Dean Roper], Revd Robert Tottenham appointed in 1835; extent of glebe 75 acres, tithes not impropriate, belong to rector.

Parish of Ballybay, County Monaghan

Statistical Report by Lieutenant John Chaytor, October 1835

NATURAL STATE

Name

The parish of Ballybay is of recent date. It was formed from portions of the adjacent parishes Aughnamullen and Tullycorbet, and called Ballybay from the town which is supposed to be derived from *Bel-aith-beithe*, signifying "mouth of the ford of birches." This is applicable to the locality of the town, at the southern extremity of which there is a ford; and near it, on the hill called Knocknamaddy, are birch trees. In old documents it is written Ballibea, at present Ballybay or Ballibay, the former of which is more general.

Locality

It is situated in the south western part of the county of Monaghan and centre of the barony of Cremorne, with the exception of 1 townland, Carrowbofin, which is in the barony of Monaghan.

It is bounded on the north by the parish of Tullycorbet, north east by Clontibret, south east, south and west by the parish of Aughnamullen.

Its length is 8 miles, breadth at the western end 3 miles, and 1 and three-quarters at the eastern; area 8,550 acres 1 rood 27 perches of land and 190 acres 3 roods 7 perches of woodland. Of the land, 7,932 acres are under cultivation, the remainder bog and rough pasture. The average valuation to county cess is 470 pounds per annum.

NATURAL FEATURES

Hills

There are no hills of any importance. The highest is called Greagh. It is a ridge extending east and west 1 and a half miles and in altitude 712 feet above the level of the sea. The other heights are: in the eastern part Drumhawens, 626 feet, Drumlane, 610 feet, Shane, 563 feet; and in the western part Drummar, 458 feet, Drummuck, 392 feet and Annaneese, 423 feet; all of which are cultivated to the summit.

Lakes

The only lakes of any consideration are those which are formed by a small river which passes close to the southern extremity of the town of Ballybay. This river has its source in the parish of Tullycorbet and, after passing through a portion of Clontibret parish, enters the northern part of Ballybay and immediately opens out, forming a lake called Terrygreeghan lough which, from north to south, is five-eighths of a mile, mean breadth 400 feet and area 50 acres. It contains several small islands, one of which, nearly in the centre of the lake, is covered with fir trees.

The height of this lake above the sea is 284 feet. The river flows from the southern part of this lake over a rocky bed 5 feet in height, and at a short distance changes its direction to the west. One mile from Terrygreeghan lough the river again expands, forming the Major's lough. This is half a mile long and a quarter of a mile broad, and covers a space of 64 and a quarter acres, being [crossed out: 259] feet above the level of the sea.

The river leaves the west extremity of this lake and passes close to the south end of Ballybay town. A quarter of a mile from the town, it again opens and forms a most irregular figure, curving in various directions for a mile (the average breadth being 300 feet), when it again assumes the form of a river and 1 mile further enters the parish of Aughnamullen.

During the winter season this river is subject to considerable floods and the meadows adjacent to the town are overflown to a considerable extent, but the water quickly subsides and these floods are considered very beneficial to the land.

Bogs

There are several bogs in various parts of the parish but none of great extent. The principal are: Greagh bog, in area 60 acres, and the altitude above the sea from 601 feet to 607 feet; Carrickinara, 60 acres in extent and 565 feet above the sea; Balladian bog, 45 and a quarter acres in area and 277 feet above the sea; and Clogher bog, area 42 acres, Knocknamaddy bog, area 34 acres, altitude 287 feet.

In addition to the above, there are several patches varying in extent from 5 acres to 20 acres, in all of which timber is found, principally oak and sally and sometimes fir. [In] the 2 former are found the roots and stumps separate, and the fir, in all cases, whole. These are found more generally in the smaller bogs than the larger, and round the edges of the bogs, lying indiscriminately.

Parish of Ballybay

The depth of the bogs varies from 5 to 15 feet. The substratum is either a white gritty clay, a hard sand of a reddish colour, or a black or blue clay.

Woods

The only appearance of natural woods in this parish is in the townland of Edinaneane, in extent 2 acres, consisting principally of birch; and on the hill called Knocknamaddy a portion of the woods bear the appearance of natural woods. They are birch, alders and beech.

Climate

The climate in this part of the country is moist and the harvest season very variable. The meadow-cutting generally commences early in July and reaping in the month of August, but in the eastern part of the parish it is not uncommon to see reaping at a very advanced period in September, and the farmer is frequently caught by heavy rains which render the saving of oats very laborious. Slight frosts occur in the early part of May, which are rather injurious to the crops.

NATURAL HISTORY

Botany

Within the last few years rye grass, perennial with clover, and trefoil have been sown by the better class of farmers, with varied success, perennial in particular, which thrives in the neighbourhood of the town and the western part of the parish but fails in the eastern parts.

Beech, birch, alder, elm, ash and Scotch spruce and larch fir, with a great variety of willow, flourish, but oak does not appear to be congenial to the soil. They are rare and stunted.

Zoology

Pike, perch, bream, roach and eels are taken in all the lakes, and trout in the rivers and principal streams. Hares, rabbits and weasels are the principal animals. Foxes, badgers and hedgehogs are very rare. Snipe, partridges, wild ducks and teal are general throughout the parish. Grouse are very scarce.

MODERN TOPOGRAPHY

Towns: Ballybay

See parish name. The town of Ballybay is situated 54 Irish miles north north west of Dublin. It is in the diocese of Clogher, ecclesiastical province of Armagh and north west circuit of assize. It consists of 1 street extending nearly north north west and south south east 1,800 feet. The centre of this street is the highest part of the town.

The scenery in the neighbourhood is varied and pleasing. On the east of the town is the Major's lough backed by the demesne of C.A. Leslie Esquire, on the west the river runs through a flat vale and on the north and south the country is in a high state of cultivation.

General History

By whom the town of Ballybay was founded, or what led to its creation, is not known. 80 years ago it consisted of a few miserable cottages, not more than a quarter of its present extent. About this period a Mr Jackson, seeing that the supply of water in the vicinity was favourable to the establishment of bleaching greens and machinery, took up his residence in Ballybay and built the present market house for the sale of flax and linen yarn and cloth, and thereby established a market in the town which at this present date, notwithstanding the depression in the linen trade, is very considerable.

We have no tradition of its having been distinguished for any remarkable circumstances, nor are there any ruins of ancient buildings in the neighbourhood.

Public Buildings

The parish church is a neat building with a tower but no spire. It is situated on the summit of the hill on the north east side of the town and is surrounded by a well-enclosed graveyard. It was erected in 1797 and cost 800 pounds. In 1822 it underwent considerable repairs costing 500 pounds. It is capable of accommodating 300 persons.

A small building in the north east part of the town is used occasionally as a Roman Catholic chapel. It was built by subscriptions by the inhabitants that the aged, infirm and other individuals, who could not go to the parish chapel, might attend divine service there. The parish chapel is 1 and a half miles distant from the town.

A new meeting house of very large dimensions is at present in progress at the west side of the town. The walls are built and roof nearly completed. It is estimated to accommodate between 800 and 900 persons at worship. The funds are raised by subscription and the building is under the management of a committee of subscribers who have difficulty in obtaining the necessary amount, in consequence of which the work is delayed.

The only public building in Ballybay, besides the houses of worship, is the market house which was built 80 years ago and is in a very bad state of repair.

Houses

In the town there are not more than 8 tolerably good houses. The remainder are very poor. The street is very dirty and is neither lighted nor paved. The inhabitants of the town of Ballybay may be divided into 3 classes, viz. shopkeepers, tradesmen and labourers.

PRODUCTIVE ECONOMY

Markets and Fairs

Since the establishment of the branch Bank of Ireland in Monaghan, the manager of that branch attends at Ballybay every market day for the purpose of cashing bills and doing other banking business for the yarn and cloth merchants and dealers who frequent the markets. These markets are held every Saturday, except the third Saturday in each month which is a fair, differing only from the markets in the sale of horses, black cattle and sheep.

The flax exposed for sale is the produce of the neighbouring country and affords the principal business of these markets and fairs. The linen and yarn is manufactured in the vicinity and meets a very ready market. Dealers in horses and cattle attend these fairs and purchase for the English market.

Building Materials

Timber and other articles, except stones and lime required for building, are obtained from Dundalk. Limestone is brought either from Carrickmacross or Clones, where it is purchased for 4d to 6d per cart-load. Goods for the merchants and other persons of the town who employ carters are conveyed from Dundalk at the rate of 8s to 10s per ton.

Conveyances

No stage-coach passes through the town of Ballybay; the Dublin, Londonderry and Belfast post bags are carried by a boy on horseback to Monaghan, distant 8 miles. There is also a direct post to Newry by a caravan which leaves Ballybay every morning at 4 o'clock and, passing through the towns of Castleblayney and Newtownhamilton, returns at 8 o'clock in the evening.

SOCIAL ECONOMY

Dispensary and Schools

A dispensary has been established in the town which is supported by subscription and a grant from the county, which is in all cases equal to the amount subscribed. This, from the 2nd March 1834 to the 10th January 1835, was 50 pounds 5s, during which period 1,036 patients were relieved.

There are 3 private schools in the town.

MODERN TOPOGRAPHY

Public Buildings

Besides the church, the new meeting house and small Roman Catholic chapel in the town of Ballybay, the parish contains the following, viz. a Roman Catholic chapel in the townland of Tonyglassan, erected in the years 1787 and 1788 by subscriptions. It contains accommodation for 400 persons and estimated at 400 pounds.

A Presbyterian meeting house in the townland of Derryvolley, 1 and a half miles west of the town. It is a plain stone building with slated roof and erected in the year 1786 at the expense of 500 pounds; contains a gallery and accommodation for 400 persons at worship.

A Seceding meeting house, situated in the same townland as the [blank], and a very short distance north of the former, which it very much resembles but is rather smaller. It was erected in 1800 and contains accommodation for 300 persons.

Bridge

The only bridge of any consideration is that which crosses the river between the townlands of Balladian and Edenanean, 1 and a half miles south west of Ballybay town. It consists of 4 small arches of very rude architecture.

Gentlemen's Seats

The Castle, as it is sometimes called by the inhabitants, is situated three-quarters of a mile east north east of Ballybay, on the opposite side of Major's lough. It is an extensive house of 2-storeys and basement. The demesne is 110 acres in extent, of which 50 acres are wood and plantations. It is the property of C.A. Leslie Esquire, who is a non-resident.

The Glebe House, situated in the townland of Derrynaloobinagh, is the residence of the present rector, the Reverend Hercules Langrishe. It is a good house of 2-storeys, built in the year 1799 at the expense of 1,800 pounds. It stands on an eminence on the west side of the Clones road and commands a fine view of the country to the west of Ballybay.

There is a small dwelling house with very good offices and plantations to the extent of 10 acres in Agheraban townland, the property of Mr A. Horner of Ballybay.

Mills

There are in the parish the following mills: Shantanna flax and corn mills, situated 2 miles west of Ballybay town; D. Roper is the proprietor. The diameter of the corn mill wheel is 13 and a half feet, breadth 2 and a half feet, with a breast fall. The mill contains 2 pairs of millstones and a cleaning fan which is wrought by the water wheel. The flax mill wheel is 12 feet in diameter and 2 and a half feet in breadth, also a breast wheel. Both buildings are of stone and thatched, and the latter in very bad order.

Ballintra mill, in Knappagh townland, is the property of Mrs McLellan. It is divided into 2 apartments, one for corn, the other for flax, and has 2 wheels. The diameter of the corn machinery wheel is 13 feet, breadth 3 and a half feet; and that of the flax is 8 feet in diameter and 3 and a half feet in breadth. The corn mill contains 2 pairs of millstones and a fan and sifters, all worked by water wheels.

The water is led from Terrygreeghan lough and in the summer season the supply is scanty. The mills are consequently idle.

Drumlane corn mill is the property of D. Keenan. The diameter of the wheel is 12 feet and breadth 2 and a half feet. It is rarely worked in the summer season, in consequence of the want of water. It is a breast wheel.

Communications

The principal roads in the parish branch from the town of Ballybay to the neighbouring towns of Clones, Cootehill, Shercock, Carrickmacross, Castleblaney and Monaghan. The whole length of these roads in the parish is 16 miles, kept in very bad order.

Of by-roads in the parish there 14 miles, also in a bad state, which may be attributed to the bad materials used in repairing them, viz. clay, slate and coarse grauwacke.

ANCIENT TOPOGRAPHY AND ANTIQUITY

Ancient Battle

Tradition exists of a battle having been fought between DeCourcy, first Earl of Ulster, and the McMahons and O'Carrols, in the townland of Balladian, which is vague, and at present there is no trace of it.

Giant's Grave and Forts

In the townland of Carrickanean may be seen a giant's grave. Large stones stand in the form of a rectangle 7 feet by 3 and a half feet; some of these stones are 3 and a half feet above the surface of the ground. There are 12 old forts in the parish, situated in the following townlands, viz. 2 in Annyneese townland, 1 in Carrickanean, 1 in Drumgoolagh, 2 in Drumlane, 1 in Drummar, 1 in Tunnyglassen, 1 in Drummurrish, 1 in Cornihore, 1 in Cabragh, 1 in Lara, [total] 12.

MODERN TOPOGRAPHY

General Appearance and Scenery

The scenery of the parish is diversified, but there is nothing particularly striking. The western part is highly cultivated with good fences, occasional clumps of trees, and plantations around the houses. In the immediate neighbourhood of Ballybay town the plantations of the demesne of Mr Leslie, with the lakes to the east and west of the town, and the river in connection with these lakes, the neat and well-cultivated appearance of the country on the west and south, and the prominent situation of the church have a pleasing effect; but as the rest of the country is poor and rocky, and although the hand of cultivation may be traced upon every part of it, it bears a bleak and barren appearance.

SOCIAL ECONOMY

Progress of Improvement

The establishment of a market in the town of Ballybay, and the bleaching greens at Creeve in the vicinity of the town, have tended much to the improvement of this neighbourhood. A leading obstruction to the further improvement is the small size of the farms, held without leases at a high rent, the occupants receiving no encouragement from the landlords who are all non-residents.

Local Government

There is no magistrate resident in the parish.

Petty sessions are held regularly in the town of Ballybay every alternate Thursday. T. Lucas Esquire, Mr Swansea of Clontibret and Major Richardson of Monaghan are the magistrates who attend. The cases that come before them are rarely of a serious nature. Trifling debts and assaults are the most general crimes.

Ballybay is a police station for 1 constable and 5 subconstables under the direction of the chief residing in Castleblayney. Illicit distillation is not practised in the neighbourhood, but selling spirits without licences is general in the town and surrounding country, though it is occasionally visited by revenue police from Clones.

Dispensary: see Ballybay town and tables.

Schools and Poor

The introduction of schools do not appear to have had much good effect upon the morals of the people. The children attend regularly except in such seasons as they are employed by their parents in the fields.

There is no provision for the poor who are very numerous.

Religion

There are 3 denominations of religion, viz. the Established Church, the Roman Catholic and Presbyterian, in the following proportions 1, 5 and a half, and 2.

Habits of the People

The habitations of the people for the most part are very poor. In all cases they are built of stone and thatched. The windows are small and rarely glazed. Little attention is paid to cleanliness, either in their persons or the interior or exterior of their cabins. They marry early, females at 17 and males at 19. The average number in a family is 5.

They enjoy very little amusement except in dancing at fairs and markets. Horse-racing, hunting and cock-fighting are very rare. Shooting at a target with muskets or fowling pieces is a general recreation at Christmas time. Card-playing prevails, particularly in the town of Ballybay. This, and the strong party feeling existing, causes much quarrelling and disturbances in the town.

Emigration

In the spring of each year a few families emigrate to America, sometimes to the United States, but more generally to British America; few of them return.

PRODUCTIVE ECONOMY

Occupations

Agricultural employment occupies the greatest portion of the time of the inhabitants, but weaving is very general in the winter season. There are many of the better class of farmers in the parish who keep looms, purchase yarn in the fairs and markets of the vicinity, and employ persons to weave by the piece, which is 52 yards long. In weaving this, they are commonly employed 15 days, for which they receive 6s and board and lodging. The linen made is of a coarse quality, 10 or 11 hundreds. The former brings in the market from 8d to 9d per yard and the latter 10d ha'penny, and 12 hundred, 14d.

Spinning flax is the general employment of the females, but they are by no means so expert as in the more northern counties. Yarn of 4 hanks to the cwt is the finest, but they spin in general 2 and 3 hanks to the lb. A hank of yarn per diem is considered good work for a woman, the average price paid for spinning which is 2d.

An active hackler is able to hackle 5 stones of flax per diem and receives from 5d to 6d per stone, but his business is only good during the early part of the winter seasons, the inhabitants being too much engaged during the summer in agricultural labour to prepare their flax for the hackler.

Rural: Proprietors

The principal proprietor in the parish is C.A Leslie Esquire: 24 out of the 36 townlands in the parish belong to him. He has not resided in the last 4 years. Major Richardson of Monaghan is the agent. Lord Blayney has a few of the eastern townlands. His lordship resides occasionally in Castleblayney. Mr Bellingham of Castle Bellingham is his agent.

Mining

About 10 years ago in the townland of Laragh, a quarter of a mile east of Ballybay town, on the summit of a rocky hill of grauwacke, some lead ore was discovered and a company from England opened 3 shafts to the depths of 25 feet, but the vein was found too poor to repay the expense of working. It was therefore abandoned and the shafts closed.

Farms

Of the farms, there are 200 above 10 acres, 8 above 20 acres, 3 above 50 acres and 2 above 10 acres. This leaves a great many below 10 acres

Parish of Ballybay

The majority of these are held without leases and the few leases that are granted are only for 1 life or 21 years. In the immediate neighbourhood of the town the rent per acre is 4 pounds, in the western part of the parish it varies from 1 pound 10s to 1 pound 15s and in the eastern part the average rent is 15s per acre. Considerable portions of land are let yearly in conacre at from 8 pounds to 10 pounds per acre.

The fields vary much both in size and figure: square ones from 1 and a half to 2 and a half acres are preferred.

Fences and Fields

In the western part of the parish the fences are good, composed of banks of earth fenced with stones and well set with quicks, but in the eastern part they are of loose stones and for the most part in very bad order. Farmhouses and offices in all cases are built and repaired by the tenants and, as before observed, they are by no means comfortable or commodious. No farms are kept expressly as examples, but Mr McCullagh's farm of Derryvolley is kept in superior order.

Soil and Manures

The soil in the west is good, of a clayey nature, resting upon a hard sand and gravel of a reddish colour. In the east the soil is light and poor, and so stony as to render cultivation very difficult.

The manure most required is lime. This is obtained in Carrickmacross and Clones, and burnt by the farmers upon the ground. Burning the ground for manure is considered so injurious that the landlords have put a stop to this practice.

Implements of husbandry are in an improving state. Iron ploughs have been introduced and carts have succeeded the wheel cars. Oxen are not used in draft. 2 horses form a team.

Crops

Wheat and barley are rarely sown. The usual crops are potatoes, oats and flax. The quantity of land required for an acre (Irish) is as follows: white oats 20 stones, black oats 26 stones; flax 150 lbs or 15 pecks; potatoes 6 barrels; wheat 14 stones; barley 16 stones.

And the average crop from the above seeds is: oats 11 to 12 barrels of 14 stones; wheat 8 barrels of 20 stones; flax 75 stones prepared for the hacklers; potatoes 56 barrels of 32 stones; barley 12 barrels of 16 stones.

And the prices vary thus: oats 7s to 9s 6d per barrel; wheat 17s 6d to 1 pound 1s per barrel; potatoes 5s 4d to 7s 6d per barrel; flax 6s 8d to 9s 6d per stone in the following markets, Castleblayney, Carrickmacross, Ballybay and Monaghan. The principal port for exportation is Dundalk.

Grazing

Grazing is very little attended to in the parish. Farm servants hired by the year commonly receive: males from 4 pounds to 5 pounds with board and lodging, and females from 1 pound 4s to 2 pounds per annum. The general rate of day labourers in the summer is 6d with board and 10d without, and in winter 4d and 8d.

Cattle of the Ayrshire and Devonshire breeds are common in this parish. Pigs, goats and asses are very plenty in this parish. The latter are much used in agriculture.

Uses made of Bogs

The bogs in this country are used only for fuel, and supply the farmers and neighbouring towns. The turf is cut in the month of June and carried to the towns for sale either in creels or carts. The average price of a pair of creels full of turf is 4d and that of a cart-load 2s. The turf is never made into charcoal: smiths and other mechanics find it cheaper to procure coals from Dundalk.

Drainage and Planting

Drainage: rarely practised in this parish.

The little planting there is in the parish appears to thrive well. A south west exposure is the only one which is found injurious. There is no nursery in the parish.

General Remarks

The soil generally in this parish is not good, neither is the situation favourable for procuring lime, the manure most required. No part of the parish is so high as to preclude cultivation, the highest point being only 712 feet above the level of the sea.

The country has the advantage of several good market towns, none of which are very distant, viz. Ballybay, Monaghan, Castleblayney, Cootehill and Carrickmacross. [Signed] John Chaytor, Lieutenant Royal Engineers, 30th October 1835.

PRODUCTIVE AND SOCIAL ECONOMY

List of Townlands

[Table contains the following headings: name of townland, proprietor].

Acres, C.A. Leslie Esquire.
Annaniese, H. Ellis Esquire.
Augheralane, A. Horner Esquire.
Balladian, C.A. Leslie Esquire.
Cabragh, Lord Blayney.
Carrickanear, C.A. Leslie Esquire.
Clogher, C.A. Leslie Esquire.
Corbofin, Colonel Kerr.
Corbrack, part A. Horner Esquire.
Corfadd, C.A. Leslie Esquire.
Corkeeran, C.A. Leslie Esquire.
Cornihoe, C.A. Leslie Esquire.
Cornamuckleglash, C.A. Leslie Esquire.
Corrybrannon, C.A. Leslie Esquire.
Derrynaloobinagh, C.A. Leslie Esquire.
Derryvalley, C.A. Leslie Esquire.
Drummar, C.A. Leslie Esquire.
Drumgara, Lord Blayney.
Drumgrole, C.A. Leslie Esquire.
Drumgoolagh Upper, Lord Blaney.
Drumgoolagh Lower, Lord Blaney.
Drumhawan, C.A. Leslie Esquire.
Drumhillagh, Henry Ellis Esquire.
Drumbane, C.A. Leslie Esquire.
Drummuck, A.N. Montgomery Esquire.
Dunmurrish, C.A. Leslie Esquire.
Edinanay, E. Fitzgerald Esquire.
Edenaneane, C.A. Leslie Esquire.
Greagh, C.A. Leslie Esquire.
Knappagh, C.A. Leslie Esquire.
Knocknamadue, C.A. Leslie Esquire.
Laragh, C.A. Leslie Esquire.
Monantin, C.A. Leslie Esquire.
Shane, Lord Blayney.
Shantonagh, A. Kerr Esquire.
Terrygreehan, C.A. Leslie Esquire.
Tunnyglassin, C.A. Leslie Esquire.

Ecclesiastical Register

[Table] Parish Ballybay, diocese Clogher, province Armagh, rectory and vicarage, union none, patron Bishop of Clogher, incumbent Revd H. Langrishe, extent of glebe 25 acres, tithes not impropriate, belong to rector, amount 353 pounds 1s 3d per year.

Dispensary Return

Ballybay dispensary return for 1834. [Table contains the following headings: diseases, surgical diseases, diseases of the skin, number of cases].

Diseases: typhus mitior 92, intermittent fever 11, opthalmia 9, cynanche 10, cynanche tonsillaris 12, pneumonia 31, hepatitis 14, rheumatisms 11, catarrhus 13, dysenteria 9, dyspepsia 87, asthma 7, pertussis 6, colica 21, diarrhoea 17, anasarca 5, ascites 7, scrophula 6, icterus 2.

Surgical diseases: injuries of the head 3, dislocations 5, fractures 4, hernia 3, hydrocele 2, hoemorrhois 9, midwifery cases 31.

Diseases of the skin: rubeola 8, scarlatina 22, varicella 6, psora 25, tinea 6, diseases not particularly named 319, slight complaints and other diseases of the skin 221.

Number visited at their houses from the 2nd March 1834 until 10th January 1835, 379, vaccinated 69, total number relieved from 2nd March 1834 to 10th January 1835, 1,036. Signed D. Williamson, medical attendant.

Dispensary Account

Dispensary account, 1834. Receipt: amount of subscriptions received prior to Lent assizes 50 pounds 5s, county grant, Lent assizes 1834, 50 pounds 5s, [total] 100 pounds 10s. Expenditure: medical attendant's salary 55 pounds, house, rent, fuel 7 pounds 8s, stationery, postage and lapping paper 3 pounds 1s 11d ha'penny, drugs and carriage 33 pounds 19s ha'penny, cash to cowpock institution 1 pound 1s, [total] 100 pounds 10s.

Parish of Clontibret, County Monaghan

Fair Sheets by J.C. Innes

NATURAL FEATURES

Lakes

Crossdall lake occupies a portion of the townland of Cornahoe Lower in this parish and a portion of the parish of Tynan in the county of Armagh. Its content is 5 acres and average depth 20 feet, and its height above the level of the sea 360 feet.

Drumneill lake occupies a portion of the townland of Drumneill in this parish and a portion of the parish of Tynan in the county of Armagh. Its content is 8 acres and average depth 25 feet, and its height above the level of the sea 310 feet.

NB The contents and altitudes of the above lakes are not stated in the map and are only judged.

MODERN TOPOGRAPHY

Mill

Greenmount mill, situated [in] the townland of Greenmount, is a stone house, thatched. The proprietor is Edward Lucan Esquire and the tenant John Maxwell. It was built in 1817. The water wheel is 14 feet in diameter and 2 feet 8 inches in breadth. It is an overshot wheel and has a fall of 1 and a half feet. The machinery is wood and metal. The wheel turns 1 pair of stones. [Signed] J.C. Innes.

Parish of Currin, County Monaghan

Statistical Report by Lieutenant P. Taylor, January 1835

NATURAL STATE

Name

Statistical Report of the parish of Currin <Curran>, Cootehill, 31st January 1835. Pronounced Curran in the eastern and Currin in the western portion of the parish. Derivation: unknown.

Locality

Situated in the south western extremity of the county of Monaghan and in the same position of the barony of Dartrey; it is bounded on the north by the parishes of Aughabog, Killevan and Clones, all in the county of Monaghan, on the west by the counties of Fermanagh and Cavan, on the south by the county of Cavan, and on the east by the parish of Ematris; and measuring in extreme length and breadth from east to west 7, and from north to south 2 English miles.

Contains 11,163 acres, 10,501 of which are land, 482 of bog and 180 of water, and paid in local taxation to the county cess in the year 1833 (1834 not being collected) the sum of 678 pounds.

NATURAL FEATURES

Hills

A very beautiful undulating formation of convex ridges of considerable elongation, stretching north east and south west, with intervening valleys, the receptacles of lakes and streamlets, the ridges occasionally intersected transversely, forming beautifully cone-shaped hills, comprise the natural features of the eastern section of the parish. A chain of heights, unconnected with any decided elevation of mountain ranges or extended plains, traverse from Carnroe through Cavany, Latacrussin and Callaghill in the centre portion of the parish, and attain the highest altitude.

From this line a considerable depression of the surface takes place towards the north west, from the base of which a nearly similar diversification of hill and vale as in the eastern now prevails throughout the whole extent of its western boundary: Mucklagh, Drum, Crunchigo and Drumurchur in the eastern section, standing respectively 426, 397, 447 and 444 feet above the level of the sea; Carnroe, Cavany, Lattacrossin and Callaghill in the centre, 635, 493, 519 and 450 feet; and Clinfad, Annaghreagh, Sandhills and Annies in the western section, 232, 241, 254 and 258 feet above the same level.

Lakes and Streams

Long loch, the largest within the parish, occupies the eastern extremity of a valley formed by the continuous ridges of Drum, Aughereagh and Tonytallagh on the north west, and a parallel ridge, comprising the townlands of Tonagamprey, Lisbrannon and Fortry in the parish of Ematris, on the south east. In extreme length it measures 63 chains by 14 in breadth. The drain or streamlet flowing westerly from its south western extremity traverses bog and several small lakes at nearly a dead level, rendering its waters unavailable within the parish.

Drum and Cormeen lochs occupy the valley to the north of the village of Drum and give rise to a streamlet flowing south easterly and penetrating the parish of Ematris.

Quarry loch lies in a depression formed by the parallel ridges of Drumgramph and Aughareagh, and impells a very small streamlet south east to Long loch.

Tatenacake loch occupies the centre of the valley formed by the townlands of Drumgramph and Tatenacake, and communicates with Drum loch by a small drain flowing in an easterly direction.

Dunsrim loch occupies the centre of a beautiful basin-shaped valley, formed by the gently sloping sides of the heights comprising the townlands of Cavany, Aughareagh West, Aughnaskieve, Latacrussin and Dunsrim, and opening into the townland of Killyfargy.

Annaghane loch is located in the centre of another beautiful basin, surrounded by the townlands of Cornaparte, Mullinary, Aughadrumdoney and Annaghane.

Loch Cor, Drumavail, Killyfargy and several others are small and unimportant but combine, by their diversity, in highly ornamenting the surface of the district. The general drainage of their waters flows westerly.

Springs are numerous and pure.

Bogs

Turbary is exceedingly scarce, particularly so in the eastern and central portions of the parish.

Most of the bogs are so much exhausted and sunk that the combustible matter is obliged to be collected in holes and thrown out to drain and condense, when it is formed into peat with the hand.

Great deprivation assails the peasantry from its scarcity. Many are obliged to carry their winter supply a distance of several miles. Every vegetable substance is eagerly sought after and accumulated as a substitute, and this leads directly to the naked and desolate appearance of the district, over which scarcely a tree is to be seen.

Coal is purchased in Dundalk and sold at 25s per ton, including carriage, but this supply is altogether beyond the resources of the peasantry. Enormous roots and stumps of oak and fir trees appear through the bogs, indicating the previous existence of lofty forests in these localities. None of the timber remains whereby to form an opinion of their antiquity but, from every appearance and size of the roots, they may be pronounced very ancient.

A bog in the townland of Annies affords, by the vast number and size of the stumps, a striking specimen of a primeval forest of oak and fir trees of great magnitude.

Every trace of the former existence of natural woods is completely extinguished throughout the parish, arising doubtlessly from the very great deficiency of bog, for the very old inhabitants affirm that in their own remembrance many of the hills were covered with timber of great size and value, much of which was cut down about 60 years ago on the expiration of leases, the tenantry being apprehensive of losing it by the non-renewal of their lease, and much was consumed as fuel.

The heights of Killenenagh are pointed to as localities which were covered in more recent times, and the more elevated and rocky portions of Carnroe, Killyfargy and Aughnaskieve are also mentioned; but, with the exceptions of the bogs in their vicinity, no indication of the kind now remains.

Climate

Although the climate is particularly moist, it is exceedingly healthy, arising probably from the high tableland on which a great proportion of the parish is situated and unexposed to great vicissitudes of weather by its remoteness from lofty mountain ranges and extensive lakes; and although a very large quantity of rain falls throughout the year, still it does not descend in greater proportion than in some of the surrounding parishes, which are pronounced rheumatic.

The winters are particularly mild: snow very seldom lies upon the ground for any continuance, indeed it may be pronounced an absentee for the last several years, having merely presented its fleecy white coping on the summit of the distant hills.

If any change might be desirable, a decrease of rain would be the choice; and still, in accordance with the prevailing system of agriculture, the existing climate is probably the best, for even at this season of the year, the 29th day of December, nothing can surpass in beauty the green verdure of the hills which are laying fallow, recovering from nature their future fertility and productiveness of soil.

The prevailing winds blow from south between east and west, and these are the chief conductors of rain. North easters are dry and exceedingly cold, and the apparent, almost evident, approach of Sleibgh Glass, arising from the purity and transparency of the atmosphere, is a sure indication of a cold visitation from that quarter.

The prevailing diseases are catarrhus, rheumatisms, chynanche tonsilaris, pleuritis and other inflammatory infections, arising from poverty and destitution, the clothing necessary to protect the persons of the peasantry from these calamities being either beyond their means of procuring or totally disregarded. Many instances of longevity are recorded in the parochial registries, and several above 100 years of age can now be produced.

Natural History

Botany

Plantations of considerable extent surround Hilton demesne. Elm, ash, sycamore, with every variety of fir, adorn the grounds. The most predominant are elm and its varieties, larch, Scotch, spruce, silver and Weymouth firs, ash, birch, beech and alder. Oak attains considerable magnitude. In the orchards and gardens apple, pear, peach and cherry, with every other variety of fruit trees, are in vast abundance. Sycamore, yew and poplars adorn the lawn. Several varieties of artificial grass have been introduced into the farms around, the Trifolium procumbens and Trifolium pratense are in profusion, the Poa trivialis and Poa pratensis are equally so, but the Lolium perenne is more extensively cultivated.

Zoology

Shad, bream, roach, perch, pike, trout and eels abound in the lakes. Hares, rabbits, partridges and snipe exist in the parish, but by no means abundantly. The transmigratory species of wild duck, woodcocks, plover, together with the crane and cormorant, frequent the lakes and marshes, and every other variety of avis peculiar to agricultural climates abound.

Geology

A grey or greenish-coloured rock, named by Captain Portlock grauwacke, pervades not only the parishes of Currin, Ematris and Aughabog but expands over a vast extent of the counties of Cavan, Monaghan and Armagh. How far it extends to the westward of Arklow hill in the county of Cavan will be determined hereafter, but that it traverses those counties eastward until it comes in contact with the transition limestone, the Armagh marble, in the vicinity of the town of Armagh, is a fact ascertained by personal examination. The elementary substances composing this rock appear to be hornblende and quartz in nearly equal proportions, with a small admixture of mica.

In the parish of Currin this unstratified, non-fossiliferous argillaceous rock, in a state of finely comminuted detritus, forms a rich and highly productive soil which clothes every portion of the parish, but more particularly so the eastern and central sections. In numerous localities it rises to the surface with so much irregularity, and in such indescribable confusion, as to induce a supposition of its being of igneous origin. Every attempt to discover or trace its formation to mechanical causes have proved illusory and vain.

In quarries where it is extensively wrought, it presents a massive rock from 30 to 40 feet square, from the centre of which a beautiful radiation of quartz veins diverge from a focus of the same mineral and ramify in straight lines towards the circumference. In some pits 20 or 30 yards long the rock is broken into square and oblong fragments, so small as to require removal only, and spreading upon the roads, and examination of these sections point clearly to an upheaving power as the cause of their comminution.

In a quarry of great extent in the townland of Mucklagh a silicious slate rock is associated with the grauwacke, but in no other section does this again appear.

In localities where it rises to the surface extensively, particularly in the townland of Carnroe, it assumes a red colour, varying in shade from deep crimson to a bright scarlet, and occasionally striated with pale yellow, imparting a similar shading to the surface around.

In some portions of this development a lamellated and stratified structure appears, forming horizontal steps a foot thick, but to determine its general bearing is perfectly impossible, the angles on a surface of a very few yards dipping to every point of the compass. It is also observable that this oxidised rock holds a superior position, seldom sinking more than 2 or 3 feet beneath the surface, and seems to have undergone an important change in its mineralogical character, its constituent elements blending into a remarkably pure clay.

In the townlands of Callaghill and Skerrick West the surface is covered with large blocks of the grauwacke rock, but whether upheaved in their present position or borne onwards from the heights of Clara Cairn in the county of Cavan is a question of difficult solution.

Limestone

In the townlands of Annies, Annaveagh, Clinfad and Cornaparte, on the northern boundary of the parish separating the counties of Fermanagh and Monaghan, the grauwacke rock becomes less prevalent and carboniferous limestone supervenes, of a deep blue shade and full of organic life, first in large round boulders in a grauwacke pit in Hilton demesne and subsequently in extensive stratified masses dipping 32 degrees north west.

In forming a mill-race in the townland of Cruncheys, and in the immediate locality of an extensive development of the grauwacke rock, small-sized boulders of limestone and quartz were drawn out; and very minute pebbles of limestone pervade everywhere and, mixing with the argillaceous soil of the parish, require much care in their separation from the clay in the formation of bricks.

A close and personal examination of every well-marked section, quarry or gravel pit of grauwacke rock within the parish has been made, and the faintest trace of organic life has nowhere appeared; neither has conglomerate in any size or form been observed.

Sand

The most interesting geological formation that has fallen under examination within the parish appears near the summit of the townland of Lurganboy. Several sandpits have been discov-

Parish of Currin

ered in this locality, 520 feet above the level of the sea. On removing 9 inches of vegetable mould, 18 inches of a red-coloured tenacious clay appears, and beneath the clay a beach of the purest dark-coloured sand, 4 feet thick, but how much lower it dips is not ascertained.

About 2 chains further down on the same slope of the hill several other sandpits have been exposed, exhibiting precisely the same appearance. Their deposition, covering the side of one of the highest ranges of the parish, present some difficulty in accounting for their accumulations, unless indeed the upheaving and elevating powers of Monsieur Elie deBeaumont be applied to convert the arenaceous beaches of the ocean into the beautiful parks and potato fields of Lurganboy.

That their arenaceous accumulations were formed by fluviatile or tidal currents appear manifest from the undulating lines which traverse them.

MODERN TOPOGRAPHY

Village of Drum

The village of Drum, containing 30 houses, most of them cabins, is situated in the eastern section of the parish, upon the convexity of a hill forming the townland of Drumgramph.

There is no trade or commerce of any description carried on in the village: several spirit retailers, 2 grocery shops, lodging house and the cabins of the people renting land in the vicinity, amounting in all to about 160, comprise its population.

A chapel of ease to the parochial church was erected in 1827 in its proximity, capable of accommodating 300 members; the Revd A. Foster the officiating curate. It also contains 1 Presbyterian and 1 Dissenting meeting house, the former containing 260 and the latter 320 members. It has besides the benefit of a resident surgeon and a small detachment of police, a monthly fair, but no weekly market.

The direct road from Cootehill to Scotshouse and Clones runs through the village. Situated in the diocese of Clogher, barony of Dartrey, county of Monaghan and province of Ulster; it is 3 miles north west of Cootehill, 4 east of Scotshouse, 7 south east of Clones, 3 south of Newbliss and 4 east of Rockcorry, and 53 north west of Dublin.

Village of Scotshouse

The village of Scotshouse is of still minor importance, comprising only 10 houses, most of which are built of stone. It is neither endowed with a weekly market nor monthly fair.

The parochial church, erected in 1812, stands in the village, accommodating 200 parishioners; the Revd W. Moffat, rector, and the Revd J.C. Collins, curate. There is also in its vicinity a Roman Catholic chapel, the Revd J. Goodwin, parish priest, capable of containing 800 members.

It is also the station for a small detachment of police and is 4 miles north of Ballyhare, 3 west of Redhills, 3 south of Clones, 4 south east of Newbliss and 4 west of Drum.

Public Buildings

There are no public buildings within the parish, neither market house, court house, dispensaries or asylums of any description.

Gentlemen's Seats

Hilton House, the mansion of Colonel Madden, situated in the north western extremity of the parish, is of modern construction, grand and imposing in the distance but plain on close examination. Its site in the western extremity of the demesne, having a south eastern aspect, is beautiful; the ornamental grounds and plantations, including several small lakes, are extensive; the deerpark is beautiful, affording by its undulation of surface and circular coping plantations shelter from every quarter; the trees have attained considerable magnitude.

The road from Scotshouse traverses the grounds and affords the observer a very interesting and pleasing prospect of richly diversified scenery.

Minore, the residence of Captain Cottenham, in the proximity of the village of Drum, is prettily situated near the eastern extremity of Long lough, of which it commands a pleasing prospect.

Much taste is here displayed in the formation, upon a small scale, of highly useful and ornamental plantation. The southern margin of the lake is beautifully feathered with varieties of pine, and the summit of the surrounding heights are covered with similar shading. The more regular subdivision of fields, and the neatness and improved condition of the grounds, render it, in the centre of naked and impoverished holdings, an object of much local admiration.

Mills

4 small corn mills, most of which are inactive the greater portion of the year, work up the produce

of the neighbouring districts. One in the townland of Tatenacake is driven by a streamlet flowing from the parish of Aughabog, another in the townland of Crunchigo is wrought by the same water power, and lower down the streamlet, in the townland of Drumurcher, a clothier's mill, long since unemployed, is still standing.

In the townland of Killyfargy a small corn mill is impelled by streamlets flowing from Dunsrim and Killyfargy lochs, and another is wrought by a streamlet on the parish boundary, in the townland of Corneparte.

Roads

Numbers of roads traverse the parish in every direction, affording facilities of transport to every point. Five, having the village of Drum as their centre, communicate with the towns of Ballyhare, Redhills, Scotshouse, Clones, Newbliss, Rockcorry and Cootehill. 2 of these, traversing the parish from east to west, connect Drum with Redhills and Scotshouse. A branch diverging north west from the latter communicates with Clones. A third line of road from Drum runs north to Newbliss, another communicates north easterly with Rockcorry, and the principal lines running south east connect Drum with Clementstown and Cootehill.

Several crossroads diverging from these penetrate the counties of Cavan and Fermanagh, one particularly which, connecting the town of Clones with Cavan, runs through Scotshouse, sending off a branch to Redhills.

The whole expense of making and repairing these roads is paid by the county and levied off the parish by presentments from the grand jury. A rock, locally termed greenstone, which pervades the whole district, supplies material for their formation, but the present condition of the roads and bridges is bad.

Ancient Topography and Antiquity

Forts

On almost every townland within the parish are to be found the circular domiciles of its very ancient inhabitants. Many have been obliterated by the husbandmen, whilst a superstitious veneration has preserved others. These forts generally measure 2 chains in diameter, but several with double fosse and terra plana encircle an acre.

These reliques of antiquity have generally been constructed upon the highest summit of the townlands, affording in a country anciently covered with dark impenetrable forests considerable means of defence against an incursory enemy.

Stations

In the townland of Clinfad 2 Roman Catholic stations, with the impression of St Patrick's knee in the centre of a large stone, and a holy well were frequented within these few years by members of the Roman Catholic persuasion; and about 40 years since divine service was performed by the Roman Catholic clergy on patron days at these stations.

In a large fort in the immediate vicinity 9 skeletons of the human form were dug up in cultivating the ground by the present tenant, and several coins of the reigns of Elizabeth, Mary and Henry VIII were also found. Tradition erects in the same locality a monastery, but no trace of it now remains.

Worm Ditch

A boundary of very ancient appearance, locally termed the Worm Ditch from its tortuous direction, and which tradition extends from Dundalk to Galway as the line of demarcation between 2 of Erin's kings, consisting of a rampart and double fosse, several portions of which is still very conspicuous but much of it faint or defaced, traverses a considerable extent of the parish in a north west and south easterly direction.

The height of the rampart in some places measures 9 feet above the surface of the ground and the depth of the ditch from the top of the rampart 20 feet, and the breadth of both the ditches and rampart 48 feet, the ditch contracting to 3 feet at the bottom.

The construction of the boundary, as described by Pillip Brady in the townland of Aughnaskieve, wherever it has been dug into, [is] as follows: the rampart is formed of good soil, which has been a strong inducement to the tenantry to level it. The gripes when dug out consist of 3 feet deep of mould. On this being removed, 2 feet of bog appear, and beneath the bog 2 feet of clay. In the bottom, and amongst the turf of the ditch, beams of black oak from 6 to 8 feet long and 2 feet square are found, some in perpendicular and others in longitudinal positions, with mortice and tenon joints at the extremities, and some of the timber round and having the appearance of windlasses.

One piece was found about a yard long, shaped like the oar of a boat, the feathered extremity scooped out like a spoon, with 2 circular holes an inch in diameter at the handle. Semi-fused pieces of stone, of a brown-red colour, were thrown aside in levelling the ramparts and are now scattered about the ground, 4 pieces of which accompany the geological specimens of the parish.

Tracing the ditch from the river separating the parishes of Currin and St Mary's Drumcrin, it traversed south westerly through the townland of Cornaparte and Annaghane, and is still well marked in the townland of Killack. It also appears faintly in Drumavan and Skerrick West, but becomes conspicuous in Aughnascrieve and Latacrussin, and, still pursuing its serpentine course through the townlands of Coranny, Drumurcher and Drumgrove, disappears entirely in Crunshigo.

Miscellaneous Discoveries

About 6 years ago 2 canoes were found in the bog surrounding the margin of Drum loch. One of them is still in the possession of Captain Cottenham, which measures 25 feet long, 20 inches broad on the keel and 2 feet of beam. The sides and extremities are much injured, but it still retains sufficient of its original form to identify it satisfactorily with the canoes of India.

In the same proximity the head of an elk was found embedded in a blue-coloured tenacious clay, whilst digging a drain betwixt the townlands of Cormean and Cortubber, and is also in the possession of the same gentleman.

Edward Clarkin, a tenant in the townland of Drumborisk, found, near the surface and edge of the bog near Dunnaluck Pole, 2 instruments of the shape of a hatchet, with a staple attached to the head of each, and 5 instruments resembling spear or halbert heads, each about the length of a bayonet, and one like the stand or upright portion of a candlestick.

[Drawings attached to letter: hatchet, spearhead or halbert, resembling a candlestick or canalink, diagram showing "the wound the spear would inflict"].

My Dear Sir,
The instruments found in Drumborisk bog, of which I gave you some account, were in the shape of spearheads and appear to be made of some hard and heavy metal with a large portion of brass in them. They were found in the latter end of the year 1833. If I can I will send you some of them. Yours very truly, Richard Mayne, Freame Mount, 25th June 1835.

MODERN TOPOGRAPHY

General Appearance and Scenery

Although the parish is not marked by any grand and imposing features in its general appearance and scenery, still it possesses upon a small scale a very beautiful and interesting diversity. The division of its surface into long, convex and tabulated ridges, running in an east and westerly direction, and flowing in succession from north to south, like the long swelling waves of the ocean, and separating exuberantly fertile vales, are objects that forcibly strike the mind of the observer with pleasing contemplation.

These valleys are confined on the east by the townlands of Cortubber, Mucklagh, Cormean and Dunnaluck, elevating their summits into various forms, and determining the general drainage of the district in a south westerly direction, until met by a range of heights, comprising the townlands of Carnroe, Cavany, Latacrossin and Callaghill, traversing the parish from north to south.

This chain naturally separates the parish into eastern and western divisions. The eastern descends at a very small angle but the western unfolds a considerable and rapid depression, forming a western aspect, and presents from the summit of this chain a very extensive view of the surrounding counties, embracing the Swanlinbar and Belmore mountains. It also contains within the circle of its prospect the towns of Clones, Newtownbutler, Scotshouse and Redhills, with the spires of numerous churches arising from the centre of surrounding plantations, with several small lakes, and in the distance the grand reservoir <reservoyer> of their superabundant accumulations, the magnificent and beautiful Loch Erne.

The western division assumes a more irregular but equally beautiful variety of undulation as the central and eastern sections, but upon a much smaller scale. The drums, or broad-backed ridges, are here low and numerous, and so located as to combine in forming beautiful basin-shaped valleys, some ornamented with lakes, others rich and fertile meadows; but what more particularly characterises and embellishes the features of this division is the highly improved appearance of its agriculture, ornamented with trees in hedgerows, orchards and its great extent of plantation.

The most southern of the valleys in the eastern section of the parish is closed easterly by the broad rising townland of Cortubber, flanked on the south by Tonagenasey, Lisbrinon and Fortry, a chain of heights in the parish of Ematris, and on the north by Drum, Aughareagh and Tonnytallagh, Long loch occupying a considerable extent of its eastern area.

Another valley running parallel, but curving south towards its western extremity, is closed easterly by the town[lands] of Drum, Drumgramph, Cartrain and Killencuagh forming its northern boundary.

A third and more extensive valley, running in the same parallel, is bounded on the east by the beautiful parachute-shaped hill forming the townland of Mucklagh, having for its northern range another broad, slightly convex, chain of heights comprising the townlands of Dunnaluck, Tatenacake, Maghershaffry and Crunchigo.

Another chain of heights, extending from the cone-shaped hill of Dunnaluck through Corragary, Tullyrample and Briskenagh, give rise to a valley flanked on the north by the townlands of Lurganboy and Carnroe, the highest elevation in the parish; and in the depression to the north of these lies the boundary betwixt the parishes of Currin and Aghabog.

All these valleys are closed westerly by the extremities of the ridges curving in a south westerly direction and which again form the eastern boundary of another succession of similarly parallel vales pursuing the same westerly course, until closed by the sierra traversing from Carnroe to Callaghill.

SOCIAL ECONOMY

Local Government

Colonel Madden and Captain Cottenham are the only resident magistrates within the parish; Richard Mayne Esquire of Freame Mount in the adjoining parish of Ematris, agent to Lord Cremorne, and [blank] Cochran Esquire of Clones, agent to the estate of Colonel Madden, both hold commissions of the peace for the county.

In consequence of the inconvenient form and length of the parish, the eastern division of its population attend the petty sessions at Cootehill for the adjudication of their wrongs on every Wednesday, and the western division attend at Clones on Fridays for the same purpose. The petty sessions at both places are generally attended by 3, and frequently 4, magistrates, all of whom are firm, decisive and impartial in the discharge of the legislative duties, and highly respected by the people.

Combination of any description (tithe excepted) nowhere exists within the parish and its general character is quiet and orderly. Illicit distillation does not prevail.

Dispensaries

There is no dispensary within the parish and the only resident surgeon is Mr James Taylor of Drum. Mr Taylor pronounces the parish exceedingly healthy; very few patients upon his books; slight fevers and colds the most prevalent complaints, with an occasional case of consumption, the peasantry attaining to a very great age. The eastern division of the parish has the benefit of attending a dispensary in the town of Cootehill and the western a dispensary in the town of Clones.

Schools

A very anxious desire prevails amongst the people to procure the means of a sound education for their children. Naturally acute and intelligent, they are fully alive to the benefits arising to their offspring from the possession of sound and useful learning. Great improvement has doubtlessly manifested itself in the moral habits of the rising generation from the diffusion and influence of schools, and a great increase of happiness and peace may still be anticipated from so wise and beneficial a system of legislation.

12 schools are in full and active operation. [Table contains the following headings: name of townland, number of pupils subdivided by religion and sex, remarks as to how supported, when erected].

Cortubber: Protestants 57, Roman Catholics 35, males 50, females 42, total 92; London Hibernian Society 6 pounds per annum, scholars from 1s to 3s per quarter, established 1832.

Drum: Protestants 32, Roman Catholics 8, males 26, females 14, total 40; landed proprietors 12 pounds, scholars 1s to 3s per quarter, erected 1821.

Aughareagh: Protestants 129, Roman Catholics 17, males 70, females 76, total 146; London Hibernian Society 6 pounds, scholars 1s to 3s per quarter, erected 1823.

Curtrain: Protestants 18, Roman Catholics 3, males 17, females 4, total 21; scholars 1s to 2s per quarter, erected 1814.

Corrygarry: Protestants 87, Roman Catholics 15, males 63, females 39, total 102; scholars from 1s to 3s 6d per quarter, erected 1833.

Tatenacake: Protestants 93, Roman Catholics 39, males 78, females 54, total 132; London Hibernian Society 6 pounds a year, scholars from 1s to 3s per quarter, erected 1829.

Knox West: Protestants 6, Roman Catholics 30, males 24, females 12, total 36; scholars from 1s to 3s per quarter, erected 1786.

Parish of Currin

Cornroe: Protestants 73, Roman Catholics 27, males 48, females 52, total 100; London Hibernian Society 6 pounds, scholars 1s to 3s per quarter, erected 1810.

Killyfargy: Protestants 2, Roman Catholics 84, males 50, females 36, total 86; National Board of Education 8 pounds per annum, scholars 1s to 3s per quarter, erected 1833.

Scotshouse: Protestants 22, Roman Catholics 30, males 32, females 20, total 52; London Hibernian Society 8 pounds, rector of the parish 2 pounds and scholars 6d per quarter, erected 1818.

Drumhillagh: Protestants 2, Roman Catholics 123, males 75, females 50, total 125; National Board of Education 8 pounds, scholars 1s to 3s per quarter, erected 1832.

Lislea: Protestants 6, Roman Catholics 4, males 8, females 2, total 10; scholars 1s to 2s per quarter, erected 1812.

Total 942.

Poor

No asylum of any denomination has ever been erected within the parish for the reception of the poor. Their only relief consists in the charitable donations, the benevolent and hospitable dispositions of the people. Indeed, in a parish so purely predial, very few instances of pauperism appear.

The collections and contributions at the church of Drum amount in the year to 10 pounds, and the numbers upon the poor list average 20. The collections on the sabbath day at the parochial church in Scotshouse average 8 pounds a year, and the poor 12.

In the Roman Catholic chapel at Scotshouse there is no weekly collection for the poor, nor any list of their numbers kept. In cases of great distress the circumstance is announced from the altar on a previous Sunday and a collection made on the following. The average amount on these occasions is about 1 pound 12s.

Religion

The last census of the parish taken in 1831 amounted to 6,888 souls. Of these, 4,076 were Roman Catholics and 2,812 Protestants, the latter subdividing into 1,902 Episcopalians, 624 Seceders and 286 Presbyterians. The divines of the Established Church derive their incomes from tithe, the Dissenting clergymen receive 50 pounds a year, the regium donum, and about 40 pounds a year from their parishioners; the Roman Catholic divines derive their income from the people.

Habits of the People

The apathy and indifference to every kind of comfort or the accumulation of property on the part of the people is too notorious to be in any way glossed over. Great are the evils and much to be deplored the baneful effects of absenteeism, but the residence and example of the landed proprietors do not produce that panacea for the evils of Ireland in their own proximities which is so much dwelt upon in the ameliorating principles of its benefactors.

A glance at the wretched hovels, scantily covered with straw, surrounded and almost entombed in mire, which everywhere present themselves throughout the parish, sufficiently testify that the total absence of all activity in industry is one source of the wretchedness and misery which almost overwhelms the land.

In no kingdom in the universe does so general an appearance of poverty and destitution prevail as in the persons and domiciles of this intelligent, lively but thoughtless community. The most substantial of their mud-built houses resist the elements for a few years only, and remain long in dilapidation before they are restored. There are exceptions of stone-built dwellings to this almost universal substitution of mud perceivable in the parish, the more numerous in the western section.

Potatoes and thin buttermilk constitute their chief and almost only source of subsistence. Butcher meat or butter form no part of their daily meals, and their well-fed pigs nowhere suspend in massive fletches from their dingy rafters, for the purpose of kitchen to their vegetable diet. All are transported to make up the rent, and nothing remains but the light, gay and cheerful spirits of the emaciated frames of a half-starved population. Still, amid such apparent destitution and want, many instances of longevity are recorded, and the healthiness of the people is well established by the medical practitioners in charge of its population.

No peculiarity of dress distinguishes the district: various coloured friezes and corduroys constitute the male, home-spun woollens with fancy cottons the female attire.

The most favourite amusement among the people is attendance at fairs, which are frequented with sacred punctuality. Sunday amongst the Roman Catholic population after morning service is a day of peculiar recreation.

No local customs, patrons or patrons' days are observed here, neither does the rehearsal of legendary tales or supernatural incantations prevail, as in more wild and mountainous districts.

McMahons, Maguires, McAtees, Connollys, Bradys, Armstrongs, Thomsons are common names.

Emigration

Emigration does not prevail here. The want of means to transport their families, however, alone prevents vast numbers from proceeding to the Canadas.

None go from hence to the English harvest.

Productive Economy

Manufacturing: Linen

An extensive and profitable trade in linen was carried on throughout the parish previous to the very general introduction of cottons into England, and was productive of much profit and comfort to the people. In those days the spinning wheels and looms occupied a large space in every dwelling and produced by their activity and occupation not only the full amount of the yearly rent of the holding, but a considerable surplus of income, thus enabling the population to enjoy the produce of their farms and in many instances the acquisition of much wealth.

The once flourishing condition of this branch of manufactures is still evinced by the ruins of extensive bleachfields, which are observable around the district, testifying by their magnitude the outlay of vast capital in their erection, very few of which unfortunately are now in operation.

This branch of domestic economy still exists, but so depressed that a few yarn and coarse linen dealers from Belfast and the northern towns purchase at weekly markets the whole produce of the district. The most industrious and active spinner cannot earn more than 2d a day, and the price of weaving is proportionally reduced. The profit upon a web of coarse linen, the only manufacture of the country, measuring 54 yards, seldom exceeds 14s, and the time in weaving it 3 weeks.

The same cause which led to the decline of the linen trade in this country operated similarly in many parts of Scotland, but the persevering habits of the Scot soon applied his energies to the new condition of things, and still contrives, by combined industry, to support his family, whereas in this unhappy country every spirit of enterprise and activity perished with the trade.

Fairs

The only monthly fair within the parish is held in the village of Drum, on the first Tuesday of every month, but this is no deprivation. The towns of Ballyhare, Redhills, Clones, Newbliss and Cootehill are all within a few miles, affording every facility for the sale of the produce of the district.

The fair in Drum is chiefly frequented by dealers in pigs, vast numbers of which are bought for the English market. Pork is sold in this and the neighbouring markets at 3d per lb., and the value of the animal in the fair is estimated at 2d per lb., and the low Dutch breed is preferred to all others.

Horses, cows, sheep and asses are bought and sold in the fair, but of a very inferior description. Horses from 8 to 12 pounds, cows from 3 to 5 pounds 10s, sheep from 30s to 50s, and asses from 1 to 3 pounds. Poultry of every description in the season: turkey from 10d to 15d, geese from 10d to 18d, fowls 6d and chickens 3d.

These fairs are the grand sources of amusement and recreation of the people. The whole population attend; not a soul is to be seen in the country on these gala days, and much jollity and mirth prevails; and happily much less inebriety is observable than in many other districts.

Rural Economy

The same deplorable system of agriculture so universally pursued throughout the country is pertinaciously adhered to in this district, a practice alike ruinous to the property of the landlord as pauperising to the occupying tenant of the soil, a system indefensible upon any recognised principle of either ancient or modern agriculture, and transferred from father to son as the ne plus ultra of experience, through a series of many generations, a system not arising from the Hydra-headed monster absenteeism nor the high rent of land, but emanating from a practice of subdividing farms into small tenures and subletting the same to insolvent tenantry.

Farms

The general size of the farms or holdings may be stated at 8 acres, which rents for good land 10 pounds sterling per annum, exclusive of county cess and tithe, averaging about 16s. Now the same quality of soil in England or Scotland may be estimated at 20 pounds, exclusive also of local taxation; but in pursuance with a superior system of

Parish of Currin

husbandry in those countries, every inch of the soil is submitted to the plough, not a ridge a foot broad remains inactive, whereas in this country not only are 4 acres of the farm necessarily laying waste for the want of capital and also the want of energy and industry on the part of the tenantry, but large spaces surrounding the margin of every field are wholly neglected and unemployed.

The farmers are generally cottiers of the poorest class, labouring for subsistence only. Not one in 20 possess the means of paying up their rent, and their cabins, almost universally built in a combination of mud and straw, present a most wretched appearance; and nothing will induce them to alter their system and try the experiment of green feeding, which has so admirably succeeded in several localities.

Manures

The only manure employed throughout the parish is the very scanty accumulations of the pigsty and byre. Cattle are permitted to roam throughout the year from field to field for food, and much manure is lost which, if collected by stall-feeding and mingled with the fodder, would be found of great value.

The system of feeding upon turnips and mangel-wurzel pursued in some localities, and productive of much abundance of domestic comfort, has no place here.

The scrapings of the roads and collections from the ditches, together with the burning of the soil, if not considered a superior mode of manuring, is most certainly pursued as if it were so, to the destruction of the soil and beggaring of the population.

The farms are subdivided into very small enclosures, fenced with ditches or banks thrown up.

Soil

The soil in the eastern and central sections of the parish is formed of an argillaceo-alluminous combination, naturally rich and fertile. In the townlands of Carnroe, Cavany, Coraghan, Skerrick and Callaghill the substratum rises to the surface, rendering the soil light and stony. In the western section an argillaceo-calcareous compound prevails, exuberantly productive, and capable of the highest degree of improvement. A deep blue marl abounding with minute shells and vegetable impressions is accessible in almost every drain and bog, but entirely neglected, notwithstanding its value as manure is well known.

Husbandry

The plough with 2 horses is occasionally, but rarely, observable throughout the parish. Indeed, very few of the tenantry can afford to keep a horse. Mutual accommodation of borrowing and lending during the spring season is their practice, and is withal so unskilfully handled that in all probability the very useful instrument, the loy, is the most productive. The great length of its blade, however, is not applied as might be supposed in trenching the soil, but for the purpose of turning up long narrow stripes which its shape and size effects with great facility.

The system of preparing the soil for every denomination of crop generally pursued is by dividing the ground into ridges about 4 feet broad, leaving a space for a trench about a foot broad betwixt them. The soil, exhausted by a previous succession of crops without manure, remains several years fallow, until its natural fertility and the fructifying power of the elements clothe it again with verdure, when the rotation of crops is as follows.

The ridges unbroken by plough or loy are covered with manure and potato-seed thickly deposited; a portion of the soil in the trenches is now raised and spread over the seed, and as the young vegetable rises the trenches again supply successive coverings, until a sufficiency has been raised and spread over the crop to bring it to maturity, and now the labours of the spring close.

The second year oat-seed and a small quantity of flax are sown upon the same ground, and produce exuberant crops; and these are followed by oats the third, fourth and fifth years, until the soil is no longer capable of sustaining vegetation.

In the western section of the parish, where the soil is formed of an argillaceo-calcareous combination, wheat and barley are more generally sown after potatoes, but upon precisely the same principle, for here also one-half of the farms are inactive. This practice, almost universal, is here more fully detailed to avoid repetition under the same head in reporting upon the surrounding parishes.

Produce

About 60 stones of potatoes are sown per acre, and the produce of a favourable season amounts to 1,250, the market price throughout the winter varying from 2d to 3d ha'penny per stone. 16 stones of oat-seed per acre follows the potato crop, the produce of which amounts to 180 stones, the price varying throughout the season from 6d to 11d ha'penny. The quantity of oat-seed per acre for the third, fourth and fifth years varies from 16 to 20 stones per acre, in proportion to the exhausted state of the soil, and the produce decrease proportionally.

16 stones of wheat-seed, after potatoes, produces 240 stones per acre, the price varying from 19s to 21s per barrel; and the proportions of barley are as 16 of seed to 240 of produce, price varying from 10d to 1s per stone. 12 pecks of flax-seed per acre, price 2 pounds 8s, produces 36 stones of prepared lint, price current 12s per stone.

Potatoes are the staple article of provisions of the peasantry: every other article of produce is bought up for the English market. Considerable quantities of oats are ground into meal by the mills of the district and forwarded to the same country. Butter varies from 5d to 7d per lb., and almost the whole of this produce also is transferred to England.

Labour

The general pay of the day labourer without diet is 10d in summer and 8d in winter. Farm servants capable of ploughing receive, besides board and lodging, 6 pounds a year, and female servants from 2 to 4 pounds per annum. The old Irish cart is still in general use throughout the parish, and the slide, so very suitable in many localities, is still retained, but most of the transport, either manure to the fields or produce to the markets, is conveyed upon asses, horses and in carts.

Threshing machines are unknown: the flail and centre of the road in fine weather supply the convenience of barns and threshing machines, and indeed the scanty stackyards are very speedily disposed of when submitted to the influence of a couple of active flails; and it is worthy of record, and almost incredible, how gigantic are the labours of 2 resolute Hibernians when engaged by the bulk on this duty.

Proprietors and Farms

The great landed proprietors of the parish are Lord Cremorne, Colonel Madden, John Quin Esquire, Dr Clarke and the Honourable R. Westenra. The general size of the farms upon his lordship's estate (a minor) is given by Richard Mayne Esquire, his agent, as 8 acres at 22s per acre Irish measure, on leases generally of 3 lives or 31 years, all expiring with his lordship's minority.

The general size of the farms upon Colonel Madden's estate, a resident landlord, is stated by [blank] Cochran Esquire, his agent, as 8 acres, on leases of 3 lives or 31 years at 25s per acre.

The general size of the farms upon Mr Quin's estate, as given by Captain Cottenham, his agent, is 5 acres at 30s per acre, on leases of 3 lives or 31 years.

The average size of the holdings upon Dr Clarke's townlands is 8 acres at 25s per acre, some on leases of 3 lives or 31 years, but most part are tenants at will.

The average size of the farms on the Honourable R. Westenra's estate, a resident in the county, is 10 acres at 25s per acre, on leases of 3 lives or 31 years.

There are 2 holdings upon his lordship's estate above 100 acres, 4 above 50 acres, 21 holdings above 20 acres and 72 above 10 acres, but all these are subdivided by the tenantry into farms of the average size of 8 acres, and the same fracture prevails upon every estate within the parish.

The tenure in general is direct from the proprietor, but there are many instances of middlemen also. Many of the small farms in the parish are held at the will of the landlord, a practice which leads to considerable improvement in the appearance of the country.

Grazing and Cattle

None of the soil of the parish is applied to grazing. The subdivision of its surface into small farms renders this impracticable. It is purely agricultural and wholly devoted to the cultivation of potatoes and grain.

A very superior breed of horses is raised in Hilton demesne under the management of Colonel Madden. The common horse of the district is low bred, and cows are equally so. The breeding of pigs is the grand object of the people, and the short-legged Dutch breed is most valued. Jobbers buy them up for the English market. Green feeding, unhappily, has no place here.

Uses made of the Bogs

The bogs are wholly applied to the formation of turf, and very great scarcity of this valuable article of fuel prevails. None is prepared for sale or for the use of the forges, unless in localities where it is tolerably abundant. No discovery of metal has ever been made in the bogs or mineral springs of the district.

Planting

With the exception of Hilton demesne and its

vicinity, and the localities of Laurel Hill and Cortubber, there are no plantations within the parish, neither has the formation of nurseries for young trees been anywhere established. Ash, elm and fir and beech have attained to full maturity in Colonel Madden's estate and are now cutting down for sale. Builders from the neighbouring towns purchase the timber in lots, rendering it difficult to name a fixed rate when the selection of a tree is made. Ash sells for 2s 6d per square foot, oak at 3s and fir at 1s 6d per square foot.

SOCIAL AND PRODUCTIVE ECONOMY

Ecclesiastical Summary

[Table] Name Currin, diocese Clogher, province Ulster, rectory, union none; patron bishop of the diocese, incumbent Revd William Moffat, glebe none, tithe compounded for 400 pounds per annum.

General Remarks: Improvements

Having pointed out under the preceding heads of illustration the natural resources of the parish, the facility of transport for its produce, the proximity of its markets and the established healthiness and salubrity of its climate, a question arises: from what cause, under circumstances so favourable, does such an amount of misery and destitution assail the land?

First, it arises from so tenaciously adhering to a system of husbandry which, having been pursued for many generations, entails nothing but self-evident and daily proofs of poverty and ruin upon its followers, and in not adopting the system of green feeding, not only universally practised in all agricultural parishes in England and Scotland but followed in several localities in this country with great advantage.

The feeding of cattle upon turnips, manglewurzel and clovers would ameliorate the condition of the peasantry more than a reduction of rent or any other remedy that could be applied.

A reduction of rent is of little avail, for whether the land pays 5s or 15s per acre, the condition of the tenantry is the same. But it more particularly arises from the practice of subdividing the farm into very small holdings, from 2 acres to 10, thereby depriving the farmer of the power of employing capital upon it, if he possess any, by confining his labours to so narrow a sphere that, under the existing system of one-half of his ground laying waste, the remaining portion is not sufficient to raise potatoes and corn for the subsistence of his family and payment of his arrears of rent.

But how is this subdividing system to be counteracted? By a legislative enactment that no new farm shall comprise less than 25 acres of arable ground; and in order to remove the surplus tenantry on the new holding, encouragement should be given, and the choice imperative, of buying each other out.

Thus an emulation to industry will at once be excited and the superabundant population will gradually disappear, and many will be enabled by the sale of their holdings to remove to America, which they are very desirous of doing. Neither is this a novel experiment, for its principle has been successfully acted upon in one estate of the county of Fermanagh.

But above every other desideratum in ameliorating the condition of the tenantry, that active and energetic spirit of enterprise, now so latent throughout the district, must be roused and fully developed. Habits of industry and accumulation must be acquired, every objection to the abandonment of old unprofitable, and the adoption of improved, modes of agriculture must be insisted upon; and these, and many other exalted virtues, are within the power of a people at present the most wretched, but incontestibly among the most intelligent, of any other nation upon the surface of the globe. [Signed] P. Taylor, Lieutenant 69th Regiment.

Extract from Statistical Report of Currin by Lieutenant P. Taylor, June 1835

ANCIENT TOPOGRAPHY

Worm's Ditch

[Insert query: County Fermanagh, county Monaghan]? A boundary of very ancient appearance locally termed Worm's Ditch, from its tortuous direction, consisting of a rampart and double fosse, several portions of which is still very conspicuous but much of it faint or defaced, traverses a considerable extent of the parish. The height of the rampart in some places measures 9 feet above the surface of the ground and the depth of the ditch from the top of the rampart 20 feet, and the breadth of both the ditches and ramparts 48 feet, the ditch contracting to 3 feet at the bottom. The construction of the boundary [no further text]. [Signed] P. Taylor, Lieutenant 69th Regiment, 2nd June 1835.

Parish of Donagh, County Monaghan

Memoir by T.C. McIlroy and by J.C. Innes, 1838

NATURAL STATE

Locality

The parish of Donagh is situated in the northern part of the county Monaghan and in the barony of Trough. It is bounded on the north by the parish of Errigal Trough, on the east by the counties of Tyrone and Armagh, on the west by the parish of Tydavnet and on the south by the parishes of Tyholland and Monaghan.

Its extreme length is 9 miles and extreme breadth is 6 and a half miles. Its content is 16,202 acres 1 rood 11 perches, including 241 acres 3 roods 7 perches of water.

NATURAL FEATURES

Hills

The highest hill in the parish is Golan. It is situated at the extremity of a narrow portion of the parish which runs in a north west direction. It is 650 feet above the level of the sea. It forms a portion of the Slieve Beagh range.

The average height of the hills in this parish is 300 feet above the sea. They are in general well cultivated and are connected in ridges which run north and south, the western side of which is the steepest. The lowest ground in the parish is along the River Blackwater, 115 feet above the sea.

Lakes

Emy lough occupies portions of the townlands of Derrygassan Lower, Emy, Killycooly, Portinaghy, Tiramoan. It is 156 feet above the sea and contains 118 acres 1 rood 23 perches, depth not known.

Emyvale lake occupies portions of the townlands of Carrigans, Cornacreeve, Derryhallagh and Tully. It is 163 feet above the sea and contains 15 acres 1 rood, depth not known.

Glaslough lake, situated close to the town of Glaslough, is 115 feet above level of the sea. It occupies portions of the townlands of Glaslough, Tullyree, Tonyhannigan and Killyconigan. Its depth is not known and its content is 86 acres 2 roods 28 perches.

Kilvey lake is situated in Mrs Leslie's demesne at Glaslough. It is 129 feet above the level of the sea. It occupies portions of the townlands of Kilvey, Killyconigan and Cleary. Its content is 104 acres 2 roods 2 perches, depth not known.

Killy lough, through the centre of which the boundary line of this parish runs, is situated on the boundary of the western part of the parish. The portion in this parish is in the townland of Cloghernagly. Its content is 7 acres 2 roods 19 perches. It is 315 feet above the level of the sea, depth is not known.

Rivers

The Mountain water forms the northern boundary line of this parish for 2 and a half miles. It then runs in a easterly direction from 4 and a quarter miles through the northern part of the parish. Its average breadth is 24 feet and it is from 1 to 3 feet in depth. It is usefully situated for drainage and water power. The average fall is 30 feet in the mile. The bed of the river is gravelly. It discharges itself into the River Blackwater in this parish. The parish is well supplied with water from rivulets.

The main branch of the River Blackwater forms the north eastern boundary of this parish for 2 miles. Its average breadth is 60 feet and it is from 3 to 6 feet in depth. It is usefully situated for drainage. The general fall is 10 feet per mile. The bed of the river is composed of sand and gravel. The banks are uninteresting.

The southern branch of the Blackwater forms the south boundary of this parish for 6 miles, running east; it then runs north for 2 and a half miles, forming the eastern boundary. Its average breadth is 45 feet and it is from 1 to 3 feet in depth. It is usefully situated for drainage and water power. The bed is gravel. The banks are uninteresting.

Bogs and Woods

There is a bog situated nearly in the centre of this parish, 1 mile from Glaslough. The old road leading to Monaghan passes through it. It occupies portions of 7 townlands, Donagh, Srananny, Lisgoagh, Mullaghbane, Mullaghduff, Derryveen, Rossarnell. Its extreme length is 1 mile and its extreme breadth three-quarters of a mile. It is 164 feet above the level of the sea and 4 feet above the Mountain water. Timber is found imbedded, depth of the bog is 10 feet.

There are no natural woods in this parish.

Parish of Donagh

The climate and crops are the same as those of the parish of Monaghan.

MODERN TOPOGRAPHY

Schoolhouse

Knocknagrave national schoolhouse is situated in the townland of Knocknagrave. It is a stone cottage, whitewashed and thatched, 35 feet long and 17 feet broad. It was erected in 1828, expense of building not known.

Roman Catholic Chapel

Corracrin chapel, situated in the townland of Derryhallagh, is a plain stone building, roughcast and slated, the form and dimensions of which are represented by the following figure: [ground plan, main dimensions 83 feet 6 inches by 54 feet, roughly "T" shape]. It was built in 1811, the cost not known. There is accommodation for 1,100 persons and the general attendance is 870. The parish priest is the Revd Patrick Moynagh.

Bridges

There is a bridge situated on the boundary line which separates the townlands of Aghaboy and Lettoonigan over the Mountain water. It is built of limestone and consists of 3 semicircular arches. It is 24 feet broad and 42 feet long, including the parapet walls.

There is a bridge situated on the boundary line which separates the townlands of Telayden and Glaslough. It is built of limestone and sandstone. It consists of 1 semicircular arch. It is 24 feet 6 inches broad and 26 feet long. It is over the Mountain water.

Catholic Chapel

There is a Roman Catholic chapel situated in the townland of Cloncaw. It is a very fine house built of freestone and limestone. It is 110 feet long and 52 feet broad. It has high and narrow Gothic windows; it is unfinished. It will accommodate 2,000 persons when finished. It has cost 1,000 pounds, beside a good deal of labour given gratis by the parishioners.

Bridge

Newmills bridge, over a branch of the River Blackwater, on the boundary line of this parish and on the boundary line which separates the townlands of Cornahoe and Kilcran: it is built of limestone and consists of 3 semicircular arches. It is 46 feet long and 23 feet broad, including the parapet walls.

Village: Emyvale

Emyvale is situated in the townland of Scarnageeragh or Emyvale, on the main road between Monaghan and Aughnacloy, county Tyrone, 6 and a quarter miles from the former. It consists of 1 street [blank] yards long and [blank] yards broad. The houses are regular. They consist of 67 of 1-storey and 57 of 2; of these only 3 are slated. They are for the most part built of stone.

Wesleyan Chapel

Emyvale Primitive Wesleyan chapel, situated on the east side of the street near the centre of the village, is a plain stone building, roughcast and slated. It is 33 and a half feet long and 21 feet broad. It was built in 1836.

Bridge

Emyvale bridge crosses the Mountain water at the south end of the village. It is 69 feet long and 24 and a half feet broad, including the parapet walls. The bridge consists of 4 semicircular arches.

Knockaginny bridge over the River Blackwater is on the boundary line of the parish and on the boundary which separates the townlands of Killyrean Upper and Monmurry. It is built of limestone and consists of 3 semicircular arches. It is 52 feet long and 24 feet 6 inches broad.

Glaslough: Locality

Glaslough is 65 miles distant from Dublin. It is in the diocese of Clogher, the province of Ulster, the county of Monaghan and the parish of Donagh. Its extreme length is 520 yards and its greatest breadth is 170 yards. The surrounding country is extremely picturesque and well cultivated.

Streets

The town consists of 1 principal street and a smaller one which runs off from near the centre of the main street. The houses in general are good. There have been many new houses lately built by Mrs Leslie. They are of stone, slated. The town consists of 32 houses of 1, 45 of 2 and 7 of 3-storeys; 29 of these are thatched and the remainder slated.

SOCIAL AND PRODUCTIVE ECONOMY

Habits and Occupations of People

There are no scientific or literary societies in the town, branch banks, library or reading rooms.

Fairs and Markets

There is a monthly fair held on the third Friday in every month and a small weekly market held on Fridays.

Occupations

Town of Glaslough, table of occupations. Trade or calling: doctors 1, woollen drapers 1, woollen and hardware merchants 1, grocers and hardware merchants 2, grocers and whiskey dealers 2, grocer and tallow chandlers 1, delph merchants 1, whiskey shops 5, grocers 2, painters and glaziers 1, lodgings and entertainment 3, shoemakers 2, smiths 2.

MODERN TOPOGRAPHY

Communications

The main road from Monaghan to Caledon (passing through Glaslough) runs in a northerly direction through this parish for 3 and three-quarter miles. Its average breadth is 28 feet. It is a well laid out road except for 2 miles south of Glaslough, where a new and better line has been laid out which will run into the former road. It is kept in good repair at the expense of the county.

There are several cross and by-roads also, which are kept in good repair.

Church

Glaslough church is situated at the north east end of the town. It is a neat, rectangular stone building 95 feet long and 40 feet broad. It was erected in 1670 and rebuilt in 1763; the expense of building and how defrayed not known.

The interior is plain. There is a small gallery at the north west end. The windows are Gothic. The accommodation is 250 persons and the general attendance is 250.

Tomb in Church

There is a dark stone laid in the floor of the aisle, on which is the following inscription: "Memento mori. Here lies the body of Matthew Ancketill Esquire of Anketell's Grove, who in the 37th year of his age was killed at Glaslough in defence of the Protestant religion and liberty of his country. March 13th anno 1688."

Glebe House

The Glebe House, the residence of the Revd William Pratt, vicar of the parish, is situated in the townland of Dundonagh. It is a plain stone building, slated, 2-storeys high.

Meeting Houses

Glaslough Wesleyan Methodist chapel is situated at the south end of the town. It is a stone building, slated. It was erected in 1820. It is 37 feet long and 27 and half feet 6 inches broad. The interior is plain. It is unceiled and unfloored. The windows are Gothic. The accommodation is for 100 persons and the general attendance is 50. There is no resident preacher attached to the above meeting house.

There is a Presbyterian meeting house situated in the townland of Lettoonigan. It is a rectangular stone building, slated, 73 feet long and 30 feet broad. It was erected in 1829; the expense of building and how defrayed not known. The interior is plain. The windows are Gothic. The accommodation is for 450 persons and the general attendance is 450.

Schoolhouses

Derryhallagh schoolhouse, situated in the townland of Mullaghpeak, is a neat stone cottage, roughcast, whitewashed and slated. It is 33 feet long and 18 feet broad, built in 1823 and cost 30 pounds, which was defrayed by William Murdock Esquire.

There is a schoolhouse situated in the townland of Coolcollict. It is a neat stone cottage, slated, 31 feet long and 18 feet broad. It was built in 1824 and cost 54 pounds, 27 pounds of which sum was defrayed by the Kildare Society and the remainder by subscriptions.

Bellanaman national schoolhouse, situated in the townland of Bellanaman, is a stone cottage whitewashed and thatched. It is 30 feet long and 17 feet broad.

Donagh schoolhouse, situated in the town of Glaslough at the south west end, is a good stone house, slated with Gothic windows. It is 41 feet long and 24 feet broad. It was built in 1820, expense of building and how defrayed not known.

Glaslough female schoolhouse is situated at the north west side of the town. It is a neat stone house, slated, 2-storeys high. The under part is occupied as a dwelling by the mistress. It was erected in 1830, cost defrayed by Mrs Leslie. It

Parish of Donagh

is 40 feet long and 21 feet 6 inches broad; the expense of erection not known.

PRODUCTIVE ECONOMY

Table of Mills

[Table contains the following headings: name of townland, proprietor, tenant, when built, dimensions and type of wheel, fall of water, type of machinery, stones or scutches, remarks].

Glannan, Mrs Ankle [Anketell?], Robert Aken; diameter of water wheel 12 feet, breadth 2 feet, breast wheel, wood, 1 pair of stones and a fanning machine; a stone building, thatched.

Aghnagap, Mrs Leslie, Bernard McCanagh; diameter of water wheel 15 feet, breadth 2 feet 4 inches, breast wheel, wood, 1 pair of stones; a stone house, thatched.

Kilcran, Mrs Leslie, William Young, built 1809; diameter of water wheel 15 feet, breadth 4 feet, breast wheel, metal, 1 pair of stones and a fanning machine; a stone house, slated, 2-storeyed.

Kilcran, Mrs Leslie, William Young, built 1824; diameter of water wheel 14 feet, breadth 2 feet 4 inches, breast wheel, wood and iron, 8 stocks and 1 pair of rollers; a stone house, slated.

Drumully, William Anketell Esquire, John Collins, built 1668; diameter of water wheel 13 feet, breadth 1 foot 11 inches, breast wheel, fall 1 foot 6 inches, wood and metal, 1 pair of stones and 1 set of fans; a stone house, slated.

Drumully, William Anketell Esquire, John Collins, built 1836; diameter of water wheel 13 feet, breadth 2 feet 8 inches, overshot wheel, wood and metal, 1 set of skutches and 1 set of rollers; a stone house, slated.

Scarnageeragh or Emyvale, Mrs Leslie, William Murdock, built 1836; diameter of water wheel 16 feet, breadth 4 feet, breast wheel, wood and metal, 2 pair of stones, 1 lifting machine, 2 sets of fans, 2 screens and 4 sets of elevators; a good stone house, slated. [Initialled] J.R. Ward.

SOCIAL ECONOMY

Table of Schools

[Table contains the following headings: name, situation and description, when established, income and expenditure, physical, intellectual and moral education, number of pupils subdivided by age, sex and religion, name and religious persuasion of master or mistress].

Coolcollict, a neat cottage in the townland of Coolcollict, established 1824; income: from the Donagh Education Society 7 pounds 10s, from the pupils 5 pounds per annum; intellectual education: Kildare Society books and Education Board books; moral education: visited by the Revd William Smyth, catechisms taught on Saturdays by the master, assisted by the Revd William Smyth, Authorised Version of Scriptures read daily; number of pupils: males, 22 under 10 years of age, 18 from 10 to 15, 40 total males; females, 16 under 10 years of age, 9 from 10 to 15, 25 total females; total number of pupils 65, 13 Protestants, 20 Presbyterians, 32 Roman Catholics; master William Reyney, Presbyterian. 9th February 1838.

Ballanaman national school, a cottage in the townland of Ballanaman, established 1835; income: from the National Board 8 pounds, from pupils 16 pounds; intellectual education: Education Board books; moral education: catechisms taught on Saturday by the master, Scriptures read daily; number of pupils: males, 12 under 10 years of age, 59 from 10 to 15, 5 above 15, 76 total males; females, 20 under 10 years of age, 15 from 10 to 15, 5 above 15, 40 total females; total number of pupils 116, 14 Protestants, 92 Roman Catholics; master John Campbell, Roman Catholic.

Donagh school, a good cottage in the town of Glaslough, established 1820; income: from the Donagh Education Society 6 pounds, as a bequest from the late William Maxwell 5 pounds 10s, from the Bishop of Clogher 5 pounds, from pupils 5 pounds 10s; intellectual education: Kildare Society books; moral education: visited by the Revd William Pratt, catechism taught on Saturdays by the master, Authorised Version of Scriptures read daily; number of pupils: males, 40 under 10 years of age, 56 from 10 to 15, 5 above 15, 96 total males; females, 40 under 10 years of age, 40 total females; total number of pupils 136, 81 Protestants, 35 Presbyterians, 20 Roman Catholics; master Robert Whitsitt, Established Church. 14th February 1838.

Female school, a good house in the town of Glaslough, established 1829; income: from Mrs Leslie of Leslie Castle 28 pounds per annum; moral education: visited by the Revd William Pratt; number of pupils: 40 under 10 years of age, 30 from 10 to 15, total number of pupils 70, 35 Protestants, 20 Presbyterians, 15 Roman Catholics; mistress Anne Darragh, Established Church.

Derryhallagh day school, a neat house in the townland of Mullaghbrack, established 1823; income: from Donagh Education Board 10 pounds per annum, from Baptist Johnston Barton Esquire 5 pounds per annum, from pupils 3 pounds per annum; intellectual education: Kildare Place books; moral education: visited by the Revd William Henry Pratt, vicar of Donagh, and the Revd William Smith, Presbyterian minister of Donagh, Authorised Version of Scriptures read daily, catechisms taught on Saturdays; number of pupils: males, 34 under 10 years of age, 20 from 10 to 15, 1 above 15, 55 total males; females, 24 under 10 years of age, 12 from 10 to 15, 3 above 15, 39 total females; total number of pupils 94, 20 Protestants, 71 Presbyterians, 3 Roman Catholics; master Hugh Armstrong, Presbyterian; [signed] J. Cumming Innes, 28th February 1838.

Knocknagrave national school, a cottage, thatched, in the townland of Knocknagrave, established 1833; income: from the Education Board 10 pounds per annum, from pupils 4 pounds per annum; intellectual education: books of the Education Board; moral education: visited by the Revd Patrick Moyne, parish priest, catechism taught on Saturdays; number of pupils: males, 53 under 10 years of age, 35 from 10 to 15, 12 above 15, 100 total males; females, 40 under 10 years of age, 30 from 10 to 15, 70 total females; total number of pupils 170, 6 Protestants, 164 Roman Catholics; master Charles McKenna, Roman Catholic; [signed] Thomas C. McIlroy, 28th February 1838.

Table of Benevolence

Establishments for the relief of mental and bodily disease. Name: Glaslough and Emyvale dispensary; object: to give relief to the sick and destitute; management: a committee of 11 gentlemen, 1 of whom acts as treasurer and secretary; funds from private sources 62 pounds per annum; annual expenses of management: house rent 5 pounds per annum, [crossed out: salary of surgeon 110 pounds per annum]; number relieved: varies, see printed forms; relief afforded: medicine and medical advice gratis.

Printed Reports of Glaslough and Emyvale Dispensary

Dispensary Report in 1836-7

[Printed] Report of the Glaslough and Emyvale dispensary, from 1st July 1836 to 1st January 1837. The following is an arranged list of the diseases which have been treated at the Glaslough and Emyvale dispensary from July 1836 to January 1837.

Fevers: febris remittens 2, synochus 29, synocha 11, typhus 16.

Inflammations: phlegmon 1, opthalmia memb 13, psoropthalmia 4, otitis 3, cynanche parot 2 cynanche tonsil 5, pleuritis 20, bronchitis acuta 16, bronchitis chronica 18, pneumonia 5, enteritis 1, hepatitis 1, rheumatismus acuta 23, rheumatismus chronica 16, lumbago 10.

Involuntary discharges of blood: hemoptisis phthisica 2, menorrhagia 1, haemorrhois pro. 3.

Fluxes with fever: catarrhus a frigore 12 dysenteria 2.

Soporose diseases: paralisis 3.

Defect of vital powers: vertigo 10, dyspepsia 77.

Spasmodic diseases: epilepsia 2, chorea sanct viti 1, singultus 1, pertussis 2, pyrosis 11, palpitatio cordis 9, asthma spon 17, asthma pleth 1 colica spasm 24, colica callos 2, diarrhoea bil 30 diarrhoea mucos 1, cholera morbus (ang.) 5.

Mental diseases: mania 2.

Cachectic diseases: atrophia famel 10, atrophia inan 1, atrophia debil 1, phthisis pulmon 2.

General swellings: anasarca 5, ascites 7, rachitis 5.

Impetiginous diseases: scrofula 11, scorbutu 2, icterus calculis 1.

Increased discharges: leucorrhoea 3.

Obstructions: obstipatio obst. 99, obstipatio deb. 6, dysuria ardens 3, amenorrhoea 15, mensium suppressio 3, menorrhagia diff. 2.

Tumours: bronchocele 1.

Painful affections: cephalalgia 9, hemicrania 5, odontalgia 3, gastrodynia 20, cardialgia 2, luxatio 2.

Solutions of parts: ulcus chronicum 14, vulnu contusum 26, vulnus incisum 4, vulnus laceratum 1, vulnus punctat 2, vulnus exust fact 6.

Diseases not referable to any particular class teres 1, taenia 2, ascarides 39.

Diseases of the pregnant state: abortio 2.

Diseases of the puerperal state: inflammatio mammae 4, papillae excoriatiae 1, prolapsus uter 1.

Diseases of infants: vomitus 6.

Surgical diseases: abscess (acute and chronic 10, paronychia 3, hernia umbilicalis 1, fractur rad. et uln. 2, fractura tib. et fib. 1, concussio cerebri 1, inflammatio testis 1, contractura articulos 1, bubo 2, leucoma 1, gonorrhoea 1, ozena 1.

Diseases of the skin, pimples: strophulu albidus 3, prurigo senilis 5, prurigo mitis 3.

Scaly diseases: psoriasis guttata 4, psoriasis palmaria 2; rashes: purpura hoemorrhagical 1, erysipelas errat 1; pustules: impetigo sparsa 1, impetigo rodens 1, impetigo figurata 3, porrigo favosa 2, variola discreta 5, variola confluens 8, scabies papuliformis 20, purulenta 4, lymphatica 4.

Vesicles: herpes zoster 1.

Supposed number of deaths 11, relieved, cured or still on the books 823, total 834.

173 visits have been paid during the same period and 3,463 prescriptions compounded.

Notes on Diseases

From a reference to the list of diseases, the supporters of the institution must perceive that fever has prevailed to a very great extent during the last few months; and when I add to the above number those who were under my care, independent of dispensary relief, it presents a fearful amount.

In the majority of instances the fever of this district was typhoid, and its progress in many families was of the most afflicting nature, from 3 to 6 being frequently ill at the same time. This melancholy fact is chiefly attributable to: the destitute state of the people; the want of proper clothing and nourishment calculated to sustain the friends of the patients in their incumbent duties at the bedside; and to that terrific practice which prevails to such an extravagant excess (from absolute necessity), association with the diseased during the day in the same apartment and rest during the night in the same bed.

Upwards of 70 cases of smallpox occurred in the district of this dispensary since July 1836, and very few out of this number had been vaccinated at any period during their lives. My attention was naturally arrested to this fact, which has been demonstrated by an accurate examination into the history of every case, that wherever the vaccine matter had appeared to have affected the system, the fever which preceded and accompanied the eruption was mild, and the pustules comparatively few; while those who had never been vaccinated laboured under a very severe form of fever, with local affections either of the head, chest or bowels, and had the body covered with the smallpox in its most frightful character.

From a calm consideration of this important truth, the unprejudiced mind must be convinced that if the introduction of vaccine matter into the constitution in early life conferred no greater boon upon society than that of moderating the severity of the fever, counteracting the tendency to local congestion and diminishing the amount of pustules, an incalculable good has been conferred upon the world, for the plague has been robbed of its dangers, deformities have been guarded against, and life secured.

There are none of the individual cases which demand particular notice. Those persons who suffered from "fractures" were attended in their respective homes, and cured, and the case of dislocation of the shoulder-joint was immediately reduced. [Signed] Richard Maffett M.D., surgeon.

List of Subscribers for 1837

Mrs Leslie 20 pounds, William Anketell Esquire 15 pounds, Mrs Singleton 5 pounds, Lady Cremorne 5 pounds, Major Richardson 2 pounds 2s, William Murdock Esquire 2 pounds 2s, Roger Anketell Esquire 1 pound 1s, Alexander Nixon Montgomery Esquire 1 pound 1s, Thomas Johnston Esquire 1 pound 1s, John Radcliff Esquire 1 pound 1s, Revd William Smyth 1 pound 1s, Revd Mr Hurst 1 pound 1s, Revd W.H. Pratt 1 pound 1s, Revd Allen Mitchell 1 pound 1s, John Johnson Esquire 1 pound 2s 6d, Baptist J. Barton Esquire 1 pound 1s, Samuel McClay Esquire 1 pound 1s, Robert Murray Esquire, M.D. 1 pound 1s, William Pringle Esquire 1 pound 1s, Thomas Anketell Esquire 1 pound 1s, Robert Murdock Esquire 1 pound 1s, William Cochran Esquire 1 pound 1s, Thomas Alexander Pringle Esquire 1 pound 1s, William Young Esquire 1 pound 1s, Mrs Murray 1 pound 1s, Mrs Anketell Snr 2 pounds 2s, Revd P. Moynagh 1 pound 1s, David Smith 3 pounds 15s 6d. [Signed] William Murdock, secretary.

Dispensary Report in 1837-8

Report of the Glaslough and Emyvale dispensary, from 1st January 1837 to 1st January 1838. The following is an arranged list of the diseases which have been treated at the Glaslough and Emyvale dispensary from January 1837 to January 1838.

Fevers: febris intermittens 1, febris remittens 4, synochus 20, synocha 83, typhus 72, influenza 16.

Inflammations: opthalmia memb 7, opthalmia purulent 1, psoropthalmia 3, otitis 1, cynanche tonsil 2, cynanche parot 2, cynanche pharygn 1, pleuritis 25, bronchitis acuta 19, bronchitis chronica 10, pneumonia 4, enteritis 1, peritonitis 4, hepatitis acuta 1, rheumatismus acuta 31, rheumatismus chronica 16, lumbago 13.

Involuntary discharges of blood: hemoptisis phthisica 1, hemoptisis plethor 2, menorrhagia 2, epistaxis 1, hemorrhois interna 4, hemorrhois externa 2.

Fluxes with fever: catarrhus a frigore 6, dysenteria 7, cystirrheae 1.

Soporose diseases: paralisis 5, apoplexia sang 2.

Defect of vital powers: vertigo 1, dyspepsia 53, syncope 1.

Spasmodic diseases: singultus 1, pyrosis 13, palpitatio cordis 10, asthma spontan 7, asthma plethor 1, colica spasmod 18, colica stercorea 1, colica accident 2, colica callosa 1, diarrhoea biliosa 18, diarrhoea mucosa 1, diarrhoea crapulosa 1, diarrhoea lienteria 3, diarrhoea coeliaca 1, dyspnaea sicca 1, dyspnaea catarrh 4, cholera spontan 2, angina pectoris 1, hysteria 1.

Cachectic diseases: atrophia famel 5, atrophia debil 1, phthisis pulmonal 8.

General swellings: anasarca 14, ascites 1, rachitis 4, hydrocele 1.

Impetiginous diseases: scrofula 22, icterus calculosus 3, icterus hepaticus 2.

Increased discharges: leucorrhoea 2, gonorrhoea pura 1.

Diseases of the senses: amaurosis 2, paracusis 3.

Obstructions: obstipatio obstruct 58, obstipatio debil 8, dysuria renalis 2, dysuria ardens 1, amenorrhoea 10, mensium suppressio 2, menorrhagia diff 6.

Parts displaced: prolapsus ani 1, luxatio 4.

Painful affections: cephalgia 7, hemicrania 8, odontalgia 4, gastrodynia 24, cardialgia 3.

Solutions of parts: ulcus chronicum 4, ulcus irrit. 2, ulcus (cornea) 3, vulnus contusum 24, vulnus incisum 8, vulnus laceratum 13, vulnus punctata 2, vulnus ex ust fact 8.

Diseases not referable to any particular class: ascarides 47.

Diseases of the pregnant state: abortio 1, menorrhagia 1.

Diseases of the puerperal state: inflammatio mammae 2, papillae excoriatiae 2, prolapsus uteri 1.

Diseases of infants: vomitus 8, tormina 2, convulsiones 2, excoriationes 1, apthae 1.

Defective appetite: anorexia 1.

Surgical diseases: acute abscess 5, chronic abscess 3, psoas abscess 1, hernia umbilical 1, hernia inguinal 2, fractura clavie paronychia 4, dislocatio humeri 1, dislocatio infer max 1, dislocatio ulnae post 1, contractura articulosa 1, polypus 1, carbuncle 1, cancer 1, hordeola.

Diseases of the skin, pimples: strophulus intertinct 1, strophulus candidus 3, strophulus confertus 1, strophulus albidus 2, prurigo mitis 1, prurigo senilis 2; scaly diseases: psoriasis palm 1, psoriasis guttata 4, pityriasis capitis 1; rashes: roseola annulata 1, erysipelas aedem 1, purpura hemorrh 1; pustules: porrigo favosa 1, porrigo fursurans 8, porrigo larvalis 1, variola confluens 3, variola discreta 1, scabies purulenta 12, scabies lymphatica 5, scabies papuliformis 12.

The number of persons prescribed for on recommendations for the year 1837, 932; number of individuals prescribed for on old recommendations for the year 1837, 507; total 1,439. Supposed number of deaths 32, cured relieved or still on the books 1,407, total 1,439. 243 visits have been paid during the same period, and 9,014 prescriptions compounded.

Notes on Diseases

With respect to the prevalence of fever in this district, the second report of the dispensary must be as unfavourable as the first. The numerical amount of cases are not only increased, but the type and character of the fever has been of a more formidable nature, although the causes which were naturally alleged for its production in 1836 have not been in force to the same extent during the winter of 1837, fuel having been more abundant and the articles of diet cheaper.

In the last report which was published in connection with the dispensary, I was forced by circumstances to describe the manner in which a fever case was necessarily treated at home, and the risks which the relatives of the afflicted were unavoidably exposed to. Those evils have not in any degree abated, for absolute distress and wretchedness compel the friends to abandon every resource of caution and, with a most deplorable recklessness, to associate constantly with the individuals labouring under this distressing visitation.

But as a sweeping assertion of this nature requires facts for its corroboration, I consider therefore that the governors of the institution possess all that is necessary to bear out my statement, in the following melancholy truths: in 2 families there were 8 individuals severally attacked in each, in 3 families 5, in 2 families 4, in 4 families 3 and in 11 families 2; in all, 22 families and 73 patients.

There has been a very marked decrease in the number of cases of smallpox during the last year, when contrasted with the winter of 1836, a diminution of nearly 60 cases at least. The lower orders have been warned by the distressing results occasioned by the late scourge, and consequently there is now an avidity manifested on the part of the parents to give to their offspring that safeguard which vaccination carries with it against the inroads of a pernicious pestilence, a safeguard which is easily laid hold upon and which nature points out.

I have arranged the diseases of the skin in a distinct class, as their number has increased considerably during the last year. There are none of the individual cases which require particular notice. A very large number appear in children of a certain age and are generally produced by irritation of the bowels and teething. A second extensive division is evidently caused by want of cleanliness and propagated more extensively by contact.

On the list of surgical diseases there were a few which were extremely troublesome to manage. The dislocation of the shoulder-joint and the displacement of the ulna backwards (though both cases were neglected for nearly 30 hours) were reduced.

There was 1 individual who had a complete dislocation of the lower jaw. It had occurred in a female residing in Emyvale and was caused by the jaw being forced open beyond its natural limits in the act of "yawning." Some difficulty was experienced in reducing it to its natural situation, in consequence of 4 days having elapsed before the individual presented herself for relief. However, the reduction was perfect and no inconvenience has been complained of since. [Signed] Richard Maffett M.D., surgeon.

Dispensary Rules

Glaslough and Emyvale dispensary rules and regulations.

First: each subscriber to be entitled to give 2 visiting tickets and 10 tickets of recommendation each year for each guinea of his subscription to the dispensary. Any subscriber granting a greater number of recommendatory or visiting tickets than the above shall pay to the funds of the dispensary in the proportion above mentioned.

Second: that the medical officer of the dispensary shall attend at Glaslough on Tuesday and Friday, and at Emyvale on Monday and Thursday, in each week from 10 till 2 o'clock, and that he shall keep an account containing the name, residence and disease of each person recommended as a patient of the dispensary, with the name of the subscriber recommending such patient; also the visits paid by him to patients who have been certified as unable to attend the dispensary, with the names of the subscribers recommending them.

Third: that the tenants of those landed proprietors who have not subscribed to the funds of the dispensary shall not be entitled to medical advice for attendance from the dispensary, and that the secretary be requested to notify this regulation to the different landed proprietors in the district and to request their subscriptions.

Fourth: that any family residing within the district of the dispensary, whose house rent does not exceed 5 pounds per annum, who shall subscribe to the funds of the dispensary 1d per week for each member of the family shall be entitled to medical attendance, advice and medicine from the dispensary free from any further charge.

Fifth: that the following committee be appointed, which shall meet on the third Friday of January, April, July and October in each year, 3 to form a quorum. William Anketell Esquire, chairman, Major Edward Richardson, Roger Anketell, Thomas Johnston, William Pringle, Robert Murdock, Revd William Hurst, Revd W.H. Pratt, Revd William Smyth, Thomas Anketell, John S. Radcliff. [Signed] William Murdock, treasurer and secretary.

Dispensary Certificate

Glaslough and Emyvale dispensary. Observe that recommending persons who are able to pay for medical assistance is a fraud upon the charity. [Insert number] I recommend [blank] of [blank] as a patient of this dispensary and believe [blank] to be a proper person to receive medicine and advice gratis. Dated [blank], signed [blank], subscriber.

Attend on Mondays and Thursdays from 10 o'clock until 2 at Emyvale, and at Glaslough on Tuesdays and Fridays from 10 until 2 o'clock. Patients neglecting for one fortnight to send an account of their health to the surgeon will be struck off the list.

Parish of Donaghmoyne, County Monaghan

Statistical Return by Lieutenant R. Boteler, November 1835

NATURAL STATE

Name and Locality

Its received name is Donaghmoyne but is variously spelt as Donaghmonie, Donaghmoyn, Donaghmoine, Donamoine, Donamoyne, Donaghmain. For authority, see Field Name Book.

Is situated at the southern extremity of the county Monaghan, extending north from the centre of the barony of Farney to its northern extremity. It is bounded on the north west by the parish of Aughnamullen in the barony of Cremorne, on the north by the parish of Clontibret in the same barony and by the parish of Muckno in the barony of Fews Upper and county Armagh.

On the east it is bounded by the parish of Creggan in the barony of Fews Upper and county Armagh, and by that part of the parish of Enniskeen which is in the barony of Farney. On the south it is bounded by the parish of Louth in the barony and county of Louth and by that part of Killanny which belongs to the barony of Farney. On the south also and on the south west it is bounded by the parish of Magheross in the barony of Farney.

Its extreme length north west and south east is 8 and three-quarter miles. Its breadth south west and north east averages 4 and three-quarter miles. It contains 25,598 British statue acres, of which 400 are water and 565 acres waste or bog. It paid from 1,700 to 1,900 pounds county cess, summer assizes 1835.

NATURAL FEATURES

Hills

Fincarne, a hill named after the townland in which it stands, is the highest point in the parish, being 757 feet above the sea and standing nearly at the north extremity of the parish. The several heights vary from that first named to a few feet above the lowest part of the parish in the neighbourhood of Carrickmacross. The hills are uniform in appearance, being round simulated.

Lakes

The parish abounds in lakes varying in form and extent. Some are insulated, others connected by streams, drains with others. The principal are noted in the following table. [Table contains the following headings: common to or in what townland, height above the sea, content in acres].

Antyduff: Feegavla, Lurganboys, Mullnavnnog and Lievadinn, 254 feet above the sea, 34 acres.

Capragh: Rahans and Rossdreenagh, 111 feet above the sea, 31 acres.

Rosslough: Corragarry and parish of Creggan, 284 feet above the sea, about 226 acres.

Negamamon: Brackly, Crossalone, Cullintragh Duff, Dunaree and Latin, 496 feet above the sea, 60 acres.

Rivers

The Fane is the only river of any note in the parish. It takes its rise in Muckno lough, 300 feet above the sea, proceeds south east 1 and half miles when it joins Rosslough 283 feet above the sea. Proceeding south east for 4 and half miles, it forms the boundary between Enniskeen and Donaghmoyne parishes, when it enters the former parish and proceeds easterly nearly.

There are several smaller streams useful in an agricultural point of view to the county, some of them sufficient to turn a mill. There is an abundant supply of water throughout the parish.

Bogs

The supply of bog is not very abundant but sufficient for the consumption with careful nursing. The following are the principal: [table contains the following headings: name of townland, extent, height above the sea, remarks].

Aughrimbeg, Aughrimmore, Colgagh and Kelmurry, 250 acres, portions in each townland.

Corragarry, Drumgoose and Toome, 86 acres, portions in each townland.

Toome and Drumgoose, 46 acres, portions in each towland. [Insert note: Height above the sea cannot be supplied without reference to plans].

Much timber, principally oak and fir with some yews, is found in the bogs. It is used for building gateways, roofing cottages and purposes generally.

The bogs vary much in depth and have generally a blue clay or marle as a substratum. In a bog at the north east of the parish, and in a marle bed,

Parish of Donaghmoyne

was found part of an elk's antler. It is now in the possession of the parish priest [rough sketch, with annotations and dimensions, 2 feet 8 inches wide, 4 feet long].

There are no natural woods in the parish.
Coast: none.
Climate: see Magheross Statistical Memoir.

NATURAL HISTORY

Botany and Zoology

The native plants vary much and but little attention paid to them. They are the same, however, as generally sown in the country.

Zoology varies in no manner with that of Magheross see Magheross Memoir.

Geology: see plans and table, also Statistical Memoir of Magheross respecting coal mines.

MODERN TOPOGRAPHY

Modern Towns

Topography or artificial state, being a description of the objects of art within the parish, both modern and ancient.

About the centre of the parish, and on the road from Carrickmacross to Cullaville, once stood the group of houses called Peterborough. Not more than 3 or 4 cabins remain. The main road from Derry to Dublin passed through it. It is still called Peterborough.

Public Buildings

There is 1 parish church and 4 Roman Catholic chapels.

The church is a new building erected in the year 1827 and is capable of accommodating 450 persons. It stands in the townland of Donaghmoyne at the south extremity of the parish. It is situated in the old graveyard and close to the ruins of the old church. The graveyard enclosure has not been completed for want of funds, nor has the schoolhouse at one corner of and outside the wall. The following table shows the situation of the chapels.

Drumcattan; Lisdoonan; Lisdoonan, a chapel of ease; Tapla, there is a graveyard at Tapla; Tullymackilmartin, there is a graveyard at Tullymackilmartin.

[Insert note: This table has not been furnished by the priest as yet].

Gentlemen's Seats

Rahans, a comfortable residence, is situated in the townland of the same name. It is a modern building and the present residence of John Reed Esquire.

Vicarsdale, the Glebe House, is a tolerably sized building but much neglected by the present incumbent, the Revd Grey Porter, who does not reside.

Donaghmoyne House, a neat small house, the residence of James Bashford Esquire, J.P. is modern built and stands in the townland of Donaghmoyne and not far from the church.

Longfield, the residence of John Johnston Esquire, is situated in the southern extremity of the parish and appears to have been built from about 60 to 100 years.

Cabra Cottage, the residence of John B. Kernan Esquire, is neat but very small, stands between the church and Longfield.

Broomfield, a small house, the residence of Henry Kenny Esquire, is situated at a turn on the road from Carrickmacross to Castleblaney, about 7 and a half miles from Carrickmacross.

Rocksavage, at present the residence of [blank] Kenny Esquire, is situated in the townland of Coolnegratten.

Bleach Greens, Manufactories and Mills

The only mill of importance is that in the townland of Aghadrena belonging to Mr McMath. The wheel is of metal, undershot and 28 feet in diameter. It is a corn mill. There are several others but not of material importance?

Communications

The main road from Carrickmacross to Ballybay bounds the northern side of the parish for about 4 miles. That from Carrickmacross to Castleblaney enters the parish soon after leaving the Ballybay road and proceeds nearly due north through the parish for 6 and a half miles. This latter is a mail and day coach road.

In addition, there are several other main communications, all of which are kept in excellent order; and when it is observed how many old lines of road have been nearly shut up and new communications established, skill and expense having been mutually brought into play, too much praise cannot be due to those under whose superintendence and care they have been executed.

There is an immense extent of road in the way of by-communications and passes throughout the country amply sufficient for the purposes of agriculture.

The principal bridges are on the Fane river but

there are others wherever required. That called Clairbawn at Muckno lough has 3 arches.

ANCIENT TOPOGRAPHY

Old Churches

There are the remains of an old chapel called Killmurray chapel in the townland of Killmurray, a few yards off the east side of the road to Culloville. It is uninteresting in every way as a ruins and no history is retained of it.

The tower of the old church at Donaghmoyne stands close to the new church but it is not worthy of notice.

Entrenchment

In the townland of Maghernakill is an interesting entrenchment with the remains of walls with an archway forcing the entrance into the body of the fortress. The roof of the archway rises from its exterior entrance, its floor and roof line not being horizontal as is generally the case.

Graveyard

In the townland of Maghernakill is the appearance of an ancient graveyard near the river. It appears to have been laid out in a circular form. At one part of it are some large stones, on one of which is the distinctive impression of a foot. Children are still buried there. The stone with the impression of the foot is 4 and a half feet long, 3 feet wide and 1 foot thick. No tradition of it is preserved?

Fincarn Hill

[Crossed out: On the top of Fincarn are wildly arranged some blocks of stones said to be Fin McCoul or the Giant's Bed].

On the top of Fincarn hill there is a circular range of stones. The circle is 60 feet in diameter. There are in all 29 stones of a size varying from 3 feet to 2 feet in length, 1 to 2 feet in thickness and from 1 to 2 feet in height. There are, however, towards it at west side 3 stones of much larger dimensions, 5, 4 and 6 feet in length, 3 and 5 feet in height and 3, 2 and 1 foot in thickness. They are all disposed with[in] the circumference of the circle according to their length, the smaller stones being arranged occasionally between some of them [outline of circle].

Graveyard

In the townland of Drumgriston Upper is an old graveyard called Caldragh. In it is a rude stone standing about 2 feet high, out of which is hewn a basin or font, circular in shape, its diameter being 10 inches and its depth 6 inches.

MODERN TOPOGRAPHY

General Appearance and Scenery

Its general appearance is uniform and devoid of beauty. Here and there a patch of rocks and trees tend to break its sameness. The comfortless appearance of the cottages does not tend to enliven the scene, leaving the eye of reflection to indulge only in the anxiety felt to give it every advantage desirable from good communications so obviously a comparison of the old straight roads with those of a modern construction.

The view from the high ground at Toome in direction of Muckno lough is very pretty, nor is the scenery devoid of interest on the river below Culloville bridge. In addition to several caves formed by the stream occasionally bursting out from its underground course are several deep craters or pits about the centre of the parish originating in the same course.

SOCIAL ECONOMY

Early Improvements

Until a short time since a farming society was established at Carrickmacross where prizes were awarded for the best show of pigs and home-made frieze, but from some difference among the subscribers it no longer exists.

Obstructions to improvement: none exist.

Local Government

There are 8 magistrates acting for the immediate district, 5 of whom only may be considered as generally sitting at the petty sessions. These are not stipendiary. 3 of them reside at Carrickmacross (2 are the agents of the Marquis of Bath and E.J. Shirley Esquire), 1 at Coolderry 4 miles from it, 1 at Ballymackney 2 miles off, 2 near Donaghmoyne church 2 miles off, and 1 at Castleblaney. The latter is the agent of Colonel Porter for that part of his estate which is adjacent to the town. They are generally speaking firm and respected by the people.

There is a station for police at Broomfield. Its force is composed of 1 constable and 4 subconstables.

The petty sessions are always held at the market house in Carrickmacross and are generally attended by 2 or more magistrates. Much busi-

Parish of Donaghmoyne

ness is, however, prevented through the influence of the 2 agents who, as such, can reconcile the parties in many cases without the necessity of the cases being brought before the bench.

Outrages are on the decrease. The usual cases tried are principally common assault and wages. The punishments inflicted seem fully adequate to the extent of the offences. Combinations do not seem to prevail to any great extent except as to the payment of tithe, where it has been very decided and in some cases led to serious results. But little illicit distillation is carried on. Insurances very uncommon, although not proceeding from any feelings of distrust.

Dispensaries and Schools

But little sickness prevails in the district. The Farney dispensary, situated in Carrickmacross, is supported by the voluntary subscription of the principal proprietors and neighbouring gentlemen, assisted by county presentment. It is attended by 1 surgeon assisted by a compounder of medicines and conducted on truly liberal terms. For further information, see Statistical Memoir of Magheross.

Schools by their introduction have led to a slight improvement in the moral habits of the people, who seem anxious for improvement.

Poor

Further than the poor pittance collected during divine service or by the poor begging from door to door, there is no provision for them. A fund was raised in Carrickmacross a short time since but, from a difference arising among some of the contributors as to its application, it has no longer been collected.

Religion

The inhabitants of the parish are composed of Protestants and Roman Catholics, the former in proportion of about 1 to 100.

Habits of the People

The cottages are generally built of a mixture of stone and sods, being roofed with scraws first and then thatched. They have generally 2 rooms and small glazed windows. They are neither clean nor comfortable. The food of the poorer class is potatoes and salt, of others potatoes, meal, buttermilk and occasionally salted herrings. Bacon is seldom consumed except by a farmer's family when their circumstances are easy. Their fuel is turbary.

Of dress, they have no particular kind except the males who generally wear a frieze coat of their own manufacture and known as peculiar to Farney. They live to an advanced age than otherwise, in some instances having of late exceeded 100 years. 5 is the usual number of a family; early marriages are frequent.

Amusements

During a Sunday after attending divine service they amuse themselves by meeting in large numbers on a road convenient to a public house generally, where they dance, or else by shooting and hunting, football, playing, leaping, throwing the stone. Drinking on that day prevails to a great extent.

Christmas here with them is a feasting period. At this time the market is loaded with white bread, geese and pork, which articles are procured for the occasion if possibly within the compass of their means. Christmas Eve and the next night are observed particularly. The day before or proceeding market day the poor may be seen returning home with one or two candles generally mould and secured in the hat by the band or ribbon. They sit up during the night. No particular patron's day, unless that of St Patrick, is observed.

On St John's Eve bonfires are lighted, but in this custom they have been restrained as much as possible of late years since it tended to create riots in the country. During the burial of their dead the funeral cries or lamentations are uttered by the women only, who accompany the bewailing with wringing of hands. Sometimes, but not often, these cries take place on the road to the graveyard.

Emigration

Some few emigrate, principally to New York and Quebec, of whom some have returned. Many go to England and adjoining counties for work during the harvest but leave their families at home. Most of the poor rent ground and sow potatoes.

Remarkable Events

No remarkable events known of nor any remarkable person born in it. The McMahon family held the chief sway in the country and were famous during the wars of the Earls of Essex.

PRODUCTIVE ECONOMY

Spinning

But little hand-spinning takes place. Frieze is

manufactured but not to the same extent as of late years, being now only sufficient for the use of the district.

Fairs and Markets

It has none; but the country people frequent those at Carrickmacross principally, for description of which see Magheross Statistical Memoir. The inhabitants occasionally frequent the neighbouring fairs and markets.

Farms and Proprietors

The farms vary so much in size that it would be scarcely possible to give a decided opinion, but on an average they may be said to be 5 acres. Few leases are now given, the tenants holding at will. This has proceeded from the tenantry having in several instances opposed themselves to their landlord. Where leases are granted, they are for 21 years but no lives.

The principal proprietor is the Marquis of Bath (non-resident), but his agent always resides, i.e. lives at Carrickmacross. Mr Shirley is proprietor of a very small part of the parish; he occasionally resides. His agent resides at Carrickmacross. Mr Plunkett holds a very small portion also, but neither he or his agent reside.

All the tenants hold direct from the head landlord. The average rents per acre are for the best 45s (of this class they are but few instances), for the middling 25s and for the worst 10s. The rents are paid wholly in money. The farmers are scarcely anything but cottiers generally speaking.

They farm for subsistence only and very seldom keep servants. The fields vary in size depending on the size of the farms. No land let in conacre. The fences are generally stones or sod. The tenants are subject to tithe and county cess. One or two gentlemen have farms in their possession.

Manures

The general manures are marle, blue clay, lime which, if the tenants are deserving of indulgence, is given to them while preparing for the crops and paid for when the crops are taken in. This arrangement has been found productive of the best effects. In addition to the above, cow-house manure is used. Marle is tolerably abundant.

Lime is abundant in the parish; coal is used in burning it and it is sold at 6d per bushel on the spot. Burning the ground for manure is not allowed.

Agricultural Methods

No improved implements are in use. The common wheel car is that generally used. Oxen are not used.

There is no rotation of crops. The produce is generally taken to the market at Carrickmacross which is convenient, particularly since the agent is always there in his office.

Grazing and Cattle

Grazing has not been hitherto resorted to, but one or two gentlemen are preparing to lay their farms down in grass, the prices of the grain not paying for the expense of cultivation. Servants are scarcely employed [but] receive, when employed, from 3 pounds to 5 pounds annually in money and are boarded and lodged.

There are no particular herds of cattle. The poor depend upon the rearing of pigs as a means of paying their rents. The common Irish pig is most general.

Uses made of Bogs

The bogs are grazed occasionally. They are given to the adjoining tenants at low rates and in proportion to the farm. It is voluntary with the proprietor, who receives [reserves?] the right of preventing it. The bogs are wholly used in fuel and by the tenants who are not allowed to sell any. The imbedded timber is used generally for building and other domestic purposes.

The bogs have been sufficiently drained, principally by levelling the water of the numerous loughs in the parish.

Planting

No planting has been effected unless occasionally a few trees for ornamental purposes. With the quicks supplied by the proprietors a number of ash and sallow plants have also been distributed.

Sea-Coast and Fishing

Sea-coast none.

Fishing: most of the loughs more or less abound in fish, but fishing is only resorted to as a recreation or by the poor to improve their meals.

General Remarks

Little remains to be done towards the improvement of culture unless what might be effected by the addition of manure. The poor are, however, availing themselves of the liberality of their land-

Parish of Donaghmoyne

lords. Cultivation is carried to the very highest point of the parish. The communications through the country are quite sufficient for all local purposes. The climate, although at times bracing, is not injurious to the vegetation.

DIVISIONS

Townlands

No others than those usual existing in parishes in general.

For a particular description, see Field Name Books. The parish contains 157 townlands.

MEMOIR WRITING

Composition of Memoir

[Insert note: The information for this table [of schools] cannot be supplied as yet; no time shall be lost].

The information for this table [Ecclesiastical Summary] shall be supplied as soon as possible, [signed] Robert Boteler, Lieutenant Royal Engineers, 7th November 1835.

Letters to Lieutenant R. Boteler, 1835

Letters to Lieutenant Boteler

Donamine Glebe, Carrickmacross, 28th October 1835.

Mr Campbell's compliments to Lieutenant Boteler. [He] wishes to say in reply to his message received yesterday from Mr Boteler's servant that there had been a letter in the post office having inscribed on its outside "On His Majesty's Service" which contained the document alluded to in Mr B's docket, but as it was charged postage [insert superscript: 1d!], and letters on His Majesty's Service usually come to hand free, Mr C. did not release it. However, if Lieutenant Boteler will send him another form Mr Campbell will make no delay in filling it up. [To] Lieutenant Boteler, Kingscourt.

Donaghmine, 3rd November 1835.

Sir,

I had the honour of a communication from you some time back relative to schools and houses of Catholic worship in this parish. In reply, I beg to state that I am but a short time in the parish and could not, without considerable trouble and expense, procure answers to your queries.

However, I think I can answer you and save myself labour by referring you to Mr William Henry of Broomfield and Mr Robert Barren of Longfield, both in the parish of Donaghmoyne. These gentlemen were appointed by government to take the census of the parish, and in their books I believe are to be found answers to your questions. Truly yours J. McMeek. [To] Captain Boteler, Kingscourt. [Stamped] Carrickmacross, 6th November 1835.

Parish of Ematris, County Monaghan

Statistical Report by Lieutenant P. Taylor, March 1835

NATURAL STATE

Name

Statistical report of the parish of Ematris, Cootehill, 31st March 1835. Universally pronounced Ematris by the inhabitants, but in Norden's map of the country, extending from Loch Erne to Dundalk, Kill Emars. Derivation: unknown.

Situation

Situated on the south western boundary of the county of Monaghan and south eastern extremity of the barony of Dartrey; it is bounded on the north by the parishes of Aghabog and Currin, on the south by the county of Cavan and a portion of the parish of Aughnamullen in the county of Monaghan, on the east by the parish of Aughnamullen in the barony of Cremorne, county of Monaghan, and on the west by the parish of Currin in the barony of Dartrey, county of Monaghan; and measuring in extreme length and breadth from east to west 7, and from north to south 4 English miles.

Contains 12,297 acres, 11,685 of which are land, 611 water and 567 bog, and paid to the county cess in the year 1834 the sum of 632 pounds 5s 9d ha'penny.

NATURAL FEATURES

Hills

The unusual number of hills preserving the aboriginal names of cor and drum which rise throughout the parish afford a clear and well-defined idea of its peculiar character and features. The substantives were applied very fancifully, but in many instances very appropriately, in denominating their respective localities.

Drummore, or magnum dorsum, as applied to a hill very clearly defines its shape and form, but Drumbacagh, the "heifer's hill," is evidently a name suggested by the fancy of the proprietor. Cor, as applied to a number of hills, manifestly points to a conical or dome-like form, having a protuberance towards its summit.

Several were named from a peculiarity of soil or disposition to produce certain vegetables, such as Coravacan "the mushroom hill," Cordiessigo "the briar hill," Coragarr "the garden hill" and Cortubber "the fountain hill."

Assemblages of dorsa and cor-shaped hills rise very abruptly in the western division of the parish, forming an irregular and very beautiful variety of surface. Such are the elevations forming the townlands of Mucklagh, Drumcall, Drumany, Drumgarkin and Maghernakelly. This apparently tumultuous upheaving of the surface in particular localities into hills assuming the varied forms of dome, cone, dorsum and cor, interesting in the highest degree to the philosophic mind, appears to have changed its intensity and directed its influence in the centre of the parish, to the production of parallel ridges or lines of elevation of nearly equal altitude, with collateral valleys of considerable elongation.

The eastern division again assumes an irregularity approaching in character to the western, the altitude through the whole extent of the parish, from Racreehan in the western through Mucklagh, Drumgale, Cornawall, Drumanan and Coolkill in the eastern extremity, standing respectively 403, 426, 448, 394, 456 and 433 feet above the level of the sea; and a line transversely from Coragany in the northern to Feddhill in the southern point of the parish through Cornawall and Drumintin stands 424, 394, 397 and 334 feet above the same level.

Lakes

All the lakes in the centre of the parish are small and unimportant, and their streamlets, flowing through valleys so nearly level, render the application of the waters available only at considerable expense. This disadvantage was so much experienced in times of greater prosperity that a windmill was erected upon the dorsum of Drummulla to grind the corn of the district, the round tower of which is still standing.

Drumany loch, Kilnaharvey loch, Annaghybawn, Coolkill and Drumsaul lochs are all small and devoid of any peculiarity of feature; but the parish of Ematris in connection with Aghabog and Drumgoon possesses considerable extent of lakes, circumscribing its northern and southern boundaries.

Leesborrow loch, forming the boundary between the parish of Ematris and Aghabog, measures 2 miles in length and one-quarter of a mile

Parish of Ematris 113

in breadth. The drain flowing from its eastern extremity becomes available only in penetrating the parish of Currin. Its level is 309 feet above the sea.

A chain of lakes, assuming the name of the various townlands through which they flow, from Corvoo in the south eastern to the county bridge in the south western extremity, and forming the natural division betwixt the counties of Cavan and Monaghan, measures 4 miles in length and a quarter of a mile in breadth. Their waters also flow over a surface so nearly level as to render them unavailable within the parish; general level 256 feet above the sea.

Inner lake, an arm of the above chain, occupying nearly the centre of Dawson Grove demesne, measures 1 mile in length by a quarter of a mile in breadth. This chain might with propriety be named Loch Cremorne on the new plans. Springs of the purest quality abound throughout the parish.

Bogs and Woods

The same scarcity of fuel which oppresses the peasantry in the adjoining parish of Currin almost overwhelms the tenantry in the parish of Ematris. The impossibility of draining the bogs, from the uniform level throughout the parish, renders their case deplorable. What may be the consequence when the whole is exhausted is a subject worthy of the deepest consideration.

That the whole of the bogs and marshes were anciently covered with timber of the most majestic size is fully evinced by the roots and stumps of oak and fir trees which everywhere pervade them. There is not the faintest trace of the previous existence of natural woods throughout the parish, but several localities are pointed out which were covered with trees and underwood within the last 80 years. Dernamoyle, Derrykinnard, also Creenard, Drumrughill and Cordressigo are particularly enumerated.

Climate

Dr Shannon, residing within the parish, pronounces the climate healthy in a high degree, and the peasantry as living to a very great age. The absence of endemic, chronic or acute diseases, and the mildness of the seasons, although by no means uniform, altogether establish strong evidence of the salubrity of the district.

NATURAL HISTORY

Botany

In Dawson Grove, the seat of Lord Cremorne, the king of the forest in the full majesty of his grandeur and power profusely reigns around. Elm, ash and beech, birch, chestnut and sycamore, with every variety of fir, have attained to full maturity and size, Bedford and Lombardy poplars, Huntingdon and weeping willows, alder, laurel, hazel are all in vast abundance.

Thorn in all its varieties adorn the lawn, fruit trees of every denomination fill the orchard and gardens, and rye-grass and clovers have been introduced into several farms around with great advantage. The rough-stalked meadow grass, trefoil and timothy grass, and the sweet scented vernal grass are in full cultivation. The "graumph," a spontaneous garlic, strongly taints the air in some localities with its offensive perfume.

Zoology

Trout, perch and bream, shad, pike and eel swim in the lakes. Foxes, hares and rabbits, partridge and woodcock, snipe and plover abound in Dawson Grove, but not so throughout the parish. Wild duck, widgeon, teal and diver, with every other variety of their kind, frequent the lakes of the demesne and are protected. Every class and genus of the winged and warbling tribe peculiar to rural parishes abound.

Geology

The rocks composing the hills in the parish of Ematris are entirely composed of grauwacke, which everywhere pervades the district. Throughout the whole extent of its surface no other development appears, neither does the varied tints of red, brown or yellow, which characterises the rock in several localities in the adjoining parish of Currin, rise anywhere to the surface.

One unvaried mass of a grey or greenish colour, totally devoid of every appearance of stratification, and equally deprived of every trace of animal exuvia, and so extremely irregular and uncertain in its cleavage as to render it almost useless for building, universally forms the substratum of the parish; but, although unprofitable in its massive state for domestic purposes, becomes, when pulverised, a naturally rich and highly productive alluvial soil.

In the townlands of Kilmore West and Drumyale it is extensively developed, forming depots of material for the repairing of roads, and in the townland of Rakeeragh a similar development prevails; but in the eastern extremity of the townland of Bogher, on which the larger portion of the town of Rockcorry is built and from which it derives its name, the most favourable opportunity offers for its examination. The presence of small limestone pebbles mixed up with the clay, which covers the whole surface of the parish, frequently disappoints the brick manufacturer by the expulsion of carbonic and gas <gass> when heated in the kiln.

Modern Topography

Towns: Rockcorry

The town of Rockcorry is situated near the south eastern boundary of the parish, on the centre of 4 crossroads connecting it with Cootehill and Monaghan, Newbliss and Ballybay. It was built under the patronage and on the estate [of] T.C. Stewart Corry Esquire.

It is endowed with a weekly market and monthly fair, the former on Wednesdays and the latter on the last Wednesday of every month. It contains a market and petty sessions house, 1 Methodist and 1 Seceder meeting house, which accommodate about 100 members each, a dispensary and a small detachment of police. The number of houses amounts to 78, besides 5 grocery and general dealing houses, and 9 licensed spirit retailers.

The town, now in a ruinous, dilapidated state, is situated 4 miles east of Cootehill, 8 west of Monaghan, 4 south of Newbliss and 4 north of Ballybay, and 57 north west of Dublin, in the diocese of Clogher, province of Ulster and county of Monaghan.

Parish Church

The old parochial church stood in the townland of Dernamoyle, of which there is no trace remaining.

Kilcrow church was erected in the year 1729 by Richard Dawson Esquire, ancestor of the present Lord Cremorne, for the convenience and accommodation of his family. The church, a rectangular building, is capable of accommodating about 300 persons.

The Revd Nicholas Devereux is the present incumbent and rector. There is no glebe annexed to the living, but a lease of 15 acres at 2 pounds per acre late currency was granted forever by the late Lord Cremorne as an accommodation. The tithes were compounded for 365 pounds a year in 1829, and no resistance has ever been made to their payment since.

Chapels

The ancient Roman Catholic chapel and graveyard of the parish stands upon the elevated portion of the townland of Edergole; capable of accommodating 300 members, the Revd Charles Riley the officiating priest. The chapel is conveniently situated for a large portion of the congregation, but for the families remotely situated in the eastern extremity of the parish a chapel of ease was erected about 20 years ago in the townland of Coravacan, the Revd Charles McGarry the officiating clergyman.

Other Buildings

The market and petty session house in the town of Rockcorry was erected by T.C. Stewart Corry Esquire in the year 1805, and the Methodist meeting house under the patronage of the same landlord in 1807. Both are plain buildings.

Monument

A handsome Corinthian column 58 feet high, commemorating the faithful service of Richard Dawson Esquire, member for the county for 4 successive parliaments, was erected by the constituency of the county in the year 1807, upon the summit of the townland of Carson, close to and in the view of the main road connecting Cootehill and Monaghan.

Gentlemen's Seats

Dawson Grove, the residence of Lord Cremorne, containing 494 acres of land and 103 of water, ranks amongst the most handsome noblemen's seats within the province. The "magnum dorsum" of Drummore runs through his lordship's demesne, forming in combination with Fairfield, lately purchased from T.C. Stewart Corry Esquire, amounting to 585 acres of land and 165 of water, a beautiful chain of undulation, interspersed with lakes and islands, and adorned with plantations and ornamental grounds of great extent and beauty. The house, quadrangular, large and commodious, but heavy in appearance, stands upon a highly eligible site commanding a very beautiful, though not extensive, prospect.

Black Island, forming a portion of the demesne, contains a neat marine villa of Gothic style upon the margin of the lake and a temple containing 2 highly finished specimens of sculpture, and upon the same site tradition erects the principal fastness of the MacMahons, the former lords and masters of the soil.

[Insert note: The Cremorne property originated in a Cromwellian grant of the townland of

Cormeen in the parish of Currin, and was enlarged by subsequent purchase from various persons holding under the same title].

Rockcorry Castle, formerly the residence of T.C. Stewart Corry Esquire but now included in Lord Cremorne's demesne, was held under a Cromwellian grant and renewed in the reign of William and Mary in the year [blank]. The house, offices and gardens are now in a state of great dilapidation, but the grounds are in good order and plantations extensive.

Glenburnie Cottage, the residence of T.C. Stewart Corry Esquire, in the vicinity of the town of Rockcorry, is of recent erection and situated in a valley in the townland of Glen, surrounded by the cor and drum-shaped hills of Bogher, Drumulla, Coravackan and Corkeeran. The house is large and commodious, the ornamental grounds and plantations, the garden and orchard are all new and limited but, even in their present state, greatly adorn the surrounding locality.

Freame Mount, anciently Dyanmore, the residence of Richard Mayne Esquire, agent to Lord Cremorne, a commodious, well-built brick house with spacious offices, is most beautifully situated on the summit of a cor-shaped hill 360 feet above the level of the sea, commanding a most delightful and almost unbounded prospect. An old fort, still perfect in rampart and fosse, planted with elm and fir trees of considerable magnitude, adorns the cor, and well-grown plantation nearly surrounds the residence, affording full shelter and shade.

The garden and ornamental grounds are limited but tastefully arranged, the enclosures are large and well fenced, and the coach road from Dublin to Clones forms its southern and eastern boundary, affording a very pleasing prospect of a rich and highly cultivated estate.

Tamnagh, the residence of Charles Dawson Esquire, a perpetuity on the Cremorne estate, is also pleasantly situated on the southern face of a hill in the townland of the same name. The plantations, ornamental grounds and garden are all limited but neatly disposed. The house is small but well built, and the grounds around are in a high state of cultivation. The road from Cootehill to Monaghan forms its southern boundary.

Newpark, the property of J. Brien Esquire, is pleasantly situated on the broad elevated townland of Maghernakelly. The house is small but commodious, the garden and ornamental grounds are neatly arranged, the plantations are young and limited but contribute much to the embellishment and diversification of the surrounding scenery.

Dawe Hamilton Esquire, a gentleman of the highest astronomical attainments and very profound learning, residing in Newpark, gives the meridian of his observatory 28 degrees 22 minutes west in time, its latitude 54 degrees 6 degrees 36 minutes north.

Forest View is another small but delightfully situated residence upon the dorsum of the beautiful townland of Drumany, lately erected by W. Dawson Esquire. The ornamental grounds, orchards and garden are all of recent formation.

The Rectory is a very small house in the cottage style in the townland of Killcrow, near the north side of the road leading from Cootehill to Monaghan.

Communications

5 roads diverge from the town of Rockcorry: 1 north north east to Monaghan, another north north west to Smithborough, sending off 2 branches westerly, 1 to Drum, the other to Newbliss; a third line of road from Rockcorry leads south westerly to Cootehill, a fourth south to Ballytrain and a fifth south east to Ballybay. A number of crossroads bisect these in every direction, affording the utmost facility of communication. The breadth of the roads measures generally 25 feet and very few of them are in good order.

The bridges are few in number and very small. The expense of making and repairing the roads and bridges is paid by the county.

ANCIENT TOPOGRAPHY

Original Proprietors: MacMahons

Prior to the confiscation of property in 1641, the parish of Ematris and the whole barony of Dartrey was possessed by the chief of the MacMahons. Within the memory of several of the inhabitants the houses of Shean Doo MacMahon and his brother Frank MacMahon was standing, the former near the monument erected to the memory of Richard Dawson Esquire, late member of parliament, and the bog from whence he cut his turf is known by Shean Doo MacMahon's bog to this day. Frank MacMahon lived in the townland of Feddan, a subdenomination, and near the margin of the lake.

Both of these families were cut off by treachery and the lords of the soil executed upon trees before their own dwellings; sic transit.

Forts

Upon almost every cor and drum within the parish

the forts of the aborigines are particularly conspicuous, and several of these gave names to the townlands in which they were erected: Lislunshion, Liseveny, Lisbrannon contain forts prominently conspicuous and, from their etymology, evidently gave name to these respective townlands; but none throughout the parish, either in construction or size, claim more minute detail.

Giant's Grave

Contemporaneous with the circular habitations of the very ancient possessors of the soil, and in the townland of Edergole and near to the parochial Catholic chapel and churchyard, a giant's grave or cromlech commemorates the illustrious Finma-gool [sic]. The grave measures 27 feet in length, 8 across the breast and 3 feet broad at each extremity. The Cyclopean rocks which form the walls of the grave are of vast size, and the monumental boulder supported upon the head and shoulder pillars must amount to several tons weight. This relique of antiquity is preserved with particular care.

Tradition: Fir Breige

In the contiguous townland of Glenhorrick 2 fir breige preserve from time immemorial that sacred respect and veneration which their august and imposing forms demand. The present occupier of the soil, regardless of consequences, sacrilegiously prostrated one of these, and from that instant to the day of its resurrection every 4-footed animal upon his ground fell a sacrifice to his audacious presumption (traditio).

MODERN TOPOGRAPHY

General Appearance and Scenery

The general appearance and scenery of the parish is particularly interesting, the division of its surface into groups of hills, rising tumultuously in some localities, in others into long continuous ridges or lines of elevation for miles in extent, forming valleys of peculiar softness and beauty.

The most northern of these valleys is bounded on the south by the continuity of the townlands of Kilmore West, Tomany, Kilmore East, Derrylosset, Drumacrieve, Miltown and Drumsaul in the parish of Ematris, and on the north by a parallel ridge in the parish of Aghabog, the extensive and beautiful Lake Leesburrow, occupying about one-half of its length only. This valley is closed easterly by the townland of Drumrughill, determining its drainage westerly.

Another vale, parallel and south of this, has for its southern barrier a chain of dorsa forming the elevated portions of the townlands of Drumsaul, Drumgole, Tategar, Cordressigo, Aughadrumkeen, Edergole, and closed easterly by Cornawall. This valley contains the small lakes of Kilmahawey and Annaghybawn.

A third valley of still greater extent, and parallel to the former, has its southern boundary formed by the continuing townlands of Drumany, Maghernakelly, Dernamoyle, Drumintin, Tarmacanally, Claraghy and Bogher, closed on its western extremity by the townland of Mucklagh, and opening easterly at the town of Rockcorry; the drainage of the vale flowing easterly through Loch Coolkill.

This section of the parish, embracing two-thirds of its extent, owes its beauty and form to the influence of natural causes alone. The embellishments of art and science nowhere appear upon its surface: a solitary tree is scarcely observable over its whole area.

The main road connecting Cootehill and Monaghan traverses a fourth, but more irregular, valley, having Dawson Grove, Fairfield Demesne, Drumlona and Glen as its southern boundary; and south of this a chain of lakes separating the counties of Cavan and Monaghan meander through a vale at nearly a dead level, conducting the principal drainage of the district south westerly on its course to Loch Erne. All these ridges are intersected transversely, producing a diversified effect, but without interrupting the course and direction of the glens.

This section of the parish, clothed with plantations, ornamental grounds, lakes, islands, orchards and gardens, and studded with gentlemen's seats, presents rich and ever varying landscapes of very high order.

SOCIAL ECONOMY

Local Government

The petty sessions are held in the town of Rockcorry on every alternate Wednesday. 4 magistrates, all residing within the parish, are generally in attendance: Mr T.C. Stewart Corry, Mr Richard Mayne, Mr Charles Dawson and Mr John McNally.

Very few outrages have been committed within the parish for several years, and its character is quiet and orderly. A small detachment of police is stationed in Rockcorry, consisting of 1 constable and 4 subconstables. No illicit distillation is

Parish of Ematris

carried on, neither does combination of any kind exist. Tithe is duly paid.

Dispensary

Dr Shannon, residing in Rockcorry, attends the dispensary, a small house rented for the purpose, but as his district does not embrace the whole of the parish, but extends to Aghabog and every other parish around, he is unable to state the exact amount of health and disease of anyone in particular, but he pronounces the state of the town and parish as exceedingly healthy.

[Table] Average of number of patients on the books 120. Complaints: chynanche tonsillaris, dyspepsia, diarrhoea, opthalmia, asthma, haemorrhois, slight affections. Remarks as to how supported: 40 pounds 7s subscribed by the landed proprietors and gentlemen, 40 pounds 7s paid by the county.

Schools

[Table contains the following headings: name of townland, number of pupils subdivided by religion and sex, how supported, when erected].

Killcrow parochial: Protestants 59, Roman Catholics 36, males 45, females 50, total 95; 20 pounds a year from Lady Cremorne, 1s 6d a quarter from the pupils, erected 1770.

Tategar: Protestants 12, Roman Catholics 8, males 12, females 3, total 20; from 1s to 3s a quarter by the pupils, erected 1815.

Drumintin: Protestants 7, Roman Catholics 33, males 30, females 10, total 40; from 1s to 3s a quarter by the pupils, erected 1827.

Muniel: Protestants 25, Roman Catholics 35, males 30, females 30, total 60; from 1s to 3s a quarter by the pupils, erected 1815.

Coragore: Protestants 30, males 21, females 9, total 30; 6 pounds from London Hibernian Society, 6d a quarter from the scholars, erected 1825.

Unshenagh: Protestants 48, Roman Catholics 13, males 25, females 36, total 61; 8 pounds from National Board of Education, 1s to 3s per quarter from the scholars, erected 1830.

Drumrughill: Protestants 54, males 28, females 26, total 54; 6 pounds from London Hibernian Society, 6d a quarter from scholars, erected 1824.

Coolkill East: Protestants 15, Roman Catholics 25, males 25, females 15, total 40; 8 pounds from National Board of Education, 1s to 3s a quarter from scholars, erected 1830.

Rockcorry female: Protestants 6, total 6; 10 pounds a year from Revd and Mrs Devereaux, erected 1815.

Rockcorry infant: Protestants 32, males 16, females 16, total 32; 10 pounds a year from Revd and Mrs Devereaux, erected 1815.

Derrylosset: Protestants 47, Roman Catholics 24, males 40, females 31, total 71; 6 pounds from London Hibernian Society, 6d a quarter from pupils, erected 1821.

Corncivall: Protestants 17, Roman Catholics 3, males 14, females 6, total 20; 1s to 1s 6d a quarter from pupils, erected 1815.

All these schools are in full operation and contribute much to the moral improvement of the rising generation. A very ardent desire prevails amongst the people to increase the number of schools, and several applications to that effect have been made to the National Board of Education.

Poor

The donations of the charitable and weekly collections upon the Lord's Day are the only sources of supply for the aged and infirm poor within the parish. The collections at Kilcrow church, including 6 pounds a year from Lady Cremorne, average from 34 pounds to 36 pounds a year, and the number upon the poor list 35.

The Revd William Dawson, late rector of the parish, bequeathed the interest of 120 pounds forever to be paid to 12 reduced householders, who were to receive 5s each on Christmas and Easter Day to provide their dinner; but the paupers who die on the parish are provided with a coffin or 5s is paid in lieu thereof.

Religion

The population amounted in 1831 to 7,676 souls. Of these, 3,837 were members of the Roman Catholic Church, 2,379 Episcopalians, 1,029 Seceders, 296 Presbyterians, and 135 itinerant beggars were found in the parish at the taking of the census. The Dissenting ministers receive the regium donum and a salary from the hearers, the Roman Catholic clergymen are paid by the people.

Habits of the People

An argillaceous rock, which universally pervades the district, but very seldom rises to the surface, and when accessible is so exceedingly irregular and fissile in its cleavage as to render the building of stone houses expensive to the people, but as the same rock, in the form of very pure clay, becomes the alluvial soil of every portion of the parish, it forms a most valuable substitute for stone, and accounts for the universal appearance of mud and brick-built houses upon its surface.

The mud houses, divided into 3 apartments, seldom exceed 1-storey high, furnished occasionally with small glass windows but often without them, an earthen floor with no ceiling, and universally thatched with straw, one extremity appropriated as a bedroom for the family, the opposite for the cattle, and the centre a kitchen and dining-room for the whole household.

Comfort and cleanliness are little observed by the peasantry of Ireland. In truth, nothing can surpass the filth and dirtiness of their cabins and the enclosures around them.

Potatoes and buttermilk constitute their principal diet; the luxury of oatmeal is seldom indulged in. The male dress is composed of very cheap but warm frieze and corduroys, the female of fancy-coloured cottons, coarse linens and home-spun woollens. No peculiarity of colour marks the district.

The mildness of the climate conduces to longevity, and numerous instances of extreme old age can now be produced. Marriages are often hastily contracted but seldom immaturely. The members of families are usually numerous: children swarm around the cabins.

Attendance at fairs are their choice amusements. Marriages, wakes and holidays exhaust a large portion of their time. Patron days are not observed, neither does the recital of poems or legendary tales prevail.

MacMahons, McCabes, McClearys, McPhillips, Thompsons, Maxwells, Clarkes, Bradfords and Neisbits and Swans and Dawsons are common names.

Emigration

Emigration is not popular in this parish. Very few families indeed have proceeded to the colonies and none go to England during the harvest season.

PRODUCTIVE ECONOMY

Manufactures

The spinning and weaving of coarse linens, as described under this head in the parish of Currin, is carried on in precisely the same manner in the parish of Ematris. Linens of 8, 9 and 10-hundred reed are the only manufacture of the district, and the market prices from 7d ha'penny to 1s per yard.

The remunerating prices of flax and coarse yarns have increased for the last 2 seasons, and more lint appears amongst the crops this year than for a long time back.

Fairs

A fair for the sale and purchase of horses, cows, asses, sheep and pigs is held in the town of Rockcorry on the last Wednesday of every month. The whole of the cattle, with the exception of the pigs, are of a very inferior description. Horses from 8 to 12 pounds, cows from 3 to 5 pounds, asses from 1 to 2 pounds, sheep from 1 pound 10s to 2 pounds 10s, and pigs in the market about 2d per lb., which are all bought up for the English market.

Rural: Farms and Rents

The subdivision of the soil into holdings varying from 2 to 10 acres is the great cause of the desolation and misery that assail the land. The average size of the farms throughout the parish is given as 8 acres, but vast numbers are much smaller, and the average rent as 22s per acre, generally on leases of 3 lives or 31 years. A few landlords let their farms at will, but unless these holdings are frequently visited by the landlord or his agent, very little improvement is observable.

The rent is invariably paid in cash by tenants of the very poorest class, labouring for subsistence only. The soil is argillaceous and naturally productive.

Crops and Manures

Wheat is cultivated in several localities, but potatoes, oats and flax are the prevailing crops. The fields are small and well shaped, fenced with ditches and banks. The county cess and tithe average 2s per acre, and in the proximity of towns much land is let in conacre. Marl is abundant but seldom used as manure. The burning of the soil is almost universal, and to an extent highly injurious.

The wages of servants, averages of seed and produce, and market price, are all precisely the same as reported under this head in the parish of Currin.

Seed and Produce

Proportions of seed and produce of a favourable season. [Table contains the following headings: name of crop, quantity of seed and produce per acre, market price].

Potatoes: seed 60 stones per acre, produce 1,250 stones, price 1d ha'penny to 3d ha'penny per stone.

Parish of Ematris

Oats: seed 16 stones per acre, produce 180 stones, price 6d to 1s per stone.

Wheat: seed 16 stones per acre, produce 240 stones, price 19s to 21s per barrel.

Barley: seed 16 stones per acre, produce 240 stones, price 10d to 1s per stone.

Flax: 12 pecks seed cost 2 pounds 6s, produce 36 stone of lint, price 12s per stone.

Hay: price 1s to 3s 6d per cwt.

Proprietors and Leases

The great landed proprietors are Lord Cremorne, Mr Corry, Lord Plunket, Mr Stone, Mr Brunker, Misses Bellingham <Bellingem> and Colonel Leslie. Mr Corry is the only resident landlord and Richard Mayne Esquire the only resident agent.

The general size of the holdings upon his lordship's property is given by Richard Mayne Esquire as 8 acres, some on lease of lives, others tenants at will, at 23s per acre.

The average size upon Mr Corry's estate may be stated as 10 acres, mostly tenure at will, and rent 30s per acre.

Lord Plunket's holdings may be taken as 10 acres, averaging 30s per acre on leases of lives and tenants at will.

The average size of Mr Stone's holdings is 8 acres at 25s per acre, and mostly tenants at will.

Mr Brunker and Colonel Leslie's may be taken as 8 acres at 30s per acre and tenants at will; and the Misses Bellingham's property averages 10 acres at 22s per acre, the greater proportion tenants at will. But vast numbers of these holdings are subdivided by the occupying tenant as low as 2, 4 and 6 acres.

Grazing and Cattle

None of the soil is applied to grazing farms. The whole is devoted to the cultivation of grain, potatoes and flax. Very few instances of the introduction of artificial grasses are observable in the central and northern sections of the parish. Rye grass and clover is occasionally, but very rarely, seen, the dependence of the tenantry resting wholly upon spontaneous vegetation.

The horses and cows of the district are of the very worst kind. No improved breeds have been anywhere introduced unless upon the grounds of the resident landlords and gentlemen, where the Ayrshire and Durham breeds are esteemed the best.

Green-feeding upon turnips and clover is practised upon those estates, but nowhere else throughout the parish. The low Dutch breed of pigs is most preferred.

Uses made of the Bogs

The turbary of the townlands where bog is scarce is invariably subdivided amongst the tenantry. In the proximity of towns it rents at 8 and 10 pounds an acre. The bog when exhausted is converted into valuable grazing pasture, and considerable extent of valleys have in this way been formed into fertile meadows. The very great scarcity of turf renders it an expensive article in domestic economy, and at an increase of 300 and 400 per cent above the prices charged in districts where it is abundant.

No mineral deposits have ever been discovered in the bogs of the parish, neither is the bog permitted to be converted into charcoal for the forges.

Planting

There are no nurseries for young trees within the parish. Dawson Grove demesne contains timber of great size and value, which is sold by auction to builders of the district. Fir of full growth is sold at 20d the square foot, ash at 2s 6d and oak at 3s.

SOCIAL AND PRODUCTIVE ECONOMY

Ecclesiastical Summary

[Table] Name Ematris, diocese Clogher, province Ulster, rectory, no union, patron the bishop of the diocese, incumbent the Revd N. Devereux, extent of glebe none, tithes compounded for 365 pounds per annum.

General Remarks

The parish of Ematris possesses all the natural advantages capable of raising it to a high degree of agricultural prosperity. Its soil is composed of a rich alluvial clay, marl abounds in every locality, facilities of transport ramify in every direction, markets are numerous and conveniently situated, but the baneful system of subdividing farms into smallholdings blasts and paralyses the whole; and until this subletting system is entirely suppressed, the size of the farms increased, the practice of green-feeding universally adopted, no amelioration in the condition of the occupying tenants can possibly be effected.

Some practical measures, some legislative enactment must be passed to alter the present order of things, before any improvement in the condition and circumstances of the unfortunate peasantry of Ireland can be secured. [Signed] P. Taylor, Lieutenant 69th Regiment.

Parish of Errigal Truagh, County Monaghan

Fair Sheets by T.C. McIlroy, J.R. Ward and J.C. Innes, March 1838

NATURAL STATE

Locality

The parish of Errigal Truagh <Trough> is the most northerly parish in the county. It is situated in the barony of Truagh and is bounded on the north east and west by the county of Tyrone, and on the south by the parishes of Donagh and Tydavnet. Its extreme length is 9 and half miles and extreme breadth 6 miles. Its mean length is 7 miles and mean breadth 5 miles. Its content is 21,174 acres 1 rood 14 perches, including 50 acres 2 roods 20 perches of water.

NATURAL FEATURES

Hills

Part of the Slieve Beagh range of mountains (for description of which see parish of Tydavnet) occurs in the western side of this parish. The principal points are Bragan, 1,156 feet. Carricknabrock, 1,117 and Greagh, 752 feet above the level of the sea. From these there is a gradual and broken fall to the east and north east side of the parish, where the country is broken with numerous small ridges which run parallel to each other in a north and south direction; their average height is 300 feet above the sea.

The highest point in the parish is in the townland of Bragan, 1,156 feet above the level of the sea. The lowest ground is in the townland of Figanny along the River Blackwater, 123 feet above the level of the sea.

Lakes

Lough More occupies a portion of the townland of Greagh in this part of the parish, the other portion being in the county of Tyrone. It is 650 feet above the level of the sea, [blank] in content, of which 39 acres 3 roods 22 perches are in this part. The depth is not known.

Lough Bradan occupies a portion of the townland of Bradan in this parish and a portion of Knockballyroney in the parish of Tydavnet. It is 945 feet above the level of the sea, 6 acres 2 roods in extent, of which 4 roods are in this part. The depth is not known.

Lough Nahery occupies a small portion of the townland of Bradan in this parish, the other portion being in the county of Tyrone. It is 1,060 feet above the level of the sea. The depth is not known.

NB The heights and extent of the last 2 lakes are not stated in the map [signed] J.R. Ward.

Rivers

The Mountain water runs along the southern part of the parish in an easterly direction for [blank] miles, forming the south boundary for [blank] miles in that distance. Its average breadth is 15 feet and it is very shallow. It rises out of Bradan and Nahery lakes and discharges itself into the Blackwater river 9 and three-quarter miles from its source.

The river is usefully situated for drainage and water power. The general fall is 40 feet in a mile. It is subject to floods which soon subside; they do no injury. The river flows over a gravelly bed. The banks on the west part of the parish are boggy and mountainous. On the east part they are well cultivated. The scenery is in all parts very uninteresting.

The Blackwater river forms the north and north eastern boundary of this parish for 9 miles. It winds very much in its course. Its average breadth is 50 feet and depth from 1 to 5 feet. It is usefully situated for drainage. It overflows its banks in the winter months; the waters soon subside. It rises in the county of Tyrone. The bed of the river is composed of fine sand and gravel. The banks are uninteresting. The general fall is 10 feet per mile.

Bogs and Woods

There is a bog situated in the south eastern part of the parish. It occupies portions of the townlands of Knockakirwan, Annagh and Corlattallan. Its extreme length is 4 and one-quarter of a mile and extreme breadth one-third. It is 200 feet above the level of the sea and [blank] feet above the Mountain water. Timber is not found imbedded. The depth of the bog in the central parts is not known. The bog stuff is not of the heaviest kind.

No natural woods in this parish.

Climate and Crops

The climate and crops of this parish are the same

Parish of Errigal Truagh

as those of the parish of Monaghan, except in the mountainous district where vegetation is generally 10 days later than in the more cultivated parts.

Modern Topography

Public Buildings: Church

Errigal church, situated in the townland of Mullanderg, is a neat limestone building corniced with freestone. The form and dimensions of the building are represented by the following figure: [ground plan, main dimensions 77 feet by 28 feet 6 inches]. It was built in 1835 and cost 661 pounds, of which sum the Board of First Fruits give 400 pounds and the remainder was defrayed by public subscription. The accommodation is for 300 persons and the general attendance is 150. The present vicar is the Revd Francis Hurst.

Chapels

Errigal chapel, situated in the townland of Knockronan, is a plain stone building, roughcast and slated. It is 80 feet long and 40 feet broad. It was built in 1820 and cost 500 pounds, which sum was raised by subscription. There is accommodation for 2,000 persons and the general attendance is 1,500. The parish priest is the Revd Charles McDermot.

Mullylodin chapel, situated in the townland of Tavanagh, is a limestone building, slated. It was erected in 1798, expense of erection not known. The form and dimensions are represented by the following figure: [ground plan, main dimensions 82 feet by 68 feet, "T" shape]. The interior is very plain. It is not floored and is unceiled. The windows are Gothic. There is no gallery. The accommodation is for 1,000 persons and the general attendance is 1,000. The interior is in a very dilapidated state. The priest of the above chapel is the Revd Charles McDermot.

Schools

Aghamackalinn schoolhouse is situated in the townland of Aghamackalinn. It is a stone cottage, thatched, 25 feet long and 14 feet broad. It was built in 1832, expense of building and how defrayed not known. 18th March 1838.

Errigal schoolhouse, situated in the townland of Mullanacross, is a plain stone building, roughcast and slated. It is 23 feet long and 17 feet broad. Neither the time of building or the cost known.

Moy national schoolhouse, situated in the townland of Moy, is a plain stone building, thatched. It was built in 1833 and cost 30 pounds. The schoolhouse is 33 feet long and 18 feet broad.

Shanco schoolhouse, situated in the townland of Shanco, is a plain stone building, roughcast, whitewashed and slated. It was built in 1830 and cost 42 pounds, which was defrayed by the late Thomas Singleton Esquire. It is 34 feet long and 19 feet broad.

Bridges

Moy bridge crosses the River Blackwater on the boundary between the counties of Monaghan and Tyrone. It is built of limestone and consists of 3 semicircular arches. It is 57 feet long and 24 feet broad, including the parapet walls.

There is a bridge over the River Blackwater on the boundary line of the parish. It is in the townland of Derrylevick, is built of sandstone and consists of 2 semicircular arches. It is 22 feet broad and 54 feet long, including the parapet wall which is 2 feet thick.

Catholic Chapel

Drumbristan Roman Catholic chapel, situated in the townland of Drumbristan, is a rectangular sandstone building 74 feet long and 30 feet broad. It was erected in 1823 and cost 500 pounds, defrayed by subscription. The accommodation is for 1,200 persons and the general attendance is 1,200. The interior is plain. The parish priest is the Revd Charles McDermot.

Social Economy

Habits and Occupations of People

The cottages in the eastern part of the parish are built of stone and have a comfortable appearance. Those in the west or mountain district are inferior in appearance and cleanliness. They are generally of mud, thatched. The people are hospitable and, in the west, the prevailing dress amongst the men is grey woollen cloth of their own manufacture.

They have no amusements except in attending the fairs and markets held in Aughnacloy, Monaghan and Tydavnet.

Modern Topography

Communications

Towns: none in this parish.

The main road leading from Monaghan and Emyvale to Aughnacloy runs through this parish in a northerly direction for 4 miles. Its average breadth is 35 feet. It is a well laid out road and is kept in good repair at the expense of the country.

The main road from Clogher to Monaghan runs through this parish in a south east direction for 4 miles. It then runs due south for [blank] miles; its average breadth is 20 feet. It is not a well laid out road and is in bad repair.

There are several by-roads also which are not in good repair.

General Appearance and Scenery

The western part of the parish is mountainous and uncultivated. The greater of it is covered with heath. The eastern side is fertile and well cultivated, and the cottages scattered over this part of the country are neat and have a comfortable appearance. [Signed] Thomas C. McIlroy.

SOCIAL ECONOMY

Table of Schools

[Table contains the following headings: name, situation and description, when established, income and expenditure, physical, intellectual and moral instruction, number of pupils subdivided by age, sex and religion, name and religious persuasion of master or mistress, date on which visited].

Errigal school, a plain house in the townland of Mullanacross; when established: not known; income: from Revd Francis Hurst 5 pounds, from pupils 1 pound 10s; intellectual instruction: London Hibernian Society books; moral instruction: visited by the Revd Francis Hurst, vicar of Errigal Truagh, Authorised Version of Scriptures read, catechisms taught on Saturday; number of pupils: 2 under 10 years of age, 15 from 10 to 15, 3 above 15, 20 total pupils, all male, 18 Established Church, 2 Presbyterians; master James Afee, Established Church; visited 9th March 1838.

Moy national school, a plain house in the townland of Moy, established 1833; income: from National Board 10 pounds, from pupils 6 pounds; intellectual instruction: National Board books; moral instruction: visited by the Roman Catholic priest of the parish, Scripture extracts read, catechisms taught on Saturday; number of pupils: males, 7 under 10 years of age, 56 from 10 to 15, 1 above 15, 64 total males; females, 10 under 10 years of age, 9 from 10 to 15, 19 total females; total number of pupils 83, 4 Established Church, 9 Presbyterians, 70 Roman Catholics; master Hugh Lovette, Roman Catholic; visited 9th March 1838.

Shanco school, a plain house in the townland of Shanco, established 1830; income: from Mrs Singleton 4 pounds, from William Anketell Esquire 4 pounds, from Lady Cremorne 2 pounds, from pupils 3 pounds; intellectual instruction: London Hibernian Society books; moral instruction: visited by the Revd [blank], Authorised Version of Scriptures read; number of pupils: males, 18 under 10 years of age, 19 from 10 to 15, 3 above 15, 40 total males; females, 10 under 10 years of age, 20 from 10 to 15, 30 total females; total number of pupils 70, 64 Established Church, 4 Presbyterians; master James Busby, Established Church; visited 15th March 1838.

Aghnamacklinn, a cottage in the townland of Aghnamacklinn, established 1832; income from pupils 20 pounds per annum; intellectual instruction: Education Board books; moral instruction: Scriptures taught daily, catechisms heard on Saturdays by the master; number of pupils: males, 31 under 10 years of age, 8 from 10 to 15, 39 total males; females, 23 under 10 years of age, 2 from 10 to 15, 25 total females; total number of pupils 64, all Roman Catholic; master John McKenna, Roman Catholic; visited 15th March 1838 [signed] Thomas C. McIlroy.

Statistical Report by J.R. Ward, 1835

NATURAL FEATURES

Lakes

Slight and imperfect; refer to Mr Boyle [signed] R.K. Dawson, 25th September 1835.

Lough More, situated partly in Cullamore townland, the greater part being in the adjacent county of Monaghan, is {about 600 feet} above the sea. In extent it is {about 56 acres}; the depth is not known.

Lough Beg, situated in Cullamore townland, is 590 feet above the sea. It contains {about} 1 acre; depth is unknown.

Rivers

The Blackwater forms the northern boundary for 2 and three-quarter miles. It is from 20 to 30 yards in breadth and is very shallow. For particulars of this river, see parish of Aghaloo.

Bogs and Woods

Bogs: [Insert query: What is to be said]?
Woods: no natural woods in the parish. There

Parish of Errigal Truagh

are some considerable plantations and growing timber in Favor Royal demesne.

Crops: same as the parish of Clogher.

MODERN TOPOGRAPHY

Public Buildings

Towns: none.

Public Buildings: Portclare church, situated in Favor Royal demesne, is a very neat stone building. It was erected in 1835 at an expense of 1,000 pounds, which was defrayed by [blank]; [insert query: by whom]? It is in length 50 feet and in breadth 5 feet. It will accommodate 300 persons; the average attendance is 140. The present clergyman is the Revd M.J. Moutray. [Insert query: The Christian names]? The income is 77 pounds per annum.

Gentlemen's Seats

Favor Royal, the residence of Captain Moutray, is situated in Favor Royal demesne. It is a large handsome building and the office houses are commodious. The demesne is beautifully ornamented with trees and plantations. There is a garden and a deerpark in it.

Mills: none in this part of the parish.

Communications

Part of the main road between Aughnacloy and Enniskillen traverses the north part of the parish for 2 miles. For particulars of this road, see parish of Clogher.

General appearance and scenery: [insert query: what is to be said of it]?

SOCIAL ECONOMY

Local Government

Early improvements and obstructions to improvement: none.

There is 1 magistrate residing in this part of the parish; his residence is Favor Royal demesne. He is firm and much respected by the people. There are no police. Petty sessions are held in Augher.

Dispensaries: none.

General Notes

Table of schools: Fymore Moutray townland. [Insert query: The columns required to be filled for this school].

Poor: no charitable institution.

Religion: mostly Protestant. [Insert note: "Mostly;" query what other denominations and the actual proportions]?

Habits of the people: the same as in the parish of Clogher.

Emigration: [blank]. [Insert query: Is there no emigration from this parish?].

Parish of Inniskeen, County Monaghan

Statistical Report by Lieutenant R. Boteler, November 1835

Geography or Natural State

Name

Is generally spelt Enniskeen. It is, however, spelt as Inniskeen, Eniskeene and Iniskeene. For authority, see Field Name Book. A resident from the village of Inishkeen (Mr O'Hagan, a respectable shopkeeper) says that it is supposed to derive its name from a small island that once existed. Its site can now be traced about 50 yards below the place where stood the old bridge of Inniskeen. It was called [insert note: written on the spot by Mr O'Hagan *Inis-cion-a-egah*, signifying "the mild island of the fews"].

Locality

Is partly situated in the county of Monaghan and barony of Farney (on the centre of its east side and in the county of Louth and barony of Dundalk). On the north it is bounded by the county Armagh, barony of Fews and parish of Creggan, on the north east by the county Louth, barony of Dundalk Upper and the parish of Creggan, on the east by the county Louth, barony of Dundalk Upper and parish of Baronstown, on the south by the county Louth, barony of Louth and parish of Louth, and on the west by the parish of Donaghmoyne in the county Monaghan.

Its extent north and south 5 and a half miles, its breadth averaging 2 and a half miles. The Monaghan portion contains 4,990 statute acres, of which 1 acre 8 perches are water and 424 and a half acres waste. The county Louth portion contains 1,203 acres, of which 3 acres are water and 75 and a half acres waste. Monaghan portion pays summer assizes 176 pounds 3s 7d county cess, that in Louth pays 33 pounds 2d.

Natural Features

Hills

Their names depend on that of the townland in which situated. They are generally low and insignificant. The highest ground is the hill in Drummond townland called Drummond hill, which is 320 feet above the sea.

Lakes

None of any note occur in the parish. On its boundary are, however, Drumbwee lough, 241 feet above the sea, Topnass, 143 feet and Drumkeith, 137 feet above the sea.

Rivers

The Fane is the only river of note in the parish. It takes its rise in Muckno lake, 300 feet above the sea, proceeds south easterly for 1 and a half miles, where it joins Ross lough 283 feet above the sea. Proceeding south east for 4 and a half miles, it forms the boundary between Inniskeen and Donaghmoyne parishes, when it enters the former parish and proceeds easterly nearly passing through Inishkeen village and meeting the east side of the parish and county boundary. It then forms the boundary nearly in a south direction when it leaves the same.

At the point of leaving it, it is about 118 feet above the sea. From the last point upwards there are several mills on it but none of any note. The river is generally speaking narrow and rapid.

The parish is well supplied with water.

Bogs

The supply of bog is tolerable but there are none of any note or size. Wood is found in tolerable quantities and consists of oak and fir principally. It is applied to domestic and building purposes. Marl is found in some of the bogs about 5 feet below the surface and is used as manure.

Woods: there are none.

Coast: none.

Climate is mild and the crops ripen about the same time as in the neighbourhood.

Natural History

Botany

None but plants and grasses of the common kinds occur. No introduction of fresh plants seems to have taken place nor have any disappeared.

Zoology

The variety of species under this head differs in no way from the neighbouring districts. The Maine river abounds in trout which occasionally run to a large size. On the river are several eel-weirs, the property of the adjoining proprietors.

Parish of Inniskeen

Modern Topography

Village of Inishkeen

The village of Inishkeen is situated rather to the west of the centre of the parish. It is about 7 miles north west of Dundalk and the same distance east of Carrickmacross; contains a population of about 70 persons, mostly Roman Catholics. The principal part of it belongs to a Mr O'Hagan, who carries on an extensive and the only grocery business. He has very good accommodation in his house for travellers.

Public Buildings

Both the parish church (supposed to have been built about 80 years) and the Roman Catholic chapel (about 14 years) are situated in the village of Inishkeen, are modern built, the former capable of accommodating 160 persons, the latter 600.

Gentlemen's Seats

The Glebe House stands close to the church. It is prettily situated and apparently modern built.

Bleach Greens, Manufactories and Mills

The 2 principal mills are a flax and tuck mill in Edenamagh townland, also another in Drummass townland, both having breast wheels 12 feet in diameter. There are other mills but of no importance. With the exception of spinning and the making of frieze, very little manufacture is carried on, and even that is for domestic purposes alone.

Communications

No important roads cross the parish. There are several by-roads generally made at the expense of the county and kept in tolerably good order. The minor communications are sufficient for local purposes and are tolerably kept.

The principal bridge is at Inishkeen. It has 5 arches and has been built about 30 years.

Ancient Topography

Remains of Antiquity

Perhaps there are few villages in the neighbourhood more interesting from its relics and antiquity than that of Inishkeen. Its pretty scenery adds also not a little to its picturesque beauty. On approaching it from the direction of Carrickmacross the first objects that catch the eye are a high mound on the right, village church in front, having a round tower in its graveyard and a very neat, though almost deserted, schoolhouse adjoining its enclosure, and rather to the left a well-built bridge of 5 arches close to the Glebe which, with the trees surrounding it, enliven the scene in no small degree.

Immediately in rear of the mound, but not to be seen at first, are the walls of what tradition pronounces to have been a bawn or place for securing cattle.

Round Tower

The round tower appears similar to that at Armoy, but in the few last years it has been cruelly disfigured. From an intelligent shopkeeper living in the village I derived much interesting, traditional and local information.

He states that about 30 years since, the mason employed in building the new bridge made a very large hole in the base of the tower for the sake of the materials. This has since been built up and a door fitted to it. The door is now used as an entrance to the belfry, an ugly piece of masonry for the purpose of supporting the tinkling machine built on its top.

Facing the east, about 16 feet above the ground, is the original entrance or doorway, and although the original masonry forming the top and sides of the entrance have been substituted by modern patchwork, there can be no doubt of its being in its original position since the foot-slab still remains. It is 4 feet 3 inches long, 10 inches thick and 3 feet 6 inches wide, i.e. running into the thickness of the wall.

At the same height as the door-sill is a circular projection of thin coping on the inside of the tower and apparently centred as corbelling to support a floor. There is another projection similar to that described 11 feet 9 inches higher up.

The whole height of the tower is 44 feet. At base its outer diameter is 16 feet 8 inches, its interior diameter 8 feet 8 inches, making the thickness of wall therefore 4 feet. At the first coping, i.e. at the foot of the original door or entrance, the interior diameter is 7 feet 9 inches and thickness of masonry 4 feet. The stones of which the tower is built are generally solid blocks averaging from 8 inches to 14 inches and cemented very strongly. They are in parallel layers.

On the sill of the door or entrance are 2 marks [diagram] about 14 inches apart, worn as if by the ends of a ladder constantly resting against it or being drawn up it.

Round tower in Ennis

[Drawing of tower, with belfrey, original door and new door].

Inscriptions in Graveyard

The most ancient inscription in the graveyard is the following, which appears on a slab let into the wall of the vault or small roofed building and over its entrance: [drawing with inscription "IHS, this chapel was built by Ardell Macoll MacMahon for himselfe and his famelly in the year anno domini 1672"].

By the same MacMahon was erected on the crossroad a stone cross as below (a wall has since been built, the cross being in its face): [drawing of cross with coat of arms and inscription "IHS, this cross was erected by Captain Coll MacMahon as a memorial of himself and of his family and desires ye prayers of all the faithfull Christians, September 2nd anno domini, 1722"].

[Inset drawing of cross in the stone wall].

In the vault or cell adjoining that above described [outline of building with 2 roofs] is a tombstone on which is the following inscription: "Here lieth the body of the Revd Father Ross MacMahon, doctor of the cannon and civil law and lord abbot of Clonish, vicar-general of the diocese of Clogher, rector of Donamine and Enniskeen, who departed this life, June 6th 1722 aged 72 years."

Between the present graveyard and crossroads tradition states that there were buried of the MacMahon family, 1 archbishop and 9 bishops. The present occupier of the field, my authority, states that during the cultivation of it he found a great number of bones.

Mound

The old mound and its vicinity are particularly interesting; see rough plan for showing disposition [plan of area showing mound and a rectangular enclosure with key, site of old bridge, 2 roads and note indicating "island whence the name Enniskeen is supposed to be derived"].

The base of the mound is about 136 feet in diameter and upper diameter 34 feet. In direction of round tower its top is 60 feet above the ground and in direction of the bawn about 50 feet.

The mound, of which a rough description has just been given, has been recently planted and enclosed by a wall at its base. On its summit was found the foundation walls of a supposed tower

Parish of Inniskeen

which tradition says was formerly inhabited by a king of Ulster.

The present occupier of the ground says that sometime since one of his workmen lost his crowbar on the summit, it having disappeared from his hands while using it; hence he supposes it has a shaft or well on its top.

The spaces (bb) and (cd) plan) are the remains of an old ditch, the parts (bc) and (dfe) were filled up not long since by the occupier of the ground, who states that in levelling the interior space he discovered, some feet under the surface, the foundation walls of a number of cells, some of which were flagged. In one of them the soil seemed very dark as if it had been burnt. He also discovered 2 walls running parallel to each other to the foot of the mound where they ceased. They appeared as if leading to a passage or entrance into it.

The rectangular enclosure (A) is formed of a wall about 2 and a half feet thick and about 10 feet high, varying, however, with the fall of the ground, although not quite parallel to its line of surface except at the part (c).

There is a small coping to the wall (where the wall is unbroken), its cross section implying almost that it never had or was intended to have a roof, thus the coping being in the interior [section of wall showing coping]. The interior measurement is 84 feet by 71 feet, too large a space for roofing to such light walls. At the gateway the wall is higher and slenderer than at the other parts.

[Plan of pound, main dimensions 84 feet by 71 feet; outside view of arched door, 11 feet high, 8 feet 10 inches wide; inside view of arch with key; detailed drawing of window masonry with annotations]; (hhhh) are openings 6 inches square to receive wooden bars; (a) is a breastwork to strengthen the fastenings or bars. On the opposite of the gate this breastwork is 14 feet wide and the holes extend the entire length]. No part of the masonry has been chiselled or squared.

In cleaning out the space (c), the foundation of a house or other building was discovered. At this part the coping of the side wall disappears. Along the same side of the enclosure, and which faces the river, there are holes on the inside of the wall as if beams had been inserted. May they not have been used in the roofing of sheds or in protection against the weather?

Leading to the river adjacent to the enclosure is the site of an old road. There was a bridge over the river at this part about 30 years ago, but 1 window only seems to have existed in the walled enclosure above described. It has no appearance of having been secured with bars.

A part of the enclosure is at the present day used as a pound.

Forts

In addition to the above antiquities, there are a number of forts so generally peculiar to the immediate neighbourhood.

MODERN TOPOGRAPHY

General Appearance and Scenery

Nothing particular strikes the eye unless, generally speaking, its open appearance, and poverty than otherwise of the cottages. Immediately round the village the scenery is interesting and decidedly pretty.

SOCIAL ECONOMY

Obstructions to Improvement

Early improvements: none.

Obstructions to improvement: none, unless such as proceed from the habitual prejudice existing on the part of the people in favour of the use of certain tools or of setting or getting in their crops at a particular times.

Local Government

The petty sessions for the Monaghan part of the parish are held at Carrickmacross every other Friday. There is a police station consisting of 1 constable and 4 subconstables at Inniskeen. The petty sessions for the Louth part are held at Louth every Thursday.

There are no police in the Louth portion. The police force stationed at Corcreagh, and composed of 1 constable and 6 subconstables, acts for the Louth part of Inniskeen. Crimes in the parish on the decline; common assaults and wages the usual crimes tried. No illicit distilling carried on.

Dispensaries

The health of the people has gradually improved. There are no dispensaries in the parish. That for the Monaghan part is at Carrickmacross, those for the Louth part are at Louth and Ardee.

Schools

Schools have tended to general improvement of morals and habits, and the people are anxious for information.

Poor

There is no provision for the poor beyond the pittance collected at the places of worship or obtained by begging from door to door.

Religion

The greatest proportion by far is composed of Roman Catholics, perhaps in the proportion of 1 Protestant to 50 Roman Catholics.

Habits of the People

The cottages seem poor and unclean: consist of 1 floor generally and seldom more than 2 rooms, often only 1. They are generally built of stone and sods, and have small glazed windows.

The food of the poor consists of potatoes and salt, with occasionally milk also. Their clothing mostly consists of articles of home manufacture. They are long-lived, as appears on reference to the headstones in the graveyard. Usual number of a family is 5; early marriages are frequent.

Hurling and wrestling the principal amusement. There is a rude stone in the churchyard having a hole in its centre, for the purpose of receiving a stick on which used to be suspended articles of wearing apparel to be given as prizes to the best wrestlers. This amusement took place during the Christmas [season].

Emigration

Emigration prevails but not to any great extent. Many go to England and to the adjoining counties during the harvest. They leave their families at home. All have generally a patch of potatoe ground.

Remarkable Events

There are more than one fairy traditions, but no remarkable events known as having positively occurred. The MacMahons were certainly remarkable persons in their day. Whether Captain MacMahon belonged or not to Inniskeen is not known, but it is said of him that at a fair held in Mullaghcrew on the 17th June (the cross put up by him, see Ancient Topography, was dated 1729), he appeared with his 16 sons all riding on white horses.

PRODUCTIVE ECONOMY

Manufacturing or Commercial

With the exception of spinning and making of frieze, very little manufacturing is carried on and even that is for domestic purposes alone.

Fairs and markets: Louth, Dundalk and Carrickmacross are attended.

Rural Economy

The principal proprietors are the Marquis of Bath, William Filgate Esquire, resident, Joseph Plunkett Esquire, [blank] Kenny Esquire of Rocksavage, his agent, the greater portion of the remainder being college land for which Mr Pentland, non-resident, is agent.

The usual size of the holdings vary from 5 to 10 acres, the yearly rent being from 15s to 26s, which is wholly paid in money. The farmers are partly yeomen and cottiers. Very little land is let in conacre. The size of the fields varies from 1 to 4 acres. The fences are generally quickset hedges, faced with stone built. The tenants are merely liable to county cess and tithes.

The soil is tolerably productive. The usual manures are marl, blue clay, lime, cow-house dung and the scrapings of roads, cleaning of drains. Marl is abundant in many parts of the parish. There are several minor lime-kilns. Burning the ground for manure is not permitted.

No improved implements of husbandry have been introduced. The common wheel car and dray are generally used. Oxen are not used in agriculture and never more than 2 horses to a plough. The rotation crops are barley, oats and potatoes, and the produce generally taken to Louth or Dundalk.

Grazing and Cattle

Same as I described in Killanny statistics, with the exception of a deerpark in the townland of Dromeril containing 78 statute acres, the property of William Filgate Esquire.

No particular breeds are reared. On the sale of pigs the poor in a great measure often depend as a means of paying their rents. The common Irish pig principally and the Dutch pig rarely are the usual breeds.

Uses made of the Bogs

The bogs are but little grazed, and even when so used it is merely by suffrance. The turf is not sold but wholly used in the neighbourhood. A small patch of turbary is generally granted (but not as a matter of course) to those holding adjoining farms. In some instances it is paid for at a low rate.

Parish of Inniskeen

Drainage and Planting

Drainage not required.

Planting is merely resorted to for ornament, and that in few instances or to a very limited extent.

Sea-Coast and Fishing

Sea-coast none. Fishing is merely resorted to as a recreation or for immediate and private use.

General Remarks

Generally speaking, the soil seems so poor as to hold out little chance of being improved. The whole of the parish is cultivated except the bogs and the deerpark of William Filgate Esquire.

Little wasteground may be said to exist. The roads and communications appear sufficient.

DIVISIONS

Townlands

None but those noted as occurring in the generality of parishes. In the county Monaghan part of the parish are 27 townlands and in that of Louth county 8. For further information as to proprietors, see Field Name Books.

SOCIAL ECONOMY

Schools

[Table] Inishkeen, 25 Protestants, 40 Catholics, 44 males, 21 females, total 65; supported by the parishioners; established 1823.

In addition to the above are 2 or 3 hedge schools supported by the scholars' poor offerings.

Ecclesiastical Summary

[Table] Inniskeen, county Monaghan: diocese Clogher, province Armagh; Inniskeen, county Louth: [blank].

[Insert note: As soon as the information for this table is procured it shall be forwarded. [Signed] Robert Boteler, Lieutenant Royal Engineers, 7th November 1835.

Parish of Killanny, County Monaghan

Statistical Report by Lieutenant R. Boteler, November 1835

NATURAL STATE

Name

Killanny is the received name. It is variously also spelt as Killany, Killanney, Killaney, but Killany seems to be the proper orthography; for different authorities, vide Field Name Book.

Locality

The greater portion of this parish is situated in the south east part of the barony of Farney and county Monaghan. The remaining part is in the barony of Louth and county of Louth. On the north it is bounded by the parish of Donaghmoyne, on the east by the parish, barony and county of Louth, on the south east by the parish of Arthurstown in the barony of Ardee and county Louth, on the western and south west by the parish of Magheracloone and on the north west by Magheross parish (Donaghmoyne, Magheracloone and Magheross being in the barony of Farney in county Monaghan).

Its extreme length north and south is 5 statute miles, its extreme breadth east and west is 4 miles, its mean breadth about 2 miles. Its Monaghan portion contains 5,188 acres, of which 680 are waste and 128 acres of water. Its county Louth portion contains 1,939 acres, of which 345 are waste and 9 water. It paid at the summer assizes of 1835 to Monaghan county cess 216 pounds 5s 4d ha'penny and to that of Louth 79 pounds 11s 10d.

NATURAL FEATURES

Hills

Their names depend upon those in the townland in which they are situated and whence they are derived. They are generally insulated, round in form, and not exceeding an average height of about 200 feet above the surrounding country. The highest is in Coolnemony townland, standing 311 feet above the sea.

Lakes

There are no lakes of importance except those on the parish boundary common to Magheross, viz. Lough-na-glack and Monalty lough, for description of which see Magheross parish.

Rivers

There are only 2 rivers of any importance: one, which can scarcely be called a river, runs south east from Monalty lough. About three-quarters of a mile on, it passes Ballymackney village, about 1 and a quarter mile further runs through the village of Killanny, joining half a mile farther and forming the parish boundary for about a mile, when it meets the other river of any note.

This last forms the boundary of the parish at the point where it and Magheracloone parish meet and continues the same, flowing north east for about 2 and a quarter miles to the point above described where the 2 join and leave the parish.

This last river is called the Lagan. The former has no regular name unless generally termed the Ballymackney river. As a means of draining and preventing from being flooded the north west side of the parish and also portions of the parishes of Magheross and Donaghmoyne, it is essentially useful. The bed of it has been sunk of late in more than one part to admit of a sufficient fall for the water.

The parish is very well, perhaps too well, supplied with water.

Bogs

Bogs are very numerous and extensive in the parish. Those mentioned below are the principal. [Table contains the following headings: name of townland, acreage, remarks].

Annacroff 60 acres; Annahean 72 acres; Annamarran 120 acres; Carrickavallan 55 acres; Essexford and Dunelty 80 acres, portion in this parish; Lannat 97 acres; Tullynaskeagh East, Tullynaskeagh West and Nuremore 103 acres, portion in this parish.

Very little timber is found except in the immediate vicinity of the loughs, in fact on their very shores, and this consists merely of roots and stumps, all of which are oak and mostly all standing. They have the appearance of having been broken by means of excessive violence. Some of the bogs contain much marl. At a few feet below the surface in some cases the marl abounds in various kinds of small shells.

Woods: there are none.

Coast: none.

Parish of Killanny

Climate

No means of ascertaining the climate exist. It is generally considered very salubrious, so much so that families have moved to the neighbourhood for the benefit of its pure air. The crops generally speaking are rather forward than otherwise. See table [in] Statistical Memoir of Magheross parish, of a register of the state of the thermometer taken at various times at Carrickmacross.

NATURAL HISTORY

Botany and Zoology

No particular plants occur, nor can it be ascertained whether any have disappeared. Few of the bogs have heather. Most of them are covered with bog myrtle or fir, each a kind of rush and occasionally cotton grass.

Most of the loughs abound in trout, perch and bream, in others are found pike which run to a considerable size. Eels are also found in most of them. The streams, being very small, but few fish are found in them and these, it would seem, merely in moving from one lough to another.

Besides birds of the common species generally found throughout the country, the inland lakes are frequented during the hard weather by seafowl of every description, from the cormorant to the small diver and teal. During the summer, and particularly in the spring, a vast number of seagulls of different kinds may be observed throughout the district but particularly in the lower or eastern extremity of the parish. There are but few partridges but a great abundance of landrails and quails, announcing their existence during the breeding season in every direction by their respective and peculiar calls.

Hares and rabbits are also to be met with but in no great abundance except in the vicinity of Monalty House. Weasels are numerous and occasionally a badger is seen. In addition to the birds already enumerated as frequenting the loughs throughout the year, may be seen the bald coote, water-hen and rail and the small diver. The two latter are not, however, common, particularly the diver. Woodcocks are scarce but snipes are very abundant, some few remaining throughout the year.

Otters are very numerous in Monalty lough, where some of a very large size have been shot. Foxes occasionally frequent but, not having a good cover, they are scarce.

MODERN TOPOGRAPHY

Villages

There are no towns. The village of Ballymackney, containing a population of about 134 persons, being 6 Roman Catholics to 1 Protestant, is situated in the townland of Aghafad; that of Killanny is situated in a townland of the same name. It contains a population of 65 persons, all Roman Catholics. It is by no means picturesque but is interesting from its having the ruins of an old abbey and graveyard, the latter still used, and a very remarkable Danish monument.

Neither markets nor fairs are held at either village. No houses in Ballymackney licensed to sell spirits; it contains 1 forge. Killanny has 4 licensed spirit shops.

Public Buildings

The parish church stands in the village of Ballymackney. It is very small and of insignificant appearance, is capable of containing 100 persons. A graveyard is attached to it.

The only Roman Catholic chapel in the parish is situated in the village of Killanny. It is capable of accommodating 600 persons and was built in 1789.

1750 is the oldest date on the tombstones in Killanny churchyard.

Gentlemen's Seats

The Glebe House, situated in Essexford townland and called Drummoey Glebe, seems a substantial and commodious house but has nothing striking in appearance.

Monalty, the residence of Thomas Gartlan Esquire, stands in the townland of Monalty Bann, about 231 yards off the north side of the Ardee road. It is prettily situated and appears a very comfortable residence.

Ballymackney House, the residence of William Daniel Esquire, stands about 200 yards from the village of Ballymackney. It is small but seems very compact and comfortable.

Bleach Greens, Manufactures and Mills

In the townland of Annaghean is an extensive tannery conducted by Mr I. Kelly, brother to a magistrate of the same name at Carrickmacross.

At Killanny is an extensive corn mill, the wheel of which is undershot. It is 15 feet 6 inches in diameter.

Communications

The principal roads crossing this parish are: the turnpike road from Carrickmacross to Dundalk. It runs for about 2 and a third miles through the northern extremity of the parish.

Another leading road is from Carrickmacross to Ardee, which enters the west side of the parish at the broken bridge and runs easterly across the centre of the parish in direction of Corcreagh. Of it, 3 and one-eighth miles are in the parish.

There are apparent by-roads sufficient for the use of the parish. The main roads average 50 feet in width, the leading crossroads 33 and the by-roads 24 feet. The roads in the Monaghan part of the parish are kept much better than the others, particularly the by-roads which, in the Louth part, are bad.

There are no bridges of any importance. Such as do exist are sufficient in every respect for their purpose.

ANCIENT TOPOGRAPHY

Old Abbey

Close to the village of Killanny is a graveyard in which are the ruins of an old abbey. The walls are roughly built, averaging in thickness 3 and a half feet: [plan and rough sketch of abbey with annotations and dimensions].

It would be difficult to ascertain the exact original shape of the building, and perhaps part of its site has been destroyed and the building added to since being first erected, as at C. There is the appearance of a side wall being broken down and no bond with the 2 walls as they now stand. The wall at C throws the end windows D in the centre of the gable.

In the graveyard the oldest inscription is on a cross and is as follows: "Here lieth the body of Thomas Feine, who departed this life February the 1st in the year of our Lord God 1713."

On a stone let into the end wall, and over the door of a cell or vault, is a coat of arms with an inscription stating it to belong to the family of Byrne and dated June 14th 1714. On a tombstone is another coat of arms dated 1755. [Drawing of coats of arms, one with inscription "Certavi vici"].

There are also tombstones of the MacMahon family but no very ancient date.

Remains of Antiquity

Not more than 132 yards from the village is an old mound similar to that at Inniskeen but concerning which no traditions are known. Its dimensions are as under [blank].

In the townland of Annaghean is situated an old graveyard but is not at present used as such.

In addition to the above are several forts of a minor kind throughout the parish and generally on the summit of the highest hills.

In the churchyard at Ballymackney is a tombstone on which is the accompanying coat of arms [drawing] and inscription: "Here lyeth the body of William Tenison Esquire, who departed this life on the 2nd day of April 1750 aged 35 years."

MODERN TOPOGRAPHY

General Appearance and Scenery

Its general appearance is flat than otherwise, although less bare and open than the adjoining districts.

SOCIAL ECONOMY

Improvements

No early improvements are on record, nor does it appear that there is a probability of any modern improvements taking place.

Obstructions to improvement: there are none.

Local Government

There are 8 magistrates acting for the immediate district, 5 of whom may be considered as generally sitting at the petty sessions. These are not stipendiary. 3 of them reside at Carrickmacross, 2 are the agents of the Marquis of Bath and E.J. Shirley Esquire, 1 at Coolderry 4 miles from it, 1 at Ballymackney 2 miles off, 2 near Donaghmoyne church 2 miles off and 1 at Castleblayney.

The latter is the agent of Colonel Porter for that part of his estate which is is adjacent to the town of Carrickmacross, where the petty sessions are held. They are generally speaking firm and respected by the people.

There are no police stations in the parish [crossed out: 2 stations, 1 in Magorey townland, consisting of 1 constable and [blank] subconstables, and 1 in [blank], consisting of 1 constable and [blank] subconstables]. The petty sessions are generally attended by 2 or more magistrates. Much business is, however, prevented through the influence of the 2 agents who, as such, can reconcile the parties in many cases without the necessity of the cases being brought before the bench.

Outrages are on the decrease. The usual cases

Parish of Killanny

tried are principally common assaults and wages. The punishment inflicted seem fully adequate to the extent of the offence.

Combinations do not seem to prevail to any great extent, except as to the payment of tithe where it has been very decided and in some cases led to serious results. But little illicit distillation is carried on. Insurances are very uncommon, although not proceeding from any feelings of distrust.

Of the above magistrates, William Daniel Esquire of Drumreaver only resides in the parish.

The petty sessions for the Monaghan part of the parish are held at Carrickmacross every other Friday and at Louth every Thursday. But one magistrate, William Daniel Esquire, resides in the parish. Crimes in the parish are on the decline; common assaults and wages the usual cases tried. No illicit distilling carried on.

Dispensaries

But little sickness prevails in the district. The Farney dispensary, situated in Carrickmacross, is supported by the voluntary subscription of the principal proprietors and neighbouring gentlemen, assisted by county presentment. It is attended by 1 surgeon assisted by compounder of medicines and is conducted on truly liberal terms, see Magheross statistics; for Louth part, see Inniskeen notes.

Schools

See table; their introduction has been attended with partial improvement in the morals of the people, who are anxious for knowledge.

Poor

Further to the poor pittance collected during divine service or by the poor begging from door to door, there is no provision for them.

Religion

The greatest proportion of the population is composed of Roman Catholics, that of the Protestants which is composed principally of members of the Established Church. The Church clergymen is supported by the tithe and the priests by contribution from their own people.

Habits of the People

The cottages are generally built of a mixture of stone and sods, being roofed with scraws first and then thatched. They have generally 2 rooms and small glazed windows. They are neither clean nor comfortable. The food of the poorer class is potatoes and salt, of others, potatoes, meal, buttermilk and occasionally salt herrings. Bacon is seldom consumed except by a farmer's family when their circumstances are easy. Their fuel is turbary.

Of dress, they have no particular kind except the males who generally wear a frieze coat of their own manufacture and known as peculiar to Farney. They live to an advanced age than otherwise, in some instances having of late exceeded 100 years. 5 is the usual number of a family. Early marriages are frequent.

Amusements

During a Sunday after attending divine service, they amuse themselves by meeting in large numbers on a road convenient to a public house generally, where they dance or else by shooting and hunting, football playing, leaping, throwing the stone. Drinking on that day prevails to a great extent.

Christmas here with them is a feasting period. At this time the markets are loaded with white bread, geese and pork, which articles are procured for the occasion, if possibly within the compass of their means. Christmas Eve and the next night are observed, particularly the day before or proceeding market day. The poor may be seen returning home with one or two candles generally moulded and secured in the hat by the band or ribbon. They sit up during the night.

No particular patron's day unless that of St Patrick is observed. On St John's Eve bonfires are lighted, but in this custom they have been restrained as much as possible of late years since it tended to create riots in the country.

During the burial of their dead the funeral cries or lamentations are uttered but by the women only, who accompany their bewailing with wringing of hands. Sometimes, but not often, these cries take place on the road to the graveyard.

Emigration

Emigration prevails but not to a great extent. Many go to England and to the adjoining counties during the harvest. They leave their families at home. All have generally a patch of potatoe ground.

Remarkable Events

This and the adjoining parishes are noted for the

wars of Lord Essex with the chief of the soil, principally the MacMahons, whose direct descendants cannot be traced at this day, although there are many of the name in existence.

Productive Economy

Manufacturing

But little hand-spinning is done in the country. The manufacturing of frieze is carried on but not to such an extent as formerly. At present they only make sufficient to supply the immediate consumption of the country.

Fairs and markets: none. Produce or commodities taken to adjoining towns of Carrickmacross principally, also to Louth and Dundalk.

Rural: Land Ownership

The great proprietors of the parish are the Marquis of Bath, E.J. Shirley Esquire and Sir E.J. Foster Bart; E.J. Shirley Esquire only residing and this for a short period in the year. His agent Alexander Mitchell Esquire, however, always resides at Carrickmacross as does James Evatt Esquire, agent of the Marquis of Bath. They are paid percentage on the rents collected. Usual sizes of the holdings varies from 5 to 20 acres. Few leases are now granted and the farms are held direct from the head landlords. The proprietors of the Louth part are Mr Balfour, agent Mr Henry of Broomfield, Sir Augustus John Forster Bart, agent Mr Pentland, none of whom reside in the parish.

The primate has also a portion of the parish.

Rural: Farms

It would be difficult to ascertain the rates per acre as they vary so much. The rent is wholly paid in money. The farmers are partly yeomen, partly cottiers and farm for subsistence only. A very little land is let in conacre. The general size of the fields varies with that of the farms, but of late that part of the parish forming a portion of the Shirley estate has been much improved by a new laying out of the fields, which are now regular and uniform. The fences are generally quickset hedges faced with stone built very compactly on their edges. The tenants are merely liable to county cess tithes.

None of the landlords, resident gentry or agent have farms to any extent in their possession.

Soil and Manures

The soil is tolerably productive but varies very much. The county Louth portion of this parish is much better than that of Monaghan. The usual manures are marl, blue, clay, lime, cow-house dung and the scrapings of roads, cleanings of drains. In some parts of the parish marl is abundant.

There are several minor lime-kilns in the parish, the property of the farmers on Mr Shirley's part of the estate, and belonging to him is a very extensive lime-kiln at a place called Reilly's Rocks in Magheross parish, also Mason Lodge in Magheracloone parish.

On the Shirley estate tenants pay 6d on the spot for lime on its delivery.

The Marquis of Bath gives the lime at a very low rate and is paid after the crops are raised or got in. Burning the ground for manure is not permitted and is only occasionally resorted to as a progress of reclaiming wasteground.

Husbandry and Crops

No improved implements of husbandry have been introduced; threshing machines only used by one or two more opulent individuals. The common wheel car and dray are generally used, although the communications would admit of good carts and wagons.

Oxen are not used in agriculture and never more than 2 horses to a plough. The system of 1 man managing a plough without a helper is gradually becoming customary.

There are no rotation crops. Potatoes are the preparation crops. The soil varies so much that it would be impossible to state the crop per acre. The produce is generally taken either to Carrickmacross, Louth or Dundalk.

Grazing and Cattle

There are no farms devoted extensively to grazing. Draining is effected when necessary. Farm servants are rarely employed, are paid at from 3 pounds to 5 pounds per annum. They are boarded and lodged.

No particular breeds are reared. On the sale of pigs the poor in a great measure often depend as a means of paying their rents. The common Irish pig principally and the Dutch pig rarely are the usual breeds.

Uses made of the Bogs

The bogs are seldom grazed, being used wholly as fuel by the tenants who pay a moderate rent for their turbary. The imbedded timber is used for

Parish of Killanny

building and other domestic purposes. No turbary is made into charcoal for the forges.

Drainage and Planting

No draining further than what is usually carried into effect is required.

The only planting that has taken place has been merely for ornamental purposes. The vicinity of Dundalk renders planting unnecessary.

Sea-Coast and Fishing

Sea-coast none. Fishing but little, and only resorted to as a source of amusement.

General Remarks

Every part of the parish has been cultivated with the exception of the boggy districts, which are carefully nursed from the probability of turbary becoming eventually scarce. The climate is mild and tending to promote, than otherwise, the growth of crops. The roads and communications are amply sufficient for all local purposes.

DIVISIONS

Townlands

Divisions: there are none but those usual in all parishes.

In this parish are 43 townlands, of which 32 are in the county Monaghan and 11 in that of Louth. For proprietors' names, see Field Name Books.

SOCIAL ECONOMY

Table of Schools

[Table contains the following headings: name of townland, number of pupils subdivided by religion and sex, how supported, when established].

Essexford, 35 Catholics, 31 males, 4 females, total 35; supported by the children's parents; when established: uncertain.

Essexford, 25 Catholics, 10 males, 15 females, total 25; supported by the children's parents; when established: uncertain.

Drumreaver, 8 Catholics, 7 males, 1 female, total 8; supported by the children's parents; when established: uncertain.

Lanatt, 50 Catholics, 30 males, 20 females, total 50; supported by the children's parents; when established: uncertain.

Mullaghmeene, 70 Catholics, 50 males, 20 females, total 70; supported by the children's parents; when established: uncertain.

Drumreaver, 20 Catholics, 16 males, 4 females, total 20; supported by the children's parents; when established: uncertain.

Aghafad, 30 Catholics, 23 males, 7 females, total 30; supported by the children's parents; when established: uncertain.

The rector of the parish pays the parish clerk a stipend as schoolmaster, but no children attend him.

Ecclesiastical Summary

[Table] Killanny, county Monaghan: diocese Clogher, province Ulster, both rectory and vicarage, no union, patron Lord Bishop of Clogher, incumbent Revd Sir Harcourt Lees, extent of glebe 168 acres British; the tithes amount to 461 pounds 10s British and are not impropriate.

Killanny, county Louth: diocese Clogher, province Leinster. [Signed] Robert Boteler, Lieutenant Royal Engineers, 7th November 1835.

Brief Notes by George Scott

SOCIAL ECONOMY AND MODERN TOPOGRAPHY

Schools and Churches

School in the townland of Coolaha: total 55, males 45, females 10, Catholics 55; master a Roman Catholic. The children pay 2s per quarter.

Church in the townland of Aghafad, erected upwards of 100 years, repaired 50 years ago. Dimensions 33 feet by 31 feet; 14 seats, would accommodate 6 persons each; 40 attend on Sunday; Sir Harcourt Lees, rector.

School, same townland, total 9, males 9, Protestants 9; master a Protestant; Sir Harcourt Lees gives the master 2 pounds 2s a year, children pay 1d per week.

Parish of Kilmore, County Monaghan

Brief Notes by J.R. Ward

MODERN TOPOGRAPHY AND SOCIAL ECONOMY

Church

Kilmore church, situated in the townland of Kilnahaltar, is a stone building 60 feet long and 30 feet broad, with a tower at the west end and a small vestry at the north side. The whole is roughcast and whitewashed, and the tower is surmounted with 4 plain minarets. The inside of the church is very neat and contains a very small gallery. It accommodates 450 persons; the attendance is fully that number.

There are no monuments in the church, but on the side walls are 2 small, white marble slabs edged with black marble. That on the north wall has the following passage taken from Scripture: "Reverence my sanctuary," Leviticus, chapter 26 verse 2; that on the south wall: "I will come into thine house even upon the multitude of thy mercy, and in thy fear will I worship toward thy holy temple," Psalm 5 verse 7.

School

Kilmore parish schoolhouse, situated near the church, is a plain stone and brick building, slated, of the following form and dimensions [ground plan, main dimensions 36 feet by 36 feet, "T" shape]. It was built in 1832 and the cost was defrayed by subscription aided by a small grant from the Board for Discountenancing Vice. The present rector of the parish, the Revd George Hay Schomberg, gave an English acre of ground from the glebe for the site of the house and for the use of the schoolmaster.

Kilmore parish school was established in 1830 in a small cottage opposite the church gate. It was removed in 1832 to the present house. The master's income is from the rector 8 pounds per annum and from the pupils 8 pounds; there is no expenditure. The books used are the Dublin Reading Book and the Authorised Version of the Scriptures. The school is visited by the Revd John Thomas Whitestone, curate, weekly, and sometimes by the rector; catechisms are taught by the master.

There is at present 105 pupils, of which there are of males, 11 above 15 years, 15 between 10 and 15 and 16 under 10 years; of females, there are 8 above 15 years, 12 between 10 and 15 and 15 under 10 years. Of the whole, 87 are of the Established Church, 8 are Presbyterians and 10 Roman Catholics.

Parish of Magheracloone, County Monaghan

Statistical Return by Lieutenant Robert Boteler, November 1835

NATURAL STATE

Name

It is generally spelt Magheracloone, by which name it is usually known. It is also called Magheracloony, but Magheracloone seems to be the proper orthography; vide Field Name Book.

Locality

Is situated in the southern extremity of the county Monaghan and barony of Farney. Its extreme length east and west is about 7 and half statute miles, its breadth from north to south is about 3 and half statute miles. It contains 14,952 acres, of which 1,063 are uncultivated and 357 are water. It paid 496 pounds 6s 2d to the county cess at the summer assizes 1835.

NATURAL FEATURES

Hills

All the hills in the parish are named after the townland in which they are situated. There are none remarkable for their form or height above the others, all being round in outline and gradually rising above each other.

The highest ground is in Dromerloghmore, situated in the west part of the parish, and which is 475 feet above the sea. The lowest point is at the south east angle of the parish and on its boundary, where the river is not more than 86 feet above the sea.

Lakes

The principal lakes are Lough Fea, Raans and Ballyhoe. Lough Fea is situated on the boundary between Magheross and Magheracloone parishes, at the eastern end of the latter. It is about 111 feet above the sea and covers 109 acres of extent.

Raans lough is on the parish boundary on its south side. It is 89 feet above the sea and covers an extent of 85 acres.

Ballyhoe lough is also on the same side of the parish and about 1 mile south east of Raans lough. It covers an extent of 170 acres and it is 89 feet above the sea.

There are several other loughs varying in size dispersed throughout the parish.

Rivers

The Lagan is the principal river. It may be said to take its rise in Corlea townland about 400 feet above the sea, proceeds south easterly, joins the parish boundary in Drummond townland and, about 10 chains east of the road from Carrickmacross to Kingscourt, passes along the south side of the parish, meets and traverses Ballyhoe lough, again forms the southern boundary of the parish until its junction with that of Killanny, when the river is about 130 feet above the sea.

Bogs and Woods

The principal bogs are as follows. [Table contains the following headings: name of townland, extent in acres, height above the sea, remarks]. [Insert note: [Height] can only be obtained by reference to the plans].

Cornalaragh and Doagh, 40 acres, partly in each townland.

Corlea and Ballaghnagearn, 36 acres, partly in each townland.

Drumond, Derrynascobe and Knocknacran West, 50 acres, partly in each townland.

Clonsedy and Losset, 40 acres, partly in each townland.

Feahoe, 65 acres.

Derry, 36 acres.

Timber is frequently found, generally laying lengthwise and indiscriminately; consists of oak and fir principally.

Woods: There are none, unless a few patches of hazel, but insignificant as to size, in Mr Shirley's demesne.

Coast: none.

Climate

No means of ascertaining the climate exist: it is generally considered very salubrious, so much so that families have moved to the neighbourhood for the benefit of its pure air. The crops generally speaking are rather forward than otherwise.

Natural History

Botany and Zoology

The native plants vary much and but little attention paid to them. They are the same, however, as generally sown in the country.

Most of the loughs abound in trout, perch and bream. In others are found pike which run to a considerable size. Eels are also found in most of them. The streams being very small, but few fish are found in them, and these, it would seem, merely in moving from one lough to another.

Besides birds of the common species generally found throughout the country, the inland loughs are frequented during the hard weather by fowl of every description, from the cormorant to the small diver and teal. During the summer, and particularly in the spring, a vast number of seagulls of different kinds may be observed throughout the district, but particularly in the lower or eastern extremity in the parish.

There are but few partridges but a great abundance of landrails and quails, announcing their existence during the breeding season in every direction [by] their respective and peculiar calls.

Hares and rabbits are also to be met with, but in no great abundance except in the vicinity of Lough Fea demesne. Weasels are numerous and occasionally a badger is seen. One of the latter was caught lately about half a mile out of the town of Carrickmacross, a very handsome specimen.

In addition to the birds already enumerated as frequenting the loughs throughout the year, may be seen the bald coote, water-hen or rail and the small diver. The two latter are not, however, common, particularly the diver. Woodcocks are scarce but snipes are very abundant, some few remaining throughout the year.

Modern Topography

Public Buildings

Towns: none.

The Established church is situated near the centre of the parish, standing in the townland of Camoghy. It was built AD 1824 (the building cost 800 pounds) by the vicar of the parish at the expense of the parish. It is neatly built without being remarkable; is capable of affording accommodation to 150 people.

A small chapel of ease has been erected at Coolderry by George Forster Esquire, at his own expense and for his own use.

Situated in the centre of the parish, and in the townland of Knocknacranfy East, is a Roman Catholic chapel; is capable of accommodating 300 persons.

Also in the townland of Mullaghgarve is a chapel of ease and capable of containing 200 persons.

Gentlemen's Seats

The cottage at Lough Fea, and situated in the demesne, forms the temporary residence of E.J. Shirley Esquire. It has very little to recommend it except its neat appearance on the outside and the vast accommodation within, so far exceeding what it might be supposed to afford. It has no less than 27 bedrooms. A gong is always sounded at it to call the labourers and others to work.

For the last 2 or 3 years Mr Shirley has been erecting an extensive mansion about 200 yards from the cottage. It is of cut freestone and in the Elizabethan style. It overlooks Lough Fea and commands an extensive view of the adjoining country. A great quantity of beautifully carved oak has been brought over from Holland at a considerable expense for the purpose of panelling the library and dining-room. One specimen, the Crucifixion, is admirably executed.

The demesne may be said to be quite in its infancy, having only been partly laid out as such but a few years since. Gradual additions of ornamental planting and walks are made to it under the superintendence of the agent, Alexander Mitchell Esquire of Shirley House, Carrickmacross, to whose display of taste and judgment too much praise cannot be given.

One of the most interesting walks passes sometimes at the top of and sometimes through the heart of a planted glen running at one part over the top of the cliff, at the foot of which is shown what was said to have been the chair of Fin McCoul. The demesne is about 1 mile south west of Carrickmacross and is bounded partly by the Drumcondra and Kingscourt roads. It contains about 806 acres.

Coolderry, the residence of George Forster Esquire, oldest son of the Revd Thomas Forster Bart, is situated in the townland of the same name at the south end of the parish, the boundary of which the River Lagan runs about 100 yards in front of. The house is a substantial dwelling prettily situated. The pleasure grounds around it have been much improved by its present owner who has had it but a short time only.

Glebe House is a newly built house situated in the townland of Camohey, about half a mile north west of the church. It is of a middling size and apparently comfortable as a residence.

Parish of Magheracloone

Maghernacloy Castle, standing in Maghernacloy townland, residence of James Gartlan Esquire; further information will be supplied.

Bleach Greens, Manufactories and Mills

There are a few mills in the parish, but are of a simple construction and of trifling importance.

Communications

The following main roads pass through part of the parish. [Table] From Carrickmacross to Shercock, half a mile; from Carrickmacross to Kingscourt, 3 miles; from Carrickmacross to Drumcondra, 4 miles; from Carrickmacross to Ardee, 4 miles; all in excellent order.

Their average breadth is 40 feet. They are kept in most excellent order, having been hitherto under the superintendence of residing agent of E.J. Shirley Esquire. The change, however, in the grand jury laws affecting the roads has already evinced a change for the worst.

The parish is intersected by numerous cross and by-roads, some of which are necessary for the comfort and convenience of the parishioners: indeed too much praise cannot be given to the landlords of the soil, who have evinced the greatest regard for the comfort of their tenantry in establishing a series of useful, well laid out and particularly well kept minor communications.

Bridges

The principal, and only, bridges of any note are as follows: viz. where the Carrickmacross and Kingscourt road crosses the parish and county boundary; it is composed of 2 arches.

Another over the same river, where a by-road joins the road from Kingscourt to Coolderry; this bridge has 3 arches and is called Tobermannen bridge.

Another where the mail coach road from Carrickmacross to Drumcondra crosses the river and county boundary; this bridge was built in the year 1818 and has 3 arches.

Lower down the river is another bridge of 5 arches; is called the Lagan bridge. It is on the road from Carrickmacross to Ardee.

ANCIENT TOPOGRAPHY

Remains of Antiquity

In the townland of Maghernacloy is a castle named after the townland. It is at present in possession of James Gartlan Esquire. [Insert note: Further information will be supplied].

On the cliff bounding the eastern side of Lough Fea demesne and parish also is a steep cliff, at the foot of which is a ledge called Finn McCool's Chair.

In addition to the above are several forts throughout the parish.

MODERN TOPOGRAPHY

General Appearance and Scenery

With the exception of the north west angle of the parish, which is its highest part and composed of the poorest soil, the parish exhibits a highly picturesque and well-cultivated surface. The cottages of the poor seem of a better description, and more efforts have been made to plant the country and assist nature in giving it a more civilised appearance.

SOCIAL ECONOMY

Early Improvements

Under this head may be introduced the facility afforded to the tenantry of improving their land, and therefore the increase of its crops, by the indulgence granted by the 2 principal proprietors in the supply of lime, which is burned on the several parts of the estate and given during the necessary periods as manure at a low rate, the price of the same not being required to be paid until after the next crop has been disposed of.

On Mr Shirley's they pay 6d per barrel on delivery. During the last year or two the number of barrels given on the 2 estates has been very great.

Cattle shows have been established and premiums given, but are now discontinued.

On Lord Bath's estate during the last year upwards of 100,000 quicks were given to the tenantry to improve their fences.

Obstructions to improvement: do not exist; on the contrary, every exertion is made to encourage.

Local Government

There are 8 magistrates acting for the immediate district; 5 of them only may be considered as generally sitting at the petty sessions. They are not stipendiary. 3 of them reside at Carrickmacross, 2 are the agents of the Marquis of Bath and E.J. Shirley Esquire, 1 at Coolderry 4 miles from it, 1 at Ballymackney 2 miles off, 2 near Donaghmoyne church 2 miles off and 1 at Castleblayney. They are generally speaking firm and respected by the people.

The petty sessions are always held at the market house in Carrickmacross and are generally attended by 2 or more magistrates. Much business is, however, prevented through the influence of the 2 agents who, as such, can reconcile the parties in many cases without the necessity of the case being brought before the bench.

Outrages are on the decrease. The usual cases tried are principally common assaults and wages. The punishments inflicted seem fully adequate to the extent of the offence. Combinations do not seem to prevail to any great extent except as to payment of tithe, where it has been very decided and in some cases led to serious results. But little illicit distillation is carried on. Insurances very uncommon, although not proceeding from any feelings of distrust.

Dispensaries

But little sickness prevails in the district. The Farney dispensary, situated in Carrickmacross, is supported by the voluntary subscription of the principal proprietors and neighbouring gentlemen, assisted by county presentment. It is attended by 1 surgeon assisted by a compounder of medicines and is conducted on truly liberal terms.

Schools and Poor

Schools by their introduction have led to a slight improvement in the moral habits of the people, who seem anxious for improvement.

Poor: further than the poor pittance collected during divine service, or by the poor begging from door to door, this is no provision for them.

Religion

According to a census taken in 1831, the population of the parish amounted to 1,588 families, containing 4,132 males and 4,312 females, of whom 304 or about one-twenty-eighth part only were Protestants, the number or proportion as to religion being ascertained in 1834. The clergyman of the Established Church is paid by tithes, the Roman Catholic priests by voluntary contributions.

Habits of the People

The cottages are generally built of a mixture of stone and sods, being roofed with scraws first and then thatched. They have generally 2 rooms and small glazed windows. They appear cleaner and more comfortable than in the adjoining district.

The food of the poorer class is potatoes and salt, of others potatoes, meal, buttermilk and occasionally salted herrings. Bacon is seldom consumed except by a farmer's family when their circumstances are easy. The fuel is turbary.

Of dress, they have no particular kind except for the males, who generally wear a frieze coat of their own manufacture and known as peculiar to Farney.

They live to an advanced age than otherwise, in some instances having of late exceeded 100 years. 5 and a half is the usual number of family; early marriages are frequent.

Amusements

During a Sunday, after attending divine service, they amuse themselves by meeting in large numbers on a road (convenient to a public house generally), where they dance, or else by shooting, horse-racing and hunting, football playing, leaping and throwing the stone. Drinking on that day prevails to a great extent.

Christmas time with them is a feasting period. At this time the market is loaded with white bread, geese and pork, which articles are procured for the occasion if possibly within the compass of their means. Christmas Eve and the next night are observed particularly. The day before or proceeding market day the poor may be seen returning home with one or two candles, generally moulds, and secured in the hat by the band or ribbon. They sit up during the night.

No particular patrons' days unless that of St Patrick is observed. On St John's Eve bonfires are lighted, but in this custom they have been restrained as much as possible of late years, since it tended to create riots in the country.

During the burial of their dead the funeral cries or lamentations are uttered, but by the women only, who accompany their bewailing with wringing of hands. Sometimes, but not often, these cries take place on the road to the graveyard.

Emigration

Some few emigrate principally to New York and Quebec, of whom some have returned. Many go to England and adjoining counties for work during the harvest, but leave their families at home. Most of the poor rent ground and sow potatoes.

Parish of Magheracloone

Remarkable Events

The parish is neither known to have given birth to any remarkable person nor to have been the scene of any remarkable event, except so far as, like the rest of the immediate neighbourhood, it was partly the arena of Lord Essex's wars, during which period the MacMahons were the chiefs of the district.

PRODUCTIVE ECONOMY

Manufacturing

See description of Carrickmacross. Hand-spinning alone, and that to a very trifling extent, exists.

Fairs and Markets

There are none; few of the inhabitants of the parish frequent, except occasionally, any other than those of Carrickmacross, for a description of which see Statistical Return of Maghross parish.

Rural: Proprietors and Farms

The great proprietors of this parish are E.J. Shirley Esquire, the Revd James Brownlow, George Foster Esquire and H.E. Porter Esquire; E.J. Shirley Esquire only residing, and this for a short period in the year. His agent, Alexander Mitchell Esquire, however, always resides at Carrickmacross. The agents are paid percentage on the rents collected.

Usual size of the holdings varies from 5 to 20 acres. Few leases are now granted and the farms are held direct from the head landlords. It would be difficult to ascertain the rents per acre as they vary so much. The rent is wholly paid in money.

The farmers are partly yeomen, partly cottiers and farm for subsistence only. Very little land is let in conacre. The general size of the fields varies with that of the farms, but of late that part of the parish forming a portion of the Shirley estate has been much improved by a new laying out of the fields, which are now in general regular and uniform. The fences are principally quickset hedges and stone and sod fences. The tenants are merely liable to county cess and tithes. None of the landlords, resident gentry or agents have farms to any extent in their possession.

Soil and Manures

The soil is tolerably productive but varies very much.

The usual manures are marl, blue clay, lime, cow-house dung and the scraping of roads and cleanings of drains. In most parts of the parish marl is abundant. There are several minor lime-kilns in the parish, the property of the farmers. On Mr Shirley's part of the estate, and belonging to him, is a very extensive lime-kiln at a place called Reilly's Rocks (in Maghross parish). Also at Mason Lodge in this parish, on the Shirley estate, tenants pay 6d on the spot for lime on its delivery.

Burning the ground for manure is not permitted and is only occasionally resorted to as a progress of reclaiming wasteground.

Husbandry and Crops

No improved implements of husbandry have been introduced; threshing machines only used by one or two more opulent individuals. The common wheel car and dray are generally used, although the communications would admit of good carts and wagons.

Oxen are not used in agriculture and never more than 2 horses to a plough. The system of 1 man managing a plough without a helper is gradually becoming customary.

There are no rotation crops: potatoes are the rotation crops. The soil varies so much that it would be impossible to state the crops per acre. The produce is generally taken either to Carrickmacross, Louth, Dundalk or Kingscourt.

Grazing and Cattle

No grazing is carried on unless for domestic purposes solely. The system of grazing has probably not been adopted from the soil not answering too well and its vicinity as a district to the county Meath, so famous as a grazing county.

Cattle vary so much as to defy description. None of them can be said to be natives of the district, not at least as a particular breed, since if any are bred in the county they are so crossed with other breeds as to puzzle their origin. The pigs are generally the common Irish breed.

Uses made of the Bogs

The bogs are used wholly as fuel and consumed in the neighbourhood. The people have a right of turbary under certain restrictions necessarily imposed from its gradually decreasing. It is not converted into charcoal for the use of smithy forges. The bog is charged for in the Shirley estate at a low rate. The imbedded timber is used for building and other domestic purposes.

Drainage and Planting

Draining has been carried on to an extensive degree of late, by which means the loughs have been reduced in size and extent, swamps reclaimed and crops now obtained where was not long since a cold, rank and unprofitable bottom.

No planting has been resorted to except for the purpose of ornamenting ground, and this only about the gentlemen's seats.

Sea-Coast and Fishing

Sea-coast: none.

Fishing merely resorted to on the loughs as a recreation, or for the purpose of adding to the comforts of the poor man's meal.

General Remarks

But few can be made, except where bogs occur which, from a fear of turbary becoming scarce, are not reclaimed; but few patches of ground occur where the utmost of cultivation has not been effected. The manure of the soil and that artificially obtained is abundant enough and easily obtained.

Of the roads and communications there are sufficient for the farmers' purposes. The system of giving orders for lime during the spring, which is paid for when the crops are got in, is generally adopted.

DIVISIONS

Townlands

Divisions: none, except townlands of which there are [blank]. Townlands: see Field Name Books for the information as to proprietors and general summary.

A certain portion of the parish, composed of 15 townlands (see Name books) and situated at the southern part of the parish, goes by the name of Hadson's Fee Farm.

It is said that the Earl of Essex was taken suddenly ill while away from home and carried to the house of one Hadson, whose daughter, on his recovery, he seduced and cohabited with. To reconcile the father's feelings he gave him on leaving the above-mentioned portion of the parish, which to this day is called or known as Hadson's Fee Farm.

SOCIAL ECONOMY

Schools

[Table] Camoghy: males 45, females 25, total 70.

This school is under the direction of the National Board, allowing the schoolmaster 8 pounds per annum. The vicar of the parish allows him 3 pounds a year in addition, and he receives 1d a week from the scholars; established 1st February 1835.

The above is the parish school. In addition, there are 2 or 3 minor hedge schools, supported by the scholars' poor offerings.

Notes by George Scott

MODERN TOPOGRAPHY

Corn Mill

There is a corn mill in the townland of Clontrain; diameter of wheel 14 feet, breadth 4 feet, fall of water 6 feet, breast wheel; belongs to Peter Wood.

SOCIAL ECONOMY

Schools

School in the townland of Clontrain: total 70, males 55, females 15, Protestants 4, Catholics 66, master a Roman Catholic. The master receives from Mr Shirley 5 pounds a year, the children pay 2s, 3s and 5s per quarter. The school is established 29 years.

School in the townland of Halftate: total 71, males 50, females 21, Catholics 71, master a Roman Catholic. The children pay 1s 3d and 1s 8d and 3s 6d per quarter.

School in the townland of Drumboory: total 50, males 45, females 5, Protestants 4, Catholics 46; the master a Roman Catholic. The children pay 3s, 5s and 10s per quarter. The house erected in 1837 at the expense of John Kenny.

Parish of Magheross (Machaire Rois), County Monaghan

Statistical Return by Lieutenant Robert Boteler, November 1835

GEOGRAPHY OR NATURAL STATE

Name

Is generally spelt Magheross, by which name it is usually known. Sometimes also it is called Carrickmacross by the inhabitants of the parish, but Magheross seems to be the proper orthography from the following authorities, viz. boundary surveyor sketch and map; Marquis of Bath's maps, date 1777; McCrea's map of the barony of Farney, date 1793; Revd Dr Robinson's tithe book, rector; and the tithe book of the late Revd William Pinching, rector.

Locality

Is situated in the county Monaghan and western side of the barony of Farney, whence it extends in a south east direction to within about 1 and three-quarter miles of the east side of the barony and county Louth. The barony of Farney forms the southern extremity of the county of Monaghan.

The parish above named is bounded on the north by the parish of Aughnamullen in the barony of Cremorne and county Monaghan, on the north east by the parish of Donaghmoyne in the barony of Farney, on the south east by the parish of Killanny in the same barony, on the south by the parish of Magheracloone in the same barony also and on the west by the parishes of Shercock and Aughnamullen, the former being in the barony of Clonkee and county Cavan, the latter in the barony of Cremorne and county Monaghan.

The extreme length of the parish extending from north west to south east is 11 miles, its breadth 4 miles. It contains 16,702 acres, of which 890 are waste, 334 are water, the latter being one five-hundredth part of the whole parish. It paid 426 pounds 14s 3d to the county cess, of which 10 pounds is paid for foundlings.

NATURAL FEATURES

Hills

The principal and highest hill is Corduff, so called from the townland in which it is situated. It stands rather west of the centre of the parish and is 801 feet above the sea. The remaining hills gradually decrease in height, but not to such a degree as to give any of them a remarkable appearance contrasted with the others. The whole of them may be said to be insulated and of an uniform shape, being round and smooth in outline.

Lakes

The principal lakes are noted in the following table. [Table contains the following headings: name, common to or in what townland, height above the sea, content].

Lough Fea: townlands of Corduffkelly and Duhatty, 111 feet above the sea, 109 acres.

Stanonagh: townlands of Lissnacullen, Coraghy, and parish of Aughnamullen, 362 feet above the sea, 89 acres.

Loughnaglack: townlands of Drummond Otra and parish of Magheracloone, height above the sea 102 feet, 36 acres.

There are in all about 37 lakes, including those on the parish boundary.

Rivers and Springs

Rivers: there are none, but throughout the parish there are several small rivulets, few of which supply sufficient water to feed a mill. There is an abundance of spring wells throughout the parish in a proportion fully sufficient to supply the wants of the people.

One spring should not be left undescribed, it being remarkable for its size, depth, cleanness and pureness of water, and from its great discharge. It is situated in a bog in Coolderry townland, about 154 yards east of the Donaghmoyne road. There is always a constant stream of beautifully clear water flowing from it.

Towards the south west extremity of the parish is a very pretty group of rocks interspersed with trees and ivy called Reilly's Rocks. Close to these are 3 or 4 natural caves caused by the small stream which works its way through the rock, which at some parts has fallen in from above and between their course.

Bogs

There are several patches of bog in the parish. The principal is as follows. [Table] Lisdronturk,

Rafferagh and Corravally townlands, extent 77 acres, height above the sea [insert note: can only be taken from the plans]; common to each townland. Timber is frequently found, generally laying lengthways and indiscriminately. It consists of oak and fir principally.

Woods

There are no woods in the parish, nor does it appear that any ever existed.

Coast: none.

Climate

No means of ascertaining the climate exists. It is generally considered very salubrious, so much so that families have moved to the neighbourhood for the benefit of its pure air. The crops generally speaking are rather forward than otherwise.

NATURAL HISTORY

Botany

It does not appear that the shrubs or grass vary from those commonly met with in the country. No steps seem to have been taken to introduce fresh species, or to detect those which are unfit for the soil.

Zoology

Most of the loughs abound in trout, perch and bream. In others are found pike, which run to a considerable size. Eels are also found in most of them. The streams being very small, but few fish are found in them, and these, it would seem, merely in moving from one lough to another.

Besides birds of the common species generally found throughout the country, the inland loughs are frequented during the hard weather by fowl of every description, from the cormorant to the small diver and teal. During the summer, and particularly in the spring, vast numbers of seagulls of different kinds may be observed throughout the district, but particularly in the lower or eastern extremity of the parish. There are but few partridges, but a great abundance of landrails and quails, announcing their existence during the breeding season in every direction by their respective and peculiar calls.

Hares and rabbits are also to be met with, but in no great abundance except in the vicinity of Lough Fea Demesne. Weasels are numerous and occasionally a badger is seen. One of the latter was caught lately about half a mile out of the town of Carrickmacross, a very handsome specimen.

In addition to the birds already enumerated as frequenting the loughs throughout the year, may be seen the bald coote, water-hen or rail and the small diver. The 2 latter are not, however, common, particularly the diver. Woodcocks are scarce but snipes are very abundant, some few remaining throughout the year. Of the common and more domestic species, no variety seems to exist.

Geology

Besides referring to the plans and tables, it should be remarked that the merciful eye of providence has not overlooked the chance of fuel (turbary) becoming scarce and beyond the means of the poor man's purchase, since coal has been discovered in the parish: but either from a want of capital or its not being immediately wanted, not much endeavour to take advantage of it has been made.

MODERN TOPOGRAPHY

Church

The parish church is situated in the town of Carrickmacross and stands at the south end of the main street, which here branches off to Dundalk and Drumcondra, on the hill close to where was the old castle. It is a modern building, being erected for 600 pounds by Henry Byrne in 1792. It has rather a pretty spire and, from its situation, may be seen for a considerable distance in almost every direction. It is capable of affording accommodation for 350 persons, the usual number of congregation being about 180.

[Insert note: It appears that since the year 1792, and in addition to the sum of 600 pounds laid out in building the new church, several other sums have been expended, the exact amount of which does not appear. For instance, in the vestry book it appears that the sum of 150 pounds was laid on at 3 different vestries towards building a spire, and 2 different sums of 60 pounds towards the completion of the gallery, churchyard walls and secondly, other matters. Probably a portion of these last 2 sums went toward the repairs of the church].

Public Buildings

A large Roman Catholic chapel is situated on the eastern suburbs of the town of Carrickmacross. It was built in 1783 and is capable of containing 800 people. In the yard surrounding it is the

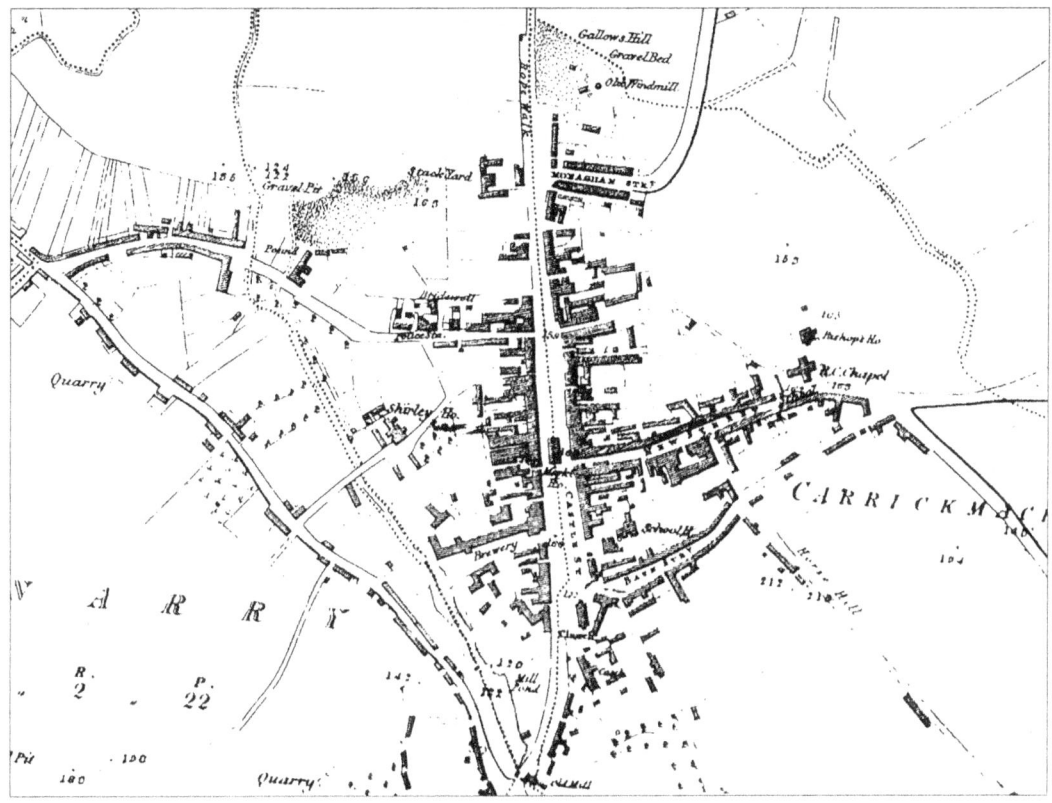

Map of Carrickmacross from the first 6" OS maps, 1830s

Roman Catholic bishop's house and a national school for children built in 1834 at the expense of the parishioners, and a sum of 100 pounds was given by government towards the completion of the house and furnishing tables and seats.

A Roman Catholic chapel stands in Corduff Mountain townland, capable of containing 700 people. There is another situated in Rafferagh townland, commonly called Corcreagh chapel, capable of containing 400 people.

In the townland of Carrickmaclim is a Presbyterian meeting house capable of containing about 300 persons. It has no gallery. A school is attached to it patronised by E.J. Shirley Esquire, who pays 5 pounds per annum to it. The scholars pay the rest towards the support of the teacher.

Gentlemen's Seats

Shirley House, the residence of Alexander Mitchell Esquire, agent to E.J. Shirley Esquire of Lough Fea, and whose property it is, is situated in the town. The house, its gardens and offices show at the first glance how much may be effected with little to work upon by taste and care. Until a very short time since it was comfortless and neglected. It is now as much the reverse. The gardens, flower and kitchen are kept in the nicest possible order.

The Glebe House stands in Derryolin Glebe. It is brick built and has apparently sufficient and good accommodation for a small family. It is conveniently situated for the clergyman, being within 10 minutes' walk of his church.

Lisaniske, the residence of Adam Gibson Esquire, is a plain and neat residence prettily situated by the edge of small lough, on the east side of the Dundalk turnpike road about half a mile from Carrickmacross.

No demesne is attached to any of the above-named houses.

Bleach Greens, Manufactories and Mills

For distillery, see account of the town of Carrickmacross. There are a few mills in the parish but all of a simple construction and of trifling importance.

Communications

From Carrickmacross the following roads diverge to the places under named, with the distance from the town to its point of crossing the parish boundary.

To Dundalk (a turnpike road) 1 mile 1 furlong; to Corcreagh and Ardee 1 mile 1 furlong; to Drumcondra and Dublin 7 furlongs; to Kingscourt 2 and half miles; to Shercock 7 and quarter miles; to Ballybay 5 miles 2 furlongs; to Castleblaney (branching from the last [blank] miles from Carrickmacross) 7 furlongs.

Their average breadth is 40 feet. They are kept in most excellent order, having been hitherto under the superintendence of the 2 residing agents of the Marquis of Bath and E.J. Shirley Esquire.

The change, however, in the grand jury laws affecting the roads has already evinced a change for the worst. The parish is intersected by numerous cross and by-roads, none of which are necessary for the comfort and convenience of the parishioners. Indeed too much praise cannot be given to the landlords of the soil, who have evinced the greatest regard for the comfort of their tenantry in establishing a series of useful, well laid out and particularly well-kept minor communications.

There are but few bridges, and these of no importance, but in no instance are they wanting. The roads have been laid down at the public expense.

ANCIENT TOPOGRAPHY

Earl of Essex

This and the adjoining parishes are treated of in many writings as having been the arena of the wars of Earl of Essex (see the *Statistical survey of county Monaghan* by Sir C. Coote Bart, Dublin, 1801).

Old Church

Close to the town of Carrickmacross, and in that part of its suburbs called Magheross, are the interesting ruins of an old church, the tower of which in a perfect state as now standing, as also the principal part of the walls of its body. In the interior of the tower is a stone slab let into the side of the wall (for inscription see below).

[Drawing of tablet with inscription: "This church was ruined in the rebellion of 1641 and rebuilt in the year 1682 at the expense of the Right Revd Dr Roger Boyle, Lord Bishop Clogher, William Barton Esquire, Robert Hill Esquire and Andrew Montgomery, clerk vicar of this parish"].

Old House and Well

Entering Carrickmacross by the Slane road, and immediately upon coming opposite to the church, stands a neat-looking house on the terrace to the right of the road. This house is built on the site of Lord Essex's Castle often alluded to in various histories of this part of the country. Scarcely any part of the walls can now be traced.

At the foot of the hill, and between the small stream and the Slane road (close to each), is a well called Tubber Inver, which probably is the well also mentioned in the history of the castle.

Inscription on Bridge

On the old road from Carrickmacross to Kingscourt, and on a bridge in the townland of Derrylavan, is a stone on which is the following inscription [drawing] much defaced: "This bridge was built by the Revd Fr Bryan Hullen, rector vicar of Magheross parish, and in the 80th year of his age anno domini 1724."

Hammer and Trough

In the bog at Corduff Kelly was recently found, about 6 feet below the surface, a stone hammer supposed to be pagan. It is now in the possession of E.J. Shirley Esquire of Lough Fea.

In his possession is also a singularly constructed cot or trough, which was found by Alexander Mitchell Esquire about 6 feet below the surface of a cut-out bog in Drumgerna townland. It is of one solid piece of oak. It is 9 and a half feet long, 10 inches broad and 6 inches deep.

Cave and Cromlech

About 1 and half miles from Carrickmacross, on the road to Ballybay, on the right side of the road is a limestone cliff, at the base of which is a cave carrying off the water from the lough on the opposite side of the road.

On the top of the cliff, and a few yards from its ledge, it is said that there once was a cromlech and that the pieces of rock of which it was composed were not long since destroyed for the purpose of being converted into lime in the kiln a the side of the cliff. This is confirmed by it being spoken of in written history.

Forts

In addition to the above are several forts o mounds scattered throughout the parish and gen erally situated on the summits of the highest ground and in sight of each other. By the country people they are much venerated, so much so that few would be hardy enough to cut a branch from any of the trees or bushes which are generally growing on their sides.

Modern Topography

General Appearance and Scenery

This and the adjoining parishes have a very open appearance, the country being almost treeless and its fences composed of stone or sods. Quicks have of late been supplied gratis to the tenantry to improve their fences within the last 2 years. Quicks have been given out to the tenantry of the 2 estates. A number of small loughs occur through the parish but by constant draining much land has been reclaimed.

The system of blasting and removing masses of rock, which not long since has occurred throughout the parish, has tended to the cultivation of the land where a waste previously existed.

On the whole the hills throughout the parish not being too steep to mar the labours of the farmer, the eye is at once, except in the north western extremity of the parish, convinced that agriculture has neither been idle nor unattended with its deserved success.

Social Economy

Early Improvements

Under this head may be introduced the facility afforded to the tenantry of improving their lands, and therefore the increase of its crops, by the indulgence granted by the 2 principal proprietors in the supply of lime, which is burned on the several parts of the estate and given during the necessary periods as manure at a low rate, the price of the same not being required to be paid until after the next crop has been disposed of. During the last year or two the number of barrels thus given to the 2 estates has been very great indeed.

Until a short time since a farming society was established at Carrickmacross, where prizes were awarded for the best show of pigs, home-made frieze and so on, but from some difference among the subscribers it no longer exists.

Obstructions to improvements do not exist: on the contrary, every exertion is made to encourage them.

Local Government

There are 8 magistrates acting for the immediate district, 5 of whom only may be considered as generally sitting at the petty sessions. These are not stipendiary. 3 of them reside at Carrickmacross, 2 are the agents of the Marquis of Bath and E.J. Shirley Esquire, 1 at Coolderry 4 miles from it, 1 at Ballymackney 2 miles off, 2 near Donaghmoyne church 2 miles off and 1 at Castleblayney. The latter is the agent of Colonel Porter for that part of his estate which is adjacent to the town. They are generally speaking firm and respected by the people.

Independent of the police force in the town, there are country stations. A detachment of infantry composed of 1 company supplied from Armagh was stationed in the town of Carrickmacross for some time and was only withdrawn at the close of the last year from want of barrack accommodation.

The petty sessions are always held at the market house in Carrickmacross and are generally attended by 2 or more magistrates. Much business is, however, prevented through the influence of the 2 agents who, as such, can reconcile the parties in many cases without the necessity of the cases being brought before the bench.

Outrages are on the decrease. The usual cases tried are principally common assaults and wages. The punishments inflicted seem fully adequate to the extent of the offence.

Combinations do not seem to prevail to any great extent except as to the payment of tithe, where it has been very decided and in some cases led to serious results. But little illicit distillation is carried on, insurances very uncommon, although not proceeding from any feelings of distrust.

Dispensaries

But little sickness prevails in the district. The Farney dispensary, situated in Carrickmacross, is supported by the voluntary subscription of the principal proprietors and neighbouring gentlemen, assisted by county presentment. It is attended by 1 surgeon, assisted by a compounder of medicines, and is conducted on truly liberal terms.

Schools and Poor

Schools by their introduction have led to a slight improvement in the moral habits of the people, who seem anxious for improvement.

Further than the poor pittance collected during divine service, or by the poor begging from door to door, there is no provision for them. A fund was raised in Carrickmacross a short time since, but from a difference arising among some of the contributors as to its application it has no longer been collected.

Religion

The greatest proportion of the population is composed of Roman Catholics who are as 50 to 1 of that of the Protestants, which is composed principally of members of the Established Church and of some Presbyterians.

The church clergymen is supported by the tithe, the Presbyterian minister by the regium donum and a stipend from his congregation, and the priests by contribution from their own people.

Habits of the People

The cottages are generally built of a mixture of stone and sods, being roofed with scraws first and then thatched. They have generally 2 rooms and small glazed windows. They are neither clean nor comfortable. The food of the poorer class is potatoes and salt; of others potatoes, meal, buttermilk and occasionally salted herrings. Bacon is seldom consumed except by a farmer's family when their circumstances are easy. Their fuel is turbary. Of dress, they have no particular kind except the males, who generally wear a frieze coat of their own manufacture and known as peculiar to Farney.

They live to an advanced age than otherwise, in some instances having of late exceeded 100 years. 5 is the usual number of a family. Early marriages are frequent. During a Sunday after attending divine service they amuse themselves by meeting in large numbers on a road convenient to a public house generally, where they dance, or else by shooting and hunting, football playing, leaping, throwing the stone etc. Drinking on that day prevails to a great extent.

Christmas here with them is a feasting period. At this time the market is loaded with white bread, geese and pork, which articles are procured for the occasion if possibly within the compass of their means. Christmas Eve and the next night are observed particularly. The day before or proceeding market day the poor may be seen returning home with 1 or 2 candles, generally mould[s] and secured in the hat by the band or ribbon. They sit up during the night.

No particular patron's day unless that of St Patrick is observed. On St John's Eve bonfires are lighted, but in this custom they have been restrained as much as possible of late years since it tended to create riots in the country. During the burial of their dead the funeral cries or lamentations are uttered, but by the women only who accompany their bewailing with wringing of hands. Sometimes, but not often, these cries take place on the road to the graveyard.

Emigration

Emigration prevails but not to a great extent. Many go to England and to the adjoining counties during the harvest. They leave their families at home. All have generally a patch of potato ground.

Remarkable Events

This and the adjoining parishes are noted for the wars of Lord Essex with the chiefs of the soil, principally the MacMahons whose direct descendants cannot be traced at this day, although there are many of the name in existence.

PRODUCTIVE ECONOMY

Manufacturing and Markets

Manufacturing or commercial: see description of Carrickmacross; but little hand-spinning is done in the country.

Fairs and markets: see description of Carrickmacross.

Rural: Proprietors and Townlands

The great proprietors of this parish are the Marquis of Bath, E.J. Shirley Esquire and the Revd Dr Robinson and Colonel Porter.

The Marquis of Bath has 6 townlands in the parish, viz. Coolderry, Coolfore, Cockrien, Corcullogue, Drummond-Otra and Trustrium.

E.J. Shirley Esquire has 60 townlands in the parish, viz. Aghalile, Ardiagh, Awary, Bardonagh, Beagh, Cargaghogue, Cargaghmore, Corravally, Carrickedny, Carrickartagh, Carrickmaclim, Coraghy, Corenenty, Corbane, Corduff Mountain, Corduff Kelly, Corensigagh, Cloghwolly Upper, Cloghwolly Lower, Cavanageragh, Corlea, Greaghlane, Greaghlaticapil, Corcrigah, Cornesasonagh, Curkisbane, Curkisduff, Greaghnaroogue, Derrylavan, Dromganney, Donogue, Dromgoan, Drumgeries, Drummond-Itra, Drombragh, Faraghy, Farthagorman, Fads, Greaghdromitt, Greaghdromwisk, Lattinalbany, Lisdromturk, Liserill, Lisnafidilly, Lisnacullen, Lisnaniske, Lisnagiseragh, Logimore, Losat, Lurgans, Magheross, Mullaghcroghery, Peast,

Parish of Magheross

Rafferagh, Rackeragh, Shancow, Streenty, Tyrnedrole, Tyrogaroan, Umerfree.

The Revd Dr Robinson has 1 townland, glebe land, viz. Derryolan, and Colonel Porter has 3 townlands, viz. Kilmactrasna, Magheraboy and Mullenary.

Mr Shirley only residing and that for a short period in the [year?]. His agent Alexander Mitchell Esquire, however, always resides at Carrickmacross, as does also James Evatt Esquire, agent of the Marquis of Bath.

A. Bellingham Esquire, the agent of the Revd Charles Brownlow, and James Reid Esquire, Colonel Porter's agent, both reside at Castleblayney. They are paid percentage on the rent collected.

Farms and Rents

The usual size of the holdings varies from 3 to 20 acres. Scarcely any leases are now granted; if any, they are for 21 years but no lives. The farms are held direct from the head landlord, the rent per acre of the best quality being 50s per acre, of the middling 25s and of the worst 15s, and is wholly paid in money.

The farmers are partly yeoman, partly cottiers, and farm for subsistence only. Little or no land is let in conacre. The general size of the fields varies with that of the farms, but of late that part of the parish forming a portion of the Shirley estate has been much improved by a new laying out of the fields, which are now regular and uniform.

The fences are generally earthen or of stone. Great endeavours have of late been made to substitute quick fences and planted hedgerows, with considerable success. The tenants are merely liable to county cess and tithes. None of the landlords, resident gentry or agents have farms to any extent in their possession.

Soil and Manures

The soil is tolerably productive but varies very much. At the Carrickmacross end, viz. the south east end of the parish, it is very rich, at the opposite extremity the reverse, the warm limestone bed being at the south east part of the parish.

The usual manures are marl, blue clay, lime, cow-house dung and the scrapings of roads and clearing of drains. In some parts of the parish marl is abundant. There are several minor lime-kilns on the parish, the property of the farmers. On Mr Shirley's part of the estate, and belonging to him, is a very extensive lime-kiln at a place called Reilly's Rocks, where the lime is quarried and burnt for the use of the poorer tenantry, and paid for at 6d per barrel on delivery.

Burning the ground for manure is not permitted and is only very occasionally resorted to as a progress of reclaiming wasteground.

Husbandry

No improved implements of husbandry have been introduced; threshing machines only used by one or two more opulent individuals. The common wheel car and dray are generally used, although the communications would admit of good carts and wagons. Oxen are not used in agriculture and never more than 2 horses to a plough. The system of 1 man managing a plough without a helper is gradually becoming customary.

There is no rotation of crops. Potatoes form generally the preparation crop.

Markets

Carrickmacross may be considered, from its locality with regard to Dundalk and Drogheda as 2 seaports, with reference also to its distillery when the consumption of grain is very great, as by far the best and most convenient market. Much of the corn is bought up for the distillery or sent to Dundalk for exportation.

Grazing and Cattle

No grazing is carried on unless for domestic purposes solely. The system of grazing has probably not been adopted from the soil not answering too well and its vicinity as a district to the county Meath, so famous as a grazing county.

Cattle vary so much as to defy description. None of them can be said to be natives of the district, not at least as a particular breed, since if any are bred in the county, they are so crossed with other breeds as to puzzle their origin. The pigs are generally the common Irish breed.

Uses made of the Bogs

The bogs are used wholly as fuel and consumed in the neighbourhood. The people have a right of turbary under certain restrictions, necessarily imposed from its gradually decreasing. It is not converted into charcoal for the use of smithy forges. The bog is charged for on the Shirley estate at a low rent. The imbedded timber is used for building and other domestic purposes.

Drainage

Draining has been carried on to an extensive degree of late, by which means the loughs have been reduced in size and extent, swamps reclaimed, and crops now obtained where there was not long since a cold, rank and unprofitable bottom.

Planting

None, nor any attempts made but on the smallest scale, and then only ornamental, when of course the fastest-growing trees and consequently the least valuable are planted.

The timber generally used in building is imported, unless in the case of the cabins and cottages, where bog wood or common wood of the country is occasionally used.

Coast and Fishing

Sea-coast: none.

Fishing merely resorted to on the loughs as a recreation, or for the purpose of adding to the comforts of the poor man's meal.

General Remarks

No parts of the parish are so light or so poor or waste in soil but that cultivation may be successfully carried on by persevering industry. The parish is under cultivation from its highest to its lowest levels, but the richest and best cultivated part is in the neighbourhood of the town, averaging 160 feet above the sea. The general aspect varies but the climate, although bracing than otherwise, is clear and free from cold chilling fogs.

DIVISIONS

Townlands

No divisions are known except those detailed in the Name Book and usually met with in the country. Townlands: see Field Name Books for particular information. The parish contains in all 70 townlands.

SOCIAL ECONOMY

Table of Schools

[Table contains the following headings: name of townland, number of pupils subdivided by religion and sex, how supported, when established].

Town of Carrickmacross: Protestants 54, Catholics 2, males 35, females 21, total 56; supported by subscriptions and very small payments from scholars, established 1828.

Carrickmaclim: Protestants 25, Catholics 45, males 52, females 18, total 70; supported by landlord, E.J. Shirley Esquire, and payment from children, established 1818.

Mullaghcroghery: Protestants 38, Catholics 14, males 32, females 20, total 52; supported by contribution of 5 pounds annually from E.J. Shirley Esquire and small payments from children, established 1825.

Carrickmacross Sunday school: Protestants 130, Catholics 1, males 63, females 68, total 131; supported by private subscription and proceeds of an annual charity sermon, established 1825.

Carrickmacross new school: Protestants 3, Catholics 250, males 130, females 121, total 253; supported by the National Board and private subscription, established 1834.

Carrickmacross: Catholics 100, males 45, females 55, total 100; supported by the scholars, established 1828.

Corduff: Protestants 4, Catholics 60, males 42, females 30, total 64; supported by the scholars, established 1808.

Cornassanagh: Catholics 50, males 30, females 20, total 50; supported by Mr Shirley and the scholars, established 1824.

Cargaghmore: Protestants 10, Catholics 60, males 30, females 40, total 70; supported by Mr Shirley and the scholars, established 1834.

Dispensary

State of the Farney dispensary from the 24th February 1834 to the 1st January 1835: remaining in attendance at last report 337; since admitted at the dispensary 2,307; visited at their homes 501; total 3,145; relieved 2,948, incurable 19, died 35, remaining in attendance 143, total 3,145.

Receipts: subscription received for 1834, 114 pounds 17s; county presentment for 1834, 114 pounds 17s; disbursements: including surgeon's and compounder's salaries, medicine and expenses, 167 pounds 17s 11d ha'penny.

Not being able to ascertain the number of cases of each class of disease, the above information has been substituted. Fever and scrofula proceeding from exposure to the weather and poor diet may be said to be the predominating diseases.

Ecclesiastical Summary

[Table] Name Magheross, diocese Clogher, province Ulster, vicarage, no union, patron:

Parish of Magheross

[insert note: will be supplied], incumbent Revd T.R. Robinson D.D., extent of glebe 113 acres Irish measure. Amount of tithes belonging to the vicar, Revd Dr Robinson, 646 pounds 3s 1d, paid by landlord E.J. Shirley Esquire, who deducts 15 percent on the whole for receiving same. The rectorial tithes, which are impropriate and repaid to John Kernan Esquire, amount to one-third of the above sum, subject to the like deductions.

Statistical Return for Town of Carrickmacross by Lieutenant R. Boteler, August 1835

NATURAL STATE

Name

Is generally written and pronounced Carrickmacross. It is sometimes written for abbreviation Ckmacross and even C.m. [insert query].

It is about 39 Irish miles from and north of Dublin, 11 from Dundalk, 7 from Castleblayney and 6 from Kingscourt; is situated in the diocese of Clogher, province of Ulster, county Monaghan, barony of Farney and south east corner of Magheross parish and Monaghan circuit of assize. It is built on the grand northern road from Omagh and Derry and Armagh to Dublin.

Its main street extends nearly north and south, is about 485 yards long. But for some of its wretched suburbs, now gradually disappearing, it would be a pretty town, its situation being by no means uninteresting.

HISTORY

General History

Distinguished in history as being the theatre of the war of Essex, of whose castle a part of the old walls and site may still be traced. In addition to the above an interesting ruin of an old church and its graveyard, much defaced during the civil wars, remains on the south west extremity of the town, and at the junction of the Kingscourt and Drumcondra roads.

MODERN TOPOGRAPHY

Public Buildings: Market House

In addition to a new church and chapel with a schoolhouse already described, are the following public buildings, viz. the market house, 2 hotels, an endowed school, a bridewell built about 4 years since, also a barrack for the accommodation of the police now building at the private expense and under the superintendence of Alexander Mitchell Esquire, agent to E.J. Shirley Esquire.

The market house is an old building and by no means an ornamental one, standing in the centre of the main street. In it are held every other week the petty sessions.

Hotels

Of the 2 hotels one, called the Shirley Arms by E.J. Shirley Esquire and built by him within the last 3 or 4 years, and situated at the northern end of the town, is exceedingly comfortable and well kept, indeed one of the best along the northern line of the road.

The other is on a much smaller scale and situated about the centre of the town. Posting of every kind to be had on the most reasonable terms of the former, the latter being supplied with cars only.

School

The Marquis of Bath's endowed school has been closed of late years. It will shortly be put under a thorough repair and be again opened. It once had among its scholars some leading and first characters in the country, Lord Enniskillen and others of high rank. It is situated on the east side of the main street and near the church.

Bridewell and Barracks

The bridewell stands close to the new police barrack on the west side of the town and on the street leading to the Shercock Road. It was built in the year 1830 and possesses good accommodation and security for its prisoners.

The police barrack now building is of cut freestone and capable of containing 14 men.

Houses

The houses in the main street are generally speaking large but badly built and, if examined, are shells only, being run up as [if] were solely for the accommodation of hordes of country people who on all days, particularly Sundays and market days, frequent them for the purpose of drinking.

The town is neither lighted, paved nor watched. The streets are tolerably clean but, during a market and the day succeeding it, the pathways are a nuisance from the dirty habits of the country people, who seem to have little ideas of delicacy.

Few, if any, new houses have been very recently built. The town, however, has been much improved, particularly its suburbs, by the demolition of some absolutely wretched hovels as much the dwelling of poverty as sinks of vice and immortality.

PRODUCTIVE ECONOMY

Banks, Fairs and Markets

A savings bank was established about 4 years since. Its present number of depositors is 46 and the annual deposits have averaged for the last year 46 pounds. The depositors are generally farmers, servants and a few artisans.

In each week are held 3 markets, viz. 2 corn markets, Wednesday and Saturday, and 1 general market on a Thursday. Fairs [blank]. No tolls or customs are now paid, they being withdrawn by sufferance of Lord Bath and Mr Shirley.

The articles sold at the fairs and markets are too numerous almost to detail. Roughly they consist of cattle, pigs, sheep, poultry and eggs (of these a good quantity are sold for the Dublin market and exportation to Liverpool via Dundalk), fresh and salt meat, salt herrings, fruit, salt, rosin, flax, meal, cottage furniture, frieze, haberdashery, nails, various articles of old iron, locks, hinges, heath and birch brooms and white bread.

General Remarks

The town is well supplied with meat, poultry, butter and milk, but indifferently with fruit and vegetables. The cattle are grazed in the townparks at various rates, timber and slates are generally procured from Dundalk, stone and lime are got in the neighbourhood. Very few houses are insured from fire.

Conveyances

A mail coach to and from Dublin to Derry passes through at 1 a.m., arriving at Dublin at 7 a.m. and at Derry at 9 every morning.

Monaghan day coach leaves Monaghan at 4 o'clock in the morning, passing through Castleblayney, Carrickmacross (at half past one in the afternoon), Drumcondra and Slane, and arrives in Dublin same day at 7 o'clock p.m. It leaves Dublin at 8 o'clock in the morning, passes through Carrickmacross at 3 o'clock p.m. and arrives in Monaghan at 6 o'clock p.m.

Omagh coach (Wonder) leaves Omagh at 6 o'clock a.m., passing through Aughnacloy, Caledon, Castleblayney and Carrickmacross (at half past one p.m.), Ardee and Drogheda, arrives in Dublin at half past four same day; leaves Dublin at 6 a.m., passes through Carrickmacross at quarter past twelve p.m. and arrives in Omagh at 8 o'clock p.m.

Strabane coach (Shareholder) leaves Strabane at half past five a.m., passes through Omagh, Aughnacloy, Monaghan, Ballybay, Carrickmacross (at 3 o'clock p.m.) and arrives in Dublin at 9 o'clock p.m.; leaves Dublin at half past five a.m., passes through Carrickmacross at 12 o'clock noon and arrives at Strabane at 9 o'clock at night.

A mail car runs from Carrickmacross to Dundalk via Corcreagh and Louth.

There is a foot-post travels from Carrickmacross to and from Kingscourt daily. There is also another foot-post travels to and from Shercock from Carrickmacross.

PRODUCTIVE AND SOCIAL ECONOMY

General Circumstances

There is 1 dispensary, see above. For schools, see table. For provision of poor, see [above].

As to general habits, perhaps there is nothing decided, except among the lower orders who are much addicted to dram-drinking. There are no places of public amusement, no saddle-horses for hire. At the principal hotel a sufficient supply of carriages is kept for the heaviest posting and at it and the other hotel numerous well-appointed cars. The inhabitants are generally well-disposed and hospitable to those of their own class.

A very extensive distillery, the property of Mr Gartlan, is carried on at the south end and outside of the town. The buildings are very extensive, and in carrying it on he gives employment to an immense number of labourers. In the town are a tallow chandler's and brewer's establishment, also another for the manufacture of tobacco.

[Table] Trades and occupations: cloth merchants 4, grocers 15, smiths 10, coopers 5, butchers 13, publicans 36, bakers 9, tailors 1, shoemakers 10, blue dyers 2.

Police

Allocation return of the constabulary of the barony of Farney. [Table contains the following headings: name of townland in which situated, parish, number of chief constables, constables, subconstables, remarks].

Carrickmacross town, Magheross parish: 1 chief constable, 1 constable, 13 subconstables. total 14.

Coolderry, Magheracloone parish: 1 constable, 3 subconstables, total 4.

Brackagh, Donaghmoyne parish: 1 constable, 3 subconstables, total 4.

Inniskeen, Inniskeen parish: 1 constable, 4 subconstables, total 5.

Magoney, Inniskeen parish: 3 subconstables, total 3.

Total: 1 chief constable, 4 constables, 26 subconstables, total 30.

Revenue Police

Return of the revenue police.

[Table] Carrickmacross town, Magheross parish: 1 lieutenant, 1 sergeant, 13 privates, total 14.

NATURAL FEATURES

Weather Journal for November and December 1834

Table showing the state of thermometer and prevailing winds and weather at Carrickmacross from 14th November to 31st December 1834.

November 1834: 14th, 47 to 58 degrees, north westerly, pleasant; 15th, 49 to 56 degrees, north westerly, pleasant; 16th, 48 to 56 degrees, westerly, calm and settled; 17th, 48 to 54 degrees, westerly, calm and settled; 18th, 50 to 55 degrees, north westerly, pleasant; 19th, 50 to 53 degrees, northerly, calm and cloudy; 20th, 46 to 50 degrees, easterly, cloudy; 21st, 46 to 50 degrees, north easterly, cold and calm; 22nd, 44 to 46 degrees, north easterly, cold and calm; 23rd, 46 to 49 degrees, easterly, pleasant; 24th, 45 to 48 degrees, south easterly, cold and cloudy; 25th, 44 to 47 degrees, southerly, cold and hazy; 26th, 43 to 44 degrees, westerly, cold and calm; 27th, 43 to 47 degrees, westerly, cold and hazy; 28th, 45 to 46 degrees, south westerly, rain and high wind; 29th, 45 to 48 degrees, westerly, rain and high wind; 30th, 45 to 47 degrees, westerly, pleasant.

December 1834: 1st, 44 to 46 degrees, westerly, hazy with rain; 2nd, 45 to 50 degrees, westerly, clear and calm; 3rd, 44 to 47 degrees, westerly, calm and cloudy; 4th, 46 to 53 degrees, south westerly, calm and cloudy; 5th, 50 to 53 degrees, south westerly, calm and cloudy; 6th, 52 to 56 degrees, southerly, dark; 7th, 50 to 53 degrees, westerly, calm and cloudy; 8th, 49 to 46 degrees, westerly, hazy, high wind and showers; 9th, 44 to 48 degrees, south westerly, cold and cloudy; 10th, 46 to 48 degrees, south westerly, pleasant; 11th, 37 to 50 degrees, south westerly, frosty and cloudy; 12th, 40 to 44 degrees, westerly, hazy and cold; 13th, 42 to 44 degrees, southerly, fog and cold; 14th, 40 to 45 degrees, easterly, hazy and cold; 15th, 40 to 44 degrees, easterly, hazy and cold; 16th, 42 to 44 degrees, north westerly, calm and cloudy; 17th, 40 to 43 degrees, northerly, clear and cold; 18th, 39 to 43 degrees, northerly, clear and cold; 19th, 41 degrees, north westerly, hazy and frosty; 20th, 38 to 43 degrees, westerly, hazy and cold; 21st, 37 to 43 degrees, north westerly, pleasant; 22nd, 36 to 38 degrees, north westerly, dark and frosty; 23rd, 36 to 40 degrees, north westerly, cloudy and cold; 24th, 40 to 45 degrees, westerly, cold and cloudy; 25th, 38 to 43 degrees, north westerly, pleasant; 26th, 38 to 43 degrees, southerly, cloudy and cold; 27th, 40 to 44 degrees, south easterly, pleasant; 28th, 46 to 49 degrees, south easterly, cloudy and rain; 29th, 48 to 50 degrees, south easterly, cloudy and rain; 30th, 48 to 52 degrees, south westerly, cloudy and rain; 31st, 47 to 50 degrees, south westerly to northerly, slight rain.

The observations were made at 9 a.m., noon and at 3 p.m.

Weather Journal for January and February 1835

Table showing state of the thermometer and prevailing winds and weather at Carrickmacross from 1st January to 28th February 1835.

January 1835: 1st, 37 to 47 degrees, northerly, pleasant; 2nd, 34 to 38 degrees, north westerly, frosty, clear and calm; 3rd, 33 to 34 degrees, north westerly, hard frost and hazy; 4th, 35 to 42 degrees, north westerly, frosty and clear; 5th, 35 to 40 degrees, north westerly, cold and slight rain; 6th, 36 to 40 degrees, southerly, cold and damp; 7th, 38 to 42 degrees, easterly, calm and cloudy; 8th, 37 to 42 degrees, westerly, calm, cold and cloudy; 9th, 43 to 42 degrees, westerly, heavy rain; 10th, 38 to 48 degrees, westerly, cold and heavy rain; 11th, 39 to 44 degrees, westerly, heavy rain; 12th, 40 to 45 degrees, south westerly, calm and cloudy; 13th, 39 to 43 degrees, southerly, slight rain; 14th, 43 to 50 degrees, north westerly, calm and heavy rain; 15th, 44 to 40 degrees, south westerly, cold and cloudy; 16th, 33 to 34 degrees, westerly, frost and heavy snow; 17th, 33 to 39 degrees, westerly, frost, snow and slight thaw; 18th, 32 to 34 degrees, south easterly, hard frost and cloudy; 19th, 32 to 34 degrees, westerly to northerly, heavy snow and frost; 20th, 30 to 32 degrees, westerly, hard frost; 21st, 33 to 39 degrees, south westerly, hard frost and slight rain; 22nd, 36 to 43 degrees, westerly, frost and slight rain; 23rd, 41 to 50 degrees, westerly, slight rain; 24th, 45 to 49 degrees, westerly, cloudy and calm; 25th, 48 to 50 degrees, westerly, cloudy and slight rain; 26th, 49 to 50 degrees, westerly, cloudy and pleasant; 27th, 48 to 50 degrees, south westerly, cloudy and pleasant; 28th, 50 to 53 degrees, south westerly, cloudy and pleasant; 29th, 48 to 51 degrees, westerly, cloudy and pleasant; 30th, 50 to 52 degrees, southerly, calm and cloudy; 31st, 44 to 58 degrees, south westerly, settled and pleasant.

February 1835: 1st, 48 to 54 degrees, south westerly, heavy rain and high wind; 2nd, 54 to 56 degrees, westerly, pleasant; 3rd, 50 to 56 degrees, westerly, cloudy and pleasant; 4th, 48 to 56 degrees, south westerly, calm and pleasant; 5th, 49 to 50 degrees, westerly, heavy rain and high wind; 6th, 42 to 52 degrees, westerly, calm and slight rain; 7th, 47 to 52 degrees, westerly, heavy rain and high wind; 8th, 38 to 44 degrees, westerly, cold and rain; 9th, 36 to 48 degrees, westerly, slight rain and cold; 10th, 38 to 48 degrees, westerly, hazy and calm; 11th, 48 to 53 degrees, westerly, calm and cloudy; 12th, 48 to 54 degrees, north westerly, calm and heavy showers; 13th, 50 to 58 degrees, westerly, calm and heavy rain; 14th, 49 to 58 degrees, westerly, heavy rain; 15th, 44 to 58 degrees, westerly, calm and cloudy; 16th, 44 to 50 degrees, westerly, cloudy and pleasant; 17th, 42 to 52 degrees, south westerly, cold and heavy rain; 18th, 40 to 50 degrees, westerly, clear and pleasant; 19th, 37 to 48 degrees, westerly, cold and heavy rain; 20th, 36 to 46 degrees, westerly, hard frost and pleasant; 21st, 35 to 40 degrees, westerly, heavy snow; 22nd, 38 to 46 degrees, westerly, heavy rain; 23rd, 36 to 44 degrees, south westerly, stormy, hail and snow; 24th, 33 to 46 degrees, south westerly, hard frost and cloudy; 25th, 36 to 45 degrees, westerly, heavy rain and high wind; 26th, 35 to 49 degrees, westerly, frost and heavy rain; 27th, 40 to 53 degrees, westerly to northerly, rain and calm; 28th, 40 to 53 degrees, westerly, rain and high wind.

The observations made were at 9 a.m., noon and 3 p.m.

Weather Journal for March and April 1835

Table showing the state of thermometer and prevailing winds and weather at Carrickmacross from 1st March to 30th April 1835.

March 1835: 1st, 38 to 44 degrees, northerly, rain and high wind; 2nd, 44 to 50 degrees, westerly, hazy and slight rain; 3rd, 38 to 48 degrees, north westerly, stormy and heavy rain; 4th, 38 to 42 degrees, westerly, cold and slight rain; 5th, 40 to 43 degrees, westerly, rain and hazy; 6th, 40 to 45 degrees, westerly, cloudy and calm; 7th, 36 to 42 degrees, north westerly, rain and high wind; 8th, 36 to 43 degrees, south westerly, pleasant; 9th, 38 to 43 degrees, westerly, rain, cold and calm; 10th, 36 to 43 degrees, westerly, cloudy and frost; 11th, 38 to 44 degrees, westerly, cloudy and rain; 12th, 40 to 50 degrees, westerly, calm and cloudy; 13th, 40 to 48 degrees, south westerly, stormy and cloudy; 14th, 40 to 47 degrees, westerly, slight rain; 15th, 40 to 47 degrees, westerly, pleasant; 16th, 43 to 54 degrees, westerly, cloudy and pleasant; 17th, 42 to 56 degrees, north westerly, rain and high wind; 18th, 48 to 58 degrees, northerly, pleasant; 19th, 48 to 59 degrees, south westerly, pleasant; 20th, 49 to 55 degrees, south westerly, calm and cloudy; 21st, 48 to 56 degrees, westerly, pleasant; 22nd, 50 to 55 degrees, southerly, pleasant; 23rd, 44 to 56 degrees, easterly, calm and cloudy; 24th, 44 to 53 degrees, easterly, pleasant; 25th, 40 to 50 degrees, north easterly, clear and calm; 26th, 45 to 52 degrees, north westerly, pleasant; 27th, 48 to 54 degrees, easterly, calm and hazy; 28th, 47 to 56 degrees, easterly, pleasant; 29th, 46 to 57 degrees, south easterly, pleasant; 30th, 48 to 54 degrees, south easterly, cloudy; 31st, 50 to 56 degrees, southerly, calm and rain.

April 1835: 1st, 53 to 60 degrees, south westerly, calm and rain; 2nd, 54 to 60 degrees, southerly, pleasant; 3rd, 56 to 60 degrees, easterly, fine; 4th, 52 to 58 degrees, easterly, cloudy and slight rain; 5th, 54 to 59 degrees, easterly, cloudy and slight rain; 6th, 52 to 58 degrees, south westerly, calm and cloudy; 7th, 53 to 59 degrees, south westerly, pleasant; 8th, 51 to 58 degrees, westerly, pleasant; 9th, 50 to 58 degrees, westerly, high wind and rain; 10th, 50 to 54 degrees, north westerly, calm and cloudy; 11th, 51 to 53 degrees, northerly, rain and calm; 12th, 52 to 56 degrees, north westerly, pleasant; 13th, 52 to 54 degrees, westerly, pleasant; 14th, 50 to 54 degrees, north westerly, cloudy and pleasant; 15th, 44 to 48 degrees, northerly, cold and showery; 16th, 42 to 46 degrees, northerly, high wind and hail; 17th, 41 to 44 degrees, north westerly, high wind and rain; 18th, 46 to 50 degrees, north westerly, high wind and rain; 19th, 48 to 54 degrees, north westerly, pleasant; 20th, 48 to 58 degrees, westerly, cloudy; 21st, 46 to 58 degrees, westerly, rain and calm; 22nd, 50 to 55 degrees, north westerly, pleasant; 23rd, 50 to 64 degrees, north westerly, pleasant; 24th, 50 to 61 degrees,

Parish of Magheross

north westerly, cloudy and high wind; 25th, 48 to 52 degrees, north westerly, cloudy and high wind; 26th, 40 to 46 degrees, northerly, rain and snow; 27th, 40 to 50 degrees, north easterly, cold and stormy; 28th, 44 to 53 degrees, north easterly, pleasant; 29th, 42 to 56 degrees, north easterly, cold and cloudy; 30th, 46 to 52 degrees, north easterly, high wind and rain.

The observations made were at 9 a.m., noon and 3 p.m.

Weather Journal for May and June 1835

Table showing the state of thermometer and prevailing winds and weather at Carrickmacross from 1st May to 30th June 1835.

May 1835: 1st, 50 to 60 degrees, north easterly, pleasant; 2nd, 48 to 52 degrees, north easterly, cold and cloudy; 3rd, 50 to 62 degrees, north easterly, pleasant; 4th, 54 to 64 degrees, north easterly to southerly, pleasant; 5th, 50 to 54 degrees, south westerly, heavy rain; 6th, 48 to 56 degrees, south westerly to westerly, high wind and rain; 7th, 52 to 62 degrees, westerly, high wind; 8th, 54 to 64 degrees, westerly to south easterly, cloudy and showers; 9th, 56 to 59 degrees, westerly, heavy rain; 10th, 52 to 64 degrees, westerly, showery; 11th, 50 to 60 degrees, south westerly, heavy rain; 12th, 54 to 56 degrees, westerly, heavy rain; 13th, 54 to 56 degrees, westerly to south easterly, showery; 14th, 44 to 49 degrees, easterly, cloudy; 15th, 48 to 50 degrees, easterly, heavy rain; 16th, 50 to 55 degrees, southerly, high wind and rain; 17th, 52 to 56 degrees, southerly, heavy rain; 18th, 52 to 58 degrees, south easterly, pleasant; 19th, 56 to 58 degrees, south easterly, pleasant; 20th, 56 to 60 degrees, south easterly to westerly, pleasant; 21st, 56 to 62 degrees, south easterly, pleasant; 22nd, 57 to 64 degrees, westerly, rain; 23rd, 58 to 62 degrees, south westerly to westerly, rain; 24th, 56 to 58 degrees, westerly to southerly, heavy rain, high wind; 25th, 58 to 60 degrees, westerly, cloudy, slight rain; 26th, 50 to 59 degrees, northerly to north westerly, pleasant; 27th, 52 to 60 degrees, northerly to north westerly, pleasant; 28th, 49 to 58 degrees, north westerly, pleasant; 29th, 52 to 62 degrees, north westerly, pleasant; 30th, 58 to 66 degrees, northerly to south westerly, pleasant; 31st, 56 to 64 degrees, northerly, slight showers.

June 1835: 1st, 52 to 56 degrees, north easterly, cloudy; 2nd, 56 to 65 degrees, easterly to south easterly, pleasant; 3rd, 58 to 66 degrees, easterly to south westerly, pleasant; 4th, 62 to 72 degrees, north easterly to northerly, pleasant; 5th, 60 to 70 degrees, north easterly, high wind, pleasant; 6th, 61 to 70 degrees, north easterly to easterly, pleasant; 7th, 68 to 78 degrees, easterly to south easterly, very fine; 8th, 68 to 77 degrees, south easterly to southerly, heavy thunder and lightning; 9th, 69 to 78 degrees, north westerly to easterly, very fine; 10th, 68 to 78 degrees, south westerly to southerly, pleasant; 11th, 64 to 70 degrees, south westerly to westerly, cloudy; 12th, 64 to 78 degrees, north westerly to westerly, fine; 13th, 67 to 78 degrees, northerly, very fine; 14th, 68 to 78 degrees, north westerly, very fine; 15th, 66 to 72 degrees, northerly, cloudy and calm; 16th, 62 to 68 degrees, northerly, cloudy; 17th, 58 to 62 degrees, north westerly to northerly, cloudy and calm; 18th, 62 to 72 degrees, westerly to north westerly, cloudy and calm; 19th, 60 to 66 degrees, westerly, cloudy and calm; 20th, 58 to 66 degrees, westerly to north westerly, cloudy; 21st, 58 to 60 degrees, westerly, cloudy and high wind; 22nd, 58 to 60 degrees, westerly, heavy rain and high wind; 23rd, 56 to 60 degrees, westerly, rain and high wind; 24th, 52 to 54 degrees, north westerly to northerly, cloudy and high wind; 25th, 50 to 58 degrees, northerly to north westerly, cloudy and high wind; 26th, 50 to 56 degrees, easterly to north easterly, heavy rain; 27th, 52 to 58 degrees, northerly to north westerly, cloudy; 28th, 54 to 62 degrees, north easterly to south easterly, fine; 29th, 58 to 66 degrees, easterly, pleasant; 30th, 54 to 62 degrees, easterly to south easterly, cloudy and rain.

The observations made were at 9 a.m., noon and 3 p.m.

Weather Journal for July and August 1835

Table showing state of the thermometer and prevailing winds and weather at Carrickmacross from the 1st July to 31st August 1835.

July 1835: 1st, 60 to 64 degrees, easterly, cloudy and calm; 2nd, 64 to 66 degrees, south westerly, pleasant; 3rd, 58 to 62 degrees, southerly and westerly, heavy cloud; 4th, 58 to 62 degrees, south westerly and southerly, cloudy, heavy rain; 5th, 58 to 66 degrees, westerly and northerly, slight rain and thunder; 6th, 57 to 60 degrees, westerly, heavy showers; 7th, 58 to 62 degrees, westerly and south westerly, slight rain and high wind; 8th, 56 to 60 degrees, westerly, cloudy and high wind; 9th, 58 to 63 degrees, westerly, cloudy and calm; 10th, 56 to 66 degrees, northerly to north westerly, heavy showers; 11th, 58 to 62 degrees, south westerly, constant rain;

12th, 58 to 64 degrees, westerly, constant rain, calm; 13th, 58 to 66 degrees, westerly, showery; 14th, 58 to 64 degrees, westerly, heavy cloud; 15th, 58 to 64 degrees, westerly, heavy showers and cloudy; 16th, 60 to 64 degrees, westerly to south westerly, cloudy, unpleasant; 17th, 57 to 62 degrees, south westerly and westerly, showery; 18th, 60 to 64 degrees, westerly, cloudy and calm; 19th, 58 to 62 degrees, westerly, slight showers; 20th, 60 to 66 degrees, westerly, pleasant; 21st, 60 to 68 degrees, southerly and easterly, pleasant; 22nd, 66 to 68 degrees, easterly and south easterly, clear and moderate breeze; 23rd, 62 to 64 degrees, south easterly, cloudy and calm; 24th, 62 to 68 degrees, south easterly, pleasant; 25th, 64 to 70 degrees, south easterly, cloudy and calm; 26th, 66 to 72 degrees, south easterly, hazy and calm; 27th, 66 to 75 degrees, south easterly, pleasant; 28th, 62 to 69 degrees, northerly, cloudy and pleasant; 29th, 65 to 78 degrees, westerly, calm and clear; 30th, 64 to 70 degrees, westerly, calm and clear; 31st, 58 to 76 degrees, north westerly and westerly, calm and clear.

August 1835: 1st, 62 to 75 degrees, westerly and south westerly, very fine; 2nd, 63 to 76 degrees, southerly, very fine; 3rd, 66 to 70 degrees, southerly and easterly, very fine; 4th, 64 to 74 degrees, westerly, cloudy and heavy showers; 5th, 64 to 70 degrees, westerly, slight rain and calm; 6th, 66 to 70 degrees, westerly, heavy showers and calm; 7th, 60 to 64 degrees, north westerly, pleasant; 8th, 58 to 70 degrees, north westerly and westerly, cloudy and calm; 9th, 60 to 72 degrees, south westerly and southerly, clear and fine; 10th, 64 to 70 degrees, southerly and south westerly, clear and fine; 11th, 70 to 80 degrees, southerly and westerly, fine; 12th, 58 to 64 degrees, westerly and north westerly, cloudy and high wind; 13th, 62 to 72 degrees, westerly and southerly, cloudy and calm; 14th, 66 to 70 degrees, south westerly, slight rain and calm; 15th, 68 to 70 degrees, south westerly, slight rain and calm; 16th, 68 to 72 degrees, south westerly, fair; 17th, 68 to 72 degrees, south westerly, fair; 18th, 68 to 72 degrees, south westerly, fair; 19th, 70 to 74 degrees, westerly, cloudy but pleasant; 20th, 70 to 73 degrees, south westerly and southerly, cloudy but pleasant; 21st, 70 to 72 degrees, southerly, cloudy and pleasant; 22nd, 67 to 70 degrees, southerly, clear and strong breeze; 23rd, 66 to 68 degrees, southerly, heavy rain and calm; 24th, 64 to 66 degrees, southerly, slight rain and cloudy; 25th, 64 to 66 degrees, south easterly and north easterly, cloudy; 26th, 60 to 62 degrees, northerly, showery; 27th, 62 to 63 degrees, northerly, dark and cloudy; 28th, 60 to 64 degrees, north easterly, cloudy and calm; 29th, 64 to 66 degrees, easterly and south easterly, pleasant; 30th, 64 to 68 degrees, north easterly, calm and pleasant; 31st, 64 to 67 degrees, north easterly, calm and pleasant.

The observations made were at 9 a.m., noon and 3 p.m. [Signed] Robert Boteler, Lieutenant Royal Engineers, 7th August 1835.

Fair Sheets for Carrickmacross by George Scott

SOCIAL ECONOMY

School

There is a small school held in a man's cabin in the townland of Derrylavin. He receives from the children 1d per week. He is not under any board. Boys 55, girls 20, total 75, Protestants 7, Catholics 68, master a Catholic. Under 10 years of age 40, between 10 and 15, 35.

MODERN TOPOGRAPHY

Gentlemen's Seats

Monalty House, the residence of Thomas McIllvoy Gartlan, situated in the townland of Monaltybane: the plantations are not extensive. There are several small lakes contiguous to the plantations in which there is some fishing.

Lough Fea House, the residence of [blank] Shirley, is in the townland of Doohatty. The plantations throughout the demesne are very extensive. They are at present in their infancy. They are tastefully laid out and in a few years will appear to great advantage. The house is a fine building, in rather an unusual style of architecture.

NATURAL FEATURES

Lakes

Lough Fea is partly in the townland[s] of Doohatty, Nuremore, Losset, Corduff and Derrylavin. It is upwards of half a mile in its greatest length and little more than a quarter at the broadest part. It is almost surrounded by Evalt's wood, part of Mr Shirley's demesne, to which it is a great ornament. The lake is 111 feet above the level of the sea. It abounds with small fish, viz. trout, pike, roach, and at times salmon are taken. The streams flowing into the lake are not large.

Parish of Magheross

Lough Fea discharges itself into Rahan's lough immediately adjoining the River Lagan, in the townlands of Rahans and Deseart. The last-mentioned lake is 89 feet above the level of the sea and 2 miles from Lough Fea. The ground to the east and west of Lough Fea is steep, to the north and south it is principally bog and marsh. Wild duck and other birds are frequently to be shot in this piece of water.

Ancient Topography

Remains of Antiquity

In the eastern part of Mr Shirley's demesne, almost at the base of some rocks (the top of which are 208 feet above the level of the sea and the bottom 160), there is an indenture of 10 inches in depth, 3 feet 4 inches in height and 2 feet 6 inches in breadth which is called Fin McCoul's Chair.

Modern Topography

Communications

The main road from Drumcondra to Castleblayney passes through the parish for the distance of 1 mile and three-quarters, the main road from Drumcondra to Ballybay for the distance of 2 miles and a quarter, the main road from Carrickmacross to Bellatrain for the distance of 5 miles and a half, the main road from Carrickmacross to Kingscourt for the distance of 1 mile, the main road from Carrickmacross to Shercock for the distance of 4 miles, the main road from Carrickmacross to Dundalk for the distance of three-quarters of a mile. The main roads are kept in good repair, particularly the mail roads.

Social Economy

Conveyances

The night mail passes through Carrickmacross for Dublin about 1 o'clock in the morning.

The Dublin mail to Derry passes through Carrickmacross about 10 minutes before 1. The Armagh and Dublin Day Coach passes through the town for Dublin every Monday, Wednesday and Friday about half past 1 o'clock p.m. and returns through here every Tuesday, Thursday and Saturday about quarter past 2 p.m.

The Armagh and Dublin Day Coach passes through this town for Dublin on Tuesday, Thursday and Saturday about 5 minutes past 10 a.m. and returns on Monday, Wednesday and Friday, passing through here at half past 1 a.m.

Modern Topography

Town of Carrickmacross

Carrickmacross, situated on the main road from Dublin to Londonderry, 39 miles from Dublin: it consists of 1 principal street and 3 smaller ones, containing about 25 3-storey houses, 115 2-storey houses and 113 cabins, the larger houses principally slated, the smaller thatched. There is also a church, chapel, national school and market house.

There appears to be little or no trade by the shops. The shops are principally spirit shops, there being a considerable quantity of whiskey consumed in the town, owing to the 4 markets in the week. The main street is particularly broad for a country town; the cause is attributed to one side of the street belonging to the Marquis of Bath, the other to Mr Shirley.

Chapel

Chapel erected in 1782, dimensions: [ground plan, overall dimensions 87 by 84 feet, cruciform]; would accommodate 1,000 persons, 67 seats contain 4 persons each. Cost 584 pounds 1s, 33 pounds 2s 1d added in 1794, 15 pounds 11s 4d ha'penny added in 1796, 156 pounds 11s added in 1806, 86 pounds 8s added in 1809, total 875 pounds 12s 5d ha'penny, paid by public contributions. 3 masses held in this chapel each Sunday. 2,000 persons are supposed to attend at the 12 o'clock mass.

School

National school erected in 1834, cost about 280 pounds, one-third paid by the National Board, the remainder by public subscription. The master receives 13 pounds from the National Board and 12 pounds a year from the committee, nothing from the children. The master is a Catholic; total number 214, males 214, Protestants 1, Catholics 213.

Female department: mistress a Catholic, receives 10 pounds a year from board and 8 pounds a year from the committee, nothing from the children. Total number 200, Catholics 200, average number in attendance 165.

Distillery

Distillery adjoining the town, belongs to Mr Gartlan. Diameter of wheel 15 feet, breadth of wheel 7 feet, fall of water 8 feet, breast wheel. Second wheel: diameter 14 feet, breadth 20 inches, fall of water 10 feet, breast wheel. Steam engine, 16 horsepower.

Social Economy

Police

7 constabulary men are stationed in the town. No stipendiary magistrate, the magistrates much respected, no troops in the town.

Houses are not generally insured, houses principally of stone, a few of brick. No combination exists.

Dispensary

Open 3 days in the week for the relief of the poor: dispensaries are of general use.

Religion

The inhabitants of the town and surrounding country are almost exclusively Catholics.

Habits of the People

Cottages generally stone, thatched, some of mud. In each cottage there are some window-frames, in most instances wanting glass. Cleanliness seldom attended to. Early marriages appear to be general. Principal amusement appears to be assembling in the town, especially on Sundays.

The inhabitants have no spirit for recruiting; a recruiting party scarcely was seen in the town. The great frieze coat is most universal. The women generally wear red cloaks and no bonnets.

Productive Economy

Markets

There is a corn market 3 times a week, viz. Monday, Wednesday and Friday, and a general market on Thursday. The markets in this town are more like fairs. Booths are erected for the sale of hardware, soft goods and leather, ready-made clothes, adapted for both male and female, sold in great abundance, boots, shoes, china, hats, horses and pigs, and woollen frieze.

Natural Features

Hills

The hills throughout the parish are small oblong features, without character, connection or expression. There are not any rivers, very little bog. Bog is dear, and turf the fuel that is burnt.

Caves

In the parish [sic] of Cloughbally Lower there is a very fine cave upwards of 200 yards in length. A stream runs through it. The entrance is through a small and steep aperture in a field.

There is also a cave in the townland of Tiragarvan, said to be extensive.

Parish of Monaghan, County Monaghan

Fair Sheets by J.R. Ward, April 1838

NATURAL STATE

Locality

The parish of Monaghan is situated almost in the centre of the north part of the county of Monaghan and in the east of the barony of Monaghan. It is bounded by the following parishes, viz. on the north by Tydavnet and Donagh, on the north east by Tyholland, on the east by Clontibret, on the south by Tullycorbet and on the south west and west by Kilmore.

Its length is 6 miles and breadth 6 miles (extreme), its mean length 4 and breadth 4 and a half miles. Its content, including 26 acres 2 roods 6 perches of water, is 13,547 acres 2 roods.

NATURAL FEATURES

Hills and Lakes

The greater part of the parish was sketched by Mr Tait's party.

Aghnasedagh lough, situated in the townland of Aghnasedagh, is 200 feet above the level of the sea, 9 acres 1 rood 8 perches in content and averages 10 feet in depth.

Aghananimy lough occupies portions of 3 townlands, viz. Aghananimy, Killygowan and Latlorcan. It is 220 feet above the level of the sea, 3 roods in content and averages 10 feet in depth.

Ballyleck lake occupies a portion of the townland of Camla in this parish and a portion of Ballyleck townland in the adjacent parish of Kilmore. It is 243 feet above the level of the sea, 3 acres 2 roods in content, averages 10 feet in depth.

Monaghan lake, situated north of the town of Monaghan, occupies portions of 3 townlands, viz. Kilmacloy, Mullaghmonaghan and Roosky. It is 200 feet above the level of the sea, 5 acres in content and averages 15 feet in depth.

Mullaghadun lake, situated in the townlands of Mullaghadun and Mullaghmonaghan, is 215 feet above the sea, 2 roods in content and averages 8 feet in depth. [Insert footnote: The content of these lakes and altitudes, not being given on the map, are only guessed or measured as accurately as possible on it].

Sparks lake, situated in the south west corner of the town of Monaghan, occupies portions of 4 townlands, viz. Mullaghcroghery, Mullaghmonaghan, Tirkeenan and Tully. It is [blank] feet above the sea, 4 acres 2 roods in content and averages feet in depth. NB The height above the sea and content only guessed.

Rivers

A minor branch of the River Blackwater forms the north boundary of the parish for 2 miles and a quarter. It runs in a north east direction by east, averages 30 feet in breadth and is very shallow. It rises in the parish of Tydavnet near the western boundary of the county. It is usefully situated for drainage and water power. There are no considerable falls or rapids in it. The average fall is 30 feet in an English mile. Its velocity is about 3 and half miles per hour.

It is subject to floods in wet seasons; they soon subside without artificial means to carry the water off. The floods deposit sand and slime which do no injury to the land but rather help it, particularly the meadows. The river impedes communication in its natural state and flows over a gravelly bed. The banks are well cultivated and apparently fertile. The scenery is not interesting.

The Cor river forms the west boundary of the parish for [blank] miles. It runs in a north direction, averages 15 feet broad and is very shallow. For further particulars of this river, see Memoir of the parish of Tyholland. Note: The greater part of the west boundary being in Mr Tait's district, the distance to be given by him or party.

Bogs and Woods

Bogs: there are none of any consideration in the north part of the parish.

Woods: no natural woods.

Climate and Crops

No meteorological register kept. The weather journal following was kept by me in Monaghan.

The crops in this parish are wheat, oats, potatoes and flax. Wheat is sown in November and December and cut in August and September. Oats are sown in April and cut in September and October. Potatoes are set in April and dug in October and November. Flax is sown in April and pulled in July. There are also green crops such as clover, turnips and mangel-wurzel cultivated in the parish for cattle.

Weather Journal

Weather journal kept in the town of Monaghan from 1st February to [10th April]. [Table contains the following headings: date, state of the day at morning, noon, afternoon, wind direction, remarks].

February 1838; 1st, rain, cloudy, fair, north easterly; 2nd, fair, fair, fair, north easterly; 3rd, snow, snow, snow, northerly, frost hard in the evening; 4th, fair, fair, fair, northerly, freezing hard; 5th, fair, fair, fair, north easterly, freezing hard; 6th, fair, fair, fair, south easterly by easterly, thawing; 7th, rain, rain, rain, southerly; 8th, rain, fair, fair, changeable; 9th, drizzly, fair, fair, south easterly, freezing; 10th, fair, fair, snow, south easterly, freezing; 11th, fair, fair, fair, south easterly, freezing very hard; 12th, fair, fair, fair, south easterly, freezing; 13th, fair, fair, misty, easterly, freezing; 14th, fair, fair, fair, easterly, freezing; 15th, fair, fair, fair, easterly, freezing; 16th, fair, snow, snow, south easterly, freezing; 17th, snow, fair, fair, changeable; 18th, fair, foggy, foggy, north easterly; 19th, wet, wet, fair, southerly; 20th, fair, fair, fair, easterly; 21st, fair, fair, fair, south easterly; 22nd, fair, fair, fair, south easterly; 23rd, drizzly, drizzly, drizzly, south easterly by easterly, blowing hard; 24th, rain, snow, snow, changeable, blowing hard; 25th, rain, rain, rain, north north easterly; 26th, fair, fair, fair, north easterly; 27th, snow, sleet, sleet, northerly; 28th, fair, fair, fair, north easterly, cloudy all day.

March: 1st, rain, rain, rain, changeable; 2nd, fair, fair, fair, changeable; 3rd, fair, very fine, very fine, north easterly; 4th, fair, very fine, very fine, north easterly; 5th, fair, very fine, very fine, north easterly, change of wind to north westerly in the evening; 6th, fair, showers, showers, south westerly by westerly; 7th, showery, showery, showery, westerly, wind high; 8th, fair, fair, fair, westerly; 9th, fair, fair, fair, changeable; 10th, showery, showery, drizzling, south westerly; 11th, rain, rain, rain, changeable; 12th, fair, fair, fair, northerly; 13th, showery, showery, showery, south westerly; 14th, showery, fair, showery, north westerly westerly; 15th, fair, showery, very fine, north westerly by westerly; 16th, showery, showery, fine, north westerly by westerly; 17th, snow showers, snow showers, snow showers, changeable; 18th, fair, fair, fair, changeable; 19th, fair, light rain, rain, north westerly by westerly; 20th, rain, rain, showery, north westerly, high;

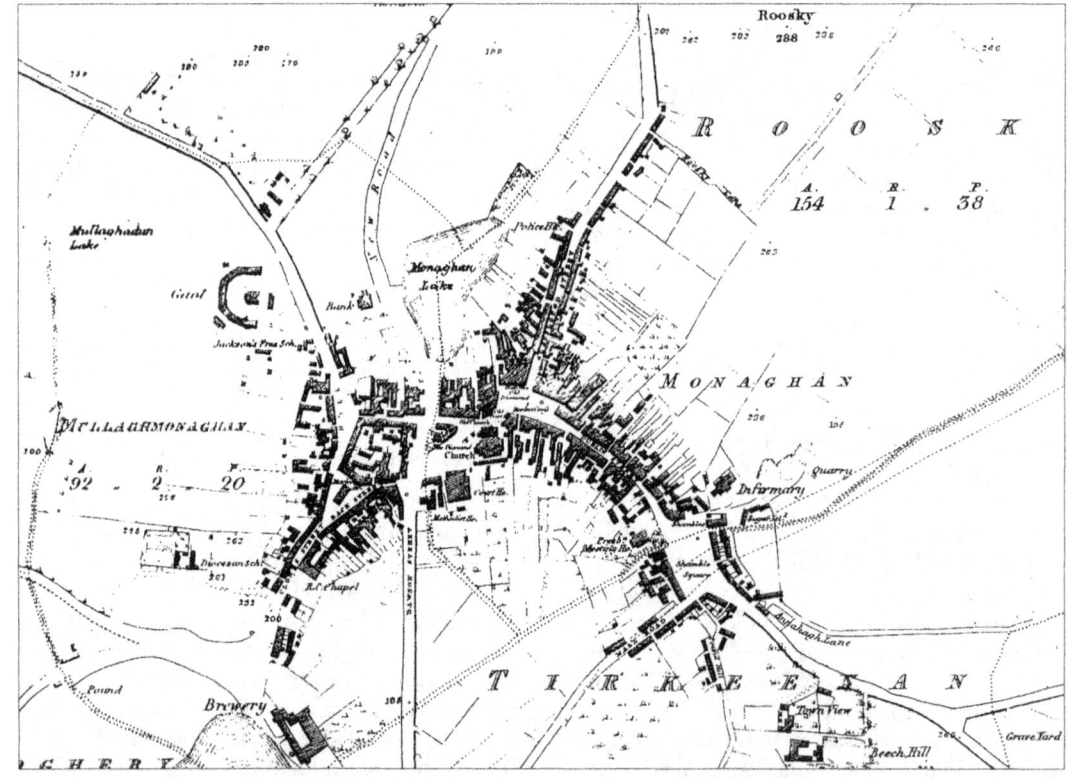

Map of Monaghan town from the first 6" OS maps, 1830s

Parish of Monaghan 161

21st, fair, fair, fair, northerly, high; 22nd, fair, snow showers, fair, northerly; 23rd, fair, showery, fair, north westerly; 24th, fair, snow, fair, north westerly by westerly; 25th, fair, fine, fair, north westerly by westerly; 26th, fair, fine, fair, southerly; 27th, fine, very fine, fine, southerly; 28th, fog, fine, fine, southerly; 29th, fair, fair, fair, northerly; 30th, fair, fair, fair, northerly; 31st, fair, fair, fair, northerly.

April: 1st, fair, fair, fair, northerly; 2nd, fair, fair, fair, north westerly by westerly; 3rd, showery, showery, showery, north westerly by westerly; 4th, showery, fair, fair, north westerly by westerly; 5th, showery, fair, fair, north westerly; 6th, showery, fair, showery, south westerly; 7th, very wet, very wet, very wet, southerly; 8th, showery, showery, showery, south easterly; 9th, fair, fair, fair, easterly, wind changed to south about 4 p.m., rain at 5; 10th, fair, fair, fair.

PRODUCTIVE ECONOMY

Table of Mills

Aghantamy townland, proprietor [blank], tenant James Hanna, diameter of water wheel 14 feet, breadth 1 foot 10 inches, breast wheel, fall of water 3 feet, machinery wood, 1 pair of stones; a stone house, thatched. [Signed] J.R. Ward.

Parish of Muckno, County Monaghan

Statistical Report by Lieutenant J. Chaytor, November 1835

NATURAL STATE

Name

This parish is said to have taken its name from the circumstance of a pig having swam across the lake from Concra hill to Church hill where the burial ground now stands, *Muc Shnamha* signifying "pig swimming." The orthography used in *Carlisle's Topographical dictionary* is Mucknoe, which is also adopted in the Irish Annals and Sir C. Coote's *Statistical survey of Monaghan county*. Beaufort and McCrea's maps give it Muckno, which is the manner it is usually spelled by the inhabitants.

Locality

It is situated in the eastern part of the country of Monaghan and in the barony of Cremorne, bounded on the north by the parishes of Keady and Derrynoose, east by the parishes of Newtownhamilton and Creggan, south by Donaghmoyne and Clontibret, and west by Clontibret. It is a very compact parish, the greatest length from north to south being 7 and three-quarter miles and greatest breadth 5 and five-eighths miles, containing 16,442 acres 2 roods 11 perches, of which [blank] are cultivated, 1,256 uncultivated and the remainder water. The average valuation to the county cess is 843 pounds per annum.

NATURAL FEATURES

Hills

The only hill of any importance is Mullyash, situated in the north east part of the parish. It is a ridge extending north and south for 1 and half miles, and the highest point, upon which stands a rude stone tower, is 1,034 feet above the level of the sea. It falls abruptly upon every side except towards the north where the slope is very gradual.

The other principal heights are as follows: Aughadamph, 733 feet, Lisseenan, 747 feet, Tattenclave, 737 feet, Loughbrottogue, 808 feet, Thompson's hill, 808 feet, Derllough, 663 feet, Killycracken North, 547 feet, Drummullard, 484 feet, Church Hill North, 426 feet, Drumacon North, 476 feet, Bree, 553 feet.

Lakes

Muckno lough, situated on the east side of the town of Castleblayney, contains portions of the parishes of Muckno, Clontibret and Donaghmoyne. It is an extensive sheet of water and very irregular. The extreme length from north north west to south south east is 3 miles, the breadth varies 380 feet to 1 mile. It is 302 feet above the level of the sea and empties itself by an inconsiderable stream from its south east extremity. I contains several islands, 2 only of which are o any consideration, viz. Black Isle and White Island.

The former, situated in the north north wes extremity, is 4,620 feet in length and averag breadth 1,300 feet. It is thickly planted and 11(acres in area. White Island is situated near the western shore of the lough, 1,800 feet long an 350 feet in breadth. It contains 13 acres, of which a great portion is planted. Besides these 2 island the following, which are very small and for th most part wooded, belong to the parish of Muckno Harper's, Blind Island, Garmany Island, Smal Otter Island and Crane Island.

Muckno Mill lough (so called in consequenc of the stream from it supplying a mill which wa formerly the mill for the Castleblayney estate) i situated 2 miles north east of the town o Castleblayney. It is [blank] acres in area. Th shore on the north and west is a loose shingle, o the south a heavy clay and at the south wes extremity rocky. At this point it empties itself, th water flowing over a ledge of rocks of 15 feet i height. The altitude of this lough above the sea i 338 feet. Besides the 2 lakes above described there are in the interior of the parish 14 small one and in the boundary 7 also of minor importance

Rivers

The only river in the parish is the County wate so called from having been the division betwee the counties of Armagh and Monaghan for a sho distance. It has its source in the parish of Kead and meets Muckno parish at the north eas extremity, from which point it runs south for and half miles and then turns west north wes through the parish of Muckno. It flows ver rapidly over a rocky bed and empties itself int Muckno lough, supplying in its course throug

Parish of Muckno

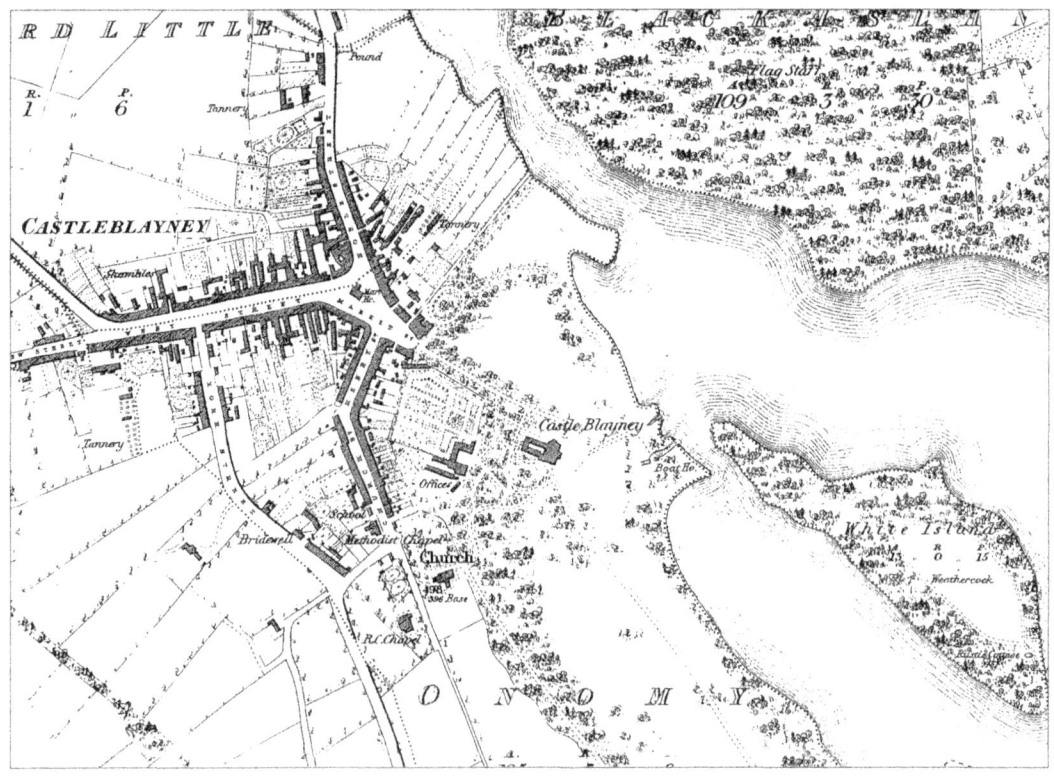

Map of Castleblayney from the first 6" OS maps, 1830s

this parish 3 mills. It is liable to overflow its banks in various places but, as the water never remains long upon the flats, these floods are very beneficial to the land.

There is a river running from Muckno lough which separates Donaghmoyne from this parish for 1 mile. It is 70 feet broad. The bed of the river is rocky and has lately been deepened 3 feet for the purpose of lowering the water in Muckno lough.

The parish is well supplied with springs and there are numerous rivulets throughout the parish.

Bogs

The principal bogs are situated in the northern part of the parish. One in the townlands of Killycracken, Corrintrough and Carrickaslean is 115 acres in extent and another on the northern side of Mullyash is 96 acres.

Adjacent to the townland of Dromacorn, in the south east part of the parish, is a considerable bog but only 30 acres lie within the parish. In addition to the above there are patches of bog conveniently situated for affording turf for the inhabitants. Timber is embedded in all these bogs, principally oak and sally and occasionally fir lying indiscriminately.

The bogs vary in depth from 4 to 16 feet and the substratum is either a white or blue clay with a mixture of stones of a kind of hard red sand called by the inhabitants "till."

Woods

There is no natural wood in the parish at present but the timber in the bogs is sufficient evidence that it formerly existed, though apparently to no great extent.

Climate

See Ballybay parish. The crops are rather later in the north east of Muckno than the eastern part of Ballybay, otherwise the harvest season commences about the same period.

NATURAL HISTORY

Botany

The spontaneous productions of this parish are little varied from the country generally. Heather would abound in the north east part, also furze which is very troublesome to the agriculturist. A field will lie a considerable time after a course of cropping before its surface is covered with spontaneous grass. The artificial grasses used are principally rye grass and perennial with clover.

Beech, birch, ash, elm, oak, alder and Scotch spruce and larch fir are found in Lord Blayney's demesne in a thriving state, though the south west winds are rather injurious to their growth when young.

Zoology

Pike, perch, roach, bream and eels are taken on the lakes, and trout and occasionally salmon on the rivers. Wild geese and ducks, teal, waterhens, crows and sometimes cormorants frequent Muckno lough.

MODERN TOPOGRAPHY

Towns: Castleblayney

Castleblayney town has its name from its proximity to a castle, the residence of the Blayney family. It is situated in the south west part of the parish of Muckno, barony of Cremorne and county of Monaghan, 51 Irish miles from Dublin, 10 miles south east of Monaghan, 7 miles west south west of Newtownhamilton and 6 miles east of Ballybay. It is in the diocese of Clogher, province of Armagh and north east circuit of assize, and junction of the Monaghan and Armagh roads to Dublin.

The town consists of 5 streets, the principal of which, called West Street, is 990 feet long. At the eastern end stands the market house and from this point Noble Street runs northward 850 feet and Henry Street southward 390 feet. From this Church Street inclines east 520 feet. York Street, which is only lately built, branches from the centre of West Street.

The appearance of the town is pleasing. West Street is wide and clear, and the buildings neat and in good order. The suburbs are not in such a filthy state as the neighbouring towns of the same size and the surrounding country is well enclosed and well cultivated, with Castleblayney demesne and Muckno lough on the east.

Castleblayney was founded by the ancestors of the present Lord Blayney, but at what date it is not known. The situation is not adapted for any purpose of manufacture and it is possible that it was chosen from being on the main road between Dublin and the towns of Armagh and Monaghan, and that its locality, with the influence and exertions of the Blayney family, have raised it to its present importance.

There are no ruins of any note in the neighbourhood.

Present State: Church

Castleblayney contains a church, a Roman Catholic chapel and a Methodist meeting house all situated at the eastern extremity of the town.

The church is a neat building with a tower and spire 136 feet high erected in the years 1808 and 1809, since which period it has been considerably improved and ornamented. The grounds was presented to the parish by Lord Blayney who, as well as Lord Templeton and Lady E. Alexander, contributed largely in money. In 1818 the gallery was fitted up and spire built, for which the parish was assessed 1,000 pounds. In 1829 another addition was made and stained-glass windows introduced by Lady Blayney, amounting to 300 pounds.

Catholic Chapel

The Roman Catholic chapel, situated a short distance west of the church, was built in 1805 under the inspection of the Revd Edmund Maguire. It is a neat building containing accommodation for 700 persons at worship and is surrounded by a small graveyard. The expense of its erection is not known.

Public Buildings

The other public buildings of the town are the market house, the sessions house and bridewell. The market house, situated at the junction of the principal street, is a substantial stone building and near it stands the sessions house. The bridewell, a neat and well-enclosed building, is in York Street, the southern part of the town.

Houses

The principal houses are the residences of W Hamilton Esquire and A.O'B. Bellingham Esquire. The inn is a good house with very good superior accommodations. There is not a thatched house in the town. Many of the inhabitants hold their property on leases forever at a low rate which induces them to build good houses, which for the most part are of stones.

SOCIAL AND PRODUCTIVE ECONOMY

Local Government

Quarter sessions are held in Castleblayney and petty sessions every alternate Thursday. Th

Parish of Muckno

magistrates who attend are William Hamilton Esquire, James McWatty Esquire, James Reid Esquire and Thomas Lucas Esquire, all residents of the town, and Allan O'Brien Bellingham Esquire, agent to Lord Blayney, who is an occasional resident. The business of the petty sessions is seldom of a serious nature, most commonly riots from party feeling.

Occupations

With the exception of the magistrates mentioned above, the inhabitants of the town are either shopkeepers, tradesmen or labourers. The population is estimated at 1,800 souls. There are in the town 3 small tanyards employing each from 5 to 8 persons only. The labourers residing in the town are employed in Lord Blayney's demesnes and working for the shopkeepers who hold small farms in the neighbourhood. The wages rarely exceed 10d per diem.

Fairs and Markets

There is a weekly market in the town of Castleblayney, well attended by the inhabitants of the surrounding country. The purchase and disposal of yarn, flax, linen cloth and pigs form the principal business of these markets, though the standings offer a great variety of articles for sale. The shambles are well supplied with meat during the winter seasons but in the summer this is not the case.

Timber used for building for other purposes is commonly obtained from Dundalk and Newry, and lime either from Carrickmacross or Armagh. The former is prepared and purchased at 4d per bushel or limestone at 6d per cart-load, which they burn upon the ground. Many of the houses in the town are insured from fire.

Schools and Poor

There are 6 schools in the town, one of which, Lady Blayney's female school, is endowed by her ladyship to the amount of 30 pounds per annum. The others are supported by the pupils.

There is no provision for the poor, who are seen constantly travelling from house to house to obtain subsistence. A subscription is made in the town of Castleblayney to provide clothing for them during the winter seasons.

MODERN TOPOGRAPHY

Public Buildings

Besides the public buildings in the town of Castleblayney, the parish contains the following.

A Presbyterian meeting house in Drumalisk townland is a plain stone building with slated roof containing accommodation for 600 persons.

Covenanters' meeting house in the townland of Aughnadamph is a small building of stone with slated roof at present in a bad state of repair. It contains accommodation for 250 persons.

Oram chapel is capable of accommodating 500 persons at worship. It is a plain stone building surrounded by a small enclosure with a few fir trees. The Revd James Duffy is the parish priest.

The Grove meeting house, situated in Formill townland, is a neat stone building with slated roof and contains accommodation for 400 persons.

Frankfort meeting house is similar to the above and capable of containing the same number of persons.

Gentlemen's Seats

The residence of Lord Blayney, adjacent to the town of Castleblayney, is an extensive building of 2-storeys and a basement, situated on a gentle eminence. It commands a beautiful view of Muckno lough and its islands. The approach to the house is by a neat gate from the end of West Street. The demesne is extensive but only a portion (84 acres) is in this parish; the remainder is in the parish of Clontibret.

Church Hill House, formerly a residence of Lord Blayney, is at present occupied by Mr Hill, and in the immediate vicinity is the residence of Mr Harrison. Surrounding these houses are some small patches of plantations and to each is attached a good garden.

The Glebe House is situated in the townland of Killygolagh. It was built in the year 1828 and cost 1,100 pounds.

Mills

In the townland of Lurganmore there is a corn mill supplied by the stream from Muckno Mill lough, diameter of which 14 feet, breadth 1 and three-quarter feet.

Drumleck corn mill, James McWatty Esquire of Castleblayney, proprietor, is a breast wheel with a fall of 15 feet from the dam head to the bottom of the wheel, the diameter of which is 18 feet and breadth 4 feet. The axle and rim of the water wheel are of metal and the interior machinery is in good order.

Lisseenan corn mill, a breast wheel, 14 feet in diameter and 2 and half feet broad; this mill has not been at work for the last 3 years in consequence of the scanty supply of water. The building is of stone with a thatched roof in a bad state of repair.

Drumacribb flax mill is a breast wheel of 12 feet in diameter and 28 feet broad. The building is small and contains only 2 sets of handles and no breakers on rollers, as the supply of water is too scanty to work heavier machinery.

Tattinclave flax mill, a breast wheel, diameter 14 feet, breadth 3 and a half feet. It contains 4 sets of handles but no breakers and has only a poor supply of water.

Carrickasleane corn and flax mills, breast wheels with a fall of 3 feet, diameter of wheel of corn mill 14 feet, breadth 2 and half feet; flax mill diameter 12 feet, breadth 2 and half feet.

Flax mill in Lurganearly is a small building of stone with a thatched roof; has a breast wheel 12 feet in diameter and 2 feet wide.

Communications

Roads diverge from Castleblayney to Dundalk, Newry, Armagh, Monaghan, Ballybay and Cootehill. These are level roads, 30 feet wide and kept in good order by the county. The length of these main roads in the parish is 16 miles. Of by-roads there are 42 miles, in the most part in good repair but very hilly.

A turnpike has been established a short distance south of the town of Castleblayney. It is one of 3 bars on the Castleblayney and Dundalk line, for which a yearly rent of 835 pounds is paid. The toll-collector receives 10s per week and 4s for an assistant to be occasionally employed.

ANCIENT TOPOGRAPHY

Remains of Antiquity

Of the early history of this parish little is known nor are there any monuments of antiquity to elucidate it. The ruins of the old church of Muckno parish can be partially traced in the old graveyard situated in the townland of Churchill, but no tradition of its erection exists among the people.

On Mullyash mountain there is a rude tower which was built by Lord Templeton's direction in the latter part of the year 1833. It is 34 feet high and stands upon a cairn 60 feet in circumference. This cairn was opened by the country people 20 years ago and found to contain human bones which appeared to have been burnt.

In the townland of Tullinangroove are the partial remains of a druidical circle, the extent of which cannot be traced.

Forts

The parish contains 14 forts, situated in the following townlands: 2 in Carrickasleane, 2 in Corratandy, 1 in Drummullard Big, 1 in Lisdonney, 1 in Tullycoghery, 1 boundary of Bree and Killicard, 1 in Drumagelvin, 1 in Moy, 1 in Dernion, 1 in Annyart, 2 in Drumalisk.

MODERN TOPOGRAPHY

General Appearance and Scenery

The general appearance of the country is bleak and barren, with the exception of the south west part. Here the town of Castleblayney and demesne join with Muckno lough in producing a lively and interesting scene. The islands and shores of the lough are for the most part covered with wood and the surrounding country in a high state of cultivation.

SOCIAL ECONOMY

Progress of Improvement

Of the early improvement and cultivation of this parish, nothing is at present known among the inhabitants. Within the memory of the present generation a considerable portion of land in the northern part of the parish which was formerly covered with heather has been cultivated and now produces reasonable crops. The principal obstruction to further improvement is the poverty of the farmers and the small size of farms.

To remedy these evils Lord Templeton is endeavouring to induce the poorer tenantry to sell their farms at the rate of 1 pound per acre to their more opulent neighbours; and to enable these poor people to remove their families, his lordship adds a small present.

Local Government

The usual force of police in the parish: in Castleblayney 1 chief constable, 1 constable and 6 or 8 subconstables; and in the townland of Drumakill, 2 and a half miles east of the town, 1 constable and 2 subconstables.

The inhabitants of the parish are at present quite well-disposed people and give the magistrates little trouble except in cases of trifling debts and quarrels at fairs and markets. Illicit distillation, which was formerly very general, is rarely heard of but the practice of selling whiskey without licence is very general.

Parish of Muckno

Schools

The inhabitants appear anxious to have their children educated in the different schools established throughout the parish and it is the general opinion that the moral habits of the young people have been considerably improved by the introduction of these schools.

Religion

There are 3 denominations of religion, the Established Church, the Roman Catholic and Presbyterian, in the following proportion: 1, 2, 6.

The clergyman of the Established Church receives tithes from the parish by composition amounting to 436 pounds 3s 1d yearly, and he has a glebe of 19 acres 2 roods 39 perches Irish at 2 pounds per acre from Lord Blayney, as the glebe of Muckno parish is not at present known. The Revd T. Hackett of Boyle, county Roscommon, is the rector and the Revd J.C. Hackett, his curate, resides in the Glebe House.

The clergymen of the other denominations are supported by dues and contributions from their own congregations.

Habits of the People

The cabins of the labouring class are very poor. They usually comprise 2 apartments, are built of stone and thatched, with small windows which are rarely glazed. Lord Blayney's tenantry have lately built some good 2-storey houses in their farms, for which his lordship has made some allowances. Lord Templeton supplies his tenantry with timber and slates to build good farmhouses and offices.

PRODUCTIVE AND SOCIAL ECONOMY

Rural: Landlords and Holdings

The parish of Muckno is divided between 2 proprietors, Lord Templeton and Lord Blayney. Sir Hedworth Williamson holds 2 townlands from Lord Blayney by lease forever. He is the only landlord who stands between the tenant and head landlord. The agents are for Lord Templeton, Mr Murdock of Glaslough, and for Lord Blayney, A.O'B. Bellingham Esquire. Neither Lord Templeton nor his agent are resident; both Lord Blayney and Mr Bellingham occasionally reside in Castleblayney. The holdings are 579 under 10 acres, 319 above 10 acres, 149 above 20 and 7 above 50. They are generally held by lease of 21 years or 2 lives, but many are held without any leases.

Sir H. Williamson grants no leases. Lord Templeton will give no lease to any tenant holding less than 20 acres. The rents of all the proprietors are nearly equal and average for the best quality 19s, middling 15s, inferior 12s per British acre, paid in all cases in money. Conacre land is common in the vicinity of Castleblayney town, at the rate of some 8 to 10 pounds per acre.

Fields vary in size and form, from 2 to 6 acres. The fences in the southern part are formed of sods and stand well-set with quicks, but in the northern part they are either loose stone walls or sod banks. Lord Templeton has lately established a nursery from which he supplies his tenantry with quicks gratis.

Considerable improvement has taken place in the farm houses and offices, in consequence of the encouragement given by the proprietors as before mentioned.

No farms are held as examples.

Manures

The soil is of a light strong nature and the manures generally used are common farmyard manures with a mixture of bog and lime. The latter when judiciously used is best adapted for the soil. It is obtained for the northern part of the parish in Armagh and for the southern part in Carrickmacross, and for the most part burned on the ground.

The burning of land for manure is strictly prohibited except in breaking up heathery ground or bog. The markets for the produce of this parish in Castleblayney, Newry and Dundalk.

Planting

Lord Templeton has a nursery in the townland of Carrintrough from which his tenantry are supplied gratis. His lordship has also planted a considerable portion of the east side of Mullyash mountain with fir and forest plants which appear to be growing well.

Table of Schools

[Table contains the following headings: name of townland, number of pupils subdivided by religion and sex, remarks as to how supported, when established].

Castleblayney (parish school): 18 Protestants, 12 Catholics, total 30; gratuity from rector 2 pounds 15s 4d ha'penny per year, scholars pay 2s to 7s 6d per quarter; when established: unknown.

Castleblayney (Lady Blayney's): 31 Protestants, 50 Catholics, 81 females, total 81; Lady Blayney allows about 30 pounds per annum, pupils pay nothing; plain sewing, reading, writing and arithmetic taught; when established: unknown.

Castleblayney: 10 Protestants, 7 Catholics, total 17; pupils pay 10s 6d to 1 guinea per quarter; classics and arithmetic taught.

Castleblayney: 4 Protestants, 18 Catholics, total 22; pupils pay 2s 6d to 3s 6d per quarter; Mr Campbell, master, established 1808.

Castleblayney: 44 Protestants, 30 Catholics, 45 males, 29 females, total 74; pupils pay 3s to 16s per quarter; classics and mathematics; when established: unknown.

Castleblayney: 7 Protestants, 78 Catholics, 68 males, 17 females, total 85; pupils pay 2s 6d to 10s per quarter; mathematics; when established: unknown.

Drumakill (Kildare Place): 53 Protestants, 46 Catholics, 72 males, 27 females, total 99; society grants books but no salary, pupils pay 1s 6d to 2s 6d and a few 10s 6d per quarter; reading, writing and mathematics, established 1826.

Tullyraghen, 3 Protestants, 27 Catholics, 12 males, 18 females, total 30; pupils pay 1s 6d to 2s 6d per quarter; reading, writing and arithmetic, established 1824.

Annyart (Kildare Place): 65 Protestants, 4 Catholics, 41 males, 28 females, total 69; society grants books but no salary, pupils pay 1s 6d to 5s per quarter; established 1821.

Drumalisk (private): 16 Protestants, 30 Catholics, 20 males, 26 females, total 46; pupils pay 1s 6d to 2s 6d per quarter; when established: unknown.

Tullynahatna (national): 75 Protestants, 5 Catholics, 54 males, 26 females, total 80; society allows 8 pounds per annum, pupils pay 1s per quarter; established January 1831.

Oram (chapel): 27 Protestants, 35 Catholics, 35 males, 27 females, total 62; pupils pay 1s 6d to 2s 6d per quarter, established 1832.

Lisseenan (national): 91 Protestants, 20 Catholics, 64 males, 47 females, total 111; society allows 8 pounds per annum, pupils pay 1d to 2s 2d per quarter; established 1824.

Drollough: no school kept at present.

Carrickasleane (national): 46 Protestants, 21 Catholics, 44 males, 23 females, total 67; Lord Templeton allows 5 pounds and society 8 pounds per annum, and pupils pay 1s 6d to 2s 6d per quarter; when established: unknown.

Drumason: 11 Protestants, 59 Catholics, 48 males, 22 females, total 70; pupils pay 1s 8d to 3s per quarter, established 1824.

Corrintrough: no school kept at present.

Ecclesiastical Summary

[Table] Name Muckno <Muckna>, diocese Clogher, province Armagh, rectory, no union, patron Bishop of Clogher, incumbent Revd T. Hackett of Boyle, county Roscommon; no glebe but 20 acres granted by Lord Blayney at 2 pounds per acre by lease forever; tithes belong to incumbent, amount 436 pounds 3s 1d.

General Remarks

The country is capable of improvement but not to a great extent. The soil is very cold and strong, and the manure most required is lime which is not easily obtained. Cultivation is carried nearly to the summit of Mullyash, which is 1,034 feet above the level of the sea. The land is by no means adapted either for pasture or sheep-walks, but might be advantageously laid out in plantations. Throughout the parish there is a good supply of water but in no case of sufficient power for heavy machinery.

The country has the full advantage of good roads to the neighbouring towns and numerous by-roads in tolerable order intersected in all directions. [Signed] John Chaytor, Lieutenant Royal Engineers, 6th November 1835.

Parish of Tydavnet, County Monaghan

Memoir by J.R. Ward and T.C. McIlroy, February and March 1838

NATURAL STATE

Locality

The parish of Tydavnet <Tydavnet> is situated in the north west part of the county of Monaghan, it being the most northern parish in the barony of Monaghan. It is bounded on the north by the parishes of Errigal Truagh and Donagh, on the east by the parish of Donagh, on the south by the parishes of Monaghan, Kilmore, Drumsnat and Clones, and on the west by the county of Fermanagh.

Its extreme length is 10 miles and extreme breadth 7 miles. Its mean length is 7 miles and mean breadth 5 miles. Its content, including 163 acres 12 perches of water, is 26,502 acres 3 perches.

NATURAL FEATURES

Hills

Part of a range of mountains which occur in the counties Tyrone and Fermanagh are situated in the north west part of this parish and run along the north boundary of it. The principal points are Eshnaglough, 1,190 feet, Eshclofin, 1,011 feet, Knockballyroney, 1,120 feet and Knockanearla, 952 feet above the level of the sea. From these points there is a gradual but broken fall to the south part of the parish in a south east direction, where the county is broken into numerous small hills running parallel to each other in a north and south direction. Their average height is 320 feet above the level of the sea.

The highest point in the parish is in the townland of Eshnaglough, 200 yards south east of Lough Sallagh, where it is about 1,230 feet above the sea. The lowest point is in the townland on Derrynagrew, along the bank of the Blackwater river, where the average height is only 170 feet above the level of the sea.

Lakes

There are a numerous quantity of small lakes situated in this parish [for] which, in order to prevent an unnecessary description of each (for none of them possess anything remarkable except the fish they may contain, which properly belong to the natural history of the parish), the following table is perhaps sufficient. [Table contains the following headings: name, townland, altitude, content, depth [not known for any].

Lough Aporton, Eshnaglough townland, 1,030 feet.

Lough Antrarer, Eshnaglough and Knockanearla townlands, 950 feet.

Lough Bradan, see parish of Errigal Truagh.

Kilmore lake, Kilmore West and Smyed townlands, 360 feet, 11 acres 8 perches.

Lough Sallagh, Eshnaglough townland, 1,206 feet, part in county Tyrone.

Lough Galluane, Eshnaglough and Barratitoppy townlands, 1,100 feet, part in county Tyrone.

Lough Meenish, Barratitoppy Upper townland.

Slacksgrove lake, Mullalishlaughlin and Annahagh townlands, 235 feet, 37 acres 28 perches.

Mont Louise lake, Aghagarr, Formoyle and Mullatigorry townlands, 220 feet, part in Clones parish.

Mullaghmore, Mullaghmore North townland, 245 feet.

Mullaghmore, Mullaghmore North and Drumsheare townlands, 252 feet.

Mullashingo North, Mullashingo, Derrydorraphy, Mullaghmore North and Aghaboy North townlands.

Mullashingo South, Mullaghshingo, Gilford and Derrydorraphy townlands.

Shee lough; Shee, Cornagiltagh and Drumoo townlands, 280 feet.

Rivers

The Blackwater river rises out of Lough Galluane, which is situated on the verge of the county and in the north part of this parish [insert marginal note: source]. It flows in a south east direction for 3 miles, then due south for 3 and a half miles, in which space it receives the Scotstown river. It then flows almost due east for 4 miles, in which distance it has many windings.

The average breadth of the river is 30 feet and it is very shallow. It is useful for drainage and for small mills. There are no considerable falls or rapids. The general fall for the first 3 miles of its course is 40 feet per mile, after that 25 feet per mile. It is subject to floods which soon subside;

they deposit sand. The river impedes communication and flows over a gravelly bed. The banks are uninteresting. The river falls into Cor river 12 miles from its source.

The Scotstown river is a small stream which rises in the townland of Derrynasell and flows almost parallel to the road between Scotstown and Brookeborough. Its average breadth is 12 feet and it is very shallow. The source of the river is 750 feet above the sea and falls into the Blackwater near Scotstown bridge, 6 miles from its source.

Bogs

The surface of the mountain district of the parish is of a boggy nature. The average height is 950 feet above the sea, the depth of the turf 1 and a half feet. There is a bog the greater part of which is situated in the townland of Derrynanamph and those townlands which border on it. Its average height is 340 feet above the sea and 20 feet above the Blackwater river. The depth of the bog in those places where it is cut is from 3 to 9 feet.

Timber is found imbedded in this bog, principally fir and birch. On the edges of it, or where the soil underneath is clay, oak is found, but it is now scarce as it has been removed, being much sought for building and other purposes by the inhabitants.

Crops

The crops in the south and east part of the parish are the same as in the parish of Monaghan, but in the west district, it being of a mountainous character, no wheat is cultivated and the other crops, viz. oats, barley and potatoes, are on the average a fortnight later in ripening.

MODERN TOPOGRAPHY

Village of Scotstown

Scotstown is a small village situated in the townland of [blank], on the main road between Monaghan and Brookeborough, county Fermanagh, [blank] miles from the former. The houses are straggling and irregular. They consist of 18 of 1-storey, 6 of 2 and 1 of 3-storeys. Of these, 6 only are slated and the remainder are thatched. They are chiefly built of stone.

Fairs

Fairs are held on the 17th of each month. Cattle, pigs and sheep are the principal commodities sold in them. They are also attended by huxters who retail callicoes, printed and plain coarse linens, stockings and socks, and a bad description of hardware, cutlery, brushes and combs.

Bridge

Scotstown bridge crosses the Blackwater river 100 yards north of the town, on the road leading to Tydavnet. It is 33 feet long and 22 feet broad, including the parapet walls which are 1 and a half feet thick. The bridge consists of 1 semicircular arch and is built of stone. It was erected in the year 1821 and the expense was defrayed by a grant from the grand jury of the county.

On the east parapet wall is a stone which was on that of the old bridge (which fell a few years before the present one was erected), [on which] is the following inscription: "The foundation stone of this bridge was laid by Henry Owen Scott Esquire on the 6th June 1791; John Mitchell and John Hawkshaw Esquires, overseers, Samuel Madden, mason." Note: The word "Madden" is erased.

Chapel

There is a Roman Catholic chapel situated in the townland of Drumdesco, 120 yards east of the main road between Scotstown and Tydavnet, half a mile from the former. It is a plain stone building 75 and a half feet long and 43 feet broad, including the walls which are 2 feet thick. There are 2 towers, 1 at each end, 12 feet by 14, in which are the entrance doors and the staircases leading to the galleries. They are the same height as the side walls and on the top of the front wall of each is a plain freestone cross. Under that on the south end is a stone on which is inscribed "1785, rebuilt from the foundation 1825."

The inside of the building is in an unfinished state. The roof is not ceiled and the floor not boarded, only partially fitted up with pews. There is an extensive gallery which also has no pews or seats at present. The building was commenced in 1823 and cost 1,400 pounds, which sum was raised by subscriptions, of which 300 pounds was given by Dr Murray. The accommodation is for 1,800 and the general attendance 1,400 persons.

On the east wall of the building there is a marble monument consisting of a white slab surmounted with a black one, on which is raised in white the arms of the Catholic bishop. On the lower slab is the following inscription: "To the memory of the Right Revd James Murphy, Catholic Bishop of Clogher for the last 20 years,

Parish of Tydavnet

He was a prelate of unshaken firmness, of inflexible integrity, of laborious zeal, the vigilant and faithful guardian of the rights and disciplines of his church. What by a discreet economy he could spare of his income was devoted to charitable purposes, to the building of chapels and to the founding of burses for the support and education of students for the mission of the diocese of Clogher.

To commend himself to the frequent prayers of the clergy and people he chose this newly erected chapel, the last effort of his zeal, as the place of interment, and beneath are deposited his remains. He fought the good fight, he finished the faith, and went to receive the crown of justice on the 19th of November 1824 in the 81st year of his age. He was appointed to the parish in 1768 and was the third pastor of it in uninterrupted succession since the year 1688."

Joining the rear of the chapel is a 2-storey house, 32 feet by 19 and half feet, for the residence of a priest and a vestry.

Village of Bellanode

Bellanode is a small straggling village situated in the townland of Mullaghmore West. It contains 29 cottages of 1-storey and a house of 2-storeys. They are all thatched and are built of stone. Their appearance is not very favourable. There are 4 publicans, 1 nailer, 1 smith, 1 tobacconist, 1 wheelwright and a schoolmaster in the village.

Church

Bellanode church, situated in the village, is a stone building, roughcast and whitewashed. The following figure will best show the form and dimensions of the building: [ground plan, "T" shape]. The tower at the south west end is 60 feet high.

The inside of the church is very neat. It contains 55 pews, beside a gallery in which are 11 seats. There are no monuments or inscriptions. The accommodation is for [blank] persons, the average attendance [blank]. The date and cost cannot be accurately ascertained.

Schoolhouse

Bellanode schoolhouse, situated at the west end of the village, is a 2-storey stone building, slated. The following figure will best show the form and dimensions: [ground plan, main dimensions approximately 50 by 30 feet, indicating schoolrooms and master's apartments]. 28th February 1838. The house was built in 18[blank].

Bridges

Bellanode bridge crosses the Blackwater river at the east end of the village. It consists of 3 arches, is built of limestone and is 50 feet long by 18 feet broad, including the parapet walls which are 1 foot 6 inches thick.

Cappog bridge crosses the River Blackwater half a mile east of Ballynode village. It is a limestone building 42 feet long and 20 feet broad, including the parapet walls which are 18 inches thick. The bridge consists of 2 semicircular arches.

MODERN TOPOGRAPHY AND SOCIAL AND PRODUCTIVE ECONOMY

Village of Tydavnet

The village of Tydavnet is situated in the eastern part of the parish, in the townlands of Mullanarockan and Tydavnet. It consists of 5 houses of 1-storey, thatched, built of stone.

Fairs and Markets

There is no weekly market in Tydavnet, but there are 5 fairs held in the year there, on the following days: 28th January, 6th February, 31st March, 24th June and 28th September.

Constabulary

The police force at present stationed in the village of Tydavnet consists of 4 men. The police force in Scotstown is a sergeant and 2 privates.

Schoolhouses

Tydavnet national schoolhouse is situated in the townland of Mullanarockan. It is a good stone house, slated, 2-storeys high, 23 feet long and 19 feet broad. It was built in 1820 and cost 70 pounds, defrayed by subscriptions. The school is held in the upper part. The under part of the house is let to a tenant.

There is a schoolhouse situated in the townland of Tullylone. It is a stone cottage, thatched. It is 37 feet 6 inches long and 19 feet broad. It was built in 1825 and cost 80 pounds, defrayed by Dacre Hamilton Esquire. The school is held in an apartment in the east end. The other part of the house is occupied by the master as a dwelling.

Catholic Chapel

There is a Roman Catholic chapel situated in the townland of Mullanarockan. It is a stone building slated, the form and dimensions of which are shown by the following figure: [ground plan, main dimensions 73 feet 4 inches by 52 feet, "T" shape].

The interior is spacious. There are 3 galleries. The house is unfloored and it is not ceiled. The windows are Gothic. The altarpiece is an oil painting of Christ crucified. The accommodation is for 1,000 persons and the general attendance is 1,000. The above chapel was built in 1784, cost not known.

Schoolhouses

Carnagilty national schoolhouse is situated in the townland of Carnagilty. It is a stone cottage, whitewashed and thatched, 33 feet long and 18 feet broad. It was built in 1831, expense of building and how defrayed not known.

Knockatallan schoolhouse, situated in the townland of Knockatallan, 200 yards north of the main road between Monaghan and Brookeborough, county Fermanagh, 7 and half miles from the former, is a 2-storey building of freestone, slated. It is 40 feet long and 20 feet broad, was built in 1836 and cost 138 pounds, which sum was raised by subscription.

A rood of ground on which the schoolhouse is built is rented at 6d, and a lease is obtained from the proprietor of the soil forever. 9th March 1838.

Table of Schools

[Table contains the following headings: name, situation and description, when established, income and expenditure, physical, intellectual and moral instruction, number of pupils subdivided by age, sex and religion, name and religion of master or mistress, date on which visited].

Tydavnet national school, a good house in the townland of Mullanarackan, established 1835; income: from the National Board 8 pounds per annum, from James Rose Esquire 1 pound per annum, from pupils 7 pounds per annum; intellectual instruction: books of the Education Board; moral instruction: visited by the Revd Peter Duffy P.P., catechism taught on Saturdays by the master; number of pupils: males, 35 under 10 years of age, 28 from 10 to 15, 4 above 15, 67 total males; females, 20 under 10 years of age, 13 from 10 to 15, 33 total females; total number of pupils 100, 6 Established Church, 3 Presbyterians, 91 Roman Catholics; master John Murtagh, Roman Catholic; visited 15th February 1838.

Tydavnet, a cottage in the townland of Tullylone, established 1825; income: from Dacre Hamilton 5 pounds, from pupils 10 pounds; intellectual education: books of no society; moral education: visited by the Revd Peter Duffy P.P., Scriptures read daily; number of pupils: males, 7 under 10 years of age, 15 from 10 to 15, 22 total males; females, 2 under 10 years of age, 6 from 10 to 15, 8 total females; total number of pupils 30, 3 Established Church, 4 Presbyterians, 23 Roman Catholics; master William McPhillips, Roman Catholic; visited 15th February 1838, [signed] T.C. McIlroy.

A stone cottage, thatched, near the chapel in Drumdesco, not known when established; income: 15 pounds from pupils; intellectual instruction: books of no society; moral instruction: visited by Peter Duffy, parish priest, no Scripture read; number of pupils: males, 30 under 10 years of age, 17 from 10 to 15, 3 above 15, 50 total males; females, 14 under 10 years of age, 25 from 10 to 15, 1 above 15, 40 total females; total number of pupils 90, 15 Established Church, 8 Presbyterians, 67 Roman Catholics; master James Whiteside, Roman Catholic; visited 2nd March.

Cornagilty national school, a cottage in the townland of Cornagilty, established 1831; income: from the Board of Education 15 pounds, from James Rose Esquire 18 pounds; intellectual instruction: books of the Education Board; moral instruction: visited by the Revd Peter Duffy, parish priest, catechisms taught on Saturdays; number of pupils: males, 14 under 10 years of age, 30 from 10 to 15, 44 total males; females, 11 under 10 years of age, 28 from 10 to 15, 1 above 15, 40 total females; total number of pupils 84, all Roman Catholics; master Arthur McGinnes, Roman Catholic; visited 2nd March 1838.

Knockatallan, a 2-storey house in Knockatallan townland, established July 1836; income from pupils 12 pounds; intellectual instruction: no society books used, *Universal spelling book*; moral instruction: visited by the Revd Peter Duffy, parish priest, catechisms taught on Saturdays; number of pupils: males, 15 under 10 years of age, 9 from 10 to 15, 2 above 15, 36 total males; females, 20 under 10 years of age, 27 from 10 to 15, 3 above 15, 50 total females; total number of pupils 86, 2 Established Church, 84 Roman Catholics; master Edward Reilly, Roman Catholic; visited 9th March 1838.

Bellanode, a convenient room in Bellanode schoolhouse; income: from parish 2 pounds, from pupils 8 pounds; intellectual instruction: no society books used, *Universal spelling book*; moral instruction: visited by the rector, catechisms

Parish of Tydavnet

taught by master, Authorised Version of Scriptures read; number of pupils: males, 17 under 10 years of age, 15 from 10 to 15, 3 above 15, 35 total males; females, 12 under 10 years of age, 10 from 10 to 15, 2 above 15, 24 total females; total number of pupils 59, 50 Established Church, 4 Presbyterians, 5 Roman Catholics; master John Welsh, Established Church; visited 15th March 1838.

Raseenan, a cottage in Raseenan townland; closed, the master having left for a more lucrative situation; visited 15th March 1838, [signed] J.R. Ward.

Table of Mills

[Table contains the following headings: townland, proprietor, tenant, when built, dimensions and type of water wheel, fall of water, type of machinery, stones and skutches, remarks].

Killymaran, proprietor James Rose Esquire, tenant James Read, when built: not known; breast wheel, 14 feet by 2 foot 6 inches, fall of water 6 feet, wood and iron, 1 pair of stones, a ruinous stone building thatched; 3rd February 1838.

Killymaran, proprietor James Rose Esquire, tenant James Read, when built: not known; machinery wood and iron, 8 sets of skutches and 1 set of rollers, a 2-storey building of stone, slated; 3rd February 1838.

Mullaghmore, proprietor Sir Thomas Foster, tenant Robert Wright, built 1837; 2 wheels: breast wheel, 16 feet by 3 feet, fall of water 4 feet, machinery wood and iron, a sifting machine, 1 pair of stones and 1 pair of fans; breast wheel, 14 feet 6 inches by 2 feet 8 inches, fall 6 and a half feet, machinery wood and iron, 1 pair of stones and 1 pair of fans; both in a stone building, slated; 28th February 1838, [signed] J.R. Ward].

Cornanure, proprietor Mrs Singleton, tenant Rodger Ankell; when built: not known; breast wheel, 16 feet by 2 feet 8 inches, fall of water 3 feet, machinery wood and iron, 2 pair of stones and a fanning machine, a stone building, thatched; 25th February 1838.

Rafeenan, tenant Andrew McCague; when built: not known; breast wheel, 14 feet 6 inches by 2 feet 8 inches, fall of water 3 feet, machinery wood and iron, 1 pair of stones, in a rough stone building, thatched. 15th March.

Quiglough, proprietor Andrew Foster, tenant Humphry Thomas, built 1796; undershot wheel, 13 foot 6 inches by 2 foot 8 inches, fall of water 2 feet, wooden wheel, iron machinery, 1 pair of stones and a fanning machine, a rough stone building, thatched.

Teraverty, proprietor Richard Westenra Esquire, tenant Thomas Read; when built: not known; breast wheel, 12 foot 6 inches by 2 foot 2 inches, fall of water 4 feet, machinery wood and iron, 1 pair of stones, a ruinous stone building, thatched.

Teraverty, proprietor Richard Westenra Esquire, tenant Thomas Read, built 1834; breast wheel, 13 foot 6 inches by 3 feet, fall of water 4 feet, machinery wood and iron, 6 sets of skutches and rollers, in a good stone building.

Drumscor, proprietor James Hamilton Esquire, tenant John Duffy, rebuilt 1835; breast wheel, 14 feet by 3 feet, fall of water 4 feet, machinery wood and iron, 1 pair of stones, in a stone building, thatched; 16th March 1838, [signed] J.R. Ward.

Parish of Tyholland, County Monaghan

Memoir by J.R. Ward and J.C. Innes

NATURAL STATE AND NATURAL FEATURES

Locality

The parish of Tyholland <Tehallan> is situated in the north east part of the county Monaghan and in the baronies of Monaghan and Cremorne. It is bounded on the north and north west by the parish of Donagh, on the south and south west by the parish of Monaghan, and on the east by the parish of Clontibret and county Armagh.

Its extreme length is 4 miles and extreme breadth 4 miles; its mean length is 2 and a half miles and mean breadth 1 mile. Its content is 5,949 acres 2 roods 20 perches.

Hills

The hills in this parish are connected in ridges which run in a north and south direction. The highest point is in the townland of Terrycaffe, which is 422 feet above the level of the sea. The lowest point is in the townland of Drumagelvin, which is 120 feet above the level of the sea. The hills are all steep on the western side and are in general well cultivated.

Rivers

The Blackwater forms the north boundary of the parish for 3 and a half miles. Its average breadth is 35 feet and it is very shallow. This river is more fully described in the Memoir of Monaghan parish.

The Corr river runs across the western part of the parish in a northerly direction for 4 miles. Its average breadth is from 15 to 40 feet and depth from 1 to 3 feet. It is usefully situated for drainage. There are no considerable falls or rapids. The river flows over a gravelly bed. The banks are cultivated.

The parish is well supplied with water from the rivulets and springs.

Bogs

There is a large bog situated in the townlands of Annacramph, Carrowkeel, Garran-Otra, Gibraltar, Killyneill, Killeef and Tamlat, the extreme length of which is 1 and a quarter miles and breadth three-quarters of a mile. It is 140 feet above the sea and 10 feet above the River Corr. Wood is found embedded, principally fir. The average depth of the bog is 6 feet.

Climate and Crops

The climate and crops of this parish are the same as in the parish of Monaghan.

MODERN TOPOGRAPHY

Church

Tyholland church, situated in the townland of Templetate, is a neat stone building, roughcast and whitewashed. The form and dimensions of the building are represented: [ground plan, main dimensions approximately 74 feet by 27 feet, rectangular shape with projections at either end].

It was built in 1787, the necessary sum, advanced by Alexander Montgomery Esquire of Bessmont Park, refunded by instalments levied off the parish. Whole sum mentioned in vestry book is 100 pounds. Besides this the seats were sold for 50 pounds 8s, which was appropriated to the finishing of the church.

In 1827 there was a tower built, which cost 66 pounds 14s 4d ha'penny.

Chapel

Tyholland chapel, situated in the townland of Leitrim, is a neat stone building, roughcast and whitewashed. It is 95 feet long and 40 feet broad.

School

Tyholland parish school, situated in the townland of Tuckmilltate, is a very neat stone house, roughcast and slated. The form and dimensions of the building are represented by the following figure: [ground plan, main dimensions 57 feet 6 inches by 24 feet, "T" shape]. It was built in 1821 and cost 250 pounds, a bequest of the late Revd John Maxwell D.D.

Communications

The main road from Monaghan to Armagh, which is also the mail coach line from Enniskillen to Belfast, runs in an easterly direction through the northern part of the parish for 4 and a half miles. Its average breadth is 36 feet. It is a well laid out road and is kept in very good repair by the Turnpike Trustees.

The old line of road from Monaghan to Armagh runs in an easterly direction through the centre of the parish for 3 miles. Its average is 33 feet. This

Parish of Tyholland

is a hilly road, but in other respects kept in good repair at the expense of the county.

The main road from Glaslough to Castleblayney runs in a northerly direction through the western part of the parish for 5 miles. Its average breadth is 25 feet. It is a well laid out road and kept in good repair at the expense of the county.

About 2 miles from Monaghan, on the mail coach road above mentioned, a road branches off to Glaslough and runs in a northerly direction for 1 and a half miles. Its average breadth is 35 feet. It is a well laid out road and is kept in good repair at the expense of the county.

SOCIAL AND PRODUCTIVE ECONOMY

Table of Schools

[Table contains the following headings: name, situation and description, when established, income and expenditure, physical, intellectual and moral instruction, number of pupils subdivided by age, sex and religion, name and religion of master or mistress, date on which visited].

Tyholland parish school, a neat house in the townland of Tuckmillvale, established 1821; income: legacy by Dr Maxwell D.D. 9 pounds, from Revd John Rotheram Tarleton 2 pounds, subscriptions 5 pounds per annum, from pupils 4 pounds per annum; intellectual instruction: Kildare Place books; moral instruction: visited by the Revd John Rotheram Tarleton and William Mills, Protestant curate of Tyholland, Authorised Version of Scriptures read and Protestant and Presbyterian catechisms taught on Saturday; number of pupils: males, 10 under 10 years of age, 69 from 10 to 15, 14 above 15, 93 total males; females, 3 under 10 years of age, 15 from 10 to 15, 2 above 15, 20 total females; total number of pupils 113, 85 Established Church, 8 Presbyterians, 20 Roman Catholics; master William Hintry, Established Church, visited 12th February 1838. [Signed] J. Cumming Innes.

Mills

[Table contains the following headings: name of townland, proprietor, tenant, when built, dimensions of water wheel, fall of water, type of machinery, remarks].

Dromore, proprietor [blank] Hulchell Esquire, tenant Francis Evans, built 1833; overshot wheel, 16 feet by 3 feet, fall of water 3 feet, machinery wood and metal, 2 pair of stones; a good stone house, slated.

Tullynure, proprietor John Maxwell Esquire, tenant George Campbell Esquire; when built: not known; overshot wheel, 13 feet by 3 feet, fall of water 2 feet, machinery wood and metal, 2 pair of stones, a set of fans and a screen; a stone house, thatched, in bad repair.

Seaveagh, proprietor Edward Richardson Esquire, tenant Thomas McGlone, built 1833; undershot wheel, 14 feet by 4 feet 6 inches, machinery wood and metal, 6 sets of skutches, 1 set of rollers; a stone house, slated.

Parish of Emlaghfad <Emlafad>, County Sligo

Statistical Report by Lieutenant P. Taylor

Natural Features

Hills

The western division of the parish, bounded in the whole length by the River Ballysadare and on the east by a range of heights intruding from Slieve Conagher on its northern boundary to the town of Ballymote, spreads itself over a flat extent of country, much covered with bog and very slightly diversified by undulation, widely separated from each other but having a general bearing in their direction from south east to north west.

The eastern division, rising by a very small angle from this slightly undulating plain, is more strongly bisected by the perpendicular escarpments, cliffs and massive boulders of limestone rocks which cover considerable portions of its surface. The natural features of this division are more particularly interesting from the evidence they afford that in the convulsive action which determined its present character, a depressive movement from north to south is clearly indicated by the position of the horizontal cliffs, descending regularly at considerable distances from each other but all in a north west direction.

The altitudes of the trigonometrical stations of Cloonan, Rathdooneymore, Ballymote tower, Emlagation and Liss[aghen] stand respectively [blank] feet above the level of the sea, and Slieve Conagher, Rathdooneybeg and Upper Carrigans in the north eastern section rise [blank] feet above the same plane.

Lakes

Templehouse lake, an extensive sheet of water on the western boundary of the parish and forming a beautiful object in Templehouse demesne, measures in extreme length and breadth three-quarters of 1 English mile, its altitude being [blank] feet above the level of the sea. The waters of the River Ballysadare flow through the lake on their course to the ocean, and a tributary stream from Loch Cloonacloghan in the parish of Cloonohill flows in upon its south western shore. Several rocky patches rise upon its surface, indicating a shallowness of water, and an island covering an area of [blank] lies close upon its south eastern shore.

Lochanulla is merely an enlargement of this river surrounded with heath and bog, a short distance beneath Templehouse lake, its reedy, rushy margin being definable only in dry seasons.

The river [blank] enters the parish in the townland of Lisananybeg and, flowing elliptically round its western division, forms the natural boundary betwixt Emlaghfad on the east and the parishes of Cloonohill and Kilvarnet on the west.

The river, descending at nearly a dead level through the greater extent of the parish, through low meadow and pasture-land, fertilises their soil by its frequent inundations. Its banks are flat and marshy and thickly loaded with depositions of slimy mud and clay, its channel is seldom fordable and the bogs through which it flows, and from their drainage, darkens its turbid waters as they flow onwards to the sea, a short distance below the town of Ballysadare.

Bogs

1,400 acres of bog covers in detached and continuous portions a large extent of the western division of the parish, the altitude of which is [blank] feet above the level of the sea and its distance from the nearest inlet 7 miles, the low flats over which it is spread rendering its drainage impossible and its surface so very wet as in many places to become flow-bog, which can only be traversed by stepping from one tuft of heather to another.

The Sphagnum palustre, with various other vegetable substances, appear to have formed the general mass, for very few remains of the branches or leaves of trees are discernible within it.

Woods

The faintest trace of planted woods is nowhere observable within the parish. In the bog around the trigonometrical station of Rathdooneymore 17 stems of oak of various sizes and lengths were discovered and extracted about 5 years ago, and throughout the whole of the bogs in the parish which have been cut into, stems of oak and fir timber have been discovered. Several stems of oak are now remaining, laying horizontally in a bog in the townland of Ballybreenan, with 4 feet of pure bog above them and an indeterminate depth of the same formation beneath them.

Parish of Emlaghfad

Climate

The close proximity of the parish to the Atlantic Ocean renders the climate exceedingly variable: the alternations of wet and dry, calm and stormy weather are incessant; west and southwesterly winds are the most prevalent, and the principal, conductor of rain. Upland crops of hay ripen in June and July, oats in September and potatoes in October. No meteorological table has been kept within the parish.

Botany

Sainfoin, trefoil, ribgrass and clover form spontaneously in the meadows and pastures. Ash, elm and birch comprise the principal trees of mature growth in the plantation, and Scotch fir, spruce and larch, alder and oak form the majority in recent formations.

Zoology

Eel, pike, perch and bream abound in the rivers and lakes. A few trout are occasionally caught, salmon are prevented ascending by the fall of Collooney and Ballysadare, and the turbid, stagnant waters of the river also check their approach.

Every variety of winged fowl are in great abundance: the mallard, widgeon, teal and diver survive in Templehouse lake. Wild geese and swans arrive in severe winters; the heron, curlew, cormorant and every variety of seagull are numerous.

Grouse, partridge, woodcock and snipe are present but not in great numbers. Foxes, hares and rabbits frequent the woods and bogs, and the otter is frequently observable on the margins of the lakes and rivers.

MODERN TOPOGRAPHY

Town of Ballymote

The town of Ballymote is situated near the centre of the eastern boundary of the parish and contains 146 dwelling houses and a population amounting to about 900 souls. The old line of road connecting the village of Collooney with Boyle passes through it from north to south and forms its principal street. The town is built upon gently rising ground, defended on the east by the elevated portion of the townland of Rathyakeeliga.

The parochial church stands in the centre. It also contains a Methodist meeting house, a Roman Catholic chapel, a barrack for the headquarters detachment of constabulary and revenue police, quarter session house and dispensary.

7 fairs are held annually for the sale of horned cattle and sheep and also of horses, pigs, asses and goats. No trade or commerce is carried within the town. The grain of the district is conveyed to the villages of Collooney and Ballysadare and Sligo for sale. A market is held for the sale of potatoes, butter, poultry and various other articles of rural industry.

Public Buildings

The church of Ballymote, erected in the year 1832 near the centre of the town, is a neat oblong building of Gothic architecture with lofty handsome spire, accommodating about 660 parishioners. The Revd John Garrit, rector of the united parishes of Emlaghfad, Toomawer, Killinorgan, Drumsnat, Killturra, and his curate, the Revd T. Carrol, are the officiating divines.

The skeleton of the old parochial church, a long narrow building with quadrangular tower, still forms a conspicuous object in the elevated portion of the townland of Emlaghfad.

The Roman Catholic chapel at the north extremity of the town is a plain modern building erected in the year 1815; accommodates about 1,000 parishioners, the Revd Bernard O'Keane and the Revd Bernard Egan, the officiating divines.

The Methodist meeting house, erected in the year 1827, is a very small building, accommodating about 150 hearers. The Revd Richard Taylor and the Revd George are the officiating clergymen.

Court House

The court house, erected in the year 1814, is plain small building in which the barrister of the county presides at quarter sessions. It contains a bench and petty jury rooms, with cells for the custody of prisoners.

Gentlemen's Seats

Earlfield House, the occasional residence of George Dodwell Esq., is delightfully situated on the western slope of the townland of Carrowcanbeg and in the immediate vicinity of the town of Ballymote. The house, quadrangular in form, is large and commodious and commands an extensive prospect of the surrounding country. The whole of the premises, orchard and gardens have been suffered to run into great dilapidation

Castle in Ballymote

and most of the grounds have been converted into a grazing farm. A very limited plantation surrounds and protects its southern and eastern face.

The Vicarage, the residence of the Revd John Garrit, is situated a short distance south of the town of Ballymote, in a low sheltered situation partially surrounded with plantation. The glebe, containing [blank] acres, is let by the bishop of the diocese to the incumbents forever at 3 pounds 16s late Irish currency.

Mills

In the immediate vicinity of Ballymote, and in the townland of Keenaghan, a corn mill, 18 feet in diameter and 3 feet 6 inches broad with an undershot water power, grinds a small proportion of the corn of the district, driven by a streamlet flowing westerly from Loch Ardree.

The absence of lakes and the low level of the general drainage of the district is the only cause assigned that other mills have not been erected in the parish.

Communications

The most abundant means of communications ramify through every section of the parish, affording the utmost facility for the transport of its produce. One Man's Lanes, measuring 5 and three-quarters English miles, traverses [it] from its northern to its southern boundary, connecting the town of Ballymote with Collooney and Boyle.

Another principal line bisects this at nearly right angles and, measuring 4 and one-half English miles, runs through the parish from east to west, opening a communication betwixt Tubbercurry, Ballymote and the mail coach road from Sligo to Dublin.

Another line, running north west from the town of Ballymote to the parish of Kilvarnet, measures 2 English miles.

A fourth line, running in a diagonal direction from north east to south west, a distance of 4 and three-quarter miles, opens the north west direction of the parish with Collooney and Tubbercurry, the average breadth of the whole being about 25 feet.

Several cross and by-roads diverge in various directions from the main lines, the whole of which are kept in poor repair, the expense of which is raised by presentments and levied off the occupiers of the land.

ANCIENT TOPOGRAPHY

Forts

Old circular forts and cairns are very interesting objects of antiquity within this parish. Many of the former, concave within the circle and surrounded with single and double fosse, present the same outlines of formation as are observable in the northern and eastern provinces of the kingdom; but in this parish the concavities in several have been filled up and formed into cairns, rising at an angle of 20 degrees from the margin of the fosse to the apex of the cove. The exterior construction of the cairn appears as if formed of rude masonry, ascending by steps which are now covered with thick grass. Many of these cairns are small, not exceeding 25 feet in diameter, and are supposed to have been formed for devotional exercises.

Some of these forts, as Rathdooneymore, erected upon abrupt irregular elevations, present a square form, the sides rising at an angle of 45 degrees and terminating in a plane. These bear the evidence of artificial formation, also ascending on each side by steps about 12 inches apart.

The rich limestone debris forming the alluvium which covers these forts and cairns support an evergreen vegetation, which renders them conspicuous and peculiarly interesting, and more particularly so when in contact with bog which frequently surrounds them.

MODERN TOPOGRAPHY

General Appearance and Scenery

Very few natural or artificial objects appear upon the surface of this parish whereby to characterise its general appearance and scenery. A very slight undulation waves throughout its western division, diversified with moats and cairns, reliques of antiquity peculiar to the district, and a great extent of bog spreads over its surface, imparting a desolate and irreclaimable character.

The eastern division is marked by loftier scenery: a range of heights extending a considerable distance from north to south, and forming a decisive line of demarcation, is covered with a soft and verdant vegetation arising from the conversion of the soil into grazing pastures.

The very limited plantations of Earlfield and Deroon, together with the localities surrounding the town of Ballymote, are the principal artificial embellishments which adorn the scenery. The old and new parochial church are prominent objects, and the old castle, with its circular turrets, commands particular observation.

SOCIAL ECONOMY

Dispensaries

The health of the tenantry and population of the parish has been greatly improved and protected by the establishment of dispensaries. No endemic or virulent diseases afflict the people. Poverty and destitution, superabundant dyspepsia and rheumatic afflictions, but the virulence of these are greatly mitigated by the salutary influence of these humane institutions.

Dr Loughead, in charge of the dispensary at Ballymote, prescribes for 86 patients on an average on Monday and Thursday of every week, besides occasional visitations to the aged in the country.

Diseases: rheumatism, consumption, catarrhs, febris, accidental affections.

Schools

The number of schools in full and active progress of instruction throughout so small a parish clearly indicates an anxious desire on the part of the peasantry for the mental improvement of their children. 7 schools, some supported by the National Board of Education, others by the bishop of the diocese and clergymen of the parish and scholars' fees, impart the useful branches of reading, writing and arithmetic to the youth of both sexes, and of all religious persuasions.

Table of Schools

[Table contains the following headings: name of townland in which situated, number of pupils subdivided by religion and sex, remarks as to how supported, when established].

Ardree, 6 Protestants, 156 Roman Catholics, 102 males, 60 females, total 162; National Board of Education 8 pounds per annum, scholars 1s to 1s 6d a quarter; founded 1834.

Ballymote, 70 Roman Catholics, 40 males, 30 females, total 70; National Board of Education 10 pounds per annum, scholars 1s to 1s 6d per quarter; founded 1832.

Ballymote court house, 52 Protestants, 21 Roman Catholics, 45 males, 28 females, total 73; bishop of diocese, vicar of Emlaghfad; founded 1815.

Carrowkeel, 55 Roman Catholics, 39 males, 16 females, total 55; supported by the scholars, 1s to 1s 6d per quarter; founded 1835.

Rathdooneymore, 36 Roman Catholics, 19 males, 17 females, total 36; supported by the scholars, 1s to 2s 6d per quarter; founded in 1834.

Religion

The census in the parish taken in the year 1834 gave the following proportions: Roman

Catholics, Protestants, Presbyterians, Methodists, [insert note: not attainable].

The vicar of the parish derives his income from tithe and glebe land. The tithe of the living was compounded in the year 1832 for 716 pounds and, through the influence of the landed proprietors, has been very generally paid. The glebe contains [blank].

The Roman Catholic clergymen derive their incomes from the fees paid by their parishioners according to the established laws of their church.

The Methodist clergymen receive about 3 pounds per annum from their congregations.

Habits of the People

The general appearance and style of the cottages of the occupying tenantry of this parish present no peculiar difference in their structure, comfort or cleanliness from the holdings in the northern and eastern provinces of the kingdom. The cottages are mostly built of stone, very few of them 2-storeys high and seldom exceeding 2 apartments with several glass windows.

6, 8 and 10 houses are thickly clustered together on many townlands under the name of villages, and possessed by cottiers carrying on the weaving of coarse linen and woollen cloth as a means of supporting their families and renting as much land by conacre as will raise a sufficiency of potatoes for their sustenance.

Potatoes and milk in the season form the principal, and almost only, support of the population. Turf is generally free to the tenantry and the only fuel burned within the parish.

6 is given as the average number of a family and, although great poverty and destitution oppress the people, many cases of great age are observable amongst them.

No decided peculiarity of dress characterises the population of this parish or district. The red cloaks and red petticoats of Connaught, so generally worn in the county of Mayo or Galway, are occasionally observable on fair days and Sundays but by no means general.

Patron days are not held within the parish.

Emigration

From many of the villages above described two-thirds of the members of families have emigrated within the last 8 years to the Canadas. In one village containing looms, in the townland of Ballytreenan, 5 only are now remaining. From 2 pounds 10s to 4 pounds is the average charge for the passage of the young and middle-aged members of the families, and nothing but the want of funds prevents a simultaneous movement of a large amount of the population. Sligo is the port from whence they take their departure and very few ever return.

Poor

The only provision for the poor of the parish is the collections at the church upon the sabbath day; the average annual amount collected is from 10s to 12 pounds and the number of poor on the church list averages 72.

Manufactures

The weaving of coarse four-hundred sacken, from six to eight-hundred sheeting and from nine to twelve-hundred linen and coarse woollen cloth are the only articles of manufacture carried on within the parish, the remunerative prices of which do not exceed 6d ha'penny a day to the weaver and 2d a day to the spinner.

Fairs and Markets

7 fairs are held in the town of Ballymote annually, on the 27th January, 11th May, 10th June, 3rd September, 13th November, 23rd December and on Easter Day, for the sale of horned cattle and pigs principally, also horses, sheep and asses and goats, and all other articles of rural industry.

Milk cows in high condition sell from 6 to 10 pounds, year-olds sell from 2 to 3 guineas, 2-year-olds from 3 to 4 guineas, and 3-year-old from 7 to 10 guineas.

Horses of inferior breed sell from 8 to 10, 12 and 14 pounds; of superior breed from 18 to 25 guineas.

Lambs sell from 12s to 20s and sheep from 34s to 50s.

Pork in the carcase is sold from 28s to 30s per cwt, in detail from 4d to 4d ha'penny per lb.

The ass sells from 15s to 40s; goats from 10s to 12s and kids from 2s to 5s.

Beef rises from 3d to 5d and mutton from 4d to 5d per lb.; geese from 15d to 18d each, turkeys from 10d to 15d, fowls from 4s to 7s a dozen and chickens from 3d to 5d each.

Collooney to Sligo are the principal linen marts, from whence it is forwarded to the linen halls of Belfast and Dublin.

PRODUCTIVE ECONOMY

Soil and Husbandry

A rich calcareous clay and gravel mixed with shale forms the alluvial soil of the parish. In some

Parish of Emlaghfad 181

localities it is light and stony, but in general it is heavy and naturally productive. The fields are small and well shaped, and mostly fenced round with stone walls.

The plough with 2 horses is much employed throughout the parish and is frequently hired by the poorer tenantry at 14s and 16s per acre, and when the ground is harrowed at 20s. 12 days' service in the year for the ploughing of an acre is also a common mode of payment. The loy is also in very general use, the whole of the hilly portions of the load being cultivated with this instrument.

Oats and potatoes are the principal crops; wheat or barley are very seldom sown, and but very little flax is cultivated. Green feeding is not adopted and in short, the prevailing system of agriculture, arising from the same cause as in other provinces of the kingdom, the subletting and subdividing system, is in the lowest possible state of depression.

Size of Farms

The farms vary in size from 2 to 4, 6, 8 and 10 acres; very few so large as 20, and are held on leases of lives of 21 or 31 years, and a very large proportion as tenants at will. Much land is let in conacre, renting as high as 10 pounds an acre for potatoes and 8 pounds for oats.

Seed and Produce

The oat seed is sown at the end of March, beginning of April and potatoes in the beginning of May. 18 stones of oat seed is sown per acre upon well-manured soil and from 22 to 24 stones upon poor soil, the produce of the former averaging 120 stone and the latter 160 stone per acre, the market price varying throughout the year from 6d ha'penny to 1s 2d per stone.

200 stones of potatoe seed is sown upon lea ground manured per acre, the produce amounting to 1,600 stones; and 160 stone of potatoe seed is sown upon stubble ground, affording a produce of 1,200 stones, the market price varying throughout the year from 3 ha'pence to 3d three farthings per stone.

Rents and Tithe

The rent of land varies from 7s to 40s per acre and townparks as high as 4 pounds per acre. County cess is equally fluctuating, varying from 1s 4d to 3s 6d per acre. The tithe of the living formed of the united parishes of Emlaghfad, Toomrourer, Killavorgan, Drumsnat and Killturra was compounded for 716 pounds in the year 1832, and very little resistance, through the influence of the landed proprietors, is made to its payment.

Proprietors

The principal landed proprietors of the parish are Sir R.B. Gore, Colonel Perceval, the bishop of the diocese, [blank] Phibs Esquire, neither of whom, or their agents, reside within the parish; but Colonel Perceval's mansion, Templehouse, is in the adjoining parish of Kilvarnet, and where he generally resides when not in attendance upon his parliamentary duties.

George Dodwell Esquire, agent to Sir Robert B. Gore, resides near Sligo. Neither of these gentlemen hold farms in their own hands.

Manures and Grazing

Burning the soil is occasionally practised to form manure. Lime is very seldom burned and used for that purpose; seaweed is brought to the parish and sold from 20s to 40s per cart-load, and is considered a cheap and valuable manure.

A large extent of the eastern section of the parish is applied to the grazing of horned cattle and sheep, a rich calcareous soil affording an abundant supply of spontaneous vegetation for their nourishment.

The extensive townland of Upper Carrigans is almost entirely devoted to the pasturage of sheep and cattle, but no attempt appears ever to have been made to introduce artificial grasses amongst these pastures, much of which is overrun with moss and rushes, particularly in low situations and even on the slopes of hills, from inattention to drainage and mowing frequently.

The grazing farms are fenced round with high stone walls which afford good shelter to the cattle.

Wages

The general rate of wages paid by the tenantry to male and female servants, including board and lodging, amounts to from 3 to 4 guineas per annum to the former and from 7s to 10s per quarter to the latter.

Livestock

The Ayr and Durhamshire breeds of horned cattle are introduced into the pasture and grazing farms of the parish, and a cross betwixt the

Ayrshire and long-horned Irish cow is beginning [to become] general amongst the tenantry; but the old Irish breed is still the most numerous.

The breed of horses is very inferior: a few half-bred English and Irish horses are occasionally met with.

The Leicester breed of sheep is common on the pastures and a few black-faced Scotch sheep are also observable, but a cross betwixt the Leicester ram and Irish sheep is much the most numerous.

The old Irish pig is very general, but a cross betwixt the Irish and Dutch breed is most preferred. Jobbers from Sligo and other towns purchase up the pigs of this district, which are all exported as provision to the English market.

Uses made of the Bogs

The bogs which are sufficiently hard to support the weight of the cattle are occasionally grazed, but a long continuance of pasturage upon heath destroys the cattle. The supply of turf within the parish is inexhaustible and generally free to the tenantry, and is wholly consumed within it. In the town of Ballymote 100 barrels of turf are sold for 30s the barrel measuring 3 feet long by [blank] square.

Coal from Sligo at [blank] per ton is used in the forges. No metallic deposits have ever been discovered in the bogs.

General Remarks on Improvement

A general introduction of the system of green feeding amongst the tenantry of the parish is the only means in the present condition of its agriculture that can either improve its soil or raise its farmers from a state of poverty to comparative comfort. The incumbent limestone rock, surrounded with inexhaustible supplies of fuel, renders the formation of lime manure an easy operation. The calcareous soil of the parish, naturally productive, is capable of being raised by the application of manure, which green feeding would produce to the highest degree of fertility.

The climate is soft and salubrious, and the large mills of the district, together with the towns of Ballina and Sligo, afford convenient ports for the sale and exportation of its produce.

These resources, with every facility of communication, if called into action and fully developed, would in a very few years raise the parish of Emlaghfad to a state of very high agricultural prosperity. [Signed] P. Taylor, Lieutenant 69th Regiment.

NATURAL FEATURES

Notes on Bogs

Vast extent of bog covers the surface of the parish and the impossibility of draining it.

2,000 acres of bog covers a district and contains [?] portions, a larger extent of the southern division of the parish, the altitude of which is [blank] feet above the level of the sea. The low flats over which it is spread renders the drainage of it impossible and its surface so very wet as in every place to become flow bog, and which can only be trimmed by stepping from one temple of heath to another. The Sphagnum palustre, with no other vegetable substance, appears to have formed the general moss; a very few reliques of the trunks or leaves of trees are discoverable within it.

Notes on River

The river descends at nearly a dead level throughout the greater extent of the parish, through rich and valuable portions fertilising the soil by its frequent inundations. Its banks are flat and murky and thickly loaded with deposits of mud and clay. Its channel is fordable in summer throughout its whole extent, with the exception of its passage through bogs, of which, and the surrounding district, it forms the principal drainage and, descending onwards its watery course, makes its exit in the townland Carrowmore, on its passage to the sea a short distance below the village of Ballysadare.

ANCIENT TOPOGRAPHY

Drawings

Ruins of castle, Ballymote, with tower and 3-storey building by William Groves, civil assistant.

Coat of arms, with motto and date 1627, "the generation of the righteous shall be blessed" Ps 112 v2.

Round tower in townland of Carrownanty near Ballymote.

Castle ruins situated in Templehouse demesne built by the Knights Templars AD 1303, by William Groves.

Sculpted head of man with triple crown, above southern door of ruined abbey.

Ruins of Emlaghfad church by William Groves.

Urn in Templehouse demesne.

Graveyard and ruins of abbey, with new church.

Parishes of Killoran and Kilvarnet, County Sligo

Statistics on Local Cess

SOCIAL AND PRODUCTIVE ECONOMY

Letter to Lieutenant T.A. Larcom

My Dear Larcom,

The paper herewith sent may be useful in connection with the parishes Killoran and Kilvarnet, county Sligo. You may keep them, yours R. Stotherd, 10th October 1837.

[Insert note: I forwarded a short time since 2 short papers on the early history of the trade of the towns Ballina and Killala; did you receive them [initialled] NL].

Cess in Killoran

Two quarters, Coolany, public cess 4 pounds 6d, church cess 1 pound 2s 3d, total 5 pounds 2s 9d.

One quarter, Mymlough, public cess 2 pounds 10s, church cess 15s 6d, total 3 pounds 5s 6d.

One quarter, Rathmore, public cess 2 pounds 9s 6d, church cess 15s, total 3 pounds 4s 6d.

One quarter, Carrowmacarrick, public cess 2 pounds 5s, church cess 12s 9d, total 2 pounds 17s 9d.

One quarter, Carrowmullin, public cess 1 pound 5s, church cess 6s 9d, total 11s 9d.

One quarter, Rathorey, public cess 2 pounds 9s 6d, church cess 15s, total 3 pounds 4s 6d.

One quarter, Sevenip, public cess 2 pounds, church cess 12s 6d, total 2 pounds 12s 6d.

One quarter, Shanguogh, public cess 2 pounds 8s, church cess 12s 3d, total 3 pounds 2s 3d.

One quarter, Rathbarren, public cess 3 pounds 2s, church cess 18s 6d, total 4 pounds 6d.

One quarter, Carrowlearn, public cess 1 pound 8s, church cess 7s 9d, total 1 pound 15s 9d.

One quarter, Carrowneclia, public cess 2 pounds 6s, church cess 13s, total 2 pounds 19s.

Two quarters, Killoran, public cess 5 pounds, church cess 1 pound 10s, total 6 pounds 10s.

Two quarters, Carrowloughan, public cess 4 pounds 16s, church cess 1 pound 8s, total 6 pounds 4s.

One quarter, Crevane, public cess 2 pounds 11s, church cess 15s, total 3 pounds 5s.

One quarter, Lisvilough, public cess 2 pounds 3s 6d, church cess 12s 9d, total 2 pounds 16s 3d.

One quarter, Rathtarman, public cess 2 pounds 5s, church cess 13s, total 2 pounds 18s.

One quarter, Carrownageragh, public cess 2 pounds 9s, church cess 13s 6d, total 3 pounds 2s 6d.

One quarter, Carrowclooneen, public cess 2 pounds 10s, church cess 14s 3d, total 3 pounds 4s 3d.

One quarter, Dunodis, public cess 4 pounds, church cess 1 pound 3s, total 5 pounds 11s.

One quarter, Carrowatroune, public cess 1 pound 17s, church cess 9s 9d, total 2 pounds 6s 9d.

Two quarters, Knockadoe, public cess 7 pounds 2s, church cess 2 pounds 4s, total 9 pounds 6s.

Two quarters, Knockatothane, public cess 4 pounds 5s, church cess 1 pound 3s 6d, total 5 pounds 8s 6d.

One quarter, Carrah, public cess 2 pounds 11s, church cess 15s 6d, total 3 pounds 6s 6d.

One quarter, Carrownabarry, public cess 2 pounds 7s, church cess 14s 6d, total 3 pounds 1s 6d.

One quarter, Carrownaskea, public cess 2 pounds 5s, church cess 13s 6d, total 2 pounds 18s 6d.

One quarter, Copagh, public cess 1 pound 17s, church cess 10s, total 2 pounds 7s.

One quarter, Gortakeerin, public cess 2 pounds 11s 6d, church cess 15s 6d, total 3 pounds 7s.

One quarter, Carrowgavneen, public cess 2 pounds 10s, church cess 15s, total 3 pounds 5s.

Half quarter, public cess 1 pound 9s, church cess 8s 6d, total 1 pound 17s 6d.

[Totals] public cess 89 pounds 16s, church cess 23 pounds 11s 6d, total 105 pounds 7s 6d.

Cess in Kilvarnet

[Table contains the following headings: name of townland, public cess in 1794, church cess in 1794, total].

Two quarters, Nymphsfield, public cess 7 pounds 14s 6d, church cess 2 pounds 6s 6d, total 10 pounds 1s.

One and half quarters, Ardcree, public cess 3 pounds 2s 6d, church cess 18s 6d, total 3 pounds 1s.

4 quarters, Ballinacarra, public cess 6 pounds 2s, church cess 1 pound 16s 6d, total 7 pounds 18s 6d.

One quarter, Ballymurry, public cess 1 pound 19s 6d, church cess 9s, total 2 pounds 8s 6d.

One quarter, Rathbane, public cess 2 pounds 4s 6d, church cess 10s, total 2 pounds 14s 6d.

One quarter, Carrowantavy, public cess 2 pounds 4s 6d, church cess 10s, total 2 pounds 14s 6d.

2 and a half quarters, Falnasugane, public cess 5 pounds 16s, church cess 1 pound 10s 6d, total 7 pounds 6s 6d.

4 quarters, Claragh, public cess 6 pounds 10s 6d, church cess 1 pound 18s, total 8 pounds 8s 6d.

Two quarters, Finlough, public cess 3 pounds 18s 6d, church cess 10s 6d, total 4 pounds 9s.

One quarter, Rathnarrow Brett, public cess 2 pounds 2s 6d, church cess 12s, total 3 pounds 2s 6d.

One quarter, Rathnarrow O'Hara, public cess 2 pounds 10s 6d, church cess 12s, total 3 pounds 2s 6d.

One and a half quarters, Kilvarnet, public cess 3 pounds 10s 6d, church cess 19s 6d, total 4 pounds 10s.

Half quarter, Federcan, public cess 1 pound 4s 6d, church cess 6s 9d, total 1 pound 11s 3d.

One and a half quarters, Rathgran, public cess 3 pounds 2s, church cess 18s 6d, total 4 pounds 6d.

Templehouse, public cess 4 pounds 10s, church cess 1 pound 2s 9d, total 5 pounds 12s 9d.

[Totals] Public cess 56 pounds 13s, church cess 15 pounds 9s 6d, total 72 pounds 2s 6d.

Parish of Kilmactigue

Parish of Kilmactigue <Kilmacteige>, County Sligo

Townland Information by Lance-Corporal Henry Trimble, December 1836

MEMOIR WRITING

Name of Aclare

Information in 1836 from 900 years back.

[Insert footnote: NB In the reading of those antiquities, where the black line appears thus under a road, let there be a pause or stop made there].

How the name Aclare originated is thus: in former days there was no bridge at Aclare but a ford with large stepping stones across the river, and when flooded the people had to throw a plank across those stones to get across the opposite side of river.

In them days there were 3 brothers of the name of O'Hara. Their place of residence were in 3 castles, 2 of which are in this parish and the third in the parish of Achonry, namely Bellaclare Castle, Castle Rock Castle and Ballyara Castle. The eldest brother was Clare O'Hara who lived in Bellaclare Castle. A in Irish is "a ford," and the Christian name of O'Hara being Clare, A and Clare joined together makes Aclare, being the name and true origin of this market village.

Fairs in Aclare

Until the year 1766 there were 4 extensive fairs every year in Aclare, and those fairs for the better prosperity of the inhabitants in this country in them days. Chosen days were appointed for them, namely St John's Day, St Ataney's Day, St Stephen's Day and, glorious but impious day, St Patrick's Day, which dates are according, as above named, 24th June, 11th August, 26th December and 17th March.

Every description of cattle, pigs, sheep etc. were brought there to Aclare for sale. Custom to the amount of 50 pounds annually was levied in them fairs by Patt McGooran. But from the year 1766, there has been no fair in Aclare whatever, unless 2 fairs of pleasure by the country people, horse-races, dancing etc. held on St John's Day and St Stephen's Day.

What prevented the fairs from being held as usual was in consequence of fighting and the death of a woman. On a fair morning, being St Patrick's Day, they commenced horse-races on the leading road from the village of Aclare towards Bellaclare, a Mr Robinson who kept ahead before the jockeys for the purpose of keeping the road clear.

Immediately at the ford of Aclare there was a tin woman in the way, having tins of various descriptions slung about her neck. This Mr Robinson made a lash of his whip at her, the whip caught entangled about the tins and hoop, the horse being in full gallop, and Mr Robinson being powerful strong, dragged the woman. The horse capered and pranced and kicked the woman, when she immediately died. Then in consequence of this unfortunate circumstance, the gentlemen and clergy put a stop to the fairs.

Market in Aclare

An excellent market held in Aclare each Saturday. Everything required is for sale; oats bought extensively and butter, immediately forwarded to Sligo for importation. The village of Aclare now consists of 3 grocers, 1 public houses, 2 tailors, 1 shoemaker, 4 lodging houses, 1 doctor, police barrack consisting of 1 constable and 4 subconstables. The dispensary is held at Tubbercurry, also petty sessions. Authorities Mr Williams, Michael Moran and Martin Quin, aged 93, and Dr McLarkey.

Ballyara Abbey and Clergy

In the year 1796 the Irish Defenders were encamped in the 2 adjoining forts of the townland of Rue, until Captain Courtney and his company dispersed them, who then was quartered in Tubbercurry. The principal commander or captain of the Defenders was shot and buried in the old abbey of Ballyara, parish of Achonry. On that day there was [a] friar from Rome in the graveyard; he stated it was exactly 900 years since the abbey and castle of Ballyara, Bellclare and Castle Rock was built.

In them days the only support the officiating clergyman had from the old abbey was that portion of ground consisting of about 7 acres south west of the abbey, and 10 pounds from Mr O'Hara who lived in the castle. The people say that that portion of ground was taken from the townland of Rue and given to the townland of Ballyara for the clergyman, which portion of ground is bounded on the north by a stream between

Kilmacteige and Achonry, see sketch: [ground plan showing castle ruins, abbey ruins in original glebe grounds, with river bounded by the parishes of Rue, Kilmacteige, Ballyara and Achonry].

In the year 1834 several large and most powerful skulls was dug up in the garden of James Golden, townland of Ballyara and parish of Achonry. In former days there had been a battle fought there, and the giant which is buried in the townland of Rathscanlin, parish of Achonry, was killed at that battle.

Grant of Estate to O'Hara

Several old men inform me that they heard their grandfathers say that in old times that Clare O'Hara obtained a grant there from the king: that from the village of Bellclare to whatever distance he might drive in one day with a recorbat, which means a gingle, he would obtain that quantity of ground forever, providing the gingle would not break down.

Consequently, he proceeded from Bellaclare to Knockashee and he, observing the quality of ground there much superior than where he proceeded from, drove much quicker and took a complete circular direction round the neighbourhood until he reached Annaghmore in the parish of Kilvarnet, when unfortunately the gingle broke down. Then he of course proceeded no further but returned back to Bellaclare, calculated the number of miles he went in different directions, which amounted to 20 miles, returning his calculations and rough sketch of the portion of ground he wished to have.

Consequently his majesty approved of it and bound O'Hara to build 24 castles in the province of Connaught at his own expense, Bellaclare being one of the first he built, Castle Rock the next and Ballyara and so on.

So it appears from this information that this is the way the O'Hara[s] obtained their estates. Seemingly it appears no way undoubtful, as it is a very straggling estate. Part of the O'Hara's estate is in the parish of Achonry immediately at Knocknashee, parish of Kilvarnet, parish of Killoran and parish of Ballysadare; and immediately at where the gingle broke down the estate ends, and where he observed the good quality of ground the estate commences. Authority William Brannen and John Ginty.

O'Hara Castle in Tullinaghey

In the townland of Tullinaghey there is the remains of an old castle, the ruins completely levelled to the ground but the foundations visible and on the top of foundation a carn of stones about 3 feet in height and 30 feet in circumference. No information to be derived concerning who lived in it, only built by the O'Haras. Patt Brett of Lullinaglug townland states his grandfather assisted in throwing down the ruins and bringing the stones away for the purpose of the building of Banada bridge. Authority Patt Brett.

Coorecuill Townland

Townland of Coolrecuill: in former days it was an extensive wood except about 10 acres arable which surrounded Oldtown village. This village was then inhabited by 3 families of the name of Harkin, Mulligan and Gawlagher. When their children had grown up to the years of maturity and wood cut down, they divided the townland into 4 quarters: a village of houses situated in each quarterland. Called Newtown village, which was the first village built in the year 1721, then Ballygaullagait and Muharagh village.

On the north west side of the townland there is another village called Barrotoher village. Situated on the leading road from Banada to Aclare, on the north side of this village and in the townland of Toolestraine, is the Roman Catholic chapel built in the year 1753; contains between 500 and 600 people, parish priest, Revd Daniel McLarkey, curate Revd Patt Hurl.

On the north east side of this townland runs the River Moy eastwards, meeting the Muharagh river which river rises in a bog between the townlands of Lislea, Lorroy and Coolrecuill. In this portion of the River Moy salmon is caught, of a most extensive size, also black and white trout.

Cloongooney Townland

Townland of Cloongooney in former days was ancient wood. The first portion of ground that became serviceable is that portion bounded by the River Moy called the Stock Farm, which stock farm has been the principal means of affording 8 families to cultivate as much ground as leaves them quite independent and comfortable to the present day. This portion of ground was always used as grazing pasture; well stocked at present with 90 head of horn cattle, horses, sheep etc.

In this townland there is a most beautiful planted fort situated in [a] flow bog called the Rabbit Fort, which name has originated from a burrow <burrough> being in the fort, but the rabbits at present are very scarce in it, in consequence

Parish of Kilmactigue

of [people] continually using them. When friends, marriages, confessions etc. interferes, the only resource for fresh meat is fly to the Rabbit Fort, where all wants are immediately supplied. Authority John Gawlagher.

Castle Rock Townland

Townland of Castle Rock: in this townland there is the remains of an old castle built by O'Hara and formerly the residence of John DeCourcey, Earl of Ulster; and in the reign of King John he retired from it and seems never [to have] returned. In that day it was called Castle Caragh.

On the north west of this old castle about 20 perches is the Bed of Gracey or Grania <Granny> and Dermott <McDermott>. On the head of this bed is a thorn bush and on the fort is another. Quite visible is the bed, beautifully surrounded with large rocks. How this conspicuous spot bears the name of Grania's and Dermot's Bed is when the Earl of Ulster lived in Castle Caragh, General Finn in that day and married to his daughter Grania. Dermot was an officer under General Finn and seduced Grania, so that by night Grania and Dermot held private communication with each [other], and in this bed they lay for a few hours by night occasionally in the summer season.

The season advancing towards harvest, the ground became rather cold, when Dermot conveyed some seasand from the coast of Dromaird into this bed as a preventative against damp and cold. However, on this night the intimacy between he and Grania was discovered. Then the both were placed in exile until their death. The Earl of Ulster gave the next eldest daughter in marriage to General Finn so as to compensate him for the loss of Grania. Authority Phill and Patt Durkan, historian, and John Mullaney.

[To Lieutenant Stotherd].Sir,

I understand the whole circumstance is recorded in Dr Keating's *History of Ireland*, not altogether as plain as the above statement, for this information has been related since the occurrence to the present day from age to age. [Signed] H. Trimble, Lance-Corporal Royal Sappers and Miners.

Also in this townland of Castle Rock, immediately at the trigonometrical station, is a commanding hill or fort and goes by the name of Hero's Road, called after Dermot in the year 1700. A Mr Larky built a house in this townland and changed the original name, which then was Castle Carah, to the present revised name Castle Rock.

In this townland there is a lough called Loughnabraereeagh, which means "the Blind Trout lough." It seems since the exile of the Earl of Ulster that there has been no fish caught in it.

There are 5 villages in the townland, called Bruncaurragh village, Upper Mullarney, Lower Mullarney, Cartron and Mullaney's Cross.

Mullaney's Cross

In the year 1798 David Mullaney, father to the present Mullaney, built a house, which house is yet remaining and occupied by his son. Immediately at the junction of those roads in that year the French, on their march from Killala, remained about one hour taking refreshment at those crossroads and consulting which road they would proceed to. So from that period only to the present day it bears the name of Mullaney's Cross. Now a village consisting of 2 lodging houses, 1 police barrack, 1 constable and 3 sub-constables.

Castle Rock Townland

In the townland of Castle Rock, at the garden of Patt Durkan of Lower Mullaraney on the south west side of his dwelling house, stands a holly tree called "the fern tree." It's considered to be the oldest tree in Ireland: it's there time without date.

Same townland there stands a conspicuous perpendicular rock, about 4 chains in circumference and 60 feet in height, called Crookenaboughelly rock, which means "the hill of the boys." It's a celebrated rock for courtship in the summer season for the youngsters. Many different marriages has taken place from the unexpected meetings of young men and women.

Same townland is bounded on the north side by a most powerful river called the Owanahir river. The salmon proceeds up the river, which is always on the ascending-facing mountain, as far as the waterfall. Beyond Cartron mill and Pat Cooper's Island is a principal ground where the salmon has been caught from 30 to 50 lbs weight frequently. Also trout and pike caught in same river. Authority Patt Durkin, John Mullaney.

On the north side of Castle Caragh at present is the dwelling house of Tedy O'Doud, built immediately on the gable of the old castle

Banada Townland

Townland of Banada: there is no particular reason to be ascertained from the name Banada. In this townland is the remains of an old abbey, originally called Benfaudaugh, which means "long gable." Also the remains of an old castle quite convenient to the abbey.

This abbey and castle was built by a friar of the name of Fr F. Charles Lucas, and in the reign of Queen Elizabeth, Dan Jones Esquire states to me, the castle was destroyed. Previous to the destruction of the castle, a man named Haggins lived in it, who was murdered by one of the O'Haras immediately on the stairs leading to the upper apartments, and his blood to this day is quite visible at the same spot. The blood appears quite black on the stones, the stones being stained by the blood from that period to the present.

The friars, recorded in history, has [had] in possession 20 acres of ground and an excellent house called the Friary, and the east side of townland called the convent ground, they having a lease of the same ground at 14s per acre. There are no friars these last 6 years in it but occupied now by the Revd Daniel McLarkey, parish priest, at the same rent. But the moment the friars demand the possession, no refusal can be given them in consequence of the friary and old abbey.

Fairs and Markets

That portion of ground beyond the River Moy called Drumbannadi and Convent ground is tithe free forever, and in them days were the fairs of Banada first commenced and holy days appointed by the friars, namely saints' days as follows: Whitsunmonday <Whissenmonday>, St Peter and Paul's Day, St James' Day, St Augustin's Day and the old twelfth day after Christmas, also a new fair held on Patrick's Day. Dates as follows for those days: 6th January, Whitsunmonday according to the moon, 29th June, 25th July, 28th August, 18th October and 17th March.

Every description of cattle bought and sold, horses, cows, sheep, pigs, asses and goats, pedlar's and every description of standings. The custom is levied by Philip Durkan of Downes townland. He, having a lease of lives from Mr Jones, pays 40 pounds 4s 2d annually. He states to me it is not worth more than 10 pounds profit rent to him.

Village of Banada

The village of Banada now consists of 1 public house, 1 shoemaker, 2 weavers, 1 hackler, 1 smith, 2 butchers and 2 coopers, no market. The constabulary was removed from it to Aclare in 1834. In the townland is the dwelling house of Daniel Jones Esquire, one of his majesty's justice of the peace, also his son, deputy lord lieutenant of the county Sligo. House and offices in good repair, excellent garden, young plantation and commanding view from dwelling house situated on the west side of the River Moy and north [?] of the old castle and abbey, known by the name of Banada Abbey.

The old abbey ruins has a graveyard attached to it where no person but a Roman Catholic has been interred. A beautiful breed of America pigs at Daniel Jones' Esquire brought from America by Captain Jackson. Authority Daniel Jones Esquire.

Holy Wells

In the townland of Kilmacteige there is a holy well with a large ash tree. Roman Catholics perform stations to the present day at this well. It's called Tubber Keeraion holy well, which name originates from a woman who was the name of Kiernan being the first in the year 902 who performed her prayers at it. Authority Patt Ginty and John Farrell [or Jarrett].

In the townland there is a holy well called Tubberroddy holy well adjacent to the main road leading from Banada to Aclare. On the north side of [this] townland in a bog the stream rises and runs underground to the holy well, crossing the road and terminates nearly at the junction of boundaries Beteacem, Curroy, Coolrecuill and Lislea. No station performed at the present by the Roman Catholics since the year 1755.

Mr John Curroy states to me that in that year a Mr O'Rorke built a new house on the opposite side of the road facing the well, now the property of John Kelly of Curroy, and immediately after the house was built it fell without any provocation whatever.

The reason assigned for the destruction of the house is: at this holy well stood a beautiful flag with letters engraved on it which never could be read by the first classical scholars; however, Mr O'Rorke, considering this flag lying idle at the well, removed it and placed in his house, so it's considered that's the reason why the house fell; however, in the rebuilding of the house the flag was left back, and the house stands firm to this day.

When the people heard of this circumstance they all unanimously agreed the powers had left the water and well. The people say it was the gentry threw down the house on account of the removal of the flag. Authority Mr John Kelly

Kilmacteige Townland

Townland of Kilmacteige: the remains of an old

Parish of Kilmactigue

barrack yet visible adjacent to the church on south west side. There is a portion of one of the walls yet remaining, mortar and stone. About 70 years ago the ruins was levelled by Mr Robinson and stones brought away for the purpose of building, but no army has been in it these 200 years past.

In the reign of Queen Elizabeth there was a company of men quartered in this barrack, and a lieutenant, after travelling in Europe previous to his arrival in this barrack, expressed then that the best water in the earth was in a spring well adjacent to barrack, on the south west side and within 10 feet of the river and boundary between Carrawreagh and Kilmacteige.

However, from this period to the present it's called the Lieutenant's Well. Never was known to go dry, which well becomes the rise of a river and meets the townland mearing, immediately from which point to the end of river never runs dry.

The barrack of Kilmacteige had been built many years before the church. The church was built for the purpose of the soldiers going to divine service in the reign of Oliver Cromwell. In that day there was not a single Protestant living in the parish. The first resident Protestants were 2 men and families called Evans and Williams, being soldiers under Cromwell previous to their arrival as becoming residents in the parish and originally from Wales. However, through their own simplicity and neglect they lost these lands.

A remnant of the same 2 families yet remains to the present day, forming the only number, I may say, of Protestants, amounting only to 19 families in the parish and in general of the same names, unless a few more names which dropped <dropt> in by marriage but all connected in the relationship. Excepting the rector, it seems how those 2 men happened to come to the parish was in consequence of they being quartered as soldiers in the barrack of Kilmacteige.

How the name Kilmacteige originated is thus: the first man ever was buried in the graveyard was a son to an old man of the name of O'Tedy. So Kill-mac-tigue was the original spelling, which means as thus "Killymean's grave." Mac is "son" and Tigue is "Tedy," that is "the grave of Tedy's son," which first gave origination to the name Kilmacteige in them days.

The content or boundary of the parish was not known, but the name of the whole country went by was the "black rocky lands" or Duffclughathawla. Authority Mr Williams and John Farrell and William Smith.

Brockagh Townland

In the year 1796, in the townland of Brockagh, was the residence of the chief commander of the Irish Defenders. He went by the name of King O'Grady and, previous to his encampment at Rue Forts, he collected his force in this parish, appointing his own officers and magistrates. One Sunday he entered the Roman Catholic chapel and expelled the priest from the altar and communicated verbally his orders as follows: any man disobeying his order, immediate death; any man having 2 coats, shoes, breeches or stockings should part one. And so then he marched his force with the expectation of meeting the French.

Cloonbarry Townland

Townland of Cloonbarry: in this townland is the house and offices of Mr Robinson, in excellent repair, garden and orchard also young planting surrounding the house. It's known by the name Cloonriggen, but since the marriage of Mr Robinson, which has been lately, Mrs Robinson disapproved of the name Cloonriggen and changed the name to Cloonbarry, as she considered it was a more respectable name, particularly to one made use of by a female, as the regional name tended to immodesty.

Mr Robinson resigned being magistrate through a lucrative motive of being collector of the county cess. Both commissions could not be held by one individual.

Salmon Fishing

In the River Moy salmon was extremely plenty and of a very large description. It's only since the year 1826 that perch first made their appearance in this river, and since that period the salmon is not half so plenty. The salmon in general is killed by eating the perch. The fins of the perch choke the salmon and many of them found dead floating in the water with a perch strangled in the salmon's throat, which is a satisfactory proof. Authority John Farrell and Mr Williams.

Copper Mine

Glenawoo mountain, which stands perpendicular over Lough Yalt: it's supposed [it] is a copper mine, in consequence of the lighting [lightning] making such a powerful distraction on the south east side of this conspicuous mountain. That part of the mountain even at a distance appears quite yellow and the heath completely burned. Authority Mr Garrett, H. Trimble, Lance-Corporal, Royal Sappers and Miners.

Origin of the Gap

On the leading road from Mullaney's Cross to Ballina, immediately where the townland boundary between Largan and Slieve Guff cross the road, is the entrance of the Gap. The reason of this spot being called the Gap was in consequence of the 2 range of mountains each side of road which, from a view distantly, it's just the exact form of a gap, appearingly quite conspicuous; then Lough Yalt's name originated from the word gap [sic], which means "the lough of the gap"; [insert note: the word "yalt"].

Family of Anders

The oldest and first family that became inhabitants in the parish of Kilmacteige was the name of Anders. There were 7 brothers of them and it appears they were the first that ever employed a horse beast as an assistant in reclaiming a portion of ground. However, in them days people were quite simple. This Anders found it necessary in providing a pair of creels for equipping the horse, and when tackling the horse first they brought the horse inside of their house, and when they fitted the creels each side of the horse they could not conceive how the horse would get out of the door.

Remaining some time in a deep study, they concluded the only method was to throw down the gable of the house. Consequently they done so and permitted horse and creels to get out. However, they never thought of taking the creels and tackling the horse outside of the house so as to prevent this serious trouble and expense. Authority Mr Williams, townland of Carn.

Estate and Robber

The mountain estate of John Tafe Esquire is set to the London company for 99 years at 5s per acre. The reclaiming of this mountain will be of great relief to the lower class of people. Authority John Tafe Esquire.

On this mountain and townland of Largan was the continual residence of the celebrated robber who was hanged in Castlebar, name Captain Gowlagher. He generally lay hid amongst the rocks and immediately at the Gap. He committed several robberies.

Mr Tafe, in gaining the goodwill of the people, provided a friar to read mass each Sunday, giving him 70 pounds annually. Authority John Tafe Esquire.

Roads

December 1836: present information.

The roads in the parish of Kilmacteige are in very bad repair: many pipes and bridges required, particular[ly] on the leading road from Tubbercurry to Banada. On the entrance of the townland of Eskeragh, where the river runs directly across the road, travellers on foot are forced in wet weather to wade across. Also on the leading road from Banada to Aclare, where the boundary between Curroy and Tubberroddy cross the road, no possibility in getting across in wet weather in consequence of a flood, for the want of a bridge or pipe.

Farms and Condition of the People

However, in general the inhabitants of this parish are extremely neglectful, thus complain in general of the lands being too high, rents etc., but they themselves in no shape or other are acquainted with farming. In general the farms are set by the bulk on the most moderate terms, particularly on the south east side of parish. Notwithstanding, they live in the most deplorable state for either clothing or raiment.

This poverty principally originates from the making of poteen whiskey, which is the general practice with the entire of the farmers. The grain is destroyed. The wretches themselves drink as much of that liquor as would defray the expense of car hire in sending their oats to Sligo properly for sale.

No meadow whatever, unless a little about Mr Robinson's of Cloonbarry and Daniel Jones Esquire of Banada Abbey. So the fodder is extremely scarce, which leaves the horse cattle but few and the horn cattle not half fed, which leaves the beef quite reasonable in this part of the country.

Notwithstanding the continual rain in the year 1836, the crops are in general very good and, most astonishing is it, the people in this parish states they never eat more comfortable before. The reason is the potatoes in general is very wet and by that means they are much easier swallowed than if they were dry; consequently they require no kitchen. At the present time there is upwards of 400 stills at work, so I may say the entire grain is completely consumed.

Party Spirit

The inhabitants of this parish is very much possessed with a party spirit at the present, in consequence of them not having members elected for the county agreeable to their wishes.

Parish of Kilmactigue

Crops and Grain

In many places has the potatoes in this parish been dug before the oats was reaped which, since the memory of man, the like never occurred before; and many fields amounting to acres is completely lost forever, lying rotted on the ground never to be reaped. Notwithstanding the powerful extent of bog in every direction in this parish, scarcely a dry turf to be got all through neglect and carelessness.

There is no description of grain, providing the ground being properly handled, but will produce a most plentiful crop if sown. The common turf clamps that are in the bogs are completely boast, having cags of poteen whiskey concealed; also lift the bottom stones that are in a lime-kiln and there to be found a concealment of grain; even [in] the potato pits that are in the open fields cags of whiskey also concealed; and many instances under the kitchen fire is many concealments, particularly what is called the hob stone.

Observance of Sabbath

No sabbath observed, continual work, digging potatoes, trashing oats and stacking oats, in fact every description of work performed as on a weekday, except 2 hours which is occupied in going to and from mass, although the constabulary force, particularly at Aclare, is putting a complete stop to such infamous violation of the Lord's Day.

Local Government

It's scarcely 1 out of 100 that knows the consequence of an oath, and by that means it is a matter nearly of impossibility to a magistrate in determining satisfactorily the decisive accuracy of any circumstance that may be brought before him in the legal discharge of his duty.

Religion

17 Protestant families in this parish: average number 5 to each family, population 102.

1,641 Roman Catholic families: average number to each family 6, population 9,846.

No Dissenters.

Authority Revd Daniel McLarkey P.P.

General Economy

By the sale of butter and poteen whiskey, the people is enabled in paying the rent to their landlord; very little oats sold. The butter is sent to Sligo by cars.

Table of Loughs

Names of loughs and rivers that fish is caught in and also the description and name of fish, parish of Kilmacteige.

Lough Yalt, trout from 4 oz. to 2 lbs, black and red.

Lough Yalt river, trout, black, red and white from half a lb. to 4 lbs [insert note: salmon].

Bellanamean river [insert note: stated in another return as having salmon and perch]: trout, generally black, small size.

Littlefish river: trout but scarce, small size.

Fidelawn river: trout from three-quarters of a lb. to 1 lb., scarce.

River Moy: trout from 20 oz. to 4 lbs, perch and salmon.

Loughonagally: trout (large) and eels.

Lenioee river: trout every size.

Lough Valaragh: trout of a superior description in size.

Lough Hure: trout of small size, quite yellow.

Lough Wattywee: trout of various colours.

Yeloo river: trout of weighty size.

Owanaher river [insert note: see antiquities Castle Rock, and another return by Corporal Trimble]: trout and salmon.

Lough Hoe: trout and pike of large size.

Blenil lough: trout and pike.

Entered in Field Name Book.

NB No description of quarries to be had in this parish. The authority for the above information is given in statistical sheets.

Fairs and Markets at Aclare

Town of Aclare and townland of Carns: in former days there were 4 fairs each year, but none since the year 1766. The fairs then was held on the 24th June, which was St John's Day, 11th August, St Anthony's Day, 26th December, St Stephen's day, and on the 17th March, St Patrick's Day. On the 24th June and 26th [December] are the only 2 fairs now. Nothing bought or sold excepting horse-races and a few people.

The patent was taken out in the almanac for Bellaclare, which was a mistake, instead of Aclare.

Fair at Banada

Banada: 7 fairs, each year held on the 6th January, Whitsunmonday, date according to the moon, 29th June, 25th July, 28t August, 18th October and New Year, and 17th March. Every commodity bought and sold; pedlars and standings of every description. Custom annually is worth 52 pounds. Rented by Philip Durkan of townland of Dowris from the landlord Daniel Jones Esquire of Banada.

Horses young and old, prices from 5 pounds to 20 pounds; cows and heifers young and old, from 2 pounds till 10 pounds each; asses from 20s to 50s; sheep from 20s to 25s; pigs from 6s to 120s or 6 pounds. Custom paid for every article bought and sold. All Irish cattle bought and sold at this fair. Philip Durkan levies the custom, having a lease of lives from Daniel Jones Esquire at 40 pounds 6s 2d. Durkan makes about 10 pounds profit annually from the fairs.

Produce

Average quantity of potatoes that sows one acre is generally 2 barrels, produce of which is almost 18 or 20 barrels. Average quantity of oats from 20 stones to 30 stones, will sow an acre; produce generally is from 200 stones to 230 stones. Average quantity of flax: 6 gallons flax sows 1 Irish rood of ground, produce of which is generally 120 lbs weight when dressed.

Religion

No Methodists or Presbyterians in this parish. One church and 2 Roman Catholic chapels

Plantations and Botany

Young plantation in this parish: Mr Robinson's of Cloonbarry and Mr Jones of Banada or Daniel Jones Esquire.

No drainage of bogs in this parish; no botany.

Livestock and Fodder

The description of every description of cattle and swine is Irish breed unless a few Scotch cows. Only an America true breed of pigs at Daniel Jones Esquire of Banada, brought there by Captain Jackson of America.

The oats is nearly entirely consumed into poteen whiskey. Upwards of 400 stills working at present in this parish. Horse cattle very scarce, not more than 30 horses, for which all is for hire in bringing butter and some oats to Sligo for sale in this parish.

I may say there is no meadow in this parish except a little at Banada. Therefore the cattle gives but from 6 quarts of milk to 10 quarts in the day after calfing. Fodder so very scarce and the grass poor and miserable, of a hard, stubborn nature. White cabbage is very plenty here but is given to the cattle, but none for the use of Christians either through sale or compliment, or yet given to the beggars for God's sake, which is the old Irish prayer, particularly in Connaught by poor; and the same word has spread through all Ireland which appears first originated immediately at the Gap by command of a friar to a poor man who first commenced begging publicly.

Magistrates and Poor

But 2 magistrates in this parish, Daniel Jones Esquire and his son deputy lord lieutenant. Banada Abbey is their residence.

No provision made for the poor in this parish from any gentlemen or society.

Old Barracks

In former days there was a barracks, south west side of the church of Kilmacteige. Martin Quinn, miller of Aclare now aged 100 years, states he remembers the old ruins which was thrown down in the year 1761 by old Mr Robinson in that day, for the purpose of building. The foundation of barrack is in part good and old walls, representing the exterior walls of the barrack. The country appeared in them days to be disturbed. The Earl of Ulster seems to be the cause of military being quartered there.

Migration and Abbey Ground

NB From 400 to 500 goes to Scotland and England to reap the harvest each year.

20 acres is converted ground, property of the friars in the townland of Banada, tithe free forever.

Old castle ruins and abbey ruins also. Described in statement: information now forwarded.

Communications

Bog plenty in this parish. Roads in bad repair and many bridges required or pipes required. The civil engineer or rather county surveyor appears not to exert himself.

Emigration and Population

No people going to America from this parish. 17 Protestant families and 1,641 Roman Catholic families. Authority Revd Mr Larkey.

Mountain Land

The mountain in general is excellent if reclaimed.

All required is encouragement to the poor. Mr Tafe has sold his title of his estate of mountain to the London company, giving a lease of 999 years from 1836. It's supposed these are to cut off a portion about 10 acres to each tenant for reclaiming the whole mountain containing 6,000 acres.

Table of Loughs and Fishing

[Printed table contains the following headings: List of names to be corrected if necessary, orthography as recommended to be used in the new plans, other modes of spelling the same name, authority for these other modes of spelling when known, situation, descriptive remarks or other general observations].

Between Kincullea, townland of Carrowreagh: Lough Nalackagh, trout, small sprats from one quarter to half a lb. weight.

Between townlands of Kilmacteige and Letterbrone: Lough Hume, trout and eels; Lough Naheenybawn, trout; townland of Kilmacteige, Black lough, no fish; Lough Nattywee, trout; Lough Cloghwelly; [all] entered in Field Name Book; small description of trout called sprats; authorities for the name of those loughs: Dennis Ginty, driver, townland of Kilmacteige, and John O'Donnal of Carrowreagh.

Townland of Kincullea: Lough Nagalla, no fish; entered in Field Name Book.

Townland of Culldalee: Leannalea village.

Townland of Culldalee: Drinulla village.

Townland of Culldalee: Lough Nashry or Gow's lough.

Lough Anvoran, Lough Doo, entered in Field Name Book; authority Antony Quinn and Patt Stephens, same townland.

Between the townlands of Letterbrone and Gulldalee: Lough Arubble.

Townland of Lettermore: Loughawaughran, Parkmore lough, Brawkaugh village; authority Patt Stephen, John O'Hara and John Bailey; entered in Field Name Book.

[Insert note: No lakes]. Townland of Carrowreagh: Munnalea village; authority John O'Donnoll, same townland.

Townland of Kincullea: Ballauch-carragh village, Faughamy village, Cintullogh village, Sraughmore village, Kincullea village; authority Patt Rowley, underagent, true copy from his rent book.

Townland of Bellaclare: an old ruins of castle yet remaining, Toorrara village, Bellaclare village, Crookondoela village, Lettersowrey village; authority Martin O'Donnall, same townland.

Townland of Carrowreagh: Castellchrack village, Uppertown village, Lowertown village, Bawllahear village, Gurtaskalee village; authority Dennis McAnulty, mearsman of Killasser, and Thomas Dun, same townland.

[Insert note: No lakes]. Townland of Gortemore: Newclare village, Oldclare village, Baullure village, Spotfield village, Oldtown village, Coolcorraugh village; authority John Connoll, same townland.

Information on Townlands

Names, authority of loughs, villages, gentlemen's seats, holy wells.

[Insert note: The names of village, loughs, bridges is thrown [known] by the youngest and oldest persons in the parish, so that the least doubt may not exist in inserting the same on the plans].

Townland of Carrigeennagowan: Tullycusshun lough, no fish; authority Michael Brit of Tullinaglug townland.

Townland of Eskeragh: Eskeragh townland, Cloonaree village; authority Patt Girlan of Eskeragh.

Townland of Coolrecuill: Colleen village; authority Lawrence Cook of Coolrecuill townland.

Townland of Coolrecuill: Oldtown village, Newtown village, Ballygaullagart village, Maharagh village, Maharagh river; authority Bryan May, Michael Higgins, Antony Lendy, Michael O'Hara. Described in statistical book.

[Insert note: River entered in Field Name Book: no, indeed they are not].

Townland of Cloongoonagh: Rabbit Fort; authority Michael Higgins, Cloongoonagh.

Townlands of Toolestraune and Coolrecuill: Roman Catholic chapel, Barratoher, and village of Barratoher, between the townlands of Coolrecuill and Toorlistraune on the leading road from Banada to Ardclare.

Townland of Barratoher: Roman Catholic chapel built 1753, inserted on a stone; contains 700 and 800 annually attends.

Townland of Castle Rock: Castle Caragh ruins, the Earl of Ulster's castle in the reign of King John; Dermot and Grania's Bed, everything relating to this is recorded to Dr Keating's *History of Ireland*; Heroe's rock, authority Antony McAnulty of Castle Rock and Thomas Durkan, Fern tree, authorities for villages; Mullaney's Cross, authority John Mullaney of Castle Rock; Crookenalaughilly rock, authority Thomas Durkan; Upper Mullaraney village, authority Thomas Durkan; Lower Mullaraney, authority

John Mullaney and Thomas Durkan; Cartron village, authority Thomas Durkan and Antony McAnulty, townland of Castle Rock; Bruncaurragh village, authority Patt Hannigan and John Mullaney, townland of Castle Rock.

Corn Mills

[Table] Townland of Carns: 1 corn mill, erected 1822, undershot, wheel 14 feet by 2 feet in diameter; authority Y. [blank] Leny, townland of Carns.

Townland of Drimina: 1 corn mill, erected 1632, gig wheel goes round, lies horizontal, 14 and half feet; authority Pat Butt of Tattenaglug.

Townland of Castle Rock: 1 corn mill, called Cartron mill, erected 1702, breast wheel, from 1702 to 1834, returns a gig wheel; authority Pat Durkan of Castle Rock.

Townland of Kilmacteige: 1 tuck mill, corn mill, 1760, breast wheel, 14 feet by 2 feet in diameter; authority Patt Fleming.

Townland of Banada: 1 corn mill, no date to be ascertained, wheel 14 feet by 2 feet in diameter, undershot; authority James Maxwell, proprietor.

Townland of Carrowreagh: 1 corn gig mill, built in 1834, well [wheel] 5 feet [diameter], lies horizontal.

Holy Well and School

Townland of Tubberroddy: holy well entered in Field Name Book, called Tubberroddy holy well; authority John Kelly, same townland.

Townland of Curroy: 1 schoolhouse, mud, recognised by no society, commenced 1834, 60 scholars, 40 males, 20 females, all Roman Catholic, scholars pay the teacher.

Loughs and Islands

Lough Yalt: originated from the Gap, which means "the lough of the gap," authority John Mullaney, having 3 islands, namely: Towneeany Island, property of Mr Robinson of Towneeany townland; Glenawoo according to name on trace given; Killanlug Island, which means "the little island," half of which belongs to Mr Tafe, the other half to Mr Robinson, both being landlords; authorities Thomas Mulligan, Patt Hegarty and Mr Tafe [insert note: Largan townland].

Killawnmore Island, which means "large island," property of Mrs Irwin of Dublin, belonging to the townland of Quarterslane; authority Thomas Mulligan.

Elanaghlughtoo Island, which means "black stones," property of Mrs Irwin; this island is not in Lough Yalt but immediately where at the townland [insert note: of Largan town and Quarterslane meets Lough Yalt adjacent to main road].

Lakes

Loughnoe: authority Thomas Mulligan of Quarterslane; pike caught in it.

Loughdoo: no fish.

Lougharose, townland of Townyany: authority Edward Connor.

Round lough: no fish.

Loughonmore: no fish.

Blind lough: authority Patt Hegarty's of Quarterslane townland; pike and eels in it.

Townland of Carns: there is a pound, another in townland of Kilmacteige, another in Quarterslane; no date to be ascertained about them.

Antiquities

[Printed sheet] Townland of Tullinaglug: the foundation only of an old castle, ruins thrown down, no date nor information to be had; authority Patrick Brett of Tullinaglug.

Townland of Rue: the 2 forts adjacent to leading road from Ballina to Tubbercurry; the Defenders were encamped in the year 1796; authority William Golden.

Townland of Coolrecuill: in former days was entire wood, except about 10 acres at Oldtown village; described in statistical book.

Townland of Toorlestraune: Roman Catholic chapel built 1753, contains 700, it's called Barratoher chapel; and also the village of Barratoher, between the townlands of Coolrecuill and Barratoher.

Townland of Glanawoo: Lorbawn village, authority Thomas Mulligan of Quarterslane; Towneeaney village, authority Edward Connor of Glenawoo; Townygraffey village, authority Edward Connor of Glenawoo and Patt Hegarty of Gurterslane; St Patrick's Rock, authority Glenawoo.

Natural Features

[Insert note: Entered in Field Name Book]. Townland of Castle Rock: Lough Nahrackeeagh, means "blind trout lough," no fish caught in it; authority John Mullaney of Mullaney Cross.

Bellinagraugh bridge on the parish boundary.

Parish of Kilmactigue

River Owanagher runs through it; authority Bartly Quince. River Ownaher, River Owanaher, parish boundary, trout large size; authority Thomas Durkan. Crow Island on same river and Cooper's Island also; authority Badly Quinn.

Townland of Quarterslane: Loughne river and Loughnoe lough and Yalt river, trout caught; authority Thomas Mulligan of Quarterslane.

Between the townland of Largan and Slieve Guff, on the leading road from Mullaney's Cross to Ballina, is the entrance of the Gap, 2 conspicuous range of mountains facing north each side of road.

NB Glenawoo mountain, which stands perpendicular over Lough Yalt, a very conspicuous mountain. It's supposed there is a copper mine on the south west side. The lightning a few years ago tore away the earth, which appears quite plain and conspicuous.

Schools

Townland of Kilmacteige, 1 national school.
  Townland of Banada, 1 national school.
  Townland of Largan, 1 national school.
  Townland of Kilmacteige, 1 Hibernian school.
  Townland of Curroy, 1 school under no society.

Field Name Books will give the whole information concerning these schools, number of schools etc.

Rivers and Schools

Townland of Kilmacteige: Bellanmean river, Lough Salt river entered in Field Name Book; fish caught in both rivers: salmon, trout and perch, also eels in River Bellanamean.

Townland of Kilmacteige: Kilbride village; tuck mill and corn mill under one roof; one school under the Hibernian Society, built 1802; schoolmistress, 12 scholars, 9 Roman Catholic and 3 Protestant, salary 8 pounds and 2 acres of ground annually; one national school built [crossed out: 1834], master paid by the scholars.

Townland of Kilmacteige: Lough Salt river terminates or meets Bellanamean river between the townlands of Kilmacteige, Carns and Claddagh. The salmon proceeds for a considerable distance from the River Ballanamean up Lough Salt river.

Villages

Townland of Cladagh: Raheen village, Fausetermore village, Anvaran village, Chroughnagour village, Maunrough village; authorities Patt O'Hara, Patt Ham and Patt McEntire, townland of Cladagh.

Rivers

Townland of Cladagh: Littlefish river, Fiddawn river; trout caught in both rivers; Ynough river, Bellanamean river; no fish; county boundary between Mayo and Sligo described above; authorities Patt O'Hara and Patt Ham.

The River Moy, entered in Field Name Book, runs for miles through the parish of Kilmacteige: salmon, trout and perch in the many other rivers running from it and to it, as inserted, also fish in them and salmon proceeds for considerable distance up this river, caught from 30 to 40 lbs weight.

NB In the River Moy there is salmon trout and perch. It is only since the year 1826 that perch was caught in the River Moy, and great destruction the perch is upon the salmon in consequence of the young salmon eating the perch. The fins of the perch choke the salmon: they immediately die. Since the year 1826 the salmon is very scarce. The country people state this as fact from different proofs. Many description of trout caught, black, white and red trout. Average wealth of the Moy river, 5 perch; depth 6 feet, current mild.

Townlands

Townland of Tullaghaglass: Loughonayally, fish in it, trout and eels; Gleeneask Cottage, residence of Mr Tafe; River Linwee, trout caught in it; authority Mr Tafe, landlord, and Patt Doughill, herd.

Townland of Ouanagh: Sion Hill Cottage, formerly the residence of Mr Dean of Dublin, now in bad repair; in consequence of a most beautiful round commanding hill or [on] south west side of house is how the name Sion originated.

Townland of Cloonbarry: Luchughore village; Cloonbarn House, residence of Mr Robinson, excellent repair, young planting, offices, orchard and garden. The house was formerly called Cloonriggeen until the marriage of Mr Robinson, when Mrs Robinson approved of the appellation Cloonbarry instead of Cloonriggeen, as it appeared to be a more respectable word or name. Authority John Welsh, tenant, same townland.

Townland of Cauran: Oldtown village; it's the first village that ever has been in townland; authority Patt Hierman, same townland.

Townland of Knockahoney: Bunnananey village, Middletown village, Bollonfortey village, Posstuey village, Oldtown village which is the oldest village in townland; authorities Michael Marrin and John Killmaster, same townland.

Townland of Lislea: Grey Fort, authority Mrs Evans, same townland.

Townland of Killure: a graveyard, only for young children that die unbaptised; authority Dinnis O'Hara.

Townland of Banada: old castle and abbey ruins called Cloonyandaugh, which means "long gable"; authority Hugh Maxwell.

Drumbanada: convent ground and friary, residence of parish priest; Ballaher village, Moneenroe village; authority Hugh Maxwell of Banada.

Townland of Oghavel: Crookoneaurrough village, Parknohoran village, Gowlan village; authority Patt Ham and James Horoley [or Howley], same townland.

Townland of Kilmacteige: Cloonyhamey village, Moneneull village, Cloughoughe village, barrack ruins, in former days was a barrack; authorities Patt Ham and Bryan Ginty, same townland.

Lieutenant's Well: authority Mr Williams of townland of Carns; holy well called Tubberkeerawn; stations made to the present day by Roman Catholics.

Tullymay: Knockglass village, Stang village; authority Matthew Killoran, same townland.

Carrownlobane: Killalavin village, Teenlaur village; authority Patt Larchfield, same townland.

Knockbrack: Stone Park village, authority John O'Hara.

Cloonca: Clooncabeg village, same townland.

Middle Cloonca: Battlefield village, Ouanaher village; authority Patt Reid, same townland.

Glenwoo: Crummisbeg village, Tubberronagh village, Parkmore village, St Atey's holy well, St Barbara's holy well; authority Matthew Doonagh, same townland.

In the townland of Knockbrack there is a school, which makes 6 in the parish. Field Name Book will give every information also. Also in the townland of Glenwoo 2 holy wells, which makes 4 in the parish.

Townland Names in 1836

[Table contains the following headings: name of townland and variants listed by boundary surveyor, Dr McLarky, and Mr Thomas Evans, clerk of church].

1. Annagh, Aunnagh, Anaugh.
2. Banada, Bannada, Bannada.
3. Belclare, Bellclare, Bellclare.
4. Carrane, Cawrane, Carrann.
5. Carriganagowna, Corrigeenagowna, Carriganagouna.
6. Carrownlobane, Corrownlobane, Carrownlabane.
7. Carrowreagh, Corrawreagh, Carrowrea.
8. Carrownagoppal, Carrownagupple, Carrownawgupple.
9. Castle Rock, Castle Rock, Castle Rock.
10. Carns, Carns, Carns.
11. Claddagh, Clawdaugh, Cladaugh.
12. Cloonbarry, Cloonberry, Cloonbarry.
13. Cloondeveon, Cloondeivin, Cloondeivinn.
14. Clooncagh, Clooncaugh, Cloonca.
15. Coolrecull, Coolrecuille, Coolreculle.
16. Cloongoonagh, Cloonguenough, Cloongoonagh.
17. Creecussane, Creecaussane, Creecaussawne.
18. Culdalee, Calldawlee, Culdalee.
19. Curraghbinee [insert note: wrong], Curroghbinee, Curraghbinee.
20. Curroy, Curroy, Curroy.
21. Dowris, Dowriss, Douris.
22. Drimina, Drimona, Drumina.
23. Drumartin, Drummarton, Drummartin.
24. Eskragh, Eskeraugh, Eskeragh.
25. Glunawoo, Glennawoo, Glennawoo.
26. Glebe, Glebe, Glebe.
27. Gurtermore [insert note: wrong], Gurrtermore, Gurtermore.
28. Gurterslane, Gurterslawn, Gurtorslane.
29. Kilmacteige [insert note: wrong], Kilmactigue, Killmactigue.
30. Killure, Killure, Killure.
31. Kincullia, Kincuillea, Kincullia.
32. Knockbrack, Knockbrock, Knockbrocke.
33. Knocknasligane, Knocknossligann, Knocknasligane.
34. Knockahoney, Knockahowny, Knockahony.
35. Largan, Largann, Largan.
36. Litterbrone, Lutterbrone, Letterbrone.
37. Lislea, Lislea, Lislea.
38. Meenamade, Meennamawdoe, Meenawmadoe.
39. Meenagleragh, Meenagleeraugh, Meenaglara.
40. Meenacligh, Meennacligh, Meenaligha [insert note: doubtful].
41. Oghaval, Oaghovall, Oghavol.
42. Ounagh, Ounnaugh, Ounagh.
43. Ruagh, Rue, Rugh.
44. Toorelustrane, Taurlusstrawne, Toorlustrane.

Parish of Kilmactigue

45. Townancleen, Townnanecleen, Townnanaleene.
46. Tubberruddy, Tubberroddy, Tubberroddy.
47. Tullaghaglass, Tullaghnagloss, Tullaghaglass.
48. Tullymoy, Tullamoy, Tullymoy.
49. Tullinaglug, Tullynaglug, Tullinnaglug.

Aclare, 10th December 1836, [signed] H. Trimble, Lance-Corporal Royal Sappers and Miners.

County Sligo

Quit Rents and Taxes paid by Lord Lorton, 1827

SOCIAL AND PRODUCTIVE ECONOMY

Quit Rents

Sligo collection, quit and rents paid by Lord Lorton to Easter 1827. [Table contains the following headings: number of patent, name of patentee, denominations, county, barony, acres, annual rent].

79, Nicholas, Earl of Carlingford, Emlaghnaghten, 1 trine, county Sligo, barony of Corran, 247 acres, 2 pounds 6s 2d.

79, Nicholas, Earl of Carlingford, Ardsallagh, half-quarter, county Sligo, barony of Corran, 91 acres, 17s farthing.

79, Nicholas, Earl of Carlingford, Tonnapowra, half-quarter, county Sligo, barony of Corran, 59 acres, 11s farthing.

79, Nicholas, Earl of Carlingford, Lecarrowreagh, half-quarter, county Sligo, barony of Corran, 13 acres, 8s ha'penny.

79, Nicholas, Earl of Carlingford, Lorga, half-quarter, county Sligo, barony of Corran, 56 acres, 10s 5d ha'penny.

79, Nicholas, Earl of Carlingford, Carrowne Coonany, half-quarter, county Sligo, barony of Corran, 75 acres, 14s farthing.

79, Nicholas, Earl of Carlingford, Finaghwe also Finagaie, half-quarter, county Sligo, barony of Corran, 55 acres, 10s 3d ha'penny.

119, Lord Kingston, Killawell, one-third cartron, county Sligo, barony of Corran, 9d farthing.

120, Lord Kingston, tenement of a market and fair, Carrick McDermot, county Sligo, barony of Corran, 9s 2d 3 farthings.

136, Robert King Esq., Killoges also Killavoges, 1 cartron, county Sligo, barony of Tirerill, 57 acres, 10s 7d ha'penny.

136, Robert King Esq., Cartroneighteragh also Cartroneaghtragh, 1 cartron, county Sligo, barony of Tirerill, 16 acres, 3s.

173, Lord Kingston, Mullaghfarna, one-third quarter, county Sligo, barony of Tirerill, 3s 1d.

173, Lord Kingston, Carrowkeele, county Sligo, barony of Tirerill, 9s 2d 3 farthings.

173, Lord Kingston, Drumdoony, county Sligo, barony of Tirerill, 4s 7d ha'penny.

238, Lord Kingston, Cappenagh, county Sligo, barony of Coolavin, 164 acres, 1 pound 10s 7d 3 farthings.

238, Lord Kingston, Annaghmarrow, county Sligo, barony of Coolavin, 22 acres, 4s 1d ha'penny.

238, Lord Kingston, Corrowlissan, Mogarrow and Kilscornagh, 2 quarters, 276 acres, 2 pounds 11s 7d farthing.

238, Lord Kingston, Mollewe, 1 quarter, 30 acres, 5s 7d ha'penny.

238, Lord Kingston, the woods of Callaghmore, Callaghbeg, Carrowbracken, county Sligo, barony of Coolavin.

238, Lord Kingston, Straken and Downerreruin, 127 acres, 1 pound 3s 8d farthing, whereof Lord Lorton pays, county Sligo, barony of Coolavin, 7s 1d.

242, Nil, in Cloonesallagh 1 quarter containing 245 acres, of which in charge of Lord Kingston 176 acres.

243, Nil, in Killprocliss a parcel of mountain formerly belonging to the quarter of Colltemannow, county Sligo, barony of Coolavin, 2 pounds 18s 9d 3 farthings.

245 and 246, Nil, Caskerable mountain belonging to the 5 quarters of Kilfree, grazeable and woody mountain belonging to the quarters of Cloonhagless, Mullaghwee and Romadia, county Sligo, barony of Coolavin, 17 pounds 9s 2d ha'penny.

253, Lord Kingston, tenant of Ardlee, 1 quarter, county Sligo, barony of Coolavin, 9s 2d 3 farthings.

253, Lord Kingston, Carrowmurlane, 1 quarter, county Sligo, barony of Coolavin, 9s 2d 3 farthings.

253, Lord Kingston, Carrownany, 1 quarter, county Sligo, barony of Coolavin, 9s 2d 3 farthings.

253, Lord Kingston, Ardgascin, 1 quarter, county Sligo, barony of Coolavin, 9s 2d 3 farthings.

253, Lord Kingston, Ardloane, 1 quarter, county Sligo, barony of Coolavin, 9s 2d 3 farthings.

253, Lord Kingston, Lismiskie also Derrybeg, 1 quarter, county Sligo, barony of Coolavin, 9s 2d 3 farthings.

253, Lord Kingston, Carrowmully, 1 quarter, county Sligo, barony of Coolavin, 9s 2d 3 farthings.

Miscellaneous Papers

253, Lord Kingston, Carrowardgullum, 1 quarter, county Sligo, barony of Coolavin, 9s 2d 3 farthings.

314, John, Lord Baron of Kingston, tenant of Ballymcegan, county Roscommon, barony of Boyle, 203 acres, 1 pound 17s 11d ha'penny.

314, John, Lord Kingston, Carromore, 1 quarter, county Roscommon, barony of Boyle, 79 acres, 14s 9d farthing.

314, John, Lord Kingston, Symokill, 1 quarter, county Roscommon, barony of Boyle, 79 acres, 14s 9d farthing.

314, John, Lord Kingston, Rusheem and Andrumaghta, county Roscommon, barony of Boyle, 79 acres, 14s 9d farthing.

314, John, Lord Kingston, Ardinskine, 1 quarter, county Roscommon, barony of Boyle, 79 acres, 14s 9d farthing.

314, John, Lord Kingston, Ardlughran, 1 quarter, county Roscommon, barony of Boyle, 15s 10d ha'penny.

314, John, Lord Kingston, Ballymullany and Aghacurragh, 4 quarters, 436 acres, 4 pounds 1s 6d, Lord Lorton pays, county Roscommon, barony of Boyle, 3 pounds 15s 1d 3 farthings.

314, John, Lord Kingston, Boilnecrannagh, Carrowreagh and Lurga, 3 quarters, county Roscommon, barony of Boyle, 213 acres, 1 pound 19s 9d 3 farthings.

314, John, Lord Kingston, Knockbrack and Longford, 2 quarters, county Roscommon, barony of Boyle, 146 acres, 1 pound 7s 3d ha'penny.

314, John, Lord Kingston, Cargin, 1 quarter, county Roscommon, barony of Boyle, 81 acres, 15s 1d ha'penny.

314, John, Lord Kingston, Creenagh, 1 quarter, county Roscommon, barony of Boyle, 124 acres, 1 pound 3s 2d.

314, John Lord Kingston, Mullagh half-quarter, Eilagh half-quarter, Cananegahill half-quarter, county Roscommon, barony of Boyle, 202 acres, 1 pound 17s 9d farthing.

314, John, Lord Kingston, Feenagh half-quarter, county Roscommon, barony of Boyle, 64 acres, 11s 11d ha'penny.

314, John, Lord Kingston, Smutternagh, county Roscommon, barony of Boyle, 62 acres, 11s 7d.

314, John, Lord Kingston, Lismulkieme, county Roscommon, barony of Boyle, 65 acres, 12s 1d 3 farthings.

314, John, Lord Kingston, Loorly and Clonookill, 1 quarter, county Roscommon, barony of Boyle, 49 acres, 9s 1d 3 farthings.

314, John, Lord Kingston, Fullaghraghan, Fullaghboy and Clogher, 4 quarters, county Roscommon, barony of Boyle, 288 acres, 2 pounds 13s 10d.

314, John, Lord Kingston, Aghrisingin, 1 quarter, county Roscommon, barony of Boyle, 260 acres, 2 pounds 8s 7d ha'penny.

314, John, Lord Kingston, Corper, 3 quarters, county Roscommon, barony of Boyle, 9 acres, 1s 8d.

314, John, Lord Kingston, Emlagh, 1 quarter, county Roscommon, barony of Boyle, 55 acres, 10s 3d ha'penny.

314, John, Lord Kingston, Grannagh, Ardneckennagh and Knockrow, 3 quarters, barony of Boyle, 296 acres 2 pounds 15s 4d, 1 pound 15s farthing, Lord Lorton pays.

326, John Drury, in Portnegrannagh 1 quarter and Lurga 1 quarter, county Roscommon, barony of Boyle, 30 acres, 5s 7d ha'penny.

326, Assignee of Robert King Esq. and Sir Robert King, in Carrowgskill 1 quarter, Ellagh 1 quarter, Mulloge 1 quarter, Creeve 1 quarter and Cargin 1 quarter, county Roscommon, barony of Boyle, 51 acres, 9s 6d farthing.

326, Assignee of Robert King Esq. and Sir Robert King, Knockbrack 1 quarter, Longford 1 quarter, in Carrick, county Roscommon, barony of Boyle, 100 acres, 18s 8d farthing.

326, Assignee of Robert King Esq. and Sir Robert King, in Aghrifinnigane, county Roscommon, barony of Boyle, 3 acres, 6d 3 farthings.

326, Assignee of Robert King Esq. and Sir Robert King, in Ballykenegane 3 quarters and Carrowtrukin 1 quarter, county Roscommon and barony of Boyle, 10 acres, 1s 10d ha'penny.

326, Assignee of Robert King Esq. and Sir Robert King, Denelow, half-cartron, 26 acres, 4s 10d ha'penny.

330, Richard Martin, Corkfreeth 1 quarter, county Roscommon and barony of Boyle, 68 acres, 12s 8d ha'penny.

330, John Drury.

330, Assignee of Lord Kingston, assignee of Richard Martin, in Tonneenagh 1 quarter, county Roscommon, barony of Boyle, 40 acres, 7s 5d 3 farthings.

330, Assignee of Lord Kingston, assignee of Richard Martin, in Portnecrannaght 1 quarter, Carrowreagh 1 quarter and Lurga 1 quarter, county Roscommon, barony of Boyle, 65 acres, 12s 1d ha'penny.

335, Hugh McFeighe, tenant in Gortnecrannaght, Carrowreagh and Lurga 3 quarters.

335, Fitzroy Owen, county Roscommon, barony of Boyle, 19 acres, 3s 6d ha'penny.

335, Granna McDermott, county Roscommon, barony of Boyle.

342, Richard Butler, in Knockfreeth, 1 quarter, county Roscommon, barony of Boyle, 20 acres, 3s 8d 3 farthings.

345, George French, tenant in Ballackivagan, 2 quarters, county Roscommon, barony of Boyle, county Roscommon, barony of Boyle, 20 acres, 3s 8d 3 farthings.

345, George French, Smulternagh, 1 quarter, county Roscommon, barony of Boyle, 46 acres, 8s 7d farthing.

348, Sir O. StGeorge, Drumcormick half-quarter, county Roscommon, barony of Boyle, 45 acres, 7s 10d farthing.

353, Nil, Ballykinnegar, county Roscommon, barony of Boyle, 2 acres, 4s farthing.

363, Lord Kingston, tenant of the monastery of Inchvickeeny at [blank], county Roscommon, barony of Boyle, 4 pounds 12s 3d 3 farthings.

365, Lord Kingston, tenant of the abbey or monastery of Boyle at [blank], county Roscommon, barony of Boyle, 10 pounds 10s.

366, Lord Kingston, tenant of 1 market and 2 fairs at Boyle, county Roscommon, barony of Boyle, 4s 7d ha'penny.

371, Sir E. Crofton, tenant of the monastery of the Holy Trinity of Lough Key <Keagh> at 2 pounds 6s 1d 3 farthings, of which Lord Lorton pays, county Roscommon, barony of Boyle.

381, Sir Henry King, tenant of 2 fairs at Gresviske, county Roscommon, barony of Boyle, 17s 3d 3 farthings.

385, Lord Lorton, Creeve 1 quarter, county Roscommon, barony of Boyle, 6s 1d 3 farthings.

385, Lord Lorton, Carrowkeele and Ardmaile, 2 quarters, county Roscommon, barony of Boyle, 9s 2d 3 farthings.

385, Lord Lorton, Townageeth, 1 quarter, county Roscommon, barony of Boyle, 18s 5d ha'penny.

385, Lord Lorton, Derryrough, 1 quarter, county Roscommon, barony of Boyle, 9s 2d 3 farthings.

385, Tenant of Lecarrow, 1 quarter, Knockadoo, 1 quarter, Ardoorgarmon 1 quarter, Ardmeeghan, 1 quarter, Knockinlough 1 quarter, county Roscommon, barony of Boyle, 9s 2d 3 farthings.

393, Lord Kingston: 1 quarter Ardmore, 3 cartrons Ardsallagh and Ardnegher, 1 quarter Cloon, Grange 1 quarter, Cloonemiege 2 cartrons, Kilnemannagh 1 quarter, Derryniquirke 1 quarter, Freaghencarrow and Feaghroy 1 quarter, Knockeannane 1 quarter, Killuden 1 cartron, Grange 1 quarter, 1 quarter Leame and Trillagh 2 quarters 2 cartrons, Knocknecally 1 quarter, Carrowgarrow 1 quarter, Cloonmeenagh 1 quarter, Carrowgeeragh 1 quarter, Cloonfreese 1 cartron, Ligadow half-cartron, Mamragh 1 cartron, Carrowtrasna 1 quarter, Knockadow 1 quarter, Drumin 2 cartrons, Derrinleagh and Terrom 1 quarter, Killaly and Ardkeene 1 quarter, Turbintaine and Brandight 1 quarter, Fane 1 quarter, Cloonaneenagh 1 quarter, Knockmaine 1 quarter, Tullagh also Boyle 1 quarter, Ballymagreevy 4 quarters, of all which lands there is free by indenture of composition 31 quarters belonging to the Abbey or Manor of Boyle, county Roscommon and barony of Boyle, 1 pound 15s 9d farthing, and remains charged 3 quarters half and 1 cartron, 4s 7d ha'penny.

417, Lord Kingston's tenant, in Smulternagh 2 cartrons, Derrinmonagh half-cartron, 1s 1d 3 farthings.

426, Earl Clanrickard, Crownegallagh in Stradkane 2 cartrons, county Roscommon and barony of Boyle, 4s 7d ha'penny.

426, Robert Edward, Viscount Lorton, tenant of 3 additional fairs to be held in or at the town of Boyle from Michaelmas 1819, county Roscommon and barony of Boyle, 9s 2d 3 farthings.

Total yearly rent 74 pounds 1s 9d; half-yearly rent 37 pounds 10d ha'penny.

I certify the foregoing denominations are correctly copied from the quit rent ledger in Sligo collection and that the east gale 1827, amounting to 37 pounds 10d ha'penny, has been paid by Lord Lorton's agent on the 4th June 1827. [Signed] Robert Holmes, Collector of Excise, Sligo.

[Signed] Robert W. Durnford, Lieutenant Royal Engineers, 31st August 1836.

www.ingramcontent.com/pod-product-compliance
Lightning Source LLC
Chambersburg PA
CBHW051210290426
44109CB00021B/2406